New Forces, Old Forces, and the Future of World Politics

Post–Cold War Edition

Seyom Brown

Brandeis University

 HarperCollins*CollegePublishers*

For the descendants
of Benjamin Brown,
pioneer builder of communities

Acquisitions Editor: Leo A. W. Wiegman
Project Coordination: Ruttle, Shaw & Wetherill, Inc.
Design Manager: Wendy Ann Fredericks
Text and Cover Design: Paul Lacy
Electronic Production Manager: Valerie A. Sawyer
Desktop Administrator: Hilda Koparanian
Manufacturing Manager: Helene G. Landers
Electronic Page Makeup: RR Donnelley Barbados
Printer and Binder: RR Donnelley & Sons Company
Cover Printer: The Lehigh Press, Inc.

New Forces, Old Forces, and the Future of World Politics
Post-Cold War Edition

Library of Congress Cataloging-in-Publication Data

Brown, Seyom.
    New forces, old forces, and the future of world politics / Seyom
  Brown.—Post-Cold War ed.
      p. cm.
    includes index.
    ISBN 0-673-52210-5
    1. World politics—1989-   2. World politics—1945-   I. Title.
D860.B77 1995
327'.09'045—dc20   94-9128
                                                          CIP

94 95 96 97   9 8 7 6 5 4 3 2 1

CONTENTS

PREFACE

This book offers a sustained argument about the evolution of world politics and how the future of the world polity can be shaped by current choices. As such it differs from international relations textbooks that are primarily surveys of the prominent theories and research in the field. Nor is it the kind of scholarly exercise that devotes most of its pages to the support or denigration of one or another of the contending schools of thought.

I am more concerned here with the state of the world than with the state of the discipline. So too are my target audiences in the policy community and, I believe, most of the students who enroll in undergraduate courses in international relations. Some of my academic work focuses on theory-building and methodological questions, as do many of my exchanges with professional peers. I have written *New Forces, Old Forces, and the Future of World Politics,* however, as a contribution to serious public discourse on the emerging predicament of human society; the book's substance and style of exposition reflect that purpose.

Previous editions anticipated some of the developments that are destabilizing the post–Cold War world: the universal flare-up of ethnic conflict; the spread of weapons of mass destruction; the press of population growth and industrialization on the planet's finite resources and vulnerable ecologies; worsening pockets of starvation and disease; the impact of economic transnationalism on sovereignty; terrorism; and the proliferation of contraband and illegal substances. But these were for the most part subordinated to the analysis of Cold War relationships. In the 1974 and 1988 editions, I did give a lot of attention to the intensifying centrifugal forces and pressures in the United States–led and Soviet-led coalitions; but like my colleagues in government and academia, I was taken by surprise by Gorbachev's wholesale retraction of Soviet power from Eastern Europe and Germany in 1989 and 1990, and the subsequent rapid disintegration of the USSR itself.

Thus, even a book that foresaw the eventual depolarization of world politics and evolution of global polyarchy needed to be substantially recast. The process of rewriting has deepened my understanding of the forces that are durable and those that are merely transitory. Reflecting this, the present edition is in many respects an entirely new book.

My basic argument, however, has been confirmed—indeed strengthened—by the end of the Cold War and what has been happening around the world in the post–Cold War era. Namely, the world polity itself is in crisis, a crisis of incongruence between its traditional structure of governance, the nation-state system, and the most important interactions of peoples. I show many of today's headline-grabbing events to be symptoms of this systemic crisis. But I also find in this crisis the ingredients of new policies and institutions conducive to a more safe and just world order.

Because I have been developing and refining this argument over the course of three decades, my intellectual debts to individuals, beyond those cited in footnotes, are more extensive than can be listed in this preface. I do want to acknowledge, however, the financial and collegial support that the project, in its various incarnations, has received from the following institutions: the Brookings Institution, the Ford Foundation, the Council on Foreign Relations, the Carnegie Endowment for International Peace, Harvard University's Center for International Affairs, and, of course, my current home institution, Brandeis University.

The manuscript for the present book was reviewed in whole or in part by my Brandeis colleagues Steven Burg and Mark Hulliung, by Elizabeth Prodromou of Princeton University, Joseph Lepgold of Georgetown University, and Patrick Callahan of DePaul University. Their criticisms were unfailingly constructive, even when reflecting views philosophically opposed to my basic argument. I trust I will be forgiven, however, for not incorporting some of them. This book, after all, is hardly designed to *end* debate on these matters.

I also want to thank my chief editor, Leo Wiegman, his staff at Harper-Collins, and Gloria Klaiman, Tom Conville, and Ann-Marie WongSam of Ruttle, Shaw & Wetherill, Inc. for helping me to effectively express what I intended. If the prose flows, more often than not it will be because Tina Rebane removed the silt.

Finally, my two youngest sons, Matthew and Jeremiah, deserve medals for patiently enduring their father's insistence that in devoting so much of his energies to this project he was trying to make their world a better place.

Seyom Brown

INTRODUCTION:
THE NEW, THE OLD,
AND THE DURABLE

In any era of world politics, policymakers and their advisers seek to assess which of the many new and old features of the complex reality facing them warrant the status of basic "forces"—that is, material and social conditions of sufficient durability to strongly affect the chances that contemplated policies will succeed or fail. As often as not, judgments prevailing at any particular time as to what will last and what will fade may be poorly grounded in reality. The surprise of statespersons and academics alike at the sudden end of the Cold War during the 1989–1991 period was the product of fundamentally inaccurate assessments of this kind. As will be detailed in Chapters 4 through 7, loyalties, ideologies, alliances, governments, and even states that were widely believed to be highly durable turned out to be fragile and transitory; other developments that "realists" dismissed as ephemeral, such as the human rights movement in Eastern Europe, emerged as powerful forces able to shatter the pillars of empire.

Some such mistakes in prognosis are inevitable. Our understanding of why humans behave as they do lags behind our understanding of the behavior of inanimate matter and of living beings lower on the scale of organic complexity. Much remains guesswork. Yet some of the mistakes have been the product of shallow and ahistorical analysis—a tendency to extrapolate eternal verities from the surface of contemporary events, to infer causality from mere statistical correlation, to confuse what can be counted with its often hidden underlying dynamics.

Granting the uncertainties, and admitting the tentativeness of our conjectures, we can at least attempt to minimize the avoidable mistakes by probing more comprehensively into the historical record and more deeply below the visible surface of contemporary events to discover the evolved and evolving structures and basic movements of world politics and the reasons for their evolution.

From the perspective of 1994, what does such an inquiry tell us about the features of world politics that are likely to be transitory and those that are likely to be durable? Here, in summary form, are my "findings" on how the old forces and new forces have combined at this particular juncture in history to produce a set of interrelated conditions with considerable staying power—conditions that have profound implications for basic health and well-being of the human species.

Subsequent chapters elaborate on these findings and provide the supporting arguments and evidence.

1

WEAKENED NATION-STATES

The end of the Cold War was seen in many quarters as a renaissance of the nation-state system. The Cold War had been a profoundly transnational struggle between two antithetical ways of life, whose champions felt justified in subverting and overthrowing the governments of states run by those adhering to the wrong ideology. The end of the Cold War meant that the world no longer would be polarized into two supranationally organized coalitions and, presumably, could return to its "natural" political condition: a highly decentralized, virtually anarchic society of autonomous nation-states.

But this prognosis confused the renaissance of national and ethnic self-assertiveness with the revival of the sovereign nation-state. To be sure, the collapse of the Soviet Union's totalitarian imperial domain in the late 1980s provided the basis for democratic national self-determination by the countries of Eastern Europe and allowed the ethnic republics of the USSR to secede from the Union. And in the Third World, following the unraveling of the Cold War coalitions, states that were little more than pawns in the superpower contest for global dominance now achieved a considerable measure of "freedom" to develop their own international relationships.

Formal independence, however, is not the same thing as actual *sovereignty,* the power to determine the basic norms of behavior and conditions of life within the political entity. Nor does a country's internationally recognized legal status as a sovereign state necessarily reflect the ability of that country's government to provide the populations under its jurisdiction with the kind of civic order and justice they regard as legitimate or to control who and what enters or leaves the country. Indeed, the decades of the Cold War coincided with the greatest increases in the mobility of goods, information, and people in human history, creating new transnational associations and markets, and with the dramatic proliferation of industrial practices disturbing to regional and global ecologies, much of this beyond the effective control of national governments. Meanwhile, the universal contagion in the late Cold War period of democratic and human rights ideologies demanding, more than ever before, that governments be based on the consent of the governed (especially when asserted by ethnic populations transcending the borders of existing nation-states) has called into question a significant proportion of today's international borders.

Nation-states are still the most powerful political entities in world society; but many of the subnational and transnational material and ideational forces that were exploited by the Cold War superpowers, and were turned into instruments of their rivalry, antedated the Cold War and are flourishing in its aftermath. The demise of the Cold War left even the great nation-states in a *relatively* weaker position vis-à-vis other political and economic forces than during the first half of the twentieth century—not primarily because of the Cold War, but because these other forces are in many respects more basic and durable than the national idea and structures that are the foundation of the nation-state system.

WIDENING AND DEEPENING OF MATERIAL INTERDEPENDENCE

The progressive erosion of the ability of national polities to retain sovereign control over conditions in their respective countries is a symptom of the expanding—and essentially irreversible—interdependence of peoples across national boundaries. A dependent relationship exists whenever people living in one country rely for their security, economic well-being, or other amenities on the behavior of people in other countries, or on the condition of resources used in common with other countries. None of the world's some 185 countries is totally without such relationships. The June 1992 environmental "Earth Summit" in Rio de Janeiro, attended by 100 heads of state, was an expression of the fact that international interdependence, despite the efforts of most states to remain as independent as possible, is increasingly a feature of world society. So are the recurrent "rounds" of the General Agreement on Tariffs and Trade (GATT) and the growing prominence of the International Monetary Fund (IMF).

Not all interdependent relationships are symmetrical among the parties. Some countries are more dependent on outsiders than are others; many are involved in a wide range of diverse dependency relationships. A few, being the crucial provisioners of resources or protection to certain allies or clients, are able to convert such asymmetrical interdependence into hegemonic power. But even the hegemon will be dependent on its wards to some degree; indeed, without being in need of what the ward could provide (by its location, its resources, its political support in international forums—the United States vis-à-vis Saudi Arabia, for example), the hegemon would not have bothered to cultivate the relationship in the first place; and once cultivated, various sectors of the hegemon's society tend to develop a vested interest in the maintenance of the relationship.

GLOBALIZATION OF CONFLICT BETWEEN COSMOPOLITANS AND PAROCHIALS

The increasing mobility of goods, persons, and information has brought to center stage the age-old conflict between those who welcome an expansion of contacts and competition and those who fear it. In virtually every country and in the world as a whole, some groups perceive they will be the winners in larger and more open markets and political systems, whereas others perceive they will lose—relatively, if not absolutely—in material well-being, political power, and/or social status if new groups are allowed into the marketplaces of trade, politics, and culture. The history of every region of the globe can be written in part as a dialectic, sometimes bloody, between these contrary reactions to the enlargement of spheres of societal interaction and interdependence. We find the dialectic recorded in the rise and fall of empires, in the transition from feudalism to consolidated nation-states, in the opposition between the champions of free trade and the devotees of mercantilism and protectionism, and in the clashes between internationalism and xenophobia and between principles of federalism and local autonomy.

This recurring axis of confrontation once again, and more widely than ever, divides and unites people around the world, supplanting the "East vs. West" (marxist vs. capitalist) confrontation that polarized global society during the Cold War era. Worldwide, coalitions and antagonisms are forming among the cosmopolitans and parochials over both material and cultural matters.

Currently, the phenomenon is reflected prominently in international bargaining between "Southern" (Third World) and "Northern" (industrialized) countries over trade, development, and environmental issues. A Third World coalition has been galvanized by concerns that the global market economy and environmental regulations being pressed on them by Northern governments, the IMF, and the World Bank will only enhance the competitive advantages already enjoyed by the advanced industrialized countries and by large Northern-owned multinational firms in Third World markets, leading to a de facto "neo-colonial" resubordination of the economically underdeveloped Southern countries to their former imperial overlords plus the United States and Japan.

Not all Third World countries, and certainly not all segments of society within Third World countries, are part of the coalition opposed to an open global market. Some of the newly industrializing countries (NICs), such as South Korea, Taiwan, and Singapore, have found profitable niches in the international production and trade of high-tech items; some, like Mexico in the 1990s, hope to do so. Other Third World countries, their economies vulnerable to sudden declines in global prices for their agricultural commodities, have been demanding international price-support agreements for their exports. Moreover, within many developing countries there is, on the one hand, considerable division between exporting and/or tourist sectors who welcome more commerce with the industrialized world and, on the other hand, struggling domestic industry sectors who feel they need a considerable period of protection from more advanced foreign competitors in order to survive and develop even a domestic clientele.

Similarly, in the Third World, there are deep divisions on environmental issues, reflecting the unequal costs different sectors of the economy and population will have to bear in converting to ecologically sustainable development. But in the 1992 Earth Summit on Environment and Economic Development and its follow-on negotiations on matters such as global warming, ozone depletion, and biodiversity, most of the developing countries have coalesced around the proposition that abatement policies that would cost a lot of money, at least in the short run, should be funded by the advanced industrial countries. The Third World is saying, in effect, global ecological interdependence and its corollary, shared responsibility for the health of ecologies, must be a *two*-way street.

Within the industrialized world as well, there tends to be a divergence between the weak/immobile and the strong/mobile elements of the society when it comes to determining how open international borders should be and who should have full access to national and transnational markets. In the European Union, for example, the economically less-developed countries and less-modernized sectors within countries are by and large defenders of special subsidies and protections for local enclaves of industry and agriculture that might otherwise be displaced by the community-wide competition, let alone worldwide competition, championed by the Union's technocratic elite. Similarly in the United States, it is the executives of the most successful multinational corporations—not small businessmen and leaders of labor unions—that have been the staunchest advocates of United States–Canada free trade and the incorporation of Mexico in a North American common market.

Cultural affinities and antagonisms are often interlinked with, and indeed are sometimes the source of, the cosmopolitan vs. parochial lineup on economic issues. The dramatic increases in *physical* mobility of goods, people, and ideas brought on by the technological revolutions in transportation and communication both challenge and reinforce ethnocentric attitudes, leading in many places to efforts to thicken *legal* barriers to mobility. For some elements of society, the new opportunities to come into contact with and learn about peoples of other cultures confirm beliefs in the "family of humankind" and convictions that we should be mutually concerned about one another's well-being across national borders. For others, familiarity sustains or breeds contempt or fear of having one's way of life diluted or overwhelmed by foreign influences and intercommunal fraternization, particularly among young people. Much of the agitation for tightening controls on foreign immigration, usually presented as required to preserve a supply/demand equilibrium for jobs in certain occupational categories, is a transparent cover for racial or religious xenophobia.

PROLIFERATION OF CROSS-CUTTING ASSOCIATIONS

Cumulatively, these various basic trends have been producing a multiplicity of cross-cutting relationships at all levels of society—individual, group, national, transnational, and global. Human existence, let alone the enjoyment of the varied amenities of modern life, has come to require sustained interaction among individuals and collectivities with quite different characteristics.

Typically, the modern individual will engage in these interactions as a member (formal or informal) of a variety of associations defined by location of residence, ethnicity, religion, occupation, and recreational pursuit. In contrast to traditional society, in which one's neighbors were likely to be of the same race and religion and to work at the same kind of jobs, in modern industrial or postindustrial society, one's neighbors are more and more just as likely as not to be of a different religion and to be employed in quite different occupations; co-members of one's labor union or professional organization will probably be heterogeneous in gender, ethnicity, and religion and in their memberships in other functionally specific organizations.

As a consequence, individuals are likely to find that their allies on one issue are their opponents on another; today's enemy may well be tomorrow's friend, depending on the subject matter around which conflict or cooperation is revolving at the time. There will be times when such multiple associations produce antithetical loyalties in an individual, setting up painful cross-pressures. On the positive side, such cross-pressures can induce the affected individuals to support efforts to resolve or at least moderate the intergroup conflicts that are the source of their pain.

An essentially similar dynamic to that which affects the cross-pressured individuals affects general membership *groups,* including nation-states, transnational movements, and interstate coalitions. In modern society, members of almost any large group will be heterogeneous in their socioeconomic and/or cultural characteristics, apart from that special characteristic that initially brings the group together (such as their religion, occupation, locale of residence, or special policy interest). The more general and heterogeneous the membership, the more difficult it will be to mobilize the group for action across a wide range of issues, particularly if such mobilization requires intense hostility to other groups sharing some of the characteristics and values of members of one's own group. Thus, as national societies become pervaded by such heterogeneous and transnationally interlinked membership groups, both international hostility against a definable enemy and interstate coalition-building across a range of issues become more difficult to sustain. This consequence of "modernization," as will be discussed in subsequent chapters, is significantly altering the role of force in world politics and the function of other traditional mechanisms of international statecraft such as alliances, the balance of power, and the operation of international institutions.

THE PRESS OF THE PLANET'S GROWING POPULATION ON ITS FINITE RESOURCES

Enveloping and interacting with all of these trends is the continuing growth of the world's human population, which even at its current size (over 5.4 billion in 1994) is putting alarming pressure on vital ecological relationships: a stratosphere with a chemical composition that screens out lethal rays of the sun; an atmosphere sufficiently free of heat-trapping gases to perpetuate a livable climate on Earth; and enough unpolluted soil, water, and air and biologically diverse plant and animal life to nourish and sustain the human species in a healthy condition.

Standard demographic estimates, assuming no dramatic worldwide revolution in population-control policies, project a global population approaching 8.5 billion by the year 2025 and 10 billion by the year 2050.[1] Assuming further that in the meantime there will have been no fundamental worldwide change in energy-consumption practices and in industrialization, this rough doubling in numbers of people over the next four decades is likely to strain the "carrying capacity" of the Earth's biosphere beyond tolerable limits. Credible dire predictions include exponential increases in the incidence of skin cancer and immune system failure (from unfiltered sunrays getting through holes in the ozone layer); drastic perturbations of the planet's climate (from an enhanced carbon dioxide "greenhouse effect"), leading to vast flooding of coastal regions and continental draughts and desertification in other regions; widespread shortages of healthy food and water (from inadequate means of disposing of waste products)—all of this increasing the proportion of humankind suffering from starvation and disease.

POLITICAL CONFLICT OVER WHO GETS WHAT, WHEN, AND HOW

As the inhabitants of the planet continue to create scarcities in valued natural amenities (material resources, healthy living space, and climatic conditions), conflict among peoples for preferred access to these amenities can be expected to grow and intensify. The expectation of increasing conflict rests on more than forecasts of population growth and worldwide industrialization; it also rests in large part on the universal spread of ideas of social justice and equity focused on the *distribution* of rights and privileges to the Earth's scarce bounty—ideas that, ironically, first developed and flourished in the more affluent regions that are now the target of, and most resistant to, demands for *re*distribution.

This historical irony is compounded by the fact that the free-market ideas that in previous centuries served to redistribute wealth and privilege (and were formerly called "liberal") are now used to ward off policies aimed at further redistributions; in general, except for the post-Communist countries in which the terminology has been turned completely on its head, today's

[1]Eduard Bos, My T. Vu, Ann Levin, Rodolfo A. Bulatao, *World Population Projections 1992–93 Edition: Estimates and Projections with Related Demographic Statistics* (Baltimore: Johns Hopkins University Press, 1992 [published for the World Bank]).

staunchest defenders of the free-market capitalism call themselves "conserv-ative" and apply the term "liberal" disparagingly to those who would have governments intervene in the free market in the name of social justice.

At the international level, the conflict between the advocates of laissez-faire regimes and the advocates of market-regulation/social justice regimes is particularly prominent when it comes to allocating use rights in the global "commons"—the high seas and deep seabed, the planet's life-sustaining biosphere, and the electromagnetic spectrum and geostationary orbit for communications and observational spacecraft. The 1992 Earth Summit on Environment and Development featured this dimension of political conflict, with the United States the most vociferous champion of nonregulatory mar-ket approaches for protecting the environment and the leaders of the Third World coalition and the Scandinavian countries arguing for international conventions binding on governments and firms to ensure their adherence to agreed-upon limits and standards (paralleling the alignment on the issue of who should finance the poor countries' conversion to environment-preserv-ing development policies).

INCONGRUENCE OF GOVERNANCE AND SOCIETY

These basic trends, operating within the inherited structures of the tradi-tional nation-state system, are producing, on the whole, a global pattern in which the formal institutions of governance lack congruence with the loyal-ties and associations of peoples. Increasingly, the officials of the national governments who negotiate with each other on behalf of the people within their territorial jurisdictions or who take their countries into war do not, in fact, authoritatively represent, nor can they authoritatively command the behavior of, the "citizens" of their countries.

Well-functioning political systems feature an essential congruence be-tween, on the one hand, the effective authority possessed by the society's governing *institutions* and, on the other hand, the *behaviors* that are sup-posed to be constrained by these institutions as they attempt to represent and service society's values. By contrast, where the relevant behaviors es-cape appropriate governmental constraints—as is increasingly the case in the global nation-state system—the political system can be said to be in "cri-sis."

This emerging global crisis of incongruence—its historical evolution, its contemporary sources, and what can be done about it—is a principal theme in the chapters that follow.

LEGACIES

1

THE INHERITED FOUNDATIONS: BASIC STRUCTURE AND NORMS OF THE NATION-STATE SYSTEM

My main themes, for which the Introduction serves as prelude, are (1) the incongruence between the inherited structure and norms of the nation-state system and the dominant trends in contemporary world society and (2) what this incongruence portends for the future of world politics. This chapter's overview of the system's evolved structure and norms provides a context for the historical and field-specific analysis in subsequent chapters.

BASIC STRUCTURE AND NORMS

The world's human population is divided into territorially demarcated "countries," and each person normally is assumed to belong to one of them. As of 1994, there were some 185 countries, ranging in area from sprawling Russia (encompassing 6.6 million square miles) to the tiny kingdom of Monaco (only one-tenth as large as Washington, DC) and varying in number of inhabitants from China's greater than a billion to Tuvala's fewer than 10,000.

Every country claims to be a self-governing community—a *state*—and generally is recognized by the other countries as possessing legal authority or "sovereignty" over what happens in its territory. The institutional apparatus of the state, its official organizations for formulating and enforcing the laws of the country, and those who run these organizations are commonly referred to as the government.

The ability to sustain such sovereign statehood requires substantial cooperation among the people living within the territory, even if only to conduct orderly exchanges of goods and services with one another and to protect themselves against disruptive foreign intruders. Accordingly, where a particular country has persisted for generations there usually are strong bonds of identity among its people, a sense of being a *nation*. To symbolize and help maintain this sense of nationhood, each country has a distinctive flag or banner, inspirational national anthems and oaths, and other rituals of citizenship and patriotism that are performed at public ceremonies to reinforce feelings of loyalty to the country.

In each of the nation-states, ultimate authority and power normally are lodged in a central government responsible for ensuring that the basic requirements of community life are maintained, namely, law and order (particularly physical security of persons and property), conditions that encourage industry and commerce, community norms of justice, controls on the use of natural resources and the natural environment, and a common cultural base, especially language.

Despite the existence of alternative foci of identification—religions, ethnic and cultural groups, gender, occupations and professions, multicountry alliances and regional confederations, humankind—the national government of a country usually has an overriding claim on the loyalty of its citizenry. Only the national government has generally recognized authority and power to require individuals to put their lives at stake, to draft them into armed forces, and to defend the common interests of the population. There are many subnational and transnational movements and organizations around the world whose members are willing to die for their particular causes, as, for example, the Hamas faction of the Palestinian *intifada,* extremist Sikh militants in India's Punjab, and the Irish Republican Army, but according to the state-sovereignty norms of the nation-state system, violence organized by nonstate groups is almost always illegitimate unless specifically authorized by an established government. Even then, such violence is usually condemned as "terrorism" by other governments.

It is primarily the national government that, in the name of law and order and justice, issues and implements the basic rules of community life that are to prevail throughout a country's territory. Virtually every nation-state has subordinate levels of government with which the national government shares responsibility for essential public fields of activity and for ensuring that law and order are maintained. The degree and organization of the devolution of authority vary from country to country, but in each the central government retains the ultimate authority to control the subordinate levels.

Under the assumption that each nation-state is a self-governing unit, relations among them would seem to be only a marginal feature of the system. But even prior to the contemporary age of "interdependence," international relations have been quite prominent among various groups of countries. Why? One basic reason is that many countries are far from self-sufficient in certain goods required or desired by their peoples, including, in some cases, physical security and public order, and therefore will attempt to acquire these goods from other countries, sometimes by commerce, sometimes by conquest. Another reason is that often countries commonly use the same re-source areas (oceans, rivers, the atmosphere, outer space), and the people of one country using a particular resource get in the way of or affect the condi-tion of the people of another country. The determination of who gets what, when, and how in such contested areas necessitates international negotia-tion or fighting.

In an ideally functioning nation-state system, international relations would be highly circumscribed by the system's norm of state sovereignty: No country, no world or regional organization, no foreign citizen or organi-zation would act within the territory of another country without its consent. Privileges obtained by foreigners to act within the territorial jurisdiction of a state would be negotiated. In fact, such sovereignty, although asserted as a fundamental norm of the system, is often violated in practice. Smaller and weaker countries are coerced by the more powerful into granting them priv-ileges of access and entry, which during the Cold War was the condition of the countries in Eastern Europe in relation to the Soviet Union. To guard against unwanted intervention from hostile states, potential victims form al-liances with powerful friendly countries, sometimes establishing a degree of dependence upon their protectors that, paradoxically, requires them to ac-cept an oppressive foreign presence, as happened to the South Vietnamese during the decade of American military involvement in Indochina.

Nation-States and Law and Order

Under the norms of the nation-state system, each country is responsible for maintaining sufficient law and order within its own jurisdiction to allow the inhabitants to engage in normal domestic pursuits—agriculture, industry, trade, and cultural and family life—secure from violent attacks on them-selves and their possessions.

To perform this basic law and order function, the central government of the country normally maintains a monopoly of violent weapons. Short of such monopolization of violence, the central government at least tries to arm itself to the extent that it can overwhelm any private or local violence.

The central government of the nation-state is also the locus of the main capabilities for protecting the territorial unit from invasion or externally supported subversion of the country's prevailing regime. This role is often called defending the "territorial integrity" of the country.

In the nation-state system, as traditionally viewed, adequate provision for both domestic order and the security of each country against external ag-gression requires, at a minimum, (1) clearly demarcated borders separating the countries; (2) reliable controls by each country over land, sea, and air (including telecommunications) access to the territorial area; and (3) possession by the central government of each country of the legal right and physical resources to use all means necessary, including war, to maintain the security of the territorial unit.

Because of the unequal military power of countries, some of them are unable to satisfy these minimum public order requirements without accepting material or direct help from friendly countries to balance the military power of an enemy. Thus, the nation-state system, in its public order functions, is inevitably also a system of power-balancing alliances.[1]

Historically, the nation-state/alliance system appears to have played a crucial role in preventing the planet from being convulsed by the extremes of anarchy, global empire, and world war.[2] But, as will be argued in subsequent chapters, a continued heavy reliance on the international mechanisms of military armaments and alliances is increasingly dangerous in the face of some of the emergent changes in world politics and threatens the very survival of the planet.

The global peace and security organizations of the twentieth century—the League of Nations and the United Nations—while conceived of by some of their champions as successors to the nation-state/alliance system, turned out, in operation, to be instruments of that system rather than its antithesis. Under the rules of the League, and now under the rules of the UN, participation by members in common actions to counter threats to the peace is voluntary. Only in the most extreme circumstances, such as a member state's violation of the essential norms of the system (For example, Iraq's invasion of Kuwait in 1990), can military or police forces assembled under authority of the international organization be deployed on the territory of a member country without that country's consent; and such actions require the approval of all five of the permanent members of the Security Council.

New forces (to be discussed in subsequent chapters) are challenging the capacity of the nation-state system to attend adequately to the peace and security needs of human society. But the responsibility for maintaining law and order among countries is still lodged in the nation-state system and its highly decentralized and voluntary mechanisms. As yet, there is no global institution and no process other than the formation of alliances among states to organize balances of power that can be relied upon to restrain determined and powerful aggressor nations.

---

[1]The notion that the nation-state system, relying heavily on military alliances, is the natural political system for world society is a central assumption of the "structural realist" school of international relations theory. *See* especially Kenneth N. Waltz, *Theory of International Politics* (Menlo Park: Addison-Wesley, 1979).

[2]The best exposition of the role of the power-balancing process among nation-states in maintaining world public order remains Hans Morgenthau's classic treatise, *Politics among Nations: The Struggle for Power and Peace* (New York: Knopf, 1978).

NATION-STATES AND COMMERCE

The separate nation-states also sustain the basic conditions for economic relations within and among communities. The territorial confines of a nation-state normally demarcate the boundaries of a highly organized trading community or "market." Except where multinational "common markets" have been instituted (as in the European Union and, potentially, the North American Free Trade Area of Canada, the United States, and Mexico), foreigners usually must receive permission from a country's national government to sell in its market and usually must convert their own currencies into the special national currency of the market in order to pay for purchases.

As communities of coordinated economic activity, nation-states are especially responsible for providing for the construction and availability of transportation and communications networks to facilitate commerce within their jurisdictions and among them. Frequently, the national government itself owns and runs major highways, air and water transport systems, postal services, and telecommunications and broadcasting systems. In some countries—China, for example—the national government monopolizes these systems (sometimes for reasons of political control of the population as well as for the effective provision of community services). In every country, the central government retains at least supreme regulatory power over the use of all but very private media of communication and transportation, even if for no other reasons than to avoid congestion, provide safe passage, and control conflict among users.

A considerable degree of coordination across nation-state lines does prevail in the commercial realm.[3] Firms that normally buy and sell outside their home countries have found it desirable, if not essential, to build some predictable order and standardization into what otherwise would be a fragmented world economy with each national market having unique rules of access, often designed to protect inefficient local producers against foreign competitors. Since World War II, those who feel they will benefit from a relatively open world market have persuaded their national governments to participate in negotiations under the General Agreement on Tariffs and Trade (GATT) to coordinate reductions in barriers to international trade and to subscribe to International Monetary Fund (IMF) rules for stabilizing exchange rates among the currencies of various nations. Consistent with the norms of the nation-state system, however, participation in the GATT and adherence to IMF arrangements are supposed to be voluntary on the part of each country (in practice, of course, the economically powerful members of these international institutions often do bring virtually irresistible pressures

---

[3]*See* Stephen D. Krasner, ed., *International Regimes* (Ithaca: Cornell University Press, 1983). *See also* Richard Rosecrance, *The Rise of the Trading State: Commerce and Conquest in the Modern World* (New York: Basic Books, 1986).

on other countries to conform to various international trading and monetary policies).

International coordination has also been found highly desirable in the transportation and communication fields, to establish "rules of the road" and to avoid congestion. Some of the most important "functional" international institutions operate in these fields, notably the International Maritime Organization, the International Civil Aviation Organization, and the International Telecommunication Union. Some of these agencies have been accorded international licensing authority, but the power to impose sanctions on violators of international rules is retained by the national governments or their subunits.

NATION-STATES AND SOCIAL JUSTICE

In addition to facilitating commerce, nation-states provide the principal means for giving special help to those who cannot adequately support themselves by selling their labor, products, services, or talents in the market. The regulatory and taxing powers of national governments are the mechanisms most relied on to redistribute wealth, status, power, and opportunity. And the domestic legal systems of the nation-states and their subdivisions are the sources of enforceable prohibitions and privileges of individual and group behavior—the norms that majorities impose on minorities, the rights of citizens in relation to governments, and the rights and obligations of individuals toward each other.

Efforts to develop international obligations to help the world's destitute or oppressed peoples have made little headway. Some countries unilaterally extend famine relief and even economic development assistance to others; some countries contribute to internationally organized relief efforts and to international institutions for development assistance such as the World Bank. Even in the case of humanitarian relief efforts undertaken by the United Nations, such as the provision of food and medical help to the Somalis and Rwandans in 1992–1994, national governments normally retain their sovereignty on both the receiving and giving ends.

Most national governments have signed international declarations and covenants of social justice and individual rights, as, for example, the Universal Declaration of Human Rights, the International Covenant on Economic, Social and Cultural Rights, and the International Covenant on Civil and Political Rights. Twenty-one governments have signed the European Convention on Human Rights, obligating themselves to conform in fact to the Convention's detailed substantive and procedural provisions. Citizens who feel that justice is being denied them within their own nation-states can invoke such international charters in an effort to bring pressure on their national governments to respond to their grievances. Even in Western Europe, however, where some countries allow citizens to appeal directly to the Human Rights Commission or Court, redress must be obtained through one of the national legal systems. There is no supranational institution that can compel a country to adhere to international human rights norms, not even those that a country has formally obligated itself to implement. But as the events of 1989–1991 in Eastern Europe and the Soviet Union demonstrated, the fact that a government officially subscribes to the basic international rights charters provides its citizenry with a contract, as it were, to wave in the face of that government, to undermine its domestic support, to challenge its legitimacy, often before the world's media, and to mobilize constituencies in other countries to bring pressure on their governments to internationally isolate the offending government.

As literacy and international communication intensify the perception of relatively poor and disenfranchised elements of world society that they are unjustly deprived by the existing international order, calls for new institutions for processing social justice demands are heard increasingly in international forums.

NATION-STATES AND THE USE OF NATURAL RESOURCES AND THE ENVIRONMENT

One of the main functions of government is the control of access to and exploitation of the natural resources used by a community, so that members can be assured of appropriate shares, vulnerable resources are kept in usable condition, and exhaustible resources are not too rapidly depleted. Historically, strong and centralized governments have developed out of the need to perform this function, an outstanding example being the role of ancient kingdoms in Egypt in managing the Nile.

Because the location of natural resources is not always congruent with the borders of nation-states, coordination and cooperation among groups of countries have often proven to be in their mutual self-interest. Accordingly, international associations of resources users have formed in various fields, particularly where there are commonly harvested and depletable resources such as ocean fisheries.[4]

In some fields, the responsible international institutions have been vested with limited inspection and/or licensing authority to "police" common standards. But refusal to accept international inspection or other actions that may disqualify a project from international agency certification are unlikely to be deterred by such highly limited licensing authority. A country determined to proceed with a project or action will do so without formal interna-

[4]Seyom Brown, Nina Cornell, Larry Fabian, and Edith Brown Weiss, *Regimes for the Ocean, Outer Space and Weather* (Washington: The Brookings Institution, 1977).

tional blessing. Any stronger deterrent sanctions must come from other national governments.

As evident in the 1992 "Earth Summit," the increasing utilization of technologies and industrial activities capable of grossly disturbing the natural ecological relationships that sustain human life, let alone the growing realization that undertakings in one political jurisdiction can negatively affect the health and welfare of people in neighboring jurisdictions, is stimulating new demands for mandatory international accountability. It is now a commonplace observation that some modifications in the sovereignty norms of the existing nation-state system are unavoidable in the environmental field.

NATION-STATES AND THE MAINTENANCE OF DIVERSE CULTURES

One of the most important functions the nation-state performs for human society is the provision of a home for particular ways of life. Under the protection of a national-legal political system whose autonomy is respected by other countries, special rules of morality, religious practice, language, music, and artistic and architectural creation can be encouraged and preserved in the face of those who may not value that culture sufficiently.

If such enclaves of culture were not provided with adequate protection, many of the ethnic groups that now maintain their uniqueness might be homogenized into larger and more aggressive world cultures. The loss of cultural integrity is feared especially by societies that require disciplined adherence to religious rituals and particular family and sexual mores. The national governments representing these societies often attempt to prevent the dissemination of literature from other cultures and foreign telecommunications broadcasts from contaminating the local cultural purity, and frequently maintain tight restrictions on the activities of tourists, foreign commercial enterprises, and foreign diplomatic and military personnel stationed in their societies. Thus, the soldiers of the United States and other Western countries participating in the 1990–1991 "Desert Storm" operation for liberating Kuwait and protecting Saudi Arabia from Iraqi attacks were prohibited by the Muslim theocratic Saudi government from freely mingling with the indigenous population. Military chaplains were even prevented from conducting Christian and Jewish religious ceremonies in view of Saudi military contingents.

Many nation-states also feel culturally threatened from within. Some are large multicultural countries. A few, like the United States, have dealt with their condition of ethnic diversity fairly well—with constitutional systems and laws congenial to cultural pluralism, permissive policies toward diverse social practices, protection of minority rights, and prohibitions against official favoritism toward particular religions. Other countries, for example, India, and Canada in some of its constitutional provisions, have federal structures that devolve considerable governing authority to subunits of government ("provinces," "states") in order to accommodate the various cultural groupings within the federal union.

Not all cultural groups, however, feel adequately protected or represented in the nation-states with formal legal jurisdiction over them. On numerous occasions in history, civil or interstate war has resulted from demands for self-determination or autonomy of a cultural group within a society ruled by another cultural group. Indeed, the current demarcation of the globe into nation-states is in large measure the outcome of the last round of struggles between cultural groups that defined themselves as nations and insisted on their own states in which they could set the rules. Such a re-demarcation of nation-state jurisdictions has recently transpired in the former Soviet Union. Under a professed ideology of cultural pluralism, the USSR tried to function with only the trappings of ethnic uniqueness allowed the ethnically diverse non-Russian republics—giving prominence to their languages, songs, dances, and the like—while systematically homogenizing their economies and polities into a tightly run totalitarian system controlled from Moscow. But songs and dances were not a sufficient safety valve for the resentments against the Russian overlords, and when the Gorbachev regime allowed for genuine political self-expression under perestroika and glasnost, one by one each of the republics exercised the right of "national self-determination" to establish themselves as sovereign countries independent of the USSR. A more violent shakedown occurred in Yugoslavia starting in 1991, where the federal center controlled by Serbia went to war against Croatia, Bosnia, and other member republics seeking to obtain full independence. Other prominent contemporary conflicts over cultural/national autonomy (to be discussed more fully in Chapter 12) are being waged by the Palestinians in Israel, the Sikhs in India, the Tamils in Sri Lanka, the Basques in Spain, and the Irish Catholics in Northern Ireland, to name just a few.

Some defenders of the nation-state system as the basis for world order accept such conflicts over self-determination, viewing them as periodic shakedowns of the system conducive to the restoration of its essential equilibrium. It is questionable, however, whether human civilization can continue to survive such struggles for national self-determination as modern means of mass destruction and terror become increasingly accessible to states and stateless groups alike.

2

PRECURSORS OF THE MODERN STATE SYSTEM

Human society has exhibited large variations in the size and shape of its characteristic political units. These variations have been caused partly by the natural geography of the world and partly by different rates of development of technologies for altering nature and subduing human adversaries. A crucial determinant, however, has been the unique capacity of the human species to conceive of, experiment with, and choose alternative patterns of social life.

There have been times and places where the preferred size of the polity, for example, has been a *micro*-polis confined to people in face-to-face contact (as in the ancient Greek city-states). At other times and places the ideal among statespersons and philosophers has been a *cosmo*-polis, or world state (the Roman Empire being the closest historical approximation). Indeed, many regions and historical eras have featured recurrent oscillations toward each of these extremes. Depending on where and when the political historian focuses attention, the "new forces" might appear to be those pressing for greater political integration of a region or the world's peoples, and the "old forces," those guarding the autonomy of existing states; or, vice versa, the "new forces" might appear to be those working to dismantle existing polities on grounds of national or ethnic "self-determination" against the opposition of the "old forces" attempting to maintain a centrally controlled union of diverse peoples.

This chapter looks at some prototypical pre-modern examples of vast unifying polities and of local autonomy systems, and of the tension between the integrative and disintegrative forces. The next chapter takes up the story of the evolution of world politics in the middle of the seventeenth century, when the oscillation between the extremes of world empire and highly localized parochialism seemed to have stabilized in a pluralistic "balance of power" system, which, as we shall see, turned out to be not so stable after all.

The principal purpose of this historical excursion is to gain insight into basic processes of political integration and disintegration, with a view toward better understanding what configurations of the world polity are likely to be most durable in the decades ahead.

"UNIVERSAL" EMPIRES

None of the great empires of the pre-modern world even approached being able to rule the entire inhabitable planet. The existing means of communication and transportation precluded more than regional spans of control. Some of the pre-modern empire builders were nevertheless insatiable in their appetite for expansion and thought themselves worthy of dominating all those peoples with whom they came into contact. As characterized by political historian Robert Wesson,

> the universal empire is a political world to itself, a single and essentially contained entity. Hardly aware of states beyond, or, if perhaps troubled by them at times, scornful of them as unworthy inferiors, it is an unchallengeable power standing over its world, so vast as to appear to exalted masters and humble subjects alike as infinite in grandeur. Such an empire rests upon conquest and hence can be established wherever geography permits a great state to be built and held together.[1]

There are over twenty pre-modern political systems that qualify as "universal empires" by such criteria.[2] I have selected nine as sufficiently prototypical of the elemental dynamics of political integration and disintegration: Egypt under the Pharaohs; Mesopotamia under Sargon; Assyria; Persia; the empire of Alexander the Great; the Chou dynasty; India under Chandragupta and Asoka; the classical Roman Empire; and the empire of the Mongols.

Egypt

Beginning about 3100 B.C., the region congruent with the valley of the 4100-mile Nile River was by and large a politically unified and self-sufficient empire—with intermittent periods of feudal disintegration and conquest by outsiders—until the period of modern European colonialism. The development and control of a highly centralized irrigation system for the otherwise infertile area was the principal basis of the Egyptian imperium.

The first era of unity lasted nearly 1000 years under the theocratic rule of absolute monarchs known as Pharaohs.

[1]Robert G. Wesson, *The Imperial Order* (Berkeley: University of California Press, 1967), pp. 21–22.
[2]*See* Arnold Toynbee, *A Study of History* (New York: Oxford University Press, 1947). Abridgement of Volumes I–VI by D. C. Somervell, p. 561.

The surrounding deserts and seas, given the transportation technologies of the time, provided natural protective frontiers within which the peoples of the river valley could be culturally homogenized and economically integrated.

Toward the end of this early period, however, ostentatious pyramid construction and other accoutrements of imperial grandeur, which the Pharaohs sustained by gifts of local territorial jurisdiction and amenities to provincial nobles, began to sap the center's sustenance in relation to the relative rise in power of rival provincial rulers. From about 2180 to 2040 B.C., the area was pervaded by virtual anarchy.

A new politically adept dynasty established itself at Thebes about 2060 B.C. and re-integrated the country through a combination of conquest and controlled devolution of authority to local nobility in exchange for their loyalty to the center. But by 1785 B.C., after a succession of incompetent and weak rulers, this so-called Middle Kingdom succumbed to internal chaos and then subjugation by the chariot-riding Hyskos coming out of West Asia. Two centuries of cruel domination by the Hyskos eventually resulted in Egyptian rebellions against their alien oppressors.

A third era of dynastic rule by indigenous Pharaohs was re-established about 1570 B.C. by Egyptian warrior leaders who expelled the Hyskos. To prevent further vulnerability to outside invaders, and exploiting the military mobility learned from the Hyskos, the restored Egyptian empire expanded its northeast frontier into western Asia as far as the Euphrates River of Mesopotamia. This "New Kingdom" lasted another four centuries until a new phase of internal instability (stimulated in part by the theocratic excesses of one of the later Pharaohs and reactive revolts by the suppressed cults) denuded the capacity of Egypt to effectively fend off a succession of conquerors, first from neighboring Lybia and Ethiopia, and then from Persia, Macedonia, and Rome.[3]

The Mesopotamian Empire of Sargon of Akkad

Huge by comparison to Egypt in the area it covered, the Sumerian-based empire of the Semite Sargon of Akkad, fanning out from the Mesopotamian plain bordering the Persian Gulf between the Tigris and Euphrates rivers, lasted briefly from 2350 to 2290 but it was the first of a long historical train of efforts to dominate other peoples from this strategically located crossroads of culture and commerce. Sargon himself ruled for only 61 years. His kingdom adopted the advanced writing, calendar, and business methods of the subjugated Sumerians and spread this culture throughout his vast Near Eastern domain.

[3]Tom B. Jones, *Ancient Civilization* (Chicago: Rand McNally, 1960), Chapter 4, "Egyptian Civilization," pp. 61–77. *See also* Geoffrey Barraclough, ed., *The Times Atlas of World History* (London: Times Books, 1979), pp. 58–59, and L. S. Stravrianos, *The World to 1500: A Global History* (Englewood Cliffs: Prentice Hall, 1970), pp. 55–58.

Mesopotamia's location was the source of both its strength and vulnerability: it had access to the world of the Near East and Mediterranean but was also highly accessible commercially and militarily from all directions and to a multiplicity of cultural influences. Sargon's descendants, resting on their laurels and luxuries, soon found themselves reigning, but not really ruling, over revived and self-assertive cities and states in Sumeria and the lands beyond. By 2050 B.C. another group of Semites established themselves in Sumeria and made Babylon their capital; yet even under the autocratic lawgiver Hammurabi (1948–1905 B.C.), Mesopotamia never regained the universal pretensions and regional power it had during its days of glory under Sargon of Akkad. Henceforth it was to be eclipsed if not subjugated by a succession of other empires with universal pretensions: Assyria, Chaldea, Persia, the empire of Alexander the Great, and Rome.

Assyria

Once again, after more than 1000 years of rivalry among the states in the area previously dominated by Macedonia, one of them, the highland kingdom of Assyria, was successful in establishing itself for some 200 years as imperial hegemon over the entire "Fertile Crescent" from the Persian Gulf to Eastern Turkey and along the east coast of the Mediterranean down into Egypt. The greatest conquests were achieved by Sargon II (naming himself after the great Akkadian ruler of Mesopotamia) and his descendants in the eighth and seventh centuries B.C.

An ancient prefiguration of the brutal twentieth century totalitarianism of Hitler's Third Reich and Stalin's Soviet system, imperial Assyria ruled over its vast domain through overwhelming military strength and the terrorization of peoples it subdued. One of the techniques of domination anticipatory of modern despotisms was the forceful transplantation of people from their homelands into other parts of the empire, thus atomizing otherwise ethnically homogeneous communities and precluding their capacity to mobilize resentments against their alien conqueror. Having subdued all likely sources of opposition in a region, the Assyrians would link it into their larger domain by roads and trade, thus creating cosmopolitan classes throughout the empire with a stake in its preservation. Historians generally give Assyria credit for being the most tightly and efficiently coordinated of all the ancient empires.[4]

Despite Assyria's resourceful material methods, both military and commercial, of establishing an integrated realm, its vastness and the cruelties of its despots proved to be inconsistent with the necessary maintenance of deeper loyalties and cultural identifications with Assyria. Eventually pe-

---

[4]The essential features of the Assyrian imperial system are vividly capsulized in T. Walter Wallbank and Alastair M. Taylor, *Civilization Past and Present* (Chicago: Scott, Foresman and Company, 1949), Vol. I, pp. 81–84.

ripheral areas succumbed to onslaughts of Indo-European warrior tribes, particularly on the northern frontiers of the empire. Assyria's growing weakness, partially the result of having to defend the ramparts against new predators, led to the capture of Babylon itself in 616 B.C. by the Chaldeans under the ostentatious Nebuchadnezzar. For the next few decades the Near Eastern "Fertile Crescent" was contested over by at least three imperiums— the Egyptians at its southwestern extremity, the Chaldeans between the Tigris and Euphrates, and the Medes and Persians on the east—with the Persians winning out and establishing their 200-year hegemony, starting in 549 BC with the defeat and occupation of Babylonia by Cyrus the Great.

The Persian Empire

In the tradition of the ancient universalizers, the imperial ambitions of Cyrus and his successors on the Persian throne knew no bounds. Each of them called himself "Kings of Kings," claiming to be the divinely appointed agent of "the good," which the Persian prophet Zoroaster taught was engaged in a struggle with "the bad" throughout the cosmos. Having no illusions that they could maintain basic order and control through the cultivation of religious obedience, the Persian monarchs ruled their vast realm through subservient regional potentates called "satraps," whose functions included the implementation of imperial law and the collection of imperial taxes. Each of the satrapies was buttressed and controlled by an army directly responsible to the central government, not to the regional satrap. The central government also retained a network of spies throughout the satrapies—often performing their cloak-and-dagger work under the cover of the deceptively autonomous Zoroastrian priesthood—to anticipate possible local revolts and nip them in the bud.[5]

At its largest and wealthiest, at the start of the fifth century B.C., the Persian empire extended from northern Africa to northwest India and from the Gulf of Oman to southern Russia. Cyrus himself took control of Turkey and the Greek Ionian cities and expanded the empire's eastern frontier as far as what is now Pakistan. Under Cyrus's son Cambyses, Persia also absorbed Egypt and Libya. In 491 B.C., however, with the empire's girth most bloated, Darius I imprudently overextended the Persian army, sending it deep into Greece, where it was defeated at Marathon. Darius's son Xerxes once again sent the Persian army into Greece in 480 B.C. He bested the Spartans at Thermopylae, but was defeated in subsequent battles in 479 and was compelled to withdraw from the Greek peninsula and southern Europe.

After Xerxes' last disastrous Greek venture, the central authority of the empire went into irreversible decline. Gradually, the local potentates were thrown back on their own resources and were vulnerable to absorption into

---

[5]William H. McNeil, *The Rise of the West: A History of the Human Community* (New York: Mentor Books, 1965), pp. 143–144, 438–445.

emergent neighboring imperiums. The final blow came in the 330s, when the Macedonian imperialist Alexander the Great carried his campaign of military expansion into Persia proper and the once-invincible Persian army proved no match for him.

The World of Alexander the Great

In conquering Persia and Greece, Alexander was able to accomplish the unrealized dreams of his father, Philip of Macedon. Philip, himself a great military imperialist, had subdued a good part of Greece, defeating Athens and Thebes in 338 B.C. and founding the Hellenic League, composed of all Greek states except Sparta. But Philip was assassinated in 336 before he could unite all of Greece and move on to take over Persia.

In taking up where his father left off, Alexander, imbued with admiration for the Greek way of life by his tutor, the philosopher Aristotle, developed the even more grandiose aim of Hellenizing as much of the world as he could reach.

The hegemonic arrogance of the young Macedonian king (Alexander was only 20 years old when he inherited the throne) at first alienated his Greek neighbors. Thebes went so far as to bar her gates to him; but he stormed the city, captured its inhabitants and sold them into slavery, and then destroyed its buildings. Traumatized by this brutal example, the other Greek city states felt they had no choice but to succumb to Alexander's authority and to contribute ships and men to help him fulfill his father's plan to conquer Asia Minor and Persia.[6]

With breathless speed, Alexander swept eastward in 334 B.C., through what is now Turkey then south past Syria and on into Egypt, where he founded Alexandria in 332 B.C. and totally reorganized the country. Turning his sights eastward again, Alexander swiftly traversed the Fertile Crescent, winning key battles along the way against numerically superior Persian forces before entering Babylon in triumph in 331. Not yet satisfied, he kept up the pursuit of his Persian rival Darius deep into Persia itself, where in 330, discovering that Darius had been slain by one of his own local satraps, Alexander proclaimed that he was now king of Asia.

But there was still more out there—India, in particular—that drew Alexander forward, perhaps out of a mixture of motives: personal glory and his Hellenizing mission. A mutinous refusal by his tired troops to follow him farther east than the Indus Valley finally, after 10 years of foreign campaigning, compelled Alexander to turn back toward home.

For roughly the last year of his life, Alexander established himself in Babylon, making it his capital city, claiming he was the legitimate successor to the former Persian kings, and adopting many of their accoutrements. His objective, he said, was to combine the best of East and West and make Eu-

---

[6]Jones, *Ancient Civilization*, p. 284.

rope and Asia one domain. As part of this cultural fusion he married a Persian noblewoman and sponsored mixed marriages among his troops and followers.[7] Some of the non-Persian peoples of the realm, especially the Macedonians, resented Alexander's assimilationist policies and accused him of putting on Persian airs. In 323 B.C., before major defections from his kingdom could occur, the Great One died of fever and excessive drinking at the age of 33.

Following Alexander's death, the Near East once again fragmented politically. As pointed out by the historian T. B. Jones,

> Alexander's empire was his own creation; its various parts were bound together only by the connections each had with Alexander—no ties bound them to each other or with Macedonia. Thus, when Alexander died, the empire soon disintegrated, for he made no careful provision for a successor, nor was there any man strong enough to step into his place.[8]

The Empire of the Chou

In contrast to the highly personalistic and therefore short-lived empire of Alexander, the Chinese Chou dynasty developed a durable *system* for ruling a vast domain. Lording over China from 1122 to 256 B.C., the Chou kings claimed the right to rule over all humankind by the "Mandate of Heaven." Their realm expanded to cover an area greater than the Roman Empire at its largest and, at least within the region of their hegemony, had an impact no less profound and lasting. In the words of historian Herrlee Creel, "It is doubtful that any other nation of comparable consequence has had its basic character more deeply or more lastingly influenced under a single ruling house than did China under the Chou."[9] The legacy of the Chou Empire was in no small measure the result of the remarkable contributions of its latter-day intellectuals—most notably the philosophers Confucius and Mencius, and the poet Lao Tse—who retrospectively enhanced the myth of the glory and benevolent imperium of the early ("Western") Chou dynasty, 1122 to 771 B.C.

The Chou first established their dominance in the region of the Yellow Sea by militarily subduing the more civilized Shang dynasty. Virtually insatiable in their imperial ambitions, but assimilating the relatively advanced economic and cultural attributes of the Shang, the Chou turned out to be remarkably benign overlords, excelling in the arts of governance, and maintaining control through dispensations of office and land and symbolic authority as much as through brute force.

[7]McNeil, *The Rise of the West*, pp. 305–306.
[8]Jones, *Ancient Civilization*, p. 288.
[9]Herrlee G. Creel, *The Origins of Statecraft in China—Volume One: The Western Chou Empire* (Chicago: University of Chicago Press, 1970), p. 43

The Chou system of governance was essentially "feudal." Generals who had played an important role in subduing particular territories, or sometimes previous overlords who were especially cooperative, were allowed suzerainty over the areas under their immediate control, which were deliberately parceled out in small enough domains of limited sovereignty to ensure that the provincial rulers could never threaten the central authority.[10] These semi-autonomous principalities at one point in time numbered over 1750. The vassal lords were obligated to provide and command fighting forces upon call of the Chou king and also to organize the collection of revenues to be transferred to the royal coffers. According to Creel, the greatest single contribution that the feudal lords made to the Chou state was their provision of a "stabilizing presence of governmental authority" throughout the vast Empire.

> The King's armies could repel invaders, and his officials could deal with crises, but it was essential that in every area there was the continuing presence of his resident representative, able to settle disputes and deal with local problems promptly, without the need to communicate with the capital.[11]

But the huge realm was composed of ethnically diverse peoples. How did the Chou and their locally installed authorities preclude indigenous populations from organizing against the outsiders who were now their overlords?

One means to prevent local peoples from subverting the hierarchical feudal order was the mass transportation and resettlement of groups from their indigenous habitats into other areas. Some groups particularly likely to exhibit dissident characteristics would be moved and resettled with considerable frequency.[12] But this method of control, borrowed by the Chou from their predecessors and resorted to by autocracies up through modern times, risked alienating and demoralizing the uprooted, with the attendant costs of low productivity.

Heavier reliance seems to have been put on indoctrination—persuading the subject peoples through religious instruction, symbols, and elaborate rituals that the Chou king was indeed the Son of Heaven. For such indoctrination to succeed in inducing the required loyalty and conformity, however, it would need to be reinforced by exemplary behavior on the part of the King and his enfeoffed nobles throughout the empire, lending credibility to their claim to be divinely appointed servants of the supreme deity.

Yet the realm was too vast, and the temptations on successor kings and remotely located vassal lords too great to exploit their privileged stations for egotistic and material ends, for such an empire to cohere as a legitimate whole in perpetuity. What is remarkable is not that the disintegrative forces

---

[10]Richard Louis Walker, *The Multi-State System of Ancient China* (Hamden, Connecticut: Shoe String Press, 1953), pp. 5–6.
[11]Creel, *The Origins of Statecraft in China*, p. 353.
[12]*Ibid.*, pp. 87–93.

eventually won out over the integrative forces, but that the empire was able to sustain itself as long as it did. Historians now generally date the reascendance of the disintegrative forces somewhere in the eighth century B.C.. "Lip service was still paid to the concept of a single kingdom, traditional ceremonies were still performed, but the effective power of the Chou kings had disappeared."[13] Henceforth, until the twentieth century, and except for periods of relatively short-lived dominance by regional hegemons (the Ch'in, the Han, and the T'angs) pretending to revive the "universal" empire of the Chous, China was pervaded by a volatile pattern of shifting alliances and almost constant warfare among rival sovereign states.

The Indian Mauryas—From Chandragupta to Asoka

Much of North India and what is now Pakistan and Afghanistan came under the control of the great general and administrator, Chandragupta Maurya, by about 320 B.C. Like the Persian emperors, Chandragupta ruled by a combination of force, awe-inspiring ostentation, and (like the Egyptian Pharaohs) centralized control over scarce water supplies through a vast system of irrigation projects. Heavy taxes were collected by the Maurya dynasty to sustain its far-flung forces and administrators. Royal coffers were further enlarged with revenues from the kingdom's monopoly of mining and metallurgy, particularly in copper and iron.[14]

Chandragupta's grandson Asoka, who succeeded to the Maurya throne in 273 B.C., expanded the empire into South India. Horrified at the genocidal butchery this expansionary campaign had inflicted, Asoka converted to pacifistic Buddhism. He issued edicts promulgating compassion and kindness to all living things, pardoned prisoners, established toleration throughout the realm for all religions, and generally relaxed the harsh regime he had inherited. Asoka perpetuated the empire's grandeur, however, through a vast building program, with the new architecturally elaborate structures featuring pillars engraved with the king's edicts.[15]

Asoka's gentle empire did not survive his death. Without his charismatic and benevolent leadership, India's more characteristic internecine conflict—often violent—among its many religious and cultural groups reemerged. Anarchy and shifting alliances among rival dynasties made the subcontinent vulnerable to a succession of conquerors from the north until the era of British colonization beginning in the eighteenth century.

---

[13]Evan Luard, *Types of International Society* (New York: Free Press, 1976), p. 70.
[14]Chester G. Starr, *A History of the Ancient World* (New York: Oxford University Press, 1991), p. 632.
[15]Wallbank and Taylor, *Civilization Past and Present*, Vol. I, pp. 291–292.

The Roman Empire

During the period in which the great East Asian and South Asian empires were disintegrating into anarchic multi-state systems, the city of Rome was beginning to flex its imperial muscles. Rome's military ascendence over the other city-states on the Italian peninsula and her emergence as a regional rival to Carthage and Greece coincided with the meteoric rise and fall of Macedonia as the dominant power in West Asia and the Eastern Mediterranean. Following the death of Alexander the Great in 323 B.C., the Romans, heady with local victories, embarked on their quest for world dominance. It took two centuries to accomplish, but by 130 B.C., having militarily vanquished Carthage and Greece as well as a temporarily revived Macedonia, Rome finally had her chance (which lasted over 500 years) to lord it over at least the entire "Western" world of Europe, North Africa, and the Near East.

During her first hundred years of hegemony, the Roman Empire was beset by severe internal corruption and civil strife, at times threatening to bring about the complete disintegration of the imperial state. Her most eloquent philosophers and legal theorists and, periodically, some of her enlightened statesmen favored a representative-republican regime; but the requirements of maintaining domestic tranquility and holding together the vast ethnically diverse realm proved to be incompatible with the ideals of city-state governance that had been assimilated from the Greeks.

Stability and grandeur were briefly restored across most of the empire under the benevolent dictatorship of the warrior-statesman Julius Caesar, who, having conquered the Gallic areas to the north, marched on the city of Rome itself in 49 B.C. But in 44 B.C. (as memorialized in William Shakespeare's famous play), Caesar was murdered by a rival general, Brutus, and a small group of conspirators. Another two decades of virtual anarchy and civil war ensued as Caesar's would-be successors battled for ascendancy. The victor, finally, was Caesar's grandnephew and adopted son, Octavian, who became the unrivaled master of Rome in 30 B.C. after wresting control of Egypt from Anthony and Cleopatra (both of whom committed suicide at the time of their defeat).

Octavian, under the title "Augustus," ruled from 30 B.C. to his death in 14 A.D., during which time he reconsolidated and marginally expanded the empire. His reign marked the most glorious period of Rome, one of basic external peace and domestic order, when the arts and literature flourished. A new era of internal turmoil followed the death of Augustus and included a number of incompetent and mentally unstable emperors: including Tiberius, Caligula, and Nero (the notorious persecutor of Christians)—a portent of the decline and fall that was to come.

Another phase of imperial greatness encompassed the regimes of Trajan (98–117 A.D.), under whom the empire was extended even farther north into what is now Romania; Hadrian (117–138 A.D.), who excelled in the arts of administration; and the philosopher-king Marcus Aurelius (161–180 A.D.), who reluctantly had to forsake his books to fend off Germanic barbarians invading the empire's northern communities.

Retrospectively idealized, *Pax Romana*, even during its intermittent periods of relative order, was in reality a vast overstretched crust of control over inherently eruptive forces. At its best, it surpassed all previous empires of the Mediterranean region in the arts of governance and in some respects even bested the Chou of China. In the words of an admiring historian,

> it formed a majestic system of law which through nearly all Europe gave security to life and property, incentive and continuity to industry. . . . It molded a government of separated legislative and executive powers whose checks and balances inspired the makers of constitutions as late as revolutionary America and France. For a time it united monarchy, aristocracy, and democracy so successfully as to win the applause of philosophers, historians, subjects, and enemies. It gave municipal institutions, and for a long period municipal freedom, to half a thousand cities. It administered its Empire at first with greed and cruelty, then with such tolerance and essential justice that the great realm has never again known a like content. It made the desert blossom with civilization, and atoned for its sins with the miracle of a lasting peace. Today our highest labors seek to revive the *Pax Romana* for a disordered world.[16]

But the Roman Empire's enormous size, which on the one hand was its most important contribution to world order— overriding the anarchy that previously had sapped the energies of the great civilizations of the Mediterranean and and Near East as they vied for hegemony—on the other hand was surely a key factor in its own eventual collapse. Given the transportation and communication technologies of the day, Rome's intentional reach would inevitably exceed its tangible grasp. There was, of course, more to it than that, for the empire proved to be overstretched politically and culturally as well as militarily and economically.

The picture of an overextended Rome at the end being overrun by barbarians from the steppes of Eurasia describes the outcome rather than the cause of its decline and fall. As the famous history by Edward Gibbon argues (other historians dispute him on particulars, especially the blame he lays on Christianity as a subversive movement, more than on his general thesis), the empire disintegrated more from internal weaknesses than from external pressures.[17]

The northwest barbarians and the recrudescent Persians took advantage of the decay and erosion that by the fifth century A.D. had become irreversible. Indeed, the empire had already come perilously close to total collapse from within at a number of junctures over the course of the final two

---

[16]Will Durant, *Caesar and Christ: A History of Roman Civilization and of Christianity from Their Beginnings to A.D. 325* (New York: Simon and Schuster, 1944), p. 670.

[17]Edward Gibbon, *The Decline and Fall of the Roman Empire* (New York: Knopf, 1993) [originally published in the 1770s and 1780s]. For critical assessments of Gibbons thesis, see Patricia B. Craddock, *Edward Gibbon: A Reference Guide* (Boston: G. K. Hall, 1987).

centuries of its existence. Thus, in five decades of chaos beginning in 235 A.D., more than twenty emperors were assassinated!

What were the underlying problems? Many were economic: The institution of slavery, for example, retarded the application of technology to agriculture and inhibited the development of internal markets and trade with the East, particularly India; it also meant that there would be an inadequate supply of humans for doing menial work when the inability of the empire to further expand its peripheries put an end to easy acquisition of slave labor. Scarcities of goods, over-mining, the exhaustion of soils, and overly rapid deforestation prompted the empire's dictators to institute harsh controls (punitive taxes on untilled land, price controls, export embargoes) that further destroyed the functioning of markets. The outlying estates, no longer finding it advantageous to buy and sell in the central cities, were driven back on their own resources; regional or even local autarchy and barriers to inter-regional trade became the norm; local areas resisted paying taxes to the central government; roads, the empire's unifying webs, fell into disuse and neglect, making it ever more expensive to revive wide-ranging commerce and more difficult militarily to protect the ramparts.[18]

Politically, the reliance on despotism also took a severe toll. The civic virtues of loyalty and pride in the republican empire, which had also sustained the effectiveness of the Roman legions, were ground out of the populace by a succession of narcissistic and corrupt dictators. Governments and the military at all levels attracted mediocrities and cynics rather than the most talented and patriotic. As recounted by one historian, "Men deliberately made themselves ineligible [for public service] by debasing their social category; some fled to other towns, some became farmers, some monks. . . . The imperial police pursued fugitives from political honors as it hunted evaders of taxes or conscription; it brought them back to the cities and forced them to serve"[19]

Efforts to arrest the declining authority of the imperial government with ostentatious pomp and ceremony, if anything, further undermined the legitimacy of the rulers. The corresponding growth in the appeal of Christianity at first drew imperial repression, but as this only enlarged its appeal, a wiser emperor, Constantine, reversed the strategy in the Edict of Milan (313), granting Christians the same tolerance as devotees of all other religions. Then, in a dramatic move—whether motivated by political calculation, genuine religious conviction, or both—Constantine himself converted to Christianity, claiming, as did the Egyptian and Persian kings of old, to rule by divine dispensation. Ironically, however, with the Church by this time having itself become more ritualistic and ostentatious, Constantine's effort to fuse

[18]Stravrianos, *The World to 1500*, pp. 139–145.
[19]Durant, *Caesar and Christ*, p. 668.

Church and State in the person of the emperor made the imperial court even more remote from the people of the realm.

Emperor Constantine's most historically momentous demarche was his decision in 327 to establish a new Roman capital in the East at the entrance to the Black Sea. As it turned out, the existence of the New Rome, later called Constantinople, saved not only Greco-Roman culture (within the renamed empire of Byzantium) but also Christianity from virtual extinction at the hands of the barbarian hordes that in less than a century would overrun Italy and subjugate the old imperial capital.[20]

Mongol Empire

The largest land empire ever, encompassing even more territory than the Soviets controlled during the height of the Cold War, was brutally and swiftly imposed over much of Eurasia during the first six decades of the thirteenth century by the Mongol warriors of Northern China. The great Mongol surge westward and southward was initiated in 1206 by the notorious Ghenghis Khan, the exemplar of cavalry-led siege and pillage warfare. At its most extended, the Mongol reign of terror engulfed India, Indochina, Burma, and India in the south and Russia, Poland, Hungary, and Turkestan in the west, reaching almost to Constantinople.[21]

Unlike all of the other great imperialists in this sampling, the Mongols relied almost entirely on raw force, including mass exterminations of communities that did not fully submit to them. In the process, they destroyed much of the indigenous cultures of the peoples they subdued and thereby removed the basis for durable imperial rule. Not only did the Mongols prove to be poor administrators of the lands they conquered, but they lacked a strong culture of their own with which, like the Chou or the Romans, they could assimilate others into the dominant civilization.

Thus having finally overextended themselves by moving as far as Syria, and there suffering a dramatic military defeat by an Egyptian army in 1260, the Mongols found the essence of their overlordship—their reputation of invincibility—shattered.[22] During the rest of the century and into the 1300s, they relinquished area after area, almost as rapidly as they had subdued them, leaving many ravaged and demoralized societies in their wake who were rather easy prey for the next set of imperialists: the Ottoman Turks in the Near East, the Moguls on the Indian subcontinent, the Russians in the North, the Ming dynasty in China, and, beginning in the late fifteenth century, the maritime colonial powers of Western Europe.

[20]Wallbank and Taylor, *Civilization Past and Present*, Vol. I, pp. 250–252.
[21]Barraclough, *The Times Atlas of World History*, pp. 128–129.
[22]Will Durant, *The Age of Faith* (New York: Simon and Schuster, 1950), pp. 338–341.

SYSTEMS OF INDEPENDENT STATES

An alternative reading of the world's political history does not look toward a system of governance for the human species in a universal state; rather it finds the "natural" condition of the world polity to be virtually anarchic, comprising numerous autonomous states, each encompassing a people of relatively homogeneous cultural traits. Such states may at various times and regions of the globe intensely interact with one another, sometimes cooperating, sometimes fighting—and to that extent may constitute inter-state "societies"—but they can be expected to resist subordination under an external power. Large multicultural empires of the kind reviewed above (let alone designs for world government) are artificial constructions that, because they cut too deeply against the grain of cultural *self*-determination, are bound to be eroded from within and sooner or later fragment into more natural political communities.

From this perspective, the ancient prototype for a durable design for the world's political system is the Greek city-state system of the sixth and fifth centuries B.C.. Also, the so-called Middle Ages (Europe between the fall of the Roman Empire and the emergence of the modern state system), rather than being viewed as an aberrant departure from good governance, is regarded as a period of necessary human recovery from the mistakes of the would-be universalizers—a groping, as it were, for political forms more congruent with the natural diversity of the species.

The Anarchic Interstate Society of Greece

Ancient Greece, like other regions around the Mediterranean, oscillated between phases of integration (in the name of pan-Hellenic culture and defense against imperialistic outsiders) and disintegration into separate city-states (consonant with the ideals of the greatest of the Greek philosophers). But more than with any of the other ancient societies, it is the Greece of the small and highly autonomous *polis* that is looked back upon by historians and social philosophers as the "classical" exemplar, even of future civilizations.

The Greek peninsula, featuring numerous small plains separated by rugged mountain barriers, was especially suited to the evolution of independent city-states. The typical polis was small enough to have all the state's citizens assemble for debates on public issues, which allowed for experiments with various forms of government, including democracy. Both the idealist philosopher Plato and his more realistic protege Aristotle prescribed the micro-polis as the unit of statehood. It should never contain more than 100,000 people, said Aristotle (ironically, Aristotle's most famous pupil was Alexander the Great).[23]

---

[23]*See* M. I. Finley, *The Ancient Greeks* (New York: Penguin Books, 1977), pp. 54–60.

Highly valuing their independence, the city-states of classical Greece would periodically form alliances or "leagues" to counter the hegemonic drives of some of their numbers or of hegemony-seeking external powers. But consistent with the political autonomy norms of Greek society, such defensive combinations were supposed to be temporary and dispensable once the objective of putting down a threatening imperialist state had been accomplished. Thus, after 11 years of cooperation between Athens, Sparta, and various minor city-states in repulsing a series of Persian invasions, culminating in the decisive defeat of Xerxes at Plataea in 479 B.C., Sparta and other states in the southwestern part of Peloponnesus defected from the larger anti-Persian coalition, leaving it to Athens to mobilize the other Greeks bordering the Aegean Sea to defend the eastern ramparts against Persia.

As Athens became the military and commercial master of the Aegean in the fifth century B.C., Sparta feared that its principal rival was bent on achieving hegemony over all of Greece. In opposition to the Delian Confederacy of city-states organized by Athens, Sparta competed for adherents to its countervailing Peloponnesian League.

The contest between Athens and Sparta to attract states into their respective spheres of influence, like the Cold War between the Soviet Union and the United States after World War II, operated on the ideological as well as the geopolitical plane.[24] Athens at the time was a democracy, its leaders elected by public assemblies where each adult male citizen could speak and vote (women and slaves were denied political rights). Sparta's policies, internal and external, were made by a dictatorial oligarchy. Athens and Sparta each professed that its way of organizing society was superior to the other's, and each acted as if it had an obligation to spread it throughout Greece.

Particularly during the period of the Peloponnesian War (431 to 404 B.C.), vividly chronicled by the Greek historian Thucydides, each looked beyond its current sphere of dominance to find allies within the opponent's camp who would subvert the opponent's power (at best even effecting a change of regime in a rival city state) and reduce its capacity to fight in the next round of warfare.

In contrast to the modern notion that democracies are more pacific than dictatorships, democratic Athens was the more imperialistic state, insisting that members of its alliance transform themselves into democracies in its own image. Oligarchic Sparta's ultimate victory over Athens was in part a function of its less intrusive proselytizing of allies and less punitive policies toward defectors from its coalition or toward neutral states. Paradoxically, it was Athens' unsqueamish "realism" in dealing with those who opposed its will (as recorded by Thucydides: "the strong do what they have the power to do and the weak accept what they have to accept")[25] that contributed to

[24]An excellent brief description of this era of Athenian and Spartan bipolar rivalry is provided by Barraclough, in *The Times Atlas of World History*, pp. 74–75.
[25]Thucydides, *The Peloponnesian War*, translated by Rex Warner (London: Cassell, 1954), Book V, Chapter 7, p. 360.

its defeat by a rival coalition made of states voluntarily banding together to secure their deeper and more durable self-interest in autonomy.

The victory by Sparta and its voluntarily organized coalition, however, left Greece insufficiently unified to stand up to the growing imperialistic ambitions of Macedonia. Nor could Greece revive its classical cultural glory following the death of Alexander the Great. Soon the expansive and over-bearing Roman Empire, while adopting many elements of Greek culture, sounded the death knell to the Greek political ideal of a pluralistic system of autonomous city states.

European Feudalism

By the time of the collapse of the Roman Empire in the fifth century A.D., there was nothing left of the Greek experience of self-government to establish a successor political order. Rather, for roughly a thousand years after the disintegration of the Roman Empire, most of the regions of Europe previously under imperial control had to grope their way out of brutish forms of anarchy through constructing elementary local systems of physical security and property rights.

The absence of central authority was reflected in the deterioration of the roads, bridges, and canals that under the Empire had facilitated commerce between the Empire's cities and the countryside and had sustained the specialized economic pursuits of the city dwellers. The disintegration of the imperial system left households and communities vulnerable to marauders and outlaw bands, as well as to onslaughts from barbarian tribes.

Elementary security of person and possessions required some pooling of protective resources—men skilled in physical combat, swift horses, smiths and tanners to equip them, and masons to build fortifications. A noble owning an estate of relatively large size, say a few hundred square miles, would recruit a loyal fighting force from among the householders within his estate as well as from among relatively weak nobles of his station in the region by agreeing to become their "lord" if they would agree (sometimes on the basis of coercion) to become his "vassals." With this pooled force, the lord would be expected to provide protection to all the vassals directly subordinate to him. Such vassals, in turn, would become the lords of lesser householders within their territories. The structure was rigidly hierarchical, but the obligations between lord and vassal were reciprocal: The vassal would make himself (and the men he commanded) warriors in the lord's army, and the lord would mobilize such forces throughout his realm to come to the defense of a vassal (local lord) as needed.

The local security arrangements were in most places congruent with and reinforced by a landholding system in which the lord would grant "fiefs" of land to vassals (sometimes the land was previously owned by the vassals, but now the land became theirs only by the grace of their lord) in return for vassal pledges of total loyalty. Reciprocal mutual assistance obligations parallel to the mutual protection arrangements would operate in case of special economic need, for example, when either lord or vassal had experienced a crop failure or the pillaging of fields and livestock by marauder bands. In the more developed areas, economic specialization among various land-holders might be accompanied by simple systems of barter and trade, and in some regions by rudimentary taxing and labor-conscript arrangements for the provision of "public goods" such as road builing and policing.[26]

I have been describing essential features of the highly decentralized pattern of feudalism that prevailed in Europe—except for the effort of the Frankish Carolingian dynasty (from 730 to 814) to resurrect a Christianized "Roman Empire" under Martel, Pepin, and, most impressively, Charlemagne—for over five centuries following the demise of the ancient Roman Empire. Then, paradoxically, around the year 1000, when feudalism was at its most widespread (from Bohemia in the East to Leon on the West Coast of Spain), an era of considerable political and economic development began to set in, leading eventually to the amalgamation or absorption of formerly autonomous noble estates into larger units more congruent with the scope of activities of the emergent commercial classes.

A major facilitator of the expanding interdependencies was the institution of the medieval trade fair, an open trading area, freed of the rules and hierarchical relationships of the manor (but often sponsored by local lords in order to generate revenue) that would attract buyers and sellers of goods and services from near and far. Performing an analogous function to the role of the multinational corporation vis-à-vis nation-states in the contemporary polyarchic world, the trade fairs, although they could not substitute for the institutions of feudal rule, did, as John Ruggie observes, contribute significantly to the decline of feudal authority relations. "They did so," writes Ruggie, "because the new wealth they produced, the new instruments of economic transactions they generated, the new ethos of commerce they spread, the new regulatory arrangemnents they required, and the expansion of cognitive horizons they affected all helped to undermine the personalistic ties and the modes of reasoning on which feudal authority rested."[27]

The desire for inter-town and inter-city trade, given impetus by technology-spurred specialization of production, pressed against the artificial feudal barriers to the exchange of goods—tolls and tariffs among the local communities—and created the need for common currencies to handle the exchange of goods and services and the buying and selling of land.

[26]On European feudalism, see Carl Stephenson, Medieval Feudalism (Ithaca: Columbia University Press, 1942). See also W. W. Palmer, History of the Modern World (New York: Knopf, 1956), pp. 23–26; Wallbank and Taylor, Civilization Past and Present, Vol. I, pp. 337–360; and Durant, The Age of Faith, pp. 552–579. For a comparison of the European system with feudal systems on other continents, see J. S. Critchley, Feudalism (London: George Allen & Unwin, 1978).
[27]John Gerard Ruggie, "Territoriality and Beyond; Problematizing Modernity in International Relations," International Organization, Vol. 47, No. 1 (Winter 1993), pp. 154–156.

Military innovations such as the long bow and (most dramatically) gun-powder gave ascendancy to well-provisioned and organized military forces over the nomadic barbarian hordes and mounted knights who had previously dominated the countryside, and over the fortified and largely impregnable castles of high noble lords, with their moats and high walls. The evolving situation provided new opportunities for territorial expansion and consolidation to the largest and richest estates. These estates were run by nobles with considerable administrative and financial skill, who were able to exploit and husband the new technologies of agricultural production, military firepower, and craft specialization. Increasingly, other traits in addition to individual fighting prowess and bravery would help determine the winners and losers in the new contests for territorial control and status. Innovation and wisdom in the arts of governance, including secular authorities for the resolution and adjudication of disputes, were crucial factors in the enhancement of a kingdom's power.

The road to a Europe of consolidated large nation-states, however, was still long, bumpy, and often bloody. The comparatively neat early feudal pattern of small, physically separate and virtually autonomous units of hierarchical lord–vassal relationships was no longer congruent with the dynamically evolving society. But the more appropriate geographic demarcations and economic and cultural bases for people to band together into viable states had yet to sort themselves out. The historian/sociologist Charles Tilly captures this polyarchic reality prevailing in Europe on the eve of the year 1000:

> The emperors, kings, princes, dukes, caliphs, sultans, and other potentates . . . prevailed as conquerors, tribute-takers, and rentiers, not as heads of state that durably regulated life within their realms. Inside their jurisdictions, furthermore, rivals and ostensible subordinates commonly used armed force on behalf of their own interests while paying little attention to the interests of their nominal sovereigns. Private armies proliferated through much of the continent. Nothing like a centralized national state existed anywhere in Europe.[28]

Histories of the late medieval period in Europe (the thirteenth to the fifteenth centuries) describe the growing complexity of governance–society relations in terms that could be used to describe the contemporary post-Cold War configuration of world politics: a "patchwork of overlapping and incomplete" jurisdictions that were "inextricably superimposed and tangled" containing "plural allegiances, asymmetrical suzerainties and anomalous enclaves."[29]

---

[28]Charles Tilly, *Coercion, Capital, and European States, A.D. 990–1990* (Cambridge: Basil Blackwell, 1990), pp. 39–40.
[29]The quotes are provided by Ruggie, "Territoriality and Beyond," pp. 149–150, from Joseph R. Strayer and Diana C. Munro, *The Middle Ages* (New York: Appleton-Century-Crofts, 1959), and Perry Anderson, *Lineages of the Absolutist State* (London: New Left Books, 1974).

Yet despite the political polyarchy—indeed, in many respects because of it—commerce and trade-generated economic development flourished and expanded, creating durable networks of interdependence, which in turn provided the groundwork for the emergence of larger states that were congruent with the new socioeconomic relationships.

Relations Among the City-States in Renaissance Italy

The system of relations prevailing among the city-states on the Italian peninsula during the 1400s and early 1500s can be viewed as a middle ground between medieval feudalism and the emergence of the modern state system. Indeed, the political power plays and wars in Italy during this period provide us with the closest prefiguration of the "balance of power" diplomacy that was later to characterize the modern system.

Italian renaissance diplomacy was in essence a pattern of shifting coalitions among powerful commercial city-states, each determined to retain an autonomous sphere of dominance in its region of the peninsula. Deceptive double-dealing and double-crossing diplomatic machinations—often called "machiavellian" after the famous theorist of the statecraft of that period— flourished side-by-side with a renaissance of Greek humanism and Roman cosmopolitanism. The revival of Greco-Roman secular culture might have provided the basis for Italy's political reintegration, especially if married to the new opportunities opening for peninsula-wide commercial intercourse. But feudalistic habits of heart and mind, putting a premium on territorial sovereignty and economic autarchy, now mixing with the new opportunities to expand commerce, produced instead an era of mercantilistic rivalry among the prosperous city-states that sustained and deepened the political disunity of the Italian peninsula.

Yet the fact that the commercially expansive Italian city-states (particularly Venice, Milan, Florence, and Naples)—despite their rivalrous coexistence on the same subcontinent, along with numerous smaller independent city-states—were able to prosper and keep from destroying one another was due in no small measure to arts (and crafts) of the diplomacy of the period. The principal concern of each of these states was that none of the others should become the peninsula's hegemon. Accordingly, the diplomacy of each was directed toward "balancing" the coercive power of any would-be hegemon, namely, by not allowing oneself to become inferior to it. Such power balancing required all of the states both to maintain capable military forces and form alliances. But since no state could trust all of its allies to refrain from secretly conniving with the "enemy" to switch sides, most states (big and small) played the game of cultivating opportunities for realignment. Since today's enemy might well be tomorrow's friend, and vice versa, diplomatic intrigue needed to be developed into a high art form, but so did the diplomacy of bargaining and compromise. War, too, was constrained by the reluctance to destroy a potential balancer in the next round of the power game. As summed up by diplomatic historian Adam Watson, "Renaissance Italy was a dangerous place, and a ruler who wanted to preserve and extend his *stato,* and to deal with other similar *statos* around him, had to be guided not by standards of right and wrong but by cool calculation of what was expedient."[30]

Niccolo Machiavelli's treatises on statecraft were not so much descriptive analyses of the diplomacy of the Italian city-states as they were prescriptive primers for princes on how to function most effectively in such an interstate system.[31] Not surprisingly, Machiavelli's works became must reading for statespersons and their advisers in Britain and the continent during the seventeenth and eighteenth centuries, when the general pattern of interstate relations in the era of the "classical balance of power" (see Chapter 3) developed striking resemblances to the pattern in fifteenth and sixteenth century Italy.

Meanwhile, however, north of the Pyrenees in the sixteenth century, the issue of the appropriate size and jurisdictional authority of states in the postfeudal order was not allowed to be determined as it had been in renaissance Italy by the new marriage of commerce and diplomacy. Religious conflicts over the relationship between individuals and God and over the role of the Church in society were polarizing Christians throughout central and western Europe and in Britain, and these emotionally explosive "otherworldly" issues were getting in the way of and often taking over from the more mundane material forces that were affecting the coalescence and dissolution of political communities.

RELIGION AS A FORCE FOR POLITICAL UNIFICATION AND DIVISION

Many of the ancient imperialists, as noted above, made use of the religious beliefs and institutions prevailing in their regions—often anointing themselves as the heads of such religions—in order to enhance their authority over their subjects. Some of these religious belief systems claimed universal validity; but it was not until the advent of Christianity that the leaders of a religion themselves seriously and aggressively took up the mission of overcoming the political anarchy of the world and bringing all of humanity un-

---

[30]Adam Watson, *The Evolution of International Society: A Comparative Historical Analysis* (London: Routledge, 1992), p. 191.

[31]*See especially* Niccolo Machiavelli, *The Prince* and *The Discourses.* Standard authoritative translations of these and his other treatises are found in *Machiavelli: The Chief Works and Others,* ed. and trans. Allan H. Gilbert, 3 vols. (Durham: University of North Carolina Press, 1965). My favorite interpreter is Mark Hulliung, *Citizen Machiavelli* (Princeton: Princeton University Press, 1983).

der the "kingdom of God." They were emulated in this, beginning in the seventh century A.D., by the followers of the prophet Mohammed. Inevitably, the universalizers of Islam would come into conflict with the universalizers of Christianity, especially as both religions became highly active in political contests for control of territory and governments. Centered in the Mediterranean region, but spreading throughout much of Africa and into the western and southern parts of Asia, this sometimes cold war, sometimes hot war between Islam and Christianity became a global force on its own (albeit frequently exploited by secular contestants for power) for the integration and disintegration of communities.

Christendom

With the fall of the Roman Empire at the end of the fifth century A.D. the function of moderating the resulting feudal anarchy was assumed by the Christian Church as a duty to God. Under the Pope of Rome, hierarchical legions of subordinate Church officials fanned out across the lands of the former empire to provide good offices, counsel, and mediational and adjudicatory services, and sometimes even to hand-pick and install local and regional rulers. Not surprisingly, its new exposed role as the authoritative legitimator of secular governance made the Church itself, and its governance, both an agent and a target of political power plays and intrigue.

The Christian Church actively took up the sword in a series of "crusades" against the Muslim infidel in the Near East, beginning with Pope Urban II's appeal in 1095 to retake control of the Holy Land in and around Jerusalem. Nobles were commissioned to raise armies and fleets. Much of this was facilitated by banks and commercial houses anxious to reap profits from high shipping charges on the retinues of the knights and kings and also to get on the good side of the Church. Two centuries of such military forays into the Islamic heartland, often led with romantic and self-righteous frenzy by major European kings, still left the Holy Land under the control of the Mohammedans and engendered a legacy of revengeful bitterness that helped sustain the westward military expansion of Islam as far as Spain in succeeding centuries.

By the late medieval period, the "universal" Church, even within its European domain, was no longer part of the solution to anarchy but had become part of the problem. Its Western (Roman Catholic) and Eastern (Greek Orthodox) hierarchies and petty officials were deeply embroiled in the power-grabbing turmoil of the day, as landlords, entrepreneurs, advisors to kings, and even employers of their own armed forces. Thus when in the sixteenth century the Western Church was further bifurcated by the Protestant revolution, religion became increasingly not only a cause of domestic violence within states but also a precipitant and instrument of interstate war, giving rulers of countries justification for cross-border interventions on be-half of their co-religionists. Rather than functioning primarily as a force for transnational integration and the moderation of interstate conflicts, Chris-tianity (in its rival versions of how to serve God) was now just as much a force for the *dis*integration of nations and for turning interstate conflicts into genocidal "holy wars" against the agents of the devil.

In 1555, the Peace of Augsburg temporarily called a halt to a bitter period of violent conflict in Germany between princes adhering to the Protestant doctrines of Martin Luther and those loyal to the Catholic Church. The Augsburgian formula of *cuius regio eius religio* ("whose region, his religion") allowed each prince to decide the religion of his subjects. But this only initi-ated a new era of particularly fanatic conflict between Protestants and Catholics—within states and between states—for now the determination of who would control the state would determine whether or not one could practice one's religion. British diplomatic historian Evan Luard recounts how

> the fragile truce erected on the basis of the Peace of Augsburg in 1555 was soon creating as many quarrels as it solved.... Most of Europe became engaged in this new conflict concerned now not with national or dynastic rivalries, but with the struggle for supremacy between two contending religious doctrines. . . .
>
> Moreover, this was not a series of isolated and separate national conflicts. It was, in a genuine sense, an international religious struggle.... Protestants in England helped Protestants in France and the Netherlands. Catholics in France and Spain helped the Catholics of England. German Protestant princes came to the aid of the Protestant cause in the Netherlands. Protestant kings of Sweden and Denmark came to the aid of the Protestant cause in Germany. Conversely, religious minorities looked always for support from the great power of their own persuasion.[32]

The imperialistic states of the day exploited the discontent of religious minorities in the camp of their opponents, engaging in subversion and inter-vention, to aggrandize their own power. Catholic France was notoriously re-sourceful at these stratagems, and even crossed religious lines, supporting Protestant dissidents and states within the Spanish Hapsburg's sphere of in-fluence in order to weaken its principal rival. By and large, except for the French cross-over strategy, the continental European groupings tended to polarize on north–south lines: the largely Protestant north aligned against the largely Catholic south.

Within some regions and countries, however, the contending religious communities were too highly juxtaposed in the population to allow for a sta-ble identification of the area with either the Protestant or Catholic side. This was the situation in Bohemia, the center of the horrible Thirty Years War

---

[32]Luard, *Types of International Society*, pp. 86–87.

(1618–1648). By the end of this war the intercommunal killing and attendant diseases had turned some 29,000 of Bohemia's 35,000 villages into ghost towns. In many localities the countryside was so devastated that the peasants were reduced to eating the remnants of dogs, cats, and rats; and in some places they resorted to cannibalism.[33]

By the mid 1640s, the princes and priests of Europe, sick of the seemingly endless carnage, convened in Westphalia to seek a modus vivendi. It took four years of haggling to work out the numerous border issues and the principles of coexistence among their states. Finally, in 1648 some 135 officials of states and principalities, large and small, affirmed in the Treaty of Westphalia and corollary documents that each prince was to be granted complete sovereign authority to determine the religion that was to prevail within his jurisdiction. In this respect, the Peace of Westphalia was basically a reaffirmation of the hapless Peace of Augsburg. But Westphalia added the crucial proviso that religious minorities also were to be permitted to practice their faith within each of the sovereign states.

Islam

The Islamic religion, founded by Mohammed in the seventh century, was explicitly and aggressively opposed to the territorial state system. Believing themselves to be the carriers of the mission Allah (God) gave Mohammed to unite all of humankind in the one true religion—at times by violent *jihad* (holy war) against the Christians and other infidels, often in combination with the armies of imperial powers (such as the Persians, the Ottoman Turks, and the Indian Mughals)—the prophet's disciples spread out from their Arabic core and established major Muslim communities as far west as Morocco and Spain, as far north as Siberia, as as far south as Equatorial Africa, and as far east as what are now the Philippines and Indonesia.

Although all of Islam was supposed to be a unitary theocracy, applying the law of Allah through a singular earthly representative, the *caliph*, in practice the *dar al Islam* (area of God) developed into one of the more pluralistic of the pre-modern imperial domains. Islam's relative looseness as a polity, as compared, say, with the Roman Empire, was due in large part to its de-legitimation of secular governance. Law was not to be made by humans; it was given only by God, as told to Mohammed and recorded in the Koran. There was no legislative body and no legislation for the *dar al Islam*, only interpretation of the Koran—a book combining mystical philosophy, practical homilies for everyday life, ethical precepts, and evocative poetry—by the learned legal appointees of the caliph, called *ulema*. The Koran was most explicit on matters of pure theology (its absolute monotheism) and re-

[33]Will and Ariel Durant, *The Age of Reason Begins*, Vol. 7 of *The Story of Civilization* (New York: Simon and Schuster, 1961), p. 567.

ligious ritual (praying five times a day, etc.); but it was vague and often self-contradictory when it came to issues of social justice and conflict resolution. Thus, the application of Islamic law as interpreted by the *ulema* would inevitably vary in the regional administrative departments of the caliphate; and the variations would depend on local custom and on pragmatic bargains struck with local elites. Moreover, while the Muslims were quite ready to use the sword to establish control over new territories, they did not believe in *forcible* religious conversion to Islam and, indeed, were considerably more tolerant of the practices of religious minorities in their dominions (Jews, Zoroastrians, Christians) than were the Roman Catholic, Greek Orthodox, and, later, the Lutheran and Calvinist theocrats.

Islam's formula of a unitary theocracy directed by a singular caliph on top of a pluralistic and loosely organized structure for administering the vast "nation of Mohammed" proved to be too thin an overlay on the indigenous tribalisms and old imperial loyalties it attempted to subordinate. Rival claimants to the caliphate exploited and were exploited by the old cultural forces as well as by the new commercial forces developing in the Mediterranean region from about 800 A.D. on.

In the eleventh century, the Seljuk Turks, one of the fierce ethnic communities that had been absorbed into Islam, but who had been allowed to retain their identity as mercenary troops for the caliphate centered in Baghdad, turned the tables on their former patrons by subduing all of Persia and assuming the role of the leading champion of the faith throughout Asia Minor and the Mediterranean area. It was the aggressive new leadership of Islam by the Seljuk Turks that prompted Pope Urban II to organize the first Crusade to regain Jerusalem for Christendom.[34]

Following the retreat of the Asian Mongols from Asia Minor in the fourteenth century, the Ottoman Turks, like the Seljuk Turks before them, took up the role of imperialistic leader of Islam, sacking Constantinople in 1453 and during the next century driving as far west as Vienna. One thousand years after the collapse of the Roman Empire, it appeared as if most of the world might be about to fall under the sway of a global hegemon, this time animated by a fanatic conviction that it was doing God's work. But once again, as recounted by a contemporary historian of such recurring cycles,

> the Ottoman Turks, too, were to falter, to turn inward and to lose the chance of world domination. . . . By the second half of the sixteenth century the empire was showing signs of strategical overextension, with a large army stationed in central Europe, an expensive navy operating in the Mediterranean, troops engaged in North Africa, the Aegean, Cyprus, and the Red Sea, and reinforcements needed to hold the Crimea against a rising Russian power. Even in the Near East there was no quiet flank, thanks to a disastrous religious split in the

---

[34] Wallbank and Taylor, *Civilization Past and Present*, pp. 274–275.

Muslim world which occurred when the Shi'ite branch, based in Iraq and then in Persia, challenged the prevailing Sunni practices and teachings. . . . With this array of adversaries, the Ottoman Empire would have needed remarkable leadership to have maintained its growth; but after 1566 there reigned thirteen incompetent sultans in succession.[35]

THE SIXTEENTH-CENTURY MARITIME IMPERIALISTS

Just when the Eastern empires of Ottoman Turkey and Ming China were becoming preoccupied with internal consolidation, the West European states were embarking on their rivalrous global quests for overseas possessions, establishing far-flung colonial empires that subordinated into their jurisdictions the peoples of roughly two-thirds of the globe for centuries to come.

This new phase of imperialism—which represents a transition from the pre-modern era to the modern state system (see Chapter 3)—can be dated from the transit around the Cape of Good Hope by the Portuguese explorer Vasco da Gama in 1497. Following by five years Christopher Columbus's first voyage to the New World for the Spanish monarchy and coinciding with John Cabot's exploration of the east coast of North America, da Gama's long-distance trip to India was accomplished with a new type of sailing ship requiring a small crew, which left more onboard room for heavier weapons and cargo and thus gave the Portuguese a decisive edge over the Ottoman Turks as well as their European rivals.

Portugal had a relatively free hand in East Africa and South Asia for some five decades until challenged by Holland and England and then France. Spain, Portugal's principal rival for overseas colonies at the start of the fifteenth century, was effectively taken out of the Eastern competition by the papal-sponsored Treaty of Tordesillas (1494) between the two Catholic imperial powers. This treaty gave Spain all colonization rights west of Brazil and Portugal all rights eastward in the Atlantic, Africa, and Asia.

The Iberian colonizers set the new pattern for European imperial domination of peoples half a world away in geographic distance and worlds away, as it were, in their cultural characteristics. Profoundly ignorant and disrespectful of the ways of life of the peoples they were now in a position to reach and conquer, the Portuguese and the Spaniards, blessed in their mission by the Pope, took it upon themselves to "civilize" the natives into submissive subjects.

The Spanish imperial system in the Americas appears to have been the worst. Pillaging, enslaving, often simply exterminating the proud peoples who resisted them—the Incas of western South America, the Mayas and

---

[35]Paul Kennedy, *The Rise and Fall of the Great Powers: Economic Change and Military Conflict from 1500 to 2000* (New York: Random House, 1987), p. 11.

Aztecs of Central America, and the Pueblos in the North—the *conquistadors* subordinated Spain's New World holdings economically, culturally, and politically into its monarchical realm. The kings of Spain made all the laws for the empire, which were administered under the aegis of a viceroy for the New World. The viceroy's brutality toward and/or indifference to the well-being of "los Indios" and the greediness with which the monarchy attempted to extract the natural wealth of the hemisphere for its own immediate financial benefit eventually proved the undoing of this early Spanish imperial system, as disease and liquor decimated a large proportion of the indigenous population and the productivity of those who survived. Communities of settlers, rather than just administrators, soldiers, and clerics, were required to keep at least a modicum of the New World's wealth flowing back to Spain; but such settler communities required the incentive of considerable local property rights and powers of governance, leading eventually to assertions of autonomy and self-rule that culminated in the Latin American anticolonial revolutions of the nineteenth century.

Meanwhile, starting from the sixteenth century the British, the Dutch, and the French, the other principal maritime powers, were hardly content to sit idly by while the two Iberian powers, under papal dispensation, divided up the wealth of the newly reachable continents. They too commissioned explorers, entrepreneurs, and soldiers of fortune to stake out claims and plant settler colonies in the Western Hemisphere (particularly in North America), in Africa, and in South and Southeast Asia. Following the constriction of Spanish Hapsburg power in the Peace of Westphalia (1648) ending the Thirty Years War, the three great mercantilist powers of northwest Europe divided most of the rest of the non-European world among themselves—sometimes by war, sometimes by agreeing to respect one another's spheres of control. The new imperialists of Europe, with their rapidly developing technologies of transportation and weaponry, were able to lord it over most of their southern colonial realms for the next three centuries. Eventually, however, these "global" empires too would suffer the disintegrative fate of their pre-modern antecedents.

THE DIALECTIC OF PRE-MODERN WORLD POLITICS: UNITY VS. AUTONOMY

Thus, as far back as anthropologists and historians can reconstruct the patterns of the pre-modern world, we can see a recurring dynamic, sometimes occurring simultaneously in various regions of the globe, sometimes on different time scales:

1. The weakness and disunity among the states (or tribes) of a region tempt an imperially inclined power to expand and integrate its

sphere of control. Often the would-be imperial ruler claims its expansion and/or integrative policies are required to protect the region from aggression by a foreign imperialist.

2. The successful empire's presumption of cultural superiority, combined with its material exploitation of those it dominates, stimulates local communities to seek political autonomy. The empire's coercive countermeasures provoke defections and/or combinations against it, often abetted by outside powers.

3. The empire's attempts to counter defections and hostile conspiracies, particularly in outlying areas of its sphere, stretch and distort its allocation of material and human resources in ways that weaken its overall power and result in even more defections and combinations against it.

4. The spreading weakness and disunity throughout the area formerly under effective imperial control stimulate the expansionist appetites of new aspirants to empire.[36]

This dialectical process did not cease with the emergence of the European "balance of power" in the seventeenth century; that intendedly anti-imperial system (analyzed in Chapter 3) also was unable to transcend the elemental contest between centripetal and centrifugal forces, as a succession of would-be global hegemons (Napoleonic France, commercially dominant Britain, Hitler's Germany, the Cold War superpowers) emerged to hold sway—temporarily—over large portions of the planet.

---

[36]In addition to drawing on the insights of Kennedy, *The Rise and Fall of the Great Powers,* my analysis of the rise and decline of imperial powers is informed by Robert Gilpin's *War and Change in World Politics* (Cambridge: Cambridge University Press, 1981), and George Modelski, "The Long Cycle of Global Politics and the Nation State," *Comparative Studies in Society and History,* Vol. 20, No. 2 (1978), pp. 214–238.

3

THE DEVELOPMENT OF THE MODERN INTERNATIONAL SYSTEM: FROM CLASSICAL BALANCE TO COLD WAR BIPOLARITY

The anarchy of the century of reglious wars, culminating in the awful devastation of the Thirty Years War, finally generated a determination on the part of the statespersons of Europe to devise an interstate regime of mutual respect and forebearance that, they hoped, would stop the senseless carnage and prevent it from ever happening again. The result of their efforts, which took place over a period of four years, was the historic breakthrough of 1648 called the Peace of Westphalia.

In the numerous documents signed in 1648, the monarchs of the day pledged to honor each other's sovereignty over the newly demarcated and newly reaffirmed realms of territory assigned to each of them. The jurisdictional integrity of every sovereign state was to be sacrosanct. Intervention by one state into the domestic affairs of another state, especially for the purpose of aiding co-religionists, was henceforth illegitimate. This basic regime for interstate relations is still reflected in the essential structure and legal norms of the contemporary nation-state system, which many scholars continue to call "the Westphalian system."

During the more than three centuries of its existence, however, the Westphalian regime has exihibited at least five different configurations: (1) the European "classical balance of power," lasting roughly until the start of the French Revolution; (2) the "Concert of Europe," beginning with the Congress of Vienna, 1815, and lasting, according to some diplomatic historians, until the immediate pre–World War I period; (3) the experiment with universal "collective security" from the establishment of the League of Nations to the first few years of the United Nations; (4) Cold War bipolarity; and (5) the post–Cold War "polyarchic" configuration of world politics, which will be analyzed in subsequent chapters.

Some of these variations of international relations have overlapped in time. None of the temporarily dominant patterns has disappeared completely; for even while being overtaken by successor patterns, each has transmitted its own legacy to its offspring, so to speak, like genes carried through many generations. And on occasion one or another of the historical patterns has seemed to be experiencing a full-blown reincarnation.

The Classical Balance of Power

The ideal configuration of international relations for many theorists and statespersons schooled in world history was the flexible system of shifting alliances through which the half dozen or so major dynasties of Europe kept each other's ambitions and power in check after 1648—until Napoleon Bonaparte commenced his imperial rampages in the last decade of the eighteenth century. To the extent that this balance-of-power system functioned according to its idealized potential, there would be no permanent alliances, and whenever an imperialistic power arose to challenge the prevailing equilibrium of power, it would be countered ad hoc by a fresh and appropriate combination of states. Conflicts among the various monarchies would be limited to disputes over tangible matters such as the control of land, waterways, and fisheries and overseas imperial holdings. Disputes over ways of life and ways of worshiping God, over which there could be no negotiated compromises, would be kept out of the interstate arena. Such wars as did break out over tangible issues could be terminated rather rapidly short of total defeat of the enemy.

The beauty of the idealized classical system—and why it still continues to have a theoretical or aesthetic appeal, if not an appeal as a practical design for world order—is that each state in servicing its overriding self-interest of survival as a sovereign political entity would thereby service the stability and durability of the system as a whole. States would adhere to rules of moderation, even in war. Self-interest and general interest would coincide. This coincidence of the self-interest of the major states with the maintenance requirements of the system meant that the essential behavioral norms of the classical balance of power would be largely self-enforcing. In this sense, the system could be thought of as self-equilibrating.

Drawing on the conceptual formulation of political scientist Morton Kaplan,[1] seven self-enforcing norms of the classical variant of the balance of power can be postulated:

[1] Morton A. Kaplan, *System and Process in International Politics* (New York: Wiley, 1962), pp. 49–50.

1. Normally, states would attempt to increase, or at least maintain, their territory, material resources, and military strength; but as this brought them into conflict with other states, they would prefer negotiated settlements, and even third party mediation, to war. (Neighboring states, such as the League of the Rhine, promised to resolve their disputes by conciliation. France accepted Swedish mediation of some of her conflicts at the end of the seventeenth century; similarly, Turkey and Austria-Hungary accepted British and French mediation in 1717–1718.)[2]

2. Yet states would go to war rather than accept a major decrease in, or forego an important opporunity to increase, their resources or military strength. (Indeed, the major powers of Europe were more frequently involved in wars against each other between the Peace of Westphalia and the French Revolution than during any other era of European history.)

3. States involved in warfare usually would terminate physical hostilities short of the point of total elimination of a key member of the system. (Thus, in the early 1760s, the prospect that Prussia might actually be destroyed, which would have severely destabilized the five-power European balance of the time, was a constraint even on the actions of Prussia's principal enemies, Austria, France, and Russia.)[3]

4. Key states of the system that were defeated or seriously weakened in war would be permitted by the other states to reenter the system as important actors; and previously unimportant actors were recognized and dealt with as important states as their changes in capability warranted this new status.

5. States would oppose, unilaterally or in combination with other states, any state or coalition that threatened to assume a position of overwhelming predominance within the system. (During the reign of Louis XIV, 1643–1715, the fear of hegemonial dominance centered on France, and Britain led in the formation of an anti-French coalition; but with the success of British overseas imperial expansion in the middle of the eighteenth century, Spain and The Netherlands, now more fearful of England's dominance, joined France in a coalition against Britain.)

6. Any state was potentially an acceptable coalition partner of any other state. Particularly during the first three-quarters of the eighteenth century, countries rapidly shifted alliances. (For example, in

[2]Evan Luard, *Types of International Society* (New York: Free Press, 1976), p. 328.
[3]Gordon A. Craig and Alexander L. George, *Force and Statecraft: Diplomatic Problems of Our Time* (New York: Oxford University Press, 1983), p. 21.

the War of the Austrian Succession, 1740–1748, France and Spain joined Prussia against Austria, which was supported by Great Britain; but in the Seven Years War, 1756–1763, France was an ally of Austria and Russia, while Britain was on Prussia's side.)

7. States sought to limit the interstate or trans-state activities of states and other groups who attempted to mobilize support for themselves or to build coalitions on the basis of trans-state or universal religions or ideologies.

The first two norms are often viewed as inherent to the anarchic structure of international society: Today, no less than in the seventeenth century, the survival and well-being of a state appear to require that it look out for its own interests—through diplomatic bargaining if possible, while maintaining a credible capability to go to war in the event that nonviolent diplomacy proves insufficient—since there is no international institution that can reliably ensure it of protection.

Norms 3 through 7, however, are the products of more particular historical contexts and have not operated with any consistency since the French Revolution. Thus, to understand why all seven of the norms operated between the Peace of Westphalia and the French Revolution, we must examine the collateral social and material conditions then prevailing, especially in Europe.[4]

The fact that the principal states of the last half of the seventeenth century and the first three-quarters of the eighteenth century were aristocratic monarchies—the only exception being the brief Republican Interregnum in England under the Cromwells (1653–1660)—was central to the operation of the classical balance. The monarchs of the time could arrange marriage, line-of-succession, and treasure deals with one another, form and reform alliances and counteralliances, trade colonial possessions, and even redraw the boundary lines demarcating the states of Europe, without having to worry whether the populations within their jurisdictions liked it or not. "L'etat c'est moi" (I am the state), France's Louis XIV is supposed to have said, giving expression to the prevailing sense that the rulers were unaccountable to the ruled.

The states, in a word, were not yet *nation*-states. Indeed, it was not unusual for the monarch to speak a different language and practice a different religion than the majority of his subjects. Monarchs often would recruit their top diplomats and generals from other countries (these valued professionals, themselves having no compelling emotional attachment to any particular country, offered their skills to the highest bidders). And the generals in

[4]My account of conditions in Europe during the period of the classical balance of power is informed by the accounts of Luard, *Types of International Society;* Edward V. Gullick, *Europe's Classical Balance of Power* (Ithaca: Cornell University Press, 1955); and Richard Rosecrance, *Action and Reaction in World Politics* (Boston: Little, Brown, 1963).

turn would fill their ranks with mercenaries, hired soldiers who as often as not had no prior connection with the land and peoples they were paid to defend.

The economic and social ties among peoples within each country were still quite flimsy. Trade between different sectors of society—farmers, craftsmen, merchants—was increasing; specialization and "vertical interdependence" were growing; but the exchange of goods was largely of finished products ready for use. Countrywide or "national" markets were developing, which meant that roads and waterways had to be constructed and maintained, as public works, to link geographically dispersed communities; but as yet the larger nation that these mutually reinforcing processes of integration implied was only a thin overlay on the still relatively distinct enclaves of homogeneous ethnic/linguistic subnations.

All of these social and economic conditions had a determining effect on resort by statespersons to their most important diplomatic trump card, war, and on the objectives for which war was fought and on the way it was fought.

Wars were fought by professional armies for war aims defined by an aristocratic monarchy and its professional diplomats. The citizenry at large normally were not asked to fight or even to support the wars going on around them. Thus, wars could be conducted for any of a wide range of state interests—from vital to trivial. One war could be fought to prevent a major shift in the interstate balance of power. Another war could be fought to establish rights to fish in a disputed areas. Still another war could be fought to salvage the reputation of a particular general who was outmaneuvered by a rival general in the last war. Wars could be started quickly and turned off quickly, for the ruling elite did not have to justify their actions to anyone but themselves. A war therefore did not need to involve any irretrievable political or material risks. War might be an instrument of high statecraft, based on prudential deliberation and systematic strategic assessment, but it also might be an instrument of caprice.

The recruitment, organization, and provisioning of the military were important influences on the role of war in the period of the classical balance. Some mercenary soldiers fought for the glory of it, but most mercenaries were simply in the business of renting out their bodies. If they were not fed and clothed well, if the work was too hard, or if there was too much risk of their getting killed, they would desert. Consequently, the generals of the time were constrained to avoid frequent or sustained battle. In a sustained battle, not only one's soldiers, but also their supply trains, ammunition, and weapons would be lost, and all of this was very expensive to replace.

Most states still had little revenue with which to finance costly wars, noblemen being generally exempt from taxation, so the incentives all went in the direction of limiting one's war aims and fighting highly controlled and brief wars. War, like chess, was a game of maneuver; and the brilliant general knew not only how to win without getting into a big engagement but also when to concede defeat—sometimes even prior to any major exchange of gunfire. Clever statespersons could (and did) play on these incentives in order to establish a bargaining advantage over an enemy, through attempts to convince the enemy that one's own resolve and staying power had by no means reached their limits in a particular conflict.

The crucial political constraint on statecraft in the classical balance— maintaining as much flexibility as possible in the choice of alliance part- ners—was highly interactive with the incentives to fight limited wars. In or- der to preserve the option of forming an alliance tomorrow with today's enemy, a state would refrain from pushing its advantage to the point of de- stroying or humiliating a rival power. Fortunately, because of the material and manpower constraints on warfare, there were few temptations to ex- ceed this rule of prudence.

But underneath the admirable restraint in statecraft and the surface equi- librium of the classical balance, new forces were at work undermining the necessary conditions for its survival as the dominant pattern of interstate re- lations.

It took the brutal cataclysm of the Napoleonic Wars following the French Revolution of 1789 to shock the statespersons of Europe into a recognition that the self-help, self-equilibrating features of the classical balance of power might be woefully inadequate for sustaining the requirements of civic order in the modern age. Indeed, given the new social and economic realities, the unilateral diplomacy of the classical system might well encourage the very immoderate behavior of states toward one another that nearly destroyed European civilization in the Napoleonic Wars.

Why? A short phrase sums up the complex and world-transforming metamorphosis. The state system was changing into a *nation*-state system. The territorially defined states were becoming nations, in which strong bonds were developing between ruling elites and general populace—bonds of perceived mutual material dependence between the various economic classes of the country, and the emergence of a countrywide sense of cultural identity. This general trend, as will be shown below, was to have profound effects on interstate diplomacy and war.

Much of the change was probably inevitable, being the product of the hu- man being's increasing and accelerating capacity to transform the natural world. This technological inventiveness was evident in eighteenth century Europe in the dramatic growth of complex manufacturing processes, which engulfed economies based on simple in-the-home craftsmen. Buildings, roads, vehicles, and instruments of war were constructed more and more of materials and parts that were themselves made by highly specialized labor and facilities. Different sectors of society, different professions, different classes, became increasingly dependent upon each other and upon more elaborate and widespread systems of money and credit. Countries became internally more integrated, not only economically but also culturally. Mod- erns "nations" were beginning to develop.

The functions of government in the various territorially demarcated countries, the controls on public order and commerce, the collection of taxes and tolls to construct and maintain commonly used roads and waterways, the raising of armed forces to enforce the rules of civic order within the country and to protect it against hostile outsiders—in short, the whole apparatus of the *state*—which heretofore were highly centralized in the monarchy, would need to be adapted to the emerging social and economic complexities. The state simply could not function any longer without the cooperation of many elements of society.

The adaptation of the state to the new nation-forming forces in eighteenth century Europe proceeded at a different pace and took different forms in the various countries. In England, not wishing to repeat the bloody Cromwellian revolution of the previous century, the monarchy gradually, if reluctantly, began to share power with a parliament increasingly representative of the commercial classes. In France, a more rigid and self-indulgent monarchy refused to accommodate sufficiently to the power-sharing demands of the emergent classes until it was too late—the result being the Revolution of 1789, the establishment of the French Republic, and a new cycle of chaos and terror leading to the takeover of the Republic by the would-be emperor of all Europe, Napoleon Bonaparte.

In response to the imperialistic expansion of Republican and Napoleonic France, the preexisting balance of power system did come into play, but only partially, and in a way that was so distortive of its own norms that it could not be reinstituted after Napoleon's defeat in 1815.

France, especially under Napoleon, had violated the classical system's norms by using the republican and nationalistic ideologies of the French Revolution as justification for military intervention into civil conflicts of other countries; France would come to the aid of those other people fighting for the "Rights of Man" against oppressive monarchs. Understandably, the crowned heads of Europe (to repeat the famous oxymoron) were trembling in their boots! It took fifteen years for the alliance of European monarchs and England to smash Napoleon and temporarily reverse the tide of nationalistic revolutions he helped to swell; but in so defending the old order, they too violated the classical principles of nonintervention into the domestic affairs of other countries and moderation in both the objectives and conduct of war.

CONCERTS AND CONFERENCE DILPOMACY: MANAGED EQUILIBRIUM AMONG NATION-STATES

The obsolescence of the classical balance of power was marked in 1815 by the perceived need on the part of influential statesmen to come together in a group to concert their actions, to jointly steer the system, out of a fear that the unilateral pursuit by each country of its perceived self-interest would not, as in the past, guarantee a statecraft of moderate ends and moderate means.

The older system of flexible alignment and realignment among the countries of Europe to balance each other's power was being undermined by the spread of the ideology of nationalism and by new material and social forces that were transforming dynastic states into nation-states. The combustible combination of the new culture of nationalism and the new ideology of liberalism that was now sweeping Europe from the Atlantic to the Urals, from the Baltic to the Mediterranean, would need to be managed by the enlightened leaders of the time if the Napoleonic Wars were not to have been only the first phase of a holocaust that would leave Europe even more devastated than had the seventeenth century wars of religion.

The post-Napoleonic statesmen differed among themselves over how much joint management was necessary—some wanting only occasional consultation, others favoring permanent institutions to formulate and oversee the implementation of new rules of interstate conduct. All, however, were agreed on the inadequacy of the pre-Napoleonic balance of power process for containing the explosive forces of the nineteenth century.

A web of multilateral treaties and obligations to at least consult with one another before taking action of system-wide significance was now required—in contrast to the classical pattern wherein a state's unilateral pursuit of self-interest was assumed to serve the general interest (and in those cases where it did not, the virtually automatic workings of the balance of power would restore the general equilibrium). In the face of the rising domestic forces, which might impel governing elites to respond more to nationalistically oriented constituencies than to the requirements of world order, the post-Napoleonic statesmen, in their discussions with one another and in their treaties, attempted to forge an explicit set of understandings on the "legitimate" structure and processes of the European state system. But when it came to the specific content of the norms and the particular forms of institutionalizing the new European system, the consensus of 1815 turned out to be quite flimsy.

Czar Alexander I of Russia wanted a re-Christianized Europe, with the rulers of the countries morally pledged to maintain the territorial status quo provided for in the treaties ending the Napoleonic Wars and to support one another in upholding the constitutional order. For the Czar, this meant coming to the aid of monarchies when they were threatened by republican revolutions. To promote these ends, the Czar persuaded his fellow rulers to sign the Treaty of the Holy Alliance of September 1815—a document long on pietistic affirmations of "Christian charity" and "indissoluble fraternity" and short on specific provisions for the conduct of interstate relations. Behind the Czar's back, many of the other conservative statesmen of the day ridiculed the document. Austrian Chancellor Metternich made vulgar jokes about it. "A piece of sublime mysticism and nonsense," said British Foreign Minister Castlereagh.[5]

Austria and Prussia were ready to wave the banner of the Holy Alliance as justification for their defense of monarchical principles against liberal and nationalistic movements. However, Britain and France (even after the monarchical restoration) were not particularly averse to political movements that would diminish the power of the autocrats of Central and Eastern Europe. There emerged, therefore, almost as soon as the Holy Alliance was promulgated, an embarrassing East–West schism under its aegis: The three Eastern powers (Russia, Prussia, and Austria) were often inclined to intervene in other states to prevent national or political revolutions against their existing sovereign authority, whereas Britain and France more often than not were opposed to such interventions. This partly ideological, partly geographical divide was expressed, on the one hand, in the Pact of Muchengratz (1833) against the forces of liberalism and revolution, and, on the other hand, in the countervailing Quadruple Alliance (1836) among Britain, France, Spain, and Portugal.[6]

But Europe was still far from polarized into two camps along either ideological or geographic lines. Britain supported Austria's imperial position in Italy in the 1820s against Italian nationlists, and in 1839–1840 supported the Turks in their efforts to suppress nationalist–reformist uprisings. As put by one British analyst, "The paradox . . . emerged of Britain, previously the chief liberal, anti-interventionist power, as the staunch supporter of the status quo in the Ottoman Empire, while Russia, the arch counter-revolutionary, became the main supporter of revolutionary forces in the area."[7] Throughout the nineteenth century, rivalries within the "Eastern" and "Western" blocs persisted and frequently were more salient than the East–West division: France against Britain in regard to Belgium and Italy, and especially in North Africa; Prussia againt Austria over the Germanic peoples; and variously Prussia and Austria, sometimes independently, sometimes in concert, against Russia's hegemonial designs in East and Southeast Europe.

Thus, the "classical" unilateral balancing system still operated under the veneer of multilateral cooperation. But both the revival of the old diplomacy and the new concert diplomacy were expressions (in the words of the subtitle to Henry Kissinger's doctoral dissertation on the period) of "The Politics of Conservatism in a Revolutionary Age." Highly elitist in conception and management, the Concert of Europe became increasingly anachronistic.

---

[5]Hans J. Morgenthau, *Politics Among Nations* (New York: Knopf, 1978 [5th edition, revised]), p. 449.
[6]Luard, *Types of International Society*, pp. 122–126.
[7]*Ibid.*, p. 165.

The statesmen of the nineteenth century seemed unable to fully comprehend, let alone adequately grapple with, the emerging central predicament of the nation-state system; namely, how to reconcile the requirements of a stable and moderate interstate order with the domestic political requirements of maintaining power in one's own country. Attempts to satisfy the latter might overwhelm the former as the transformation of countries into nation-states intensified the pressures on ruling elites to be first and foremost accountable to their national constituencies.

Particularly where the Industrial Revolution was most advanced, the power of a country vis-à-vis other countries—its military and economic power—came to depend upon the ability of its rulers to gain cooperation from many sectors of the country to build modern fleets and armies, to construct and maintain nationwide roads and transportation systems, and to foster industries that could engage in profitable international trade. This put the merchant and commercial elites in an especially strong bargaining position (particularly when it came to the mobilization of the country's resources for large projects, such as the expansion of the navy), since it was they who really controlled the country's industry and finances. Simple prudence compelled the hereditary dynasties and aristocracies to co-opt these new elites into the regimes, to invite them into the chambers where policy was made. And thus were born the institutions of the nation—councils of state and parliaments—to which the monarchy had to be accountable. Interstate diplomatic maneuverings and power plays were accordingly constrained by this need of governing elites to satisfy broader segments of society that particular alliances, foreign adventures, and wars were indeed in the nation's interest.

Paradoxically, therefore, ruling elites felt it necessary to cultivate and enhance the new forces that were constraining their freedom of action, thereby limiting their diplomatic flexibility even further. In order to generate sufficient popular support for the measures, domestic and international, required to secure the country's independence, let alone to increase its power, monarchs, aristocrats, and prime ministers now had to identify with the people rather than stand aloof from them. They had to speak the peoples' languages and champion their causes. They had to embrace the ideology of nationalism—the idea of the nation-state as an organic whole.

This equation of state and nation plus the spread of the ideology of nationalism was at odds with another of the cardinal norms of the classical balance of power: moderation.

Foreign adventures, particularly wars, would be more difficult to initiate because they required a rather solid national consensus for their provisioning. National fear, anger, and pride had to be whipped up in order to go to war; the reasons of state for which war was required had to be reasons of nation—its survival, its honor, its glory; the enemy had to be venal and therefore deserved to be severely punished, hobbled, if not destroyed.

Developments in weapons technology and military logistics reinforced the sociopolitical and economic factors that were making it difficult to limit the destructiveness of war. The new weapons, military transportation systems, and powerful navies required support from a militarily prepared industrial base that in turn required a virtual mobilization of the entire nation. Consequently, a belligerent country's munitions factories, transportation networks, indeed its whole industrial base, now became crucial (thus legitimate) military targets.

No longer could a country depend on hired mercenaries to fight its wars. Loyal citizens would have to be recruited to fight and to provide the generalship. This dependence on citizen armies further reinforced the requirement that wars—and military alliances—only be entered into for vital national purposes. Again, wars might be harder to start and sustain than in previous centuries, but once started, they would be more difficult to terminate short of total victory or total defeat.

The ideology of nationalism had another paradoxical effect even more threatening to the prospects for a stable and durable civic order in Europe. On the one hand, it helped to forge the vertical integration of society within countries, the identification of the rulers with the ruled, and gave "legitimacy" to the sometimes brutal suppression by national governments of dissident linguistic and religious groups. On the other hand, the ideology of nationalism (particularly when infused with the doctrines of the French and American revolutions that only those governments were legitimate that rested on the "consent of the governed") was the energizing force of groups, now claiming to be nations of their own, who resented being submerged into the dominant culture of the larger nation-state in which they resided. If states were nations, then nations had a right to states of their own. Some of these would-be nation-states transcended existing state boundaries.

These highly combustible effects of nationalism had been exploited by the French Republic and Napoleon in their international interventions on behalf of the "Rights of Man." Napoleon, although defeated by the conservative powers, taught them a lesson they would learn all too well—that nationalism in the rival imperial power's camp could be an exploitable substance for undermining the rival's power and expanding one's own power. Henceforth, the statesmen of Europe, no matter what their own liberal or conservative ideology, would respond to temptations to expand the power and territorial base of their countries by seizing upon opportunities to help ethnic or religious dissidents in a rival state. Such interventionist temptations would be especially hard for statesmen to resist when the dissidents' causes, because of religious or cultural affinity, were popular with one's own citizenry.

Yet despite all the temptations to exploit the volatile social currents of the nineteenth century, the leading post-Napoleonic statesmen of Europe—Metternich, Castlereagh, and after them Bismarck—exhibited remarkable moderation and self-restraint. Unable to master the new forces, they at least recognized that the "bad currency" of unrestrained international power plays could easily drive out the good; and they had the recent lesson of the 20-year period of the Napoeonic Wars to remind them of the consequences of such a descent into anarchy.

While the popular image of the post-Napoleonic nineteeth century as an era of basic international peace among the great powers is surely wrong, especially for the last half of the century (witness the Crimean War of 1854 between Britain and Russia, the Italian War of 1859 between Austria and France, the war between Denmark and the German states of 1864, the Austro-Prussian War of 1866, and the Franco-Prussian War of 1870),[8] it was truly at the same time an era of creative international institution-building. The wars were a continuing reminder to enlightened statespersons that the nation-state system, left to the devices of unilateral statecraft, was now no longer capable of self-equilibration. They could no longer avoid the realization that the vaunted interstate anarchy of the classical balance of power, carried over into the age of intense nationalism, was now, if anything, one of the stimulants to war-making and to immoderation in the conduct of war.

The verbal pledges among nineteenth century statesmen of mutual accountability thus were more than hypocritical homages paid to virtue by vice. And the international conferences and congresses and the creation of international organizations that characterized the period were more than a diverting charade played by the diplomatic elite between their "real" power games.

The period featured serious multilateralism and international institution-building by history's arch *realpolitik* statesmen. It is the period from which the twentieth century's most noted *realpolitik* internationalist, Henry Kissinger—architect of the Nixon administration's policies of detente with the USSR and rapprochement with China—derived most of his ideas on diplomacy.[9]

Following the initial Congress of Vienna of 1815, there were a number of other congresses (the functional equivalent of today's "summits") that accomplished results of lasting significance. The London Conference of 1830–1831 established the independence of Belgium and Greece. The London Conference of 1839 instituted the permanent neutrality of Belgium. The London Conference of 1840–1841 promulgated rules on the contentious issue of the navigation of straits; and other major navigation and sea law rules were agreed to at the Congress of Paris in 1856. The famous 1878 Congress of Berlin, orchestrated by Bismarck, resolved a bitter Russo–Turkish dispute that might have easily led to an even bloodier repeat of the Crimean War and could have directly embroiled most of the major powers. And at the

---

[8]*See* Gordon Craig's account of the workings of the balance of power between 1815 and 1914 in Gordan A. Craig and Alexander L. George, *Force and Statecraft*, pp. 28–47.
[9]Henry A. Kissinger, *A World Restored: The Politics of Conservatism in a Revolutionary Age* (New York: Grosset & Dunlop, 1964).

Conference of Berlin in 1884, rules were negotiated on the establishment of colonial territories in Africa.[10]

The subject of war itself, its causes, prevention, and control—rather than any particular disputes among countries—were addressed at the Hague Conferences, begun in 1899. These produced a comprehensive revision and restatement of the rules of warfare and set up permanent institutions for the pacific settlement of disputes (the precursors of the system of international courts created under the League of Nations): the Permanent Court of Arbitration and the International Commission of Inquiry. The Hague instrumentalities marked no intrusion on the sovereignty of the states who agreed to adhere to them; but they did represent the growing recognition by statespersons that agreed-upon international norms and dispute-resolution mechanisms were important, if for no other reason than to provide a notion of international "legitimacy" to invoke against immoderate nationalistic passions that might drive governments into unnecessary wars and mindless levels of destruction.

Finally, the least glamorous and yet probably the most innovative of accomplishments of the internationalist diplomats of the nineteenth century was their creation of public international "unions" for coordinating actions by countries in economic, technological, and social welfare fields where cooperation and/or standardization was necesssary. Precursors of the functional specialized regional and global institutions that have proliferated in the contemporary age of "interdependence," the international unions were given mandates by their member governments to hire permanent international staffs ("secretariats") to operate in implementing agreed-upon policies, conducting research, preparing future conferences, and in general serving as administrative clearing houses. The first of these permanent international functional institutions was the Bureau of the International Telegraphic Union, established in 1868 (later to become the International Telecommunication Union). Similar organizations were instituted to coordinate activities in postal affairs, health and disease control, and labor standards and unionization rights.

The evolution of a system of international accountability for the world polity has its roots in the creative statecraft of the nineteenth century. As put by Professor Inis Claude: "Most basically, the nineteenth century contributed a broadening concept of the nature and subject matter of international relations, an evolving sense of the need for joint decisions . . . [and] a growing recognition of the usefulness of international machinery."[11]

However, the interstate accountability processes and institutions, while undoubtedly an important contribution of nineteenth century statecraft to the art of human governance, were essentially conservative. They were ef-

---

[10]Luard, *Types of International Society*, pp. 330–332.
[11]Inis L. Claude, Jr. *Swords into Plowshares: The Problems and Progress of International Organization* (New York: Random House, 1984), p. 39.

forts to preserve the system of cool-headed bargaining among aristocratic elites over the drawing and redrawing of territorial jurisdictions in Europe and in the colonial arena. The bargaining was constrained by the traditional power-balancing process: The European states would form alliances among themselves as required to prevent any of their numbers from overly aggressive imperialism.

German Chancellor Bismarck, the continent's quintessential conservative of the latter half of the nineteenth century, had hoped to perpetuate the European Concert after the Franco-Prussian War by renouncing all expansionist aims and pledging to use Germany's power only to further the general peace. Perceiving correctly that a new all-European war might be catalyzed by a clash of Russian and Austrian ambitions in the Balkans, Bismarck promised St. Petersburg that Berlin would remain neutral with respect to Russian moves in the Near East but would come to the assistance of Vienna in the event of a Russian direct attack on Austria-Hungary. At the same time, he assured Vienna that Germany would use its power to help Austria-Hungary protect its present position, but not in a way that would incur strong Russian opposition[12] The Bismarckian balancing act was prototypically "classical."

But the nineteenth century, anticipated by the American and French revolutions, was a period of radical transformation in political norms and structures *within* countries, which was turning ministers of state into the creatures of nations rather than their masters. The nations of the world were defining *their* interests and *their* borders, choosing *their* governments, and insisting that governing elites be accountable to *them* rather than to the governing elites of other countries. Interstate conflicts, including wars, were no longer primarily caused by (and efforts to redress) disequilibria in the balance of power between countries; they were now just as much the product of domestic passions and crises demanding external release.

The state system, a product of the old forces, was unable to harness passionate nationalism, a manifestation of the new forces. Bismarck saw what was coming and warned: "If the monarchical governments do not understand the need for working together in the interests of political order and instead surrender to the chauvinistic sentiments of their subjects, I fear that the international and revolutionary social struggles, which we shall have to fight through, will become more dangerous. . . ."[13]

Approaching the twentieth century, the nation-state system was becoming a self-contradictory human invention, hardly amenable to control through traditional balance-of-power diplomacy of either the classical or concert variety.

[12]Hajo Holborn, *The Political Collapse of Europe* (New Haven: Yale University Press, 1957), pp. 43–50.
[13]Bismarck's warning is quoted in Holborn, p. 47.

Yet the balance of power was still the only means at the disposal of countries in conflict to protect themselves against determined international adversaries.

Nationalism was now the driving force that set country against country, coalition against coalition. The balance of power became only an *instrument* of this immoderate force. It was the clash of rival nationalisms, aided and abetted by balance-of-power diplomats, that polarized Europe into two implacably hostile camps and brought on World War I. Moreover, what was supposed to be a solution to the problem of immoderation became part of the problem, as conservative governments, on the defensive domestically against rising liberal and socialist demands, went on the offensive internationally for nationalist causes in the hope of enhancing their popularity at home.[14]

Viewed from this perspective, World War I would not be seen, in retrospect, as a war resulting from miscalculation or diplomatic ineptitude—an unnecessary war. Rather, it can be seen as given by the system itself, a war that could have been avoided in 1914 only by extraordinarily brilliant statesmanship and that was likely to break out sooner or later anyway.

It was hardly illegitimate for German nationalism to be expressed at the turn of the century in an effort to challenge British and French preponderance as colonial powers, and therefore to launch a major buildup of the German navy. Nor were the countermoves of Britain and France—their *entente cordiale* to allocate spheres of influence to themselves in the colonial world and to keep Germany out, and their subsequent link-up with autocratic Russia in the Triple Entente—inconsistent with the normal dynamics of the balance of power. Similarly, Germany's countervailing resolidification of her old Triple Alliance with Austria and Italy was in tune with "classical" principles.

This bipolarization of the European balance, when superimposed on the competitive exploitation of nationalist movements in the Balkans by Austria and Russia, put all the elements in place for the conflagration that was sparked in the summer of 1914 by the assassination of the heir to the throne of the Austro-Hungarian empire by a Serbian nationalist.

Given the overwhelming propensities in the balance-of-power system in 1914 for a test of strength between the Triple Entente (Britain, France, and Russia) and the Central European powers (Germany and Austria), the British effort at the last minute to convene the Concert to prevent an all-European war from breaking out was bound to be futile. Indeed, the British diplomatic maneuvering may well have had the perverse effect of convincing the Kaiser that the British might sit out the war even if, despite their warnings, Germany went ahead with its planned invasion of neutral Belgium.

---

[14]Rosecrance, *Action and Reaction in World Politics*, pp. 149–168.

This is not to say that World War I was inevitable. But the evidence is massive that the eighteenth and nineteenth century forms of the balance of power were no longer capable of adequately managing the contradictions of the nation-state system, which by now were weakening its very foundations. The crisis of the increasingly anachronistic old order is starkly rendered in a retrospective historical account:

> For the men and women who lived through the first week of August 1914, the outstanding impression was of the cheering, singing, marching masses. It was the same before the Winter Palace in St. Petersburg, on the Unter den Linden in Berlin, on the Champs Elysees in Paris, in Trafalgar Square in London.
>
> It was as if the expanding wealth and multiplying populations, as if the unconscious boredom of peace over so many unbroken years had stored up in the nations a terrific potential, which only waited for an accident to touch it off. Far from being innocents led to the slaughter, the peoples of Europe led their leaders. Ministers of Tsar, Kaiser, King, and President watched the press and the streets during these demented days and fell victim to the hysteria as helplessly as any of the nameless multitudes about them. It was as if some historic fatality, expressing itself in a sort of elemental mass passion, for a moment had suspended all the normal processes of reason and humanity.[15]

THE LEAGUE OF NATIONS AND THE UNITED NATIONS— EXPERIMENTS WITH "COLLECTIVE SECURITY"

The immediate legacy of the failure of balance-of-power diplomacy to prevent World War I was the effort, led by US President Woodrow Wilson, to supplant the traditional self-help/alliance system with a new system of "collective security." But this would require a more fundamental transformation of the world polity than was contemplated in the new international arrangements negotiated by Wilson, the British Prime Minister David Lloyd George, and the French Premier Georges Clemenceau in the Peace Conference of 1919. (The other principal ally at the start of the war, Russia, since October 1917 under the leadership of Lenin and his Bolshevik party, had signed a separate peace with Germany before the war's end and therefore was not regarded as one of the victor powers.)

Wilson went into the Peace Conference as a world-order idealist, asking for a peace that would be generous to the defeated countries, a peace "without victory" for either side, a peace of universal "justice." It should provide for the self-determination of peoples and for general disarmament. Above all, and of greatest urgency, the postwar arrangements should include a

---

[15]Frank P. Chambers, Christina Phelps Harris, and Charles C. Bayley, *This Age of Conflict: 1914 to the Present* (New York: Harcourt Brace, 1950), p. 16.

League of Nations to supervise the peace and promote justice through common international action to resolve conflicts and dissuade aggression.[16]

But Wilson's confreres at the Peace Conference were agents for both the historic power interests of their respective countries and for the popular nationalistic sentiments whipped up by their governments in order to sustain support for the long and bloody conflict. (The French lost over 1.5 million lives and the British 917,000, as compared with 127,000 Americans.)[17] They saw the historical moment as an opportunity to fundamentally reduce German power through a punitive peace. Lloyd George was particularly anxious to take over most of Germany's colonial commerce. Clemenceau, representing a vindictive French nation, was determined to prune Germany down to a minor weight in the new European balance by levying harsh war reparation obligations on Berlin and imposing a wholesale disarmament of the German military establishment. To discourage further collaboration between a defeated Germany and Bolshevik Russia, he insisted on establishing a *cordon sanitaire* by extending the "Polish Corridor" up to the Baltic (principally by making the ethnically German port city of Danzig a "free city" under Polish administration).

The tough negotiations between the victor powers produced the grand bargain signed at Versailles, in which Wilson got his League of Nations (somewhat watered down from his preferences) in exchange for acquiescing to a harsher peace toward Germany and her allies than he believed was just. In the bitterest of ironies, however, Wilson's own countrymen prevented him from collecting on his side of the bargain, when the Congress refused to approve the Treaty of Versailles.

The popular view has it that the League experiment with collective security was ruined by the American failure to join. To be sure, with US participation and that of Russia and Germany when they were invited in, the international organization would have approximated its goal of universal membership. But the League's inability to significantly transcend the anarchic nation-state system was for the most part predetermined by the fact of the League's being a child of that system and carrying its progenitor's genes into its own basic structure and principal organs.

Article 11 of the Covenant reflected the collective responsibility norms of the nineteenth century Concert, stating that "Any threat of war, whether immediately affecting any members of the League or not, . . . is a matter of concern to the whole League, and the League shall take any action that may be deemed wise and effective to safeguard the peace of nations."

---

[16]Arthur S. Link, *Woodrow Wilson, Revolution, War, and Peace* (Arlington Heights: Harlan Davidson, 1979); and Robert E. Osgood, *Ideals and Self-Interest in American Foreign Relations* (Chicago: University of Chicago Press, 1953).
[17]Statistics on lives lost in World War I are from Francis A. Beer, *Peace Against War: The Ecology of International Violence* (San Francisco: W. H. Freeman, 1981), p. 37.

And Articles 12 through 15 inherited and built upon the Hague approach to conflict resolution, obligating members to submit their disputes for resolution to the League Council, the Permanent Court of International Justice, or other certified international tribunals, and "in no case to resort to war until three months after the award by the arbiters or the judicial decision or the report by the Council" (the so-called cooling-off period). But, realistically, Article 15 also provided that if the appropriate League bodies were unable to render a decision in such cases, "the members of the League reserve unto themselves the right to take such action as they shall consider necessary for the maintenance of right and justice."

The heart of the League's collective security system was supposed to be Article 16, where it was stipulated that if any country resorted to war in disregard of the provisions of Articles 12 through 15, "it shall *ipso facto*, be deemed to have committed an act of war against all other Members of the League, which hereby undertake to immediately subject it to the severance of all trade or financial relations, to prohibition of all intercourse between their nationals and the nationals of the Covenant-breaking State, and the prevention of all financial, commercial or personal intercourse between the national of any other State whether a Member of the League or not." In such cases, the Council was to recommend to member countries what military forces they should contribute to a collective effort to protect the covenants of the League.[18]

Some of the League's basic premises were highly innovative: War, though still not outlawed, was an abnormal, last-resort method of dealing with international disputes—in contrast to the traditional *realpolitik* view of war as a normal instrument of statecraft. The resort to war before utilizing the League's international dispute-resolution mechanisms, or in disregard of their awards, was illegal. And illegal wars were acts of aggression against the whole international community and were to be countered by collective community action.

But the structure through which the new collective security premises were to be implemented was fundamentally conservative in design and, as such, destined for self-paralysis in important cases. League collective security decisions had to be based on unanimity, excepting the parties to a dispute; but no party to a dispute, if it was a major power, would be without friends on the Council. In any event, League collective security enforcement decisions would always be in the form of recommendatory resolutions. There was a strong "moral" obligation on the part of members to conform to League resolutions, but no country in joining the League gave up a whit of its legal sovereignty.

[18]*Covenant of the League of Nations,* Signed at Versailles 28 June 1919 (Geneva: League of Nations, 1920).

The extent of the League's power (and impotence) was most starkly exposed in 1935, when Italy, then under the dictatorship of Benito Mussolini, invaded Ethiopia. The League did brand the invasion an illegal aggression; and the Council in this case did invoke the Article 16 sanctions system, asking members to embargo sales of arms and strategic materials to Italy, excepting oil (Italy's most strategically crucial import!). Fifty-two countries made credible attempts to comply with the League's embargo resolutions, but the effects on Mussolini's ability to prosecute his bullying action were negligible.

The only two powers that might have been able to challenge Italy militarily, France and Britain, were preoccupied with domestic problems and not at all anxious to assume the burden of organizing military sanctions since none of their vital geopolitical interests were in immediate jeopardy. Within a year, Ethiopia had been totally absorbed by Italy, and the League—true to its legalistic deference to nation-state sovereignty—found itself in the anomalous position of denying a hearing to the erstwhile Ethiopian Emperor, Haile Selassie, whom it had been trying to protect from Mussolini's brutal aggression.

Other aggressor nations took note of the League's perverse role as a mechanism for mobilizing countervailing power. Not only was it unable to provide timely and decisive opposition to Mussolini's power play against hapless Ethiopia, but its existence as the world's security agency of first resort provided an excuse for countries to refrain from reacting as they might have otherwise—unilaterally or through alliances to counter acts of aggressive expansion. The Japanese invasion of China in 1937 and Hitler's moves the following year against Austria and Czechoslovakia were, if anything, tempted by the power vacuum surrounding the League's collective security system.

So irrelevant had the League become as a mechanism for managing the balance of power that when England and France finally declared war against Hitler in 1939 in response to his invasion of Poland, they did not even bother to invoke the collective security provisions of Article 16.[19]

Paradoxically, World War II, which confirmed the irrelevance of the League, was attributed by laypersons the world over to the failure of the major powers to support and utilize the world organization. The United Nations embodies this paradox in its Charter, which provides for a reincarnated collective security system that is a synthesis of divergent elite and popular notions of how the balance of power should work.

Neither Winston Churchill nor Joseph Stalin nor Franklin D. Roosevelt had any desire to resurrect the League. Their preference was to project their Big Three wartime concert into the postwar world. FDR was a Wilsonian only in his belief that the democratically ascertained "self-determination" of

[19]See the discussion of the League's collective security system in Seyom Brown, *The Causes and Prevention of War* (New York: St. Martin's Press, 1994), pp. 179–186.

peoples was the essential basis for a stable and peaceful nation-state system. In contrast to Wilson, he wanted the conflict-management tasks for the system to be provided by the Big Three, who would continue to act in concert as the "world's policemen" (each patrolling, as it were, a sphere of influence), joined eventually by France and China in a five-power concert.

The Big Three differed with each other in their wartime conferences mainly over precisely where the postwar spheres of influences would be drawn, how much autonomy was to be allowed each of the hegemons to control its own sphere, and how to deal with the defeated enemy countries. The design of a United Nations Organizaion, which they agreed to in broad outline, was worked out at a conference of foreign ministers and occupied very little of their time at the summit.

The structure of the UN surfaced as a relatively minor controversial issue at the Yalta Conference in February 1945 when Stalin asked for separate voting seats in the General Assembly for the various "autonomous republics" of the USSR. But the issue was disposed of rapidly as FDR and Churchill agreed to let Stalin have two extra seats as a compromise (one each for the Ukraine and Belorussia). The Western leaders had no qualms in allowing this without getting compensatory representation (say, for Scotland or Texas) since they regarded the Assembly as just a debating forum and assumed that only the Security Council, in which each of the Big Five would retain a veto, would have the potential for developing into a real decision-making body.[20]

There were important domestic constituencies in Britain and the United States for a revived and strengthened universal collective security system—for a League of Nations "with teeth"—to whom Roosevelt and Churchill felt necessary to cater, as well as to many of the smaller countries that helped the Allies in the war against Germany and Japan and whose cooperation would be important in the postwar world. Internationalists in the US State Department and in the British Foreign Ministry were therefore given encouragement to work out with their Soviet counterparts the outline of a possible weighty collective security apparatus for the United Nations, under the clear proviso that it would be directly controlled by the Security Council (where the veto still would prevail). The outcome of these deliberations was the unprecedented—but, during the Cold War, largely unworkable—set of provisions for a truly international military force contained in Chapter VII of the Charter.

Chapter VII stipulates that the "Security Council . . . may take action by air, sea, or land forces as may be necessary to maintain or restore international peace and security" (Article 42); and it obligates all members "to

---

[20]On Big Three wartime planning for the United Nations, *see* John Lewis Gaddis, *The United States and the Origins of the Cold War, 1941–1947* (New York: Columbia University Press, 1972), pp. 27–30, 153–154; and Daniel Yergen, *Shattered Peace: The Orgins of the Cold War and the National Security State* (Boston: Houghton Mifflin, 1977), pp. 47–48.

make available to the Security Council, on its call in accordance with a special agreement or agreements, armed forces, assistance, and facilities, including rights of passage, necessary for maintaining international peace and security" (Article 43). Anticipating such contributions of forces to UN military actions, the Charter further stipulates (in Article 47) that

1. There shall be established a Military Staff Committee to advise and assist the Security Council on all questions relating to the Security Council's military requirements for the maintenance of international peace and security, the employment and command of forces placed at its disposal, the regulation of armaments, and possible disarmament.

2. The Military Staff Committee shall consist of the Chiefs of Staff of the permanent members of the Security Council or their representatives. . . .

3. The Military Staff Committee shall be responsible under the Security Council for the strategic direction of any armed forces placed at the disposal of the Security Council. . . .[21]

If the Military Staff Committee were ever to receive the contributions of forces contemplated in Chapter VII of the Charter, it would be a full-blooded *supra*national military force, but quite clearly under the political control of an intergovernmental body (the Security Council) with no more supranational characteristics than existed when the nineteenth century statesmen came together, in the Concert System, for their big-power conferences. It was, indeed, for the purpose of reasserting Security Council control over the use by member states of armed force in 1991 to implement UN resolutions against Iraq's invasion of Kuwait that the USSR suggested placing the command of such forces under the Military Staff Committee. But it was precisely in order to maintain full control over its own armed forces being assembled in the Persian Gulf region that the US government rejected this suggestion.

Although no UN military command was formed to repel Iraq's 1990 invasion of Kuwait, the resolutions passed by the Security Council branding Iraq as an aggressor and authorizing member states to apply sanctions, including the use of military force, came closer to being a true universal collective security action than any previous actions by either the League of Nations or the United Nations. (Some of the Chapter VII collective security provisions had been invoked back in 1950 to establish the "United Nations Peace Action" to repel the North Korean invasion of South Korea. But this was actually a US response draped in the UN flag and was possible only because of the USSR's temporary absence from the Security Council during the vote on

---

[21]*Charter of the United Nations*, Chapter VII.

the authorizing resolution.[22] To preserve the definition of the Korean action as a UN collective security operation even after the USSR returned to the Security Council, the United States was compelled to resort to the device of a General Assembly "Uniting for Peace Resolution" asserting the Assembly's authority to act when the Security Council was unable, because of the veto, to exercise its primary responsibility for peace and security.)[23]

The key Security Council resolutions during August and September 1990 condemned Iraq's invasion of Kuwait as "a breach of international peace and security" and called upon all States to cease exporting and importing commodities and products to and from Iraq until Saddam Hussein withdrew his forces from Kuwait. Finally, at the end of November, still not being able to effect Iraq's withdrawal, the Security Council voted to authorize member states, if Iraq failed to comply by January 15, 1991, "to use all necessary means" to compel Iraq to withdraw.[24] Upon the expiration of the January 15 deadline, the United States, citing the UN resolutions, commenced its successful "Desert Storm" military operation, with co-participation by some of its NATO allies and friendly Middle Eastern states. Notably, however, the military phase of international response to Iraq's invasion of Kuwait was conducted by a *coalition* of states led by the United States (in the mode of traditional alliance actions) and, unlike the operation in Korea 40 years earlier, did not fly the UN flag.

United Nations police forces have been formed for limited "peace-keeping" actions (the deployment, with the permission of the disputants, of a UN presence to oversee cease-fires, truce agreements, and the like), as distinct from collective security; but these usually have been organized on an ad hoc basis under the management of the Secretary General, directly responsible to the Security Council or General Assembly, and bypassing the Military Staff Committee.

The Charter's formulators explicitly anticipated the incapacity of the UN to serve traditional but still necessary power-balancing needs in the nation-state system. Article 51 accordingly legitimizes bypassing the UN in such circumstances, by allowing for "individual or collective self-defense if an armed attack occurs against a Member of the United Nations, until the Security Council has taken the measures necessary to maintain international peace and security." To garner popular support for such bypassing strategies, the United States and its allies, when formulating the North Atlantic Treaty Organization (NATO) in 1949, cited Article 51 to back their claim that NATO was consistent with the letter and spirit of the UN Charter, as did the Soviet Union and its allies in forming the Warsaw Pact in 1955.

[22]United Nations Document S/1587.
[23]United Nations Document A/1481.
[24]United Nations Security Council Resolutions, nos. 660 (2 August 1990); 661 (6 August 1990); 662 (9 August 1990); 664 (18 August 1990); 665 (25 August 1990); 666 (13 September 1990); 667 (16 September 1990); 669 (24 September 1990); 670 (25 September 1990); 674 (29 October 1990); and 678 (29 November 1990).

The post–World War II collective security institutions, in short, were elaborated in the midst of the emergent bipolarization of international relations; more so than the institutions of the League, they were carefully designed to survive, unused if it came to that, in the basic nation-state system while more traditional balance-of-power and/or concert diplomacy took over once again.

COLD WAR BIPOLARITY

As it turned out, the bipolar configuration of world politics that developed out of World War II was in many respects a throwback to the norms of statecraft of the period of religious wars. The diplomacy of the so-called Cold War differed from the diplomacy of the classical balance-of-power, concert, and collective security systems more than any of these configurations differed from each other. In the Cold War, the great powers once again, as during the wars of religion, found justification for intervening in each other's internal affairs, for practicing subversion and sponsoring civil wars in the opposing camp, and for defining the rivalry between the coalitions as a contest between good and evil.

The roots of this modern bipolarization were at once geopolitical and ideological. On the "western" side (which not incidentally included the recently defeated far-eastern power, Japan) the geopolitical explanations for the emergence of post–World War II bipolarity went back to de Tocqueville, the early nineteenth century French observer of American democracy, who saw the United States and Russia each "marked out by the will of Heaven [in the form of their vast material endowments] to sway the destinies of half the globe."[25] More concretely, the cold war strategists sought justification for their policies in the works of the seminal Anglo-American military geopolitical theorists of the pre-World War I period—especially Captain Alfred Thayer Mahan and Sir Halford MacKinder—who postulated a fundamental contest for global ascendancy between an imperialistic Eurasian "heartland" power and the insular states: Britain, the United States, and Japan. The cold war geopoliticians seized upon the "heartland/rimland" concepts popular before World War II to propound freshly the old imperative: Hold at least the rimland around the vast Eurasian land mass, for if the resources and sea access of the rimland areas were absorbed by the power that also controlled the heartland (aims attributed to the Soviet Union), that power would dominate the world.[26]

[25]Alexis de Tocqueville, *Democracy in America*, Vol. 1 (New York: Random House, Vintage Books, 1954), p. 452.
[26]The legacy of Anglo-American geopolitical thought drawn upon by the cold war strategists is found in Alfred Thayer Mahan, *The Problem of Asia and Its Effects upon International Relations* (Boston: Little, Brown, 1900); Halford MacKinder, "The Geopolitical Pivot of History," Geographical Journal, Vol. 23 (1904), pp. 421–441; and Nicholas Spykman, *The Geography of the Peace* (New York: Harcourt Brace, 1944). My interpretation of the essential similarities among Mahan, MacKinder, and latter-day western geopoliticians finds support in Stephen B. Jones, "Global Strategic Views," *Geopolitical Review*, Vol. 45 (1955), pp. 492–508.

The thrust of Russian foreign policy since Peter the Great had a special clarity and meaning in light of new preoccupations with Soviet expansionism. The straits connecting the Black Sea and the Mediterranean, the approaches to the Gulf of Finland and the Baltic, nationalist groups along the invasion routes from the West, the Oriental populations of Sinkiang and Mongolia, the northern Japanese territories—all of these had been periodically the direct targets of Russian military threats or diplomatic power plays. And now, having emerged from World War II a first-ranking great power, second to none on the Eurasian land mass, the Russians were at it again.

The geopoliticians in the Kremlin were themselves rereading the geopolitical classics and, knowing that their American counterparts were reviving the classical assumptions, had ample grounds for their own new worries. As is characteristic of most nation-states, Russia invariably justified its expansionist moves as dictated by minimum security needs; and, to be sure, its long history of constant suffering from attacks by enemies on all sides gave considerable credence to the posture. Added to the traditional Russian suspicions of British and French ambitions on the rimland were the Bolshevik suspicions that, being a socialist nation, the Soviet Union's continued existence was now intolerable to the capitalists. The Soviets, accordingly, were prone to see the West's containment policy as nothing less than a strategy of encirclement and strangulation.[27]

Thus, by the early 1950s, the official wisdom in Moscow and Washington reflected a set of remarkably similar geopolitical notions, presumed in both capitals to be self-evident:

1. The role of the United States as the leader of a broad anticommunist coalition was inescapable, since the Soviet Union could expand into the power vacuums of Europe, Asia, and the Middle East if the nations of these areas did not have the protection of the United States.

2. The Soviet Union, even if it abandoned or postponed its professed goal of transforming the world into a system of soviets, would continue to fear imperialist world wars and capitalist encirclement and therefore was bound to secure its borders in the West, East, and South. These fears would drive it to ensure the absolute loyalty of regimes in Eastern Europe and wherever else on the periphery of the USSR allies could be signed on.

3. This historically determined power configuration—two rival superpowers separated by power vacuums—made inevitable a clash of vital interest in the areas between. War over any of these interests became an ever-present possibility.

[27]According to the *Survey of Fifty Years of the Soviet Union*, published by the Central Committee of the Soviet Communist Party in 1967, the socialist industrialization of the USSR "had to be undertaken in conditions of our country's capitalist encirclement, and of constant danger of an armed attack by the aggressive power of imperialism." Quoted by Alexander Werth, *Russia: Hopes and Fears* (New York: Simon and Schuster, 1969), p. 30.

4. Consequently, an advantageous global balance of military power and access to zones of potential combat would be sought by each superpower. This competition for military advantage created additional geopolitical imperatives—economic resources, manpower, and bases for military operations—for maintaining large and highly coordinated multilateral coalitions.

From these perspectives, national security was so dependent upon the cohesion of one's coalition that the coalition itself tended to be regarded as an end rather than a means. At the least, the strength and cohesion of the coalition were thought to be the *sine qua non* for the pursuit of other values objectives.

The geopolitical incentives for polarization were reinforced by ideology. From the outset of their formation, each of the cold war coalitions was assumed to be a community of basic common beliefs no less than an alliance to marshall power for the defense of territorial objectives. Although the standard code words such as "free world" and "socialist commonwealth" were inadequate descriptions of the values adhered to by members in each camp, they did reflect a very real difference in general approach to domestic and world order that establihsed two rival ideological centers of gravity around which most nations tended to coalesce. The collective military force of each coalition was presumed to be available to protect a "way of life" or the "rules of the international game" as well as pieces of real estate critical to the balance of power.

The socialist camp, as viewed from Moscow, was a community of communist political parties—in some countries in control of the government, elsewhere still in opposition—which represented the class interests of the proletarians. Differences in tactics and priorities that might exist between national branches of this movement were dwarfed by their common adherence to "proletarian internationalism," which put them in universal opposition to governments and parties representing the capitalist classes. The allocation of tasks for the grand struggle against the capitalists, for the time being, required all parties to support the state interests of the USSR. But specialization of effort also obligated the USSR to protect weaker elements of the community in their confrontations with locally powerful capitalists— subject to the proviso that local communist parties could not expect to be bailed out of suicidal situations that were the product of un-Marxist adventurisms; namely, moves in advance of the full ripening of revolutionary conditions in particular countries.[28]

By attaching credibility to the ideological motives in Soviet foreign policy and in the international behavior of other communist regimes and parties, the leaders of most of the free-world countries—at least those in the North

[28]Zbigniew Brzezinski, *Ideology and Power in Soviet Politics* (New York: Praeger, 1962), pp. 97–113.

Atlantic region and Japan—gave serious ideological content to the noncommunist coalition. The concept "free," however it might be stretched with respect to the character of domestic society, came to mean being anticommunist internationally. It became necessary to resist the assumption of power by communists or regimes willing to align themselves with the international communist movement on important international issues, as well as to resist the overt extension of communist control by military aggression. Who was in whose camp ideologically would largely determine the extent of military commitments by the superpowers and the lineup of military allies in case of general war. From the point of view of the United States, being against the extension of communism was usually sufficient to qualify a nation as a member of the free world coalition; and the ideologies of national self-determination and international pluralism countenanced the presence in the coalition of some rather curious species of free society (the Greek, Turkish, and Spanish autocracies, for example, plus various Latin American and other Third World military dictatorships).

The bipolar configuration of the balance of power seemed most natural from the late 1940s to the early 1960s—the "high cold war" period—when the rival coalitions had little interaction that was not confrontational, when the common assumption was that one side's gain was the other side's loss, when Moscow and Washington charged each other with understanding only the language of force, and when, therefore, the balance of power was essentially a balance of military power.

The equation of overall power with military power tended to reinforce the bipolar legacy of World War II, since even the reviving centers of economic and political energy in Europe and Japan and China could not hope to rival the "super" military power—particularly the strategic nuclear weaponry—of the United States and the Soviet Union. When push came to shove in any conflict between a lesser power and one of the superpowers, the lesser power would either have to capitulate or seek the military protection of the other superpower.

As long as the United States and the Soviet Union retained their unchallenged military superpower status relative to the other countries, the bipolar structure presumably would persist. Consistent with this expectation, the grand strategies pursued by both Moscow and Washington in the 1950s and early 1960s were designed to tighten the bipolar system so as to make it more controllable and predictable, and—consonant with the then-fashionable theories of deterrence—also safer.

But the two-camp world turned out to be much less cohesive and durable than the bipolarists of the 1950s and early 1960s hoped. Older relationships, temporarily suppressed by the devastation of World War II, and new forces spawned by the technological innovations of the twentieth century began to erode not only the Cold War structures but also the very foundations of the nation-state system itself. These developments are analyzed in the following chapters.

2

The Demise of the Cold War

4

CHANGING GEOPOLITICAL REALITIES

The demise of the Cold War, although dramatic in its final convulsions, was a process that had been at work for decades. The rigid bipolar structure that the two superpower victors in the Second World War superimposed on their defeated enemies and devastated allies was subject from the start to a set of centrifugal counterpressures. As the nations gutted by the war recovered their energies and pride, they became progressively unwilling to subordinate their own interests to the interests and preoccupations of their rivalrous superpower protectors.

Symptoms of deep coalition disunity began to affect both the US-led and Soviet-led camps even before the end of the first decade of the Cold War. In the fall of 1956, dissident national communists in Poland and Hungary (the latter provoking a bloody intervention by Soviet troops) exposed the extent to which the presumed ideological unity of the communist bloc was artificially imposed by an imperial hegemon. That same fall, in the "Suez Crisis," the most important allies of the United States, Britain and France, behind the back of the Eisenhower administration, conspired with Israel to militarily attack Egypt—an action that shocked the US President and Secretary of State into publicly rebuking their British and French counterparts and threatening them with a cutoff of US economic aid if they failed to reverse their military action.

The Suez Crisis was one of the cases in point of diverging allied strategic interests that led France to pull out of the NATO military command and to develop its own strategic nuclear force. China defected from the Soviet camp in the early 1960s. And by the end of the 1960s, the vast majority of the approximately 100 newly independent states of the Third World had made clear their determination to remain *non*aligned vis-à-vis the competing ideological camps of the superpowers.

Despite periodic efforts by each of the superpowers to impose unity and discipline on their respective coalitions during the 1970s and 1980s (e.g., the "Brezhnev Doctrine" justifying military action against counter-revolutionary dissent within the Soviet bloc and the Reagan administration's effort to reforge a "strategic consensus" of anticommunism), the centrifugal forces continued to counter, and increasingly outpull, the magnetic attraction of the polar centers on both sides.

THE CRISIS OF ALLIANCE CREDIBILITY

The disintegration of the superpower coalitions was in part the result of re-assessments among strategists and laypersons, starting in the late 1950s and intensifying in the 1960s and 1970s, of the value and liabilities of military alliances.

Military planners recognized that as the range of missiles and bombers became intercontinental, neither superpower would need distant allies anymore to extend its lethal reach into the home territory of the other. Such allies might perhaps still be strategically desirable in a US–Soviet war, for confounding enemy defenses and complicating enemy offensive targeting, but they no longer provided indispensable strategic-warfare assets to the superpowers. Nor did either superpower, with reconnaissance systems in orbit around the earth, require bases near the other's frontiers to gain adequate warning of menacing deployments or impending attack.

Meanwhile, publics, parliaments, and heads of state alike began to assimilate the implications of the genocidal dimensions of war conducted with nuclear weapons in the arsenals of the superpowers. If going to war meant placing one's national community at high risk of virtually total destruction, then no foreign interests, other than those essential to the defense of the homeland itself, would be worth a war. The "balance of terror," or Mutual Assured Destruction (MAD) as it came to be called, rather than providing an umbrella of protection for the alliance partners of each superpower, left them exposed to nuclear blackmail and bullying; for if the United States and the Soviet Union truly were deterred from attacking one another out of fear of mutual devastation, their pledges to come to the defense of their respective allies to protect them against the rival superpower would turn out to be hollow commitments at moments of truth. French President Charles de Gaulle, in justifying the need for an independent French deterrent force, told of his apocalyptic vision of a war in which Western Europe was incinerated from Moscow and Central Europe was incinerated from Washington while Russia and the United States held back from directly attacking each other's homeland. Similar fears that the Kremlin would renege on its security commitments prompted China to develop its own nuclear arsenal. The declining credibility of superpower strategic assurances also stimulated India, Pakistan, Israel, Iraq, South Africa, North Korea, and others to develop the technical option to manufacture and deploy their own nuclear weapons.

The fear by allies of the superpowers that they were dispensable pawns was further exacerbated by communications and transportation technologies that reduced the significance of distance from the zone of battle as a factor in military effectiveness even for "limited" or non-strategic wars.

By the 1980s, these various developments were producing widespread skepticism of the promises of nations to incur the awful costs of contemporary war on behalf of foreign friends. Accordingly, countries were inclining increasingly toward postures of self-reliance for protection against military attack—self-reliance meaning mass destruction capabilities under their own control and/or sufficient diplomatic flexibility to make deals unilaterally with their adversaries.

THE SLACKENING
OF IDEOLOGICAL BONDS

Once it was admitted by the Kremlin that a world war would be mutually suicidal, the standard Marxist-Leninist prediction of a final bloody struggle to bring about the worldwide victory of socialism needed revision. In a nuclear holocaust, the workers would lose more than their chains. As the Soviet Communist Party put it in one of its doctrinal disputes with the Chinese Communist Party, "The nuclear bomb does not distinguish between the imperialists and the working people, it hits great areas, and therefore millions of workers would be destroyed for one monopolist."[1] Accordingly, argued the Soviet ideologists, the primary diplomatic task of the leading Marxist states was now to stabilize relations among the great powers to the degree necessary to prevent global war, while the historical revolutionary process worked itself out in the varied domestic societies of the noncommunist world.[2]

As noted by the American Sovietologist Marshall Shulman, the strategy of peaceful coexistence, originally a tactical response to adverse situations requiring a breathing spell, became "elongated in time" and was "extended into a long-term strategy, implying a continued acceptance of the necessity for an indirect and more political way of advancing Soviet interests than the militant advocacy of revolution and the use of force."[3]

As the Kremlin adopted detente with the capitalist world as a durable policy, to be capped by Soviet–American arms limitations agreements in the common interest of avoiding war, it became increasingly difficult for Soviet Communist Party theoreticians to sustain the Marxist premise of two implacably contradictory social systems. If world politics was not simply the anticipation of the impending worldwide class war, the urgency for attaining a completely autarchic economy in the socialist commonwealth faded, as did the justification for mobilizing the camp in a rigidly hierarchical system. These implications were reflected in efforts by various communist countries to pursue their own commercial relations with the capitalist world. The con-

[1]Open letter from Communist Party of the Soviet Union Central Committee to Party Organization and All Communists of the Soviet Union, July 14, 1963; complete text in William E. Griffith, *The Sino–Soviet Rift* (Cambridge: MIT Press, 1964), pp. 289–325.
[2]For the transformation of Soviet ideology, even during the height of the Cold War, in response to the threat of nuclear extinction, *see* William Zimmerman, *Soviet Perspectives on International Relations, 1956–1967* (Princeton: Princeton University Press, 1969).
[3]Marshall D. Shulman, *Beyond the Cold War* (New Haven: Yale University Press, 1966), pp. 53–54.

cept of "many roads to socialism" was elaborated in the theoretical treatises and the practice of state parties within the Soviet-led coalition—in some cases (most dramatically the Czechoslovakian "Prague Spring" of 1968) go-ing beyond the threshold of Kremlin tolerance.

In the West, the transformation of the image of the major opponents from a monolithic band of revolutionaries into a feuding group of self-interested states also gradually eroded the ideological foundations of the extensive US system of alliances. Once it became generally accepted, as US Secretary of State Dean Rusk put it in 1964, that "the Communist world is no longer a single flock of sheep following blindly one leader,"[4] and that the Soviet Union was unflinchingly putting its state interests ahead of its missionary impulses, then it would appear unnecessary to the security of the United States and its allies to oppose each and every expansion of communist influence. Distinctions among communist countries would now seem to be in order, less on the basis of the internal character of their regimes than on the basis of their intentions and capabilities for major international aggression against important Western interests.

This reassessment of the importance and desirability of a global resistance to communism was well under way in the United States and other Western countries by the mid 1960s, when the Johnson administration revived the hyperbolic ideology of the 1950s to justify US military intervention in Vietnam. Once again, US anticommunist alliances were defined by Washington policymakers as a seamless web of commitments, which if cut in one place would unravel the whole system.[5] With the failure of the American effort to prevent the communization of Vietnam and the other Indochinese countries—a failure due in part to spreading rejection within the US policy community of the cold war premise that the success of communism anywhere in the world was a threat to the American way of life—a more restrictive set of criteria would determine whether and how the United States should intervene to redress a local imbalance of power favoring the communists.[6] The importance of a particular country's alignment for the global balance of power, the degree of involvement in the local conflict by the Soviet Union, and the symbolic or emotional importance attached to the preexisting commitment—all of these would become more weighty considerations than any general obligation to support members of the "free world" against a communist takeover.

[4]Dean Rusk, "United States Policy and Eastern Europe," address of February 25, 1964, Council on Foreign Relations, *Documents on American Foreign Relations* (1964), pp. 144–149.
[5]Leslie Gelb and Richard Betts, *The Irony of Vietnam: The System Worked* (Washington, DC: The Brookings Institution, 1979).
[6]The erosion of support within the US policy community for the universalistic anticommunist premises underlying the US Vietnam intervention is described in detail in Seyom Brown, *The Faces of Power: Constancy and Change in United States Foreign Policy from Truman to Reagan* (New York: Columbia University Press, 1983), Chapter 20.

The American souring on ideological anticommunism made Henry Kissinger's *realpolitik* concepts palatable to President Nixon and allowed Nixon, whose past political successes had been built on his anticommunist rhetoric, to preside over the distinctly nonideological policies of detente with the USSR and rapprochement with China. All high US government officials purged anticommunist rhetoric from their statements; and the President publicly allowed that "it would be a safer world and a better world if we have a healthy United States, Europe, Soviet Union, China, Japan; each balancing the other, not playing one against the other, an even balance."[7]

As it turned out, the Nixon–Kissinger *realpolitik* was perhaps too devoid of ideology, or at least prematurely so, to be sustained as American policy over the long run. Critics on the left and on the right called it "amoral," if not immoral. And a bipartisan majority in the Congress coalesced in 1974 to reject the economic centerpiece of the new Soviet–American detente (the extension of normal trading and credit privileges to the Soviets) as long as the Soviets continued to restrict Jewish emigration and to commit other human rights violations.

But, significantly, the revived emphasis on human rights and the popular insistence that "America ought once again to stand for something in the world," which helped elect Jimmy Carter in 1976, was not accompanied by a renaissance of anticommunism as such. If anything, the Carter administration officials with responsibility for implementing the new human rights policy were more inclined to bring pressure on right-wing dictators in the US-led coalition (whose transgressions had been largely ignored by previous administrations) than on repressive regimes in the communist world. The shift in attitude was reflected in President Carter's statement that "we are now free of that inordinate fear of communism which once led us to embrace any dictator who joined us in that fear."[8] The President did write a public letter to Soviet dissident Andrei Sakharov; and US representatives in various international human rights forums were not reluctant to call the Soviets on their failure to abide by their obligations under UN covenants and the 1975 Helsinki accords; but it was the Carter administration's initial policy not to let the popular human rights concern be a drag on the negotiation of a SALT II treaty, nor to substantially inhibit the elaboration of cooperative relationships with the Soviet Union and other communist countries.

By 1981, when President Reagan, using rhetoric with a stridency not heard from the top levels of the US government since the days of Secretary of State John Foster Dulles, attempted to restore the ideology of anticommunism as a motive force for US foreign policy and coalition unity, there were already too many powerful interests in both the Soviet-led and US-led coali-

---

[7]Interview with President Nixon, *Time*, January 3, 1972, p. 11.
[8]The "inordinate fear of communism" statement appeared in Carter's 1977 commencement speech at Notre Dame University. Text in *Public Papers of the President of the United States: Jimmy Carter, 1977* (Washington, DC: GPO, 1977), Vol. I, pp. 955–956.

tions and in the Third World with a practical stake in East–West detente to countenance a full international repolarization on ideological lines. Reagan's public castigation of the Soviets as untrustworthy negotiating partners because of their adherence to Leninism[9] and his characterization of communist countries as "the focus of evil in the modern world"[10] were widely dismissed in the United States and allied countries as rhetorical excesses. Foreign diplomats were privately briefed by embarrassed administration officials to pay more attention to what the administration did than to what the President sometimes said.

BRIDGES ACROSS THE DIVIDE

East–West bridge-building first got going in earnest in Europe, a good five years before the United States and the Soviet Union decided in the early 1970s to construct their own substantial ties of bilateral communication and cooperation. From the standpoint of the Europeans, the continent's bifurcation was an aberration—a temporary condition imposed on them by World War II and its immediate aftermath. Prior to the war, about 60 percent of Eastern Europe's trade was with Western Europe, and about one-fourth of this was with Germany. Accordingly, many Europeans anticipated that the revival of the economic and political health of their nations would lead to the reestablishment of a vigorous pan-European economy and civilization, which in turn would allow them to slough off their relationships of subordinate dependence on the essentially non-European superpowers.

Under the leadership of President Charles de Gaulle, France was the first to candidly assert a French and all-European interest in more intensive interaction between the West and East Europeans than might be congenial to either superpower. De Gaulle's concept of a revived and flourishing. Europe "from the Atlantic to the Urals" underlay his diplomatic demarche of 1966, which included his own visit to Moscow and visits by his foreign minister to Warsaw, Prague, Bucharest, Budapest, and Sophia. Grandly pursuing his European idea, which he sometimes referred to as a "third force," de Gaulle visited Poland and Romania with great fanfare in 1967 and 1968, and would have visited most of the other countries in Eastern Europe during the next few years had he not resigned the presidency in 1969.[11] All of de Gaulle's

[9]Ronald Reagan, News Conference of January 19, 1981, *Weekly Compilation of Presidential Documents,* Vol. 17, No. 5, pp. 66–67.

[10]Ronald Reagan, Speech of March 8, 1983, before the National Association of Evangelicals, Orlando, Florida, in *Weekly Compilation of Presidential Documents,* Vol. 19, No. 10, pp. 364–370.

[11]On de Gaulle's Eastern demarche, *see* Raymond L. Garthoff, *Detente and Confrontation: American-Soviet Relations from Nixon to Reagan* (Washington, DC: The Brookings Institution, 1985), pp. 106–107.

successors carried forward his basic Eastern policy of weaving an ever-thickening web, particularly of commercial relations, with the USSR and the other countries in the Soviet sphere.

DeGaulle's demarche made it legitimate for West Germany to experiment with a policy of enlarging contacts and commerce with the East—a reversal of Chancellor Konrad Adenauer's policy of making Soviet agreement to a reunification of Germany through free elections a precondition for detente. While still not ready to recognize the communist government in East Germany, Adenauer's successors (Chancellors Ludwig Erhard and then Kurt Kiesinger) in 1966 began to promote trade with Eastern Europe and, somewhat ambivalently, with the USSR. The Erhard government also sent a "Peace Note" to all other governments, including the communist governments in Eastern Europe, proposing an exchange of declarations to refrain from using force in international disputes.[12]

Thus, a modest *Ostpolitik* was already in place in Bonn by 1969 when Chancellor Willy Brandt, as head of the coalition of his Social Democrats and the Free Democrats, launched a more assertive Eastern diplomacy—producing the 1970 Federal Republic of Germany–USSR Non-Aggression Pact, the 1970 treaties with Poland and Czechoslovakia recognizing the post–World War II borders, the 1971 Quadrapartite Agreement on Berlin (signed by the United States, the USSR, Britain, and France), and the Basic Treaty of 1972 between the Federal Republic of Germany and the German Democratic Republic.

Under Willy Brandt's leadership, West German Ostpolitik became the catalyst of the larger movement toward East–West detente, resulting in the Nixon–Brezhnev summit of 1972. But Brandt was highly sensitive to concerns in Moscow and Washington that the European equilibrium not be destabilized. West Germany's first normalization agreements were with the Soviet Union; only then did Bonn negotiate directly with Warsaw and Prague, thus deferring to the Soviet Union's compulsion to retain authority over the detente policies of its allies. Brandt was also insistent that his program of increasing interaction with the communist countries was fully consistent with Germany's continuing support for economic and political unity in Western Europe within the larger framework of the NATO alliance.[13]

The general presumption among US policymakers before the 1970s was that the Kremlin was furthering the idea of peaceful coexistence among the overly willing Europeans mainly for the purpose of sowing dissension in the anticommunist alliance. Yet there were some notable US–Soviet agreements that in some ways prefigured the Nixon–Brezhnev detente: the Austrian Peace Treaty of 1955 providing for a mutual withdrawal of troops, demilitarization, neutralization, and a Western-style political democracy; the

---

[12]*See* Angela Stent, *From Embargo to Ostpolitik: The Political Economy of German-Soviet Relations, 1955–1980* (New York: Cambridge University Press, 1981).

[13]Willy Brandt, "Germany's *Westpolitik*," *Foreign Affairs*, Vol. 50, No. 3 (April 1972), pp. 416–426.

Nuclear Test Ban Treaty of 1963; and the 1963 agreement (growing out of the Cuban missile crisis) to establish a direct crisis-communication link, the so-called Hot Line, between the two governments; and the Nuclear Nonproliferation Treaty of 1968.

It was not until the early 1970s, however, that substantial credit was given by US policymakers to the hypothesis that the Soviet leadership, while not abandoning its goal of communizing the world, might have made a historic shift in grand strategy away from isolation and antagonism vis-à-vis the West and toward securing and developing the USSR through cooperation and commerce with the noncommunist industrial world. Actually, the Soviets had made such a shift in grand strategy in 1966, and there had been signs even earlier that they were preparing for such a reorientation of their global policy. Signals of the Soviet shift were picked up by European statesmen such as de Gaulle and Brandt and gave them to believe that efforts to help move the Soviets in this direction might be worth a try.

A strong indication that a major change was in the works in at least Soviet foreign economic policy was the Kremlin's revision, at the Twenty-Third Party Congress in 1966, of its standing doctrine that the Socialist Commonwealth ought to provide on its own for all its economic requirements. To be sure, the Soviets since Stalin's death had made periodic forays into the capitalist marketplace to purchase machinery and technology and in 1963 had to negotiate a huge wheat deal with the United States and other grain producers to make up for some disastrous crop failures. Such shopping excursions had been officially defined as ad hoc and stop-gap measures not in any way inconsistent with the policy of COMECON self-sufficiency.[14] But now before the representatives of the world's communist parties, Premier Aleksei Kosygin was admitting that "It is becoming more and more evident that the scientific and cultural revolution under way in the modern world calls for freer international contacts and creates conditions for broad economic exchanges between socialist and capitalist countries."[15]

This historic Kremlin decision to participate in the capitalist international economy was dictated by the following considerations: The technological gap between the capitalist and communist worlds was threatening to negate much of the international influence the Soviets had gained as a result of their rapid modernization, industrialization, and strategic buildup. Continuing modernization now required the Soviet Union to make a substantial reallocation of resources into many of the high-technology, largely civilian areas, which, until recently, had been given low priority in comparison with military and space needs. But taking off into the kind of advanced industrialization that would allow the Warsaw Pact countries to maintain military

[14]On the pre-1966 period, *see* Marshall Goldman, *Detente and Dollars: Doing Business with the Soviets* (New York: Basic Books, 1977), pp. 21–31.
[15]Kosygin's remarks before the Twenty-Third Party Congress are quoted by Samuel Pisar, *Coexistence and Commerce: Guidelines for Transactions between East and West* (New York: McGraw-Hill, 1970), pp. 33–34.

parity *and* satisfy rising consumer demands would require substantial inputs from the West, especially in the fields of information technology and electronics. These expensive inputs would have to be purchased in the world economy with foreign exchange assets earned in international trade, and this in turn would require a capability on the part of the Soviets for flexible economic decisions responsive to demand changes in the world market. Only a fully creditable Kremlin policy of peaceful coexistence, however, would induce the noncommunist industrial countries to extend credits, liberalize their strategic embargo lists, and otherwise let down their political barriers to East–West commerce.[16] Henceforth, Soviet decisions about whether to produce a commodity or to purchase it in the world market would be based heavily on calculations of the costs of production relative to the costs of importation. In a complementary move, producers in the USSR were to have their product specifications and quotas formulated with greater sensitivity to the world market than previously.

At the Twenty-Fourth Party Congress, General Secretary Leonid Brezhnev called special attention to the "economic, scientific, and technical ties, in some instances resting on a long-term basis," being developed "with the countries of the capitalist world." And he called for a wide range of cooperative East–West projects for "conservation of the environment, development of power and other natural resources, development of transport and communications, prevention and eradication of . . . diseases, and the exploration and development of outer space and the world oceans."[17]

Under Brezhnev, the Kremlin also developed a geostrategic rationale to justify the shift toward peaceful coexistence with the capitalists: The Soviet Union's attainment of parity with the United States in strategic nuclear forces had changed the overall "correlation of forces" (the Soviet term for the global balance of military, economic, and political power) from one in which the capitalists might contemplate initiating another world war in order to prevent the global ascendancy of socialism, to a situation in which this was no longer a real option for the capitalists. Consequently, they—the capitalist countries—now might be willing, however reluctantly, to accept the necessity of peaceful coexistence with the socialists.

On the US side, meanwhile, there was a parallel revamping of the Cold War doctrines that, prior to the 1970s, had prevented normal commerce with the Soviets and members of their coalition.

Of crucial importance to the change in US policy was the information on the Soviet policy changes revealed at the Twenty-Third and Twenty-Fourth Party Congresses and corroborated by intelligence data on the new pattern

---

[16]On the doctrinal and practical considerations underlying the 1966 Soviet shift in international economic policy, *see* Richard V. Burks, *Technological Innovation and Political Change in Communist Eastern Europe* (Santa Monica: RAND Corporation, 1969), RM-6051-PR; and Goldman, *Detente and Dollars*, pp. 35–39.

[17]*Report of the Central Committee of the Communist Party of the Soviet Union,* delivered by Leonid Brezhnev, March 30, 1971 (Moscow: Novosti Press), pp. 33, 37.

of Soviet international commercial activities. It became an accepted premise within the Nixon administration that the Soviets, because of seriously lagging modernization efforts, were sorely in need of substantial long-term economic intercourse with the noncommunist industrial countries and that the Kremlin therefore really did want a protracted period of peaceful coexistence—not (as it was previously assumed) for the purpose of destabilizing the West, but rather to allow the Soviet Union access to the advanced technologies of the leading capitalist countries and to earn the foreign exchange needed to purchase the inputs necessary for modernizing the Soviet economy.

By the late 1960s, there was also heavy lobbying by the exporting sectors of the US economy to normalize trade with the Soviet Union and its allies. As US producers faced increasingly vigorous competition globally (and in the American market itself) from the West Europeans and Japanese, the US merchandise trade balance was rapidly deteriorating. This loss of markets to foreign competitors was partly due to the American involvement in the Vietnam War and the consequent inflation that increased the price of US goods; it was partly the inevitable result of the revival of economic strength of the war-devastated countries. In this context, US self-denial of access to willing importers in the Soviet sphere seemed economically foolhardy.[18]

The readiness of the National Association of Manufacturers and the US Chamber of Commerce and large segments of American labor to support efforts to penetrate the beckoning Eastern market provided the Nixon administration the opportunity it was seeking to convert the Soviet hunger for commerce with the United States into a US political asset. Nixon and Kissinger conceived of the change in US East–West commercial policy as part of a larger grand strategy of making the Soviets pay a political price for the expansion of East–West commerce the Kremlin so desparately sought. As Kissinger delicately put it in a public explanation of the US policy shift, "We have approached the question of economic relations with deliberation and circumspection as an act of policy not primarily of commercial opportunity."[19] The containment of Soviet aggressive expansion would henceforth need to be accomplished more with "carrots" than with "sticks." The big stick of nuclear deterrence of Soviet expansion had lost most of its utility as the Soviets attained nuclear parity with the United States, and the non-nuclear sticks were being whittled down by a nondefense majority in the Congress that reflected the popular isolationist reaction to the war in Vietnam. The lever of expanded economic intercourse, combined with the new US ability to worry the Kremlin about how far the developing US–China rapprochement would go (another essential feature of Kissinger's new international "mosaic"), could supplant the previous policy of threatening US military counteraction against Soviet international power plays and threatening

[18]Goldman, *Dollars and Detente*, pp. 73–76.
[19]*Ibid.*, pp. 353–359.

major increases in the US military budget to dissuade the Kremlin from provocative buildups of Soviet military forces. East–West commerce would thus be linked to Soviet international moderation and seriousness in negotiating arms limitation agreements.

The very different purposes of the two superpowers in laying economic spans across the ideological divide was artfully finessed in the central plank of the declaration on "Basic Principles of Relations" signed by President Nixon and General Secretary Brezhnev at their May 1972 summit:

> The USA and the USSR regard commercial and economic ties as an important and necessary element in the strengthening of their bilateral relations and thus will actively promote the growth of such ties. They will facilitate cooperation between the relevant organizations and enterprises of the two countries and the conclusion of appropriate agreements and contracts, including long-term ones.[20]

Consistent with the Nixon-Kissinger strategy, the agreement to expand economic cooperation was embedded in a set of political commitments by the two superpowers to "always exercise restraint in their mutual relations," to "negotiate and settle their differences by peaceful means . . . in a spirit of reciprocity, mutual accommodation, and mutual benefit." Both sides recognized, in the words of the communique, "that efforts to obtain unilateral advantage at the expense of the other, directly or indirectly, are inconsistent with these objectives."[21]

The arms control agreements signed at the 1972 summit—the ABM Treaty and the Interim Agreement on Strategic Offensive Weapons—marked the culmination of the first round of Strategic Arms Limitation Talks (SALT) begun in 1969. In combination, they constituted a Soviet–American suicide pact against a nuclear World War III. The SALT accords reinforced the Mutual Assured Destruction basis of the balance of terror by virtually eliminating (in the ABM Treaty) the deployment of defensive weapons on either side that could substantially reduce the massive destruction each would suffer in a strategic war, and allowing each side (in the Interim Agreement) sufficient strategic offensive weapons to survive even an all-out first strike by the other superpower and still be able to retaliate in a massively destructive second strike. Each side, in effect, was to hold the other's population "hostage" against any attempt to start a strategic war.

By the end of 1972, the tally of successful Soviet–American negotiations included the following breakthroughs: (1) agreement by the Soviets to pay back $722 million, by the year 2001, of their wartime Lend Lease debt, in return for which President Nixon would now authorize the Export-Import Bank to provide credit guarantees for Soviet purchases of US goods; (2) a

---

[20]"Basic Principles of Relations Between the United States of America and the Union of Soviet Socialist Republics," *Department of State Bulletin*, Vol. 66, No. 1722 (29 June 1972), pp. 898–899.
[21]*Ibid.*

commitment by the Nixon administration to seek congressional extension to the Soviets of most-favored-nation (MFN) trading privileges in the US market; (3) arrangements for the United States to set up government-sponsored and commercial offices in Moscow to facilitate their work, and similar arrangements for the Russians in Washington; (4) the delivery of 440 million bushels of wheat to the Soviet Union; (5) a maritime accord opening 40 ports in each country to the other's shipping; (6) an agreement between the navies of the two countries to take steps to prevent high-risk incidents at sea; (7) the start of joint work on a combined space flight planned for 1975 of the US Apollo and the Soviet Soyuz; (8) a series of projects to solve environmental problems in which Soviet and American experts would work together in both countries; and (9) an agreement to set up the International Institute of Applied Systems Analysis, a multidisciplinary think tank involving social and systems scientists from both countries, as well as from Britain, France, West Germany, East Germany, Czechoslovakia, Poland, Italy, Canada, Romania, and Bulgaria, to study projects in medical research, oceanography, and environmental problems.[22]

THE CHINA CONNECTION

The Soviet Union's efforts to consolidate its detente with the Western countries and to enlarge its global commercial activities were in no small degree stimulated by the intensification during the 1960s of its rivalry with Communist China. Soviet resources were being strained by the need to maintain a balance of military power against the People's Republic of China (PRC) in the East while simultaneously maintaining a balance in the West. The Kremlin's worst nightmare was someday having to fight a two-front war.

The Sino–Soviet conflict was an even heavier determinant of China's western policy. In the PRC's active courtship of western relationships in the late 1960s and 1970s—emerging from the extreme isolation Mao Zedong had imposed on China during the period of the Cultural Revolution—other considerations were secondary to the objective of building a world-spanning structure of diplomatic counterweights to the Soviet Union. China's new international priorities were displayed in its negotiations to establish diplomatic relations with Canada and Italy, especially in its surprising flexibility on the Taiwan issue. Previously Beijing had demanded from any country with whom it was to have diplomatic relations an unequivocal endorsement of its claim to rule over Taiwan. But now it was willing that

[22]US-USSR Cooperative Agreements, Hearings before the Subcommittee on International Cooperation in Science and Space, House Committee on Science and Astronautics, 92d Cong. 2d sess. (1972).

Canada and Italy simply "take note" of its claim without requiring their explicit endorsement.

As with the Soviet Union's detente policies, the PRC's new openings to the West were first explored with Europe and Canada. Many of the West European countries, including France and Britain, had recognized the PRC as the government of China soon after the victory of the Maoists in 1949. Those who refused to extend recognition were mainly deferring to the US policy of continuing to support the "Republic of China" on Taiwan. Any possibility of early cordiality developing between the United States and the PRC was precluded by the escalation of the Korean War in 1950 into a Sino–American conflict and by their brink-of-war confrontations in the Taiwan Strait during 1954–1955 and 1958.

But in 1969 the signs of a significant attempt by China to become once again an active participant in international diplomacy coincided with the Nixon administration's search for new leverage on the Soviet Union to compensate for adverse changes in the East–West military balance. Nixon and Kissinger came quickly to the realization that Beijing's needs might mesh with their own. In the tradition of classical European balance-of-power diplomacy (one of Kissinger's academic specialties), moves toward rapprochement with China could be a means of pressuring the Kremlin to be more accommodating to US demands. There was nothing to lose (except the affection of the Nationalist Chinese on Taiwan) by trying. And if a genuine Sino–American detente did result, it could also serve other priority objectives of the administration: an early end to the Vietnam War; a reduction in overseas deployment of American troops; a dismantling of military commitments to Asian regimes that might be unstable or reckless; and simply the need to do something dramatic to convince the American public and international audiences (discouraged by US impotence in Vietnam) that the government, under Nixon's leadership, did have the capacity to act impressively on the world stage.[23]

In the fall of 1970, Nixon and Kissinger, communicating with the Chinese leaders indirectly through the Romanians and Pakistanis, let it be known that the US President would like an opportunity to visit China. The subsequent events, from China's hosting of a US ping-pong team to Kissinger's secret travels to Beijing to arrange for Nixon's historic February 1972 visit, provide a fascinating case study of the dynamic interaction of the multiple levels of world politics and how in diplomacy modalities and substance are inextricably intertwined. It is quite likely that without the artistry of both Zhou En-lai and Kissinger the opportunity to begin the process of Sino–American rapprochement might have been lost. Certainly Kissinger

---

[23]*See* my account of the calculations by Nixon and Kissinger underlying their China policy in *The Faces of Power*, pp. 344–353. *See also* Henry Kissinger, *The White House Years* (Boston: Little, Brown, 1979), pp. 163–194.

thinks so. "Chou and I spent hours together essentially giving shape to in-
tangibles of mutual understanding," he recounts in his memoirs.

> We had to build confidence; to remove the mystery. This was his fundamental
> purpose with me; as was mine with him. . . .
>   The impact of personalities on events is never easy to define. To be sure,
> China and the United States were brought together by necessity; it was not ab-
> stract goodwill but converging interests that brought me to Peking. . . . But
> that these interests were perceived clearly and acted upon decisively was due
> to leadership that—on both sides—skillfully used the margin of choice avail-
> able.[24]

Yet the underlying cause of the opportunity was deeply geopolitical on both
sides, and this sustained the 1972 rapprochement for the rest of the Cold
War period, despite the election of an American president in 1980 pledged
to restore US support for the Chinese regime on Taiwan. President Nixon
phrased it euphemistically in his statement announcing his planned trip to
China: "There can be no stable and enduring peace," he said, without the
participation of the People's Republic of China and its 750 million peoples."
Mao gave the more candid explanation in an old article he had reprinted to
help his followers understand what to many of them must have seemed like
a 180-degree turnabout, given the 20-year legacy of intense anti-American
propaganda. Mao's article, defending the wartime collaboration of the Chinese Communist Party with the "imperialists" in order to resist the Japanese
invasion, defended the wisdom of "uniting with the forces that can be
united while isolating and hitting at the most obdurate enemies."[25]

   The parameters of the new Sino–American relationship were articulated
in the Shanghai Communique of February 1972, issued by President Nixon
and Premier Zhou En-lai upon the conclusion of Nixon's visit. The Communique committed both sides to "facilitate the progressive development of
trade between their two countries" and to "broaden the understanding between the two peoples" by the further development of contacts and exchanges in such fields as science, technology, culture, sports, and journal-
ism. Diplomatic contacts at the senior level would be sustained "to further
the normalization of relations" (full diplomatic relations were established
six years later during the Carter administration); and, despite "essential differences . . . in their social systems and foreign policies," to conduct their relations "on the principles of respect for the sovereignty and territorial integrity of all states, non-aggression against other states, non-interference in
the internal affairs of other states, equality and mutual benefit, and peaceful

---

[24]Kissinger, *The White House Years*, pp. 733–787, quotes from p. 746.
[25]Mao's article was reprinted in September 1971 in one of the regime's official journals and also
broadcast over radio Beijing. Tillman Durdin, "Peking Explains Warmer US Ties," *New York
Times*, 22 August 1971. *See also* Garthoff, *Detente and Confrontation*, p. 235, for a slightly different,
but essentially the same, translation of Mao's words.

coexistence. *International* [my emphasis] disputes should be settled on this basis, without resorting to the use or threat of force."

The agreed formulation on excluding force in the settlement of "international" disputes was carefully crafted to exempt the Chinese from having to dispense with military means to dispose of the Nationalists on Taiwan—which the PRC held to be an "internal" problem. The unresolved Taiwan issue was handled in the Shanghai Communique by the device (suggested by Zhou En-lai) of explicitly including the different positions of "each side": Thus,

> The Chinese side reaffirmed its position: The Taiwan question is the crucial question obstructing the normalization of relations between China and the United States; the Government of the People's Republic of China is the sole legal government of China: Taiwan is a province of China which has long been returned to the motherland; the liberation of Taiwan is China's internal affair in which no other country has the right to interfere; and all US forces and military installations must be withdrawn from Taiwan.

But just below this paragraph, the Communique recorded:

> The US side declared: The United States acknowledges that all Chinese on either side of the Taiwan Strait maintain there is but one China and that Taiwan is a part of China. The United States Government does not challenge this position. It reaffirms its interest in a peaceful settlement of the Taiwan question by the Chinese themselves. With this prospect in mind, it affirms the ultimate objective of the withdrawal of all US forces from Taiwan. In the meantime, it will progressively reduce its forces and military installations on Taiwan as the tension in the area diminishes.

The agreement to disagree in this way on such an important matter was remarkably clear testimony to the overwhelming advantage, in the calculations of both countries, of cooperating to forge a global balance of power against the Soviet Union. But Nixon and Kissinger, in anticipation of the forthcoming detente summit in Moscow, wanted to play down any statements that could be interpreted as a Sino-American collusion against the USSR, while not totally relieving the Kremlin of anxiety that such collusion could be forced upon the Americans and Chinese by uncooperative Soviet behavior. Zhou and Mao, on the other hand, had their own anxieties about the new detente Nixon and Brezhnev were about to conceive. The result in the Communique of this convergence, yet divergence, in grand strategy was the following exquisitely nuanced section:

> [The two sides agreed that] neither should seek hegemony in the Asia-Pacific region and each is opposed to efforts by any other country or group of countries to establish such hegemony; and . . . neither is prepared to negotiate on behalf of any third party or to enter into agreements or understandings with the other directed at other states.

Both sides are of the view that it would be against the interests of the peoples of the world for any major country to collude with another against other countries, or for major countries to divide up the world into spheres of influence.[26]

For the rest of the 1970s the evolution of the Sino–American relationship was mainly elaboration of what was laid down in the Shanghai Communique. The Carter administration extended full mutual recognition to the PRC in December 1978, at which time the United States withdrew its formal diplomatic recognition of Taiwan and agreed to the complete withdrawal of its military personnel and to terminate the Taiwan–US defense treaty. The Taiwan Relations Act of 1979, however, to the displeasure of Beijing, provided that the United States should continue to "provide Taiwan with arms of a defensive character" in order to help Taiwan "maintain a sufficient self-defense capability."[27] Consistent with the terms of the legislative mandate, the Carter administration approved $280 million in sales of "selective defensive equipment" to Taiwan in January 1980, but it refused to grant Taiwan's request for fighter aircraft that could be used in offensive operations against the Chinese mainland. Beijing's anger at the 1980 arms sales to Taiwan was deflected by the Carter administration's willingness to sponsor a major military buildup of the PRC in the wake of the Soviet invasion of Afghanistan. Careful not to do or say anything that might alienate the presumably sensitive PRC leaders, the Carter administration thus found itself in the anomalous situation of basically exempting the largest totalitarian autocracy in the world from its human rights campaign.

There was heightened anxiety in Beijing following the US presidential elections of 1980 that President-elect Reagan, once in the White House, would implement his campaign promise of restoring normal relations with Taiwan. But from the vantage point of the presidency, Reagan rapidly came to appreciate, as did his three predecessors, the geostrategic reasons for keeping a friendly China as a counterweight to the USSR. In Asia, at least, anti-Soviet *realpolitik* would take precedence over ideological anticommunism. The pattern established during the Carter administration was essentially sustained: a modicum of "defensive" arms continued to be sold to Taiwan while the US arms and military-technology transfers to the PRC were steadily expanded to the point where the cooperation between the two countries' military establishments became virtually a de facto alliance. Not that there weren't issues between Washington and Beijing in addition to the Taiwan question—China's sales of nuclear technology and missiles to Middle Eastern countries, for example. But these issues now became subjects of

[26]Text of the Joint Communique Issued at Shanghai, February 27, 1972, *Department of State Bulletin,* Vol. 66, No. 1708 (20 March 1972), pp. 435–438.
[27]Taiwan Relations Act, April 10, 1979.

normal bilateral diplomatic bargaining rather than adversarial confrontation. Significantly, in 1980 China was accorded "most-favored-nation" trading access to the US market, while the USSR and most of the Warsaw Pact countries continued to be denied normal trading privileges.

The Bush administration inherited this *realpolitik* attitude toward China, rejecting congressional attempts to rescind normal commercial relations in response to the Deng government's brutal suppression of the prodemocracy demonstrations by students in Beijing's Tiananmen Square in the summer of 1989. At the same time, both the US Congress and the administration remained hesitant to extend normal trading privileges to the USSR—deferring to pressures from voter constituencies who remained unforgiving of the Kremlin for its repressive policies against members of their ethnic groups within the Soviet sphere—even as the Gorbachev regime instituted major liberal reforms (permitting national self-determination in Eastern Europe, freeing political prisoners, allowing virtually unlimited Jewish emigration, encouraging open dissent). Yet this double standard, applying much less stringent human rights criteria toward the government in Beijing for fear of once again alienating America's new Asian coalition partner against the Soviets, now had little geostrategic justification as the Soviets renounced their Cold War rivalry with the United States.[28]

HUMAN RIGHTS VS. *REALPOLITIK*

Back in the 1970s, the bridge-building between Washington and Moscow was somewhat less popular with the American public than the rapprochement between Washington and Beijing. Both policies were fully consistent with Henry Kissinger's *realpolitik* philosophy that international relationships should be forged out of geostrategic, economic, and balance-of-power calculations and not on the basis of ideological preferences. But the notion that how the Soviet government treated the people within its own jurisdiction was not the business of other countries did not sit well with broad segments of the US public, convinced since the days of the Truman Doctrine that the conflict with the Soviet Union was over two antithetical ways of life. Responsive to popular sentiment, Congress in 1974 denied the USSR "most-favored-nation" trading opportunities and Export-Import Bank credits, pending a liberalization of Soviet restrictions on Jewish emigration and other human rights violations.

The Nixon administration, committed to delivering on its side of the detente bargain, told Congress that it was naive to assume that the Kremlin's

---

[28]For an explication of the Bush administration's China policy *see* Robert S. Ross, "U.S. Policy Toward China," in Robert J. Art and Seyom Brown, eds., *U.S. Foreign Policy: The Search for a New Role* (New York: Macmillan, 1993), pp. 358–357.

motivation for commerce was so high that it would modify Soviet internal policies to obtain it, especially under a public ultimatum from the United States. "We have accomplished much," said Secretary of State Kissinger, "but we cannot demand that the Soviet Union, in effect, suddenly reverse five decades of Soviet and centuries of Russian history." He argued further, but to no avail, that if the commercial lever was to work at all, even on less sensitive matters, trade should not be subject to such political conditions before it was permitted to achieve the level that economic market conditions would allow.[29]

Again, it was the West Europeans who led the way in effectively linking the Soviet desire to expand commercial relationships with the West to the human rights issue. They saw an opportunity in the Soviets' resumed push to convene an international conference to lay the groundwork for a reconstituted greater Europe that would transcend the divisions of the Cold War. The Nixon White House was at first opposed to the idea, believing that the Kremlin was up to its old trick of luring the West Europeans into a "peace conference" to legitimize the USSR's wartime territorial gains, the division of Germany, and, by implication, the Soviet sphere of influence in Eastern Europe. But when the West Europeans and the Canadians made it clear that they had every intention of conducting this dialogue with the Soviets despite the coolness in Washington, the Nixon administration reluctantly agreed to participate.

By the time the 35-member Conference on Security and Cooperation in Europe (CSCE) concluded on August 1, 1975, in Helsinki, it had been partially transformed by the Western participants into a forum for calling the Soviet and East European governments to account for their failure to accord their citizens many of the basic human rights that members of the United Nations, including the USSR, had subscribed to in the Universal Declaration of Human Rights and various corollary protocols. The *Final Act* of the CSCE (sometimes referred to as the Helsinki Accords) reflected the conflicting Eastern and Western concepts for constructing a legitimate and durable peace in Europe.

The provisions on "Security in Europe" (Basket I) contained what the Soviets most wanted: clauses affirming respect for the sovereignty of states, the inviolability of their frontiers, and their territorial integrity. At Western insistence these provisions were juxtaposed with a clause affirming respect for human rights and fundamental freedoms. In addition, the West was successful in getting the Soviets to agree to a special document on "Confidence-Building Measures," providing for advance notification and international observation of large military exercises. The provisions on "Cooperation in the Field of Economics, of Science and Technology and the Environment"

---

[29]*Department of State Bulletin,* Vol. 71, No. 1842 (14 October 1974), pp. 505–519.

(Basket II) were rather straightforward endorsements of what was already transpiring in the atmosphere of detente. The Western delegations, however, made their acceptance of Basket I and Basket II conditional upon acceptance by the Conference of Basket III provisions on "Cooperation in Humanitarian and Other Fields," which enumerated various human rights that needed improvement, giving special emphasis to the free movement of people, ideas, and information within and between countries.[30]

The ability of the Western delegation to turn the CSCE into an instrument of face-to-face official pressure on the USSR and East European governments on human rights issues converted Secretary of State Kissinger from an early opponent of this ideological extravaganza into a public supporter. Accordingly, when President Gerald Ford flew to Helsinki for the signing of the Final Act by heads of state, he came armed with ringing rhetoric connecting what had been accomplished at the CSCE to the American rededication to the universal cause of human liberty then being celebrated in the Bicentennial of the Declaration of Independence. (In the Reagan wing of the Republican Party, however, "Helsinki" was viewed as a Western "sell-out" to the Soviets, typifying all that was wrong with the detente policy.)

Periodic CSCE follow-up conferences were in many respects recapitulations of the East–West bargaining that went on in the foundational conference of 1973–1975, with the West attempting to hold the East to account on the human rights provisions of Basket III and the Soviets attempting to separate out and give special emphasis to projects for commercial and technological cooperation. Rather than living up to its billing as a post–Cold War framework, the CSCE was turning into another arena *of* the Cold War.

DETENTE IN DIFFICULTY

Within a year of the 1972 Nixon–Brezhnev summit, even before Congress refused to extend MFN status to the Soviets on human rights grounds, the Nixon White House had started to lose hope the Soviets would honor their commitment in the Moscow Declaration of Principles to forego "efforts to obtain unilateral advantage at the expense of the other, either directly or indirectly." Nixon and Kissinger faulted the Kremlin for giving aid and encouragement to the Vietnamese communists in their violations of the 1973 Paris Accords ending the Indochina War—cynically taking advantage of the congressional restrictions on further US military assistance to the South Vietnamese.[31] The Ford administration became increasingly resentful of the Kremlin for taking advantage of the American isolationist mood in 1975 and

---

[30]Department of State, *Conference on Security and Cooperation in Europe, Final Act* (Washington, DC: Department of State, 1975), Publication 8826.
[31]Henry Kissinger, *Years of Upheaval* (Boston: Little, Brown, 1982), pp. 301–370, *passim.*

1976 by stepping up the Soviet efforts to create new client states in southern Africa upon the withdrawal of the Portuguese from Angola and Mozambique.[32]

Despite the mutual disillusionment in Washington and Moscow with how the other side was attempting to exploit detente at the economic and political levels, negotiations continued throughout most of the 1970s on the most crucial aspect of the superpower relationship: the balance of nuclear terror. The SALT II Treaty signed by Brezhnev and Jimmy Carter in Vienna on June 18, 1979, was held by both presidents to represent "a substantial contribution to the prevention of nuclear war and the deepening of detente."[33] But this time, in contrast to the general public approval that greeted SALT I, opponents of SALT II in the United States had marshaled their forces to put in doubt its approval by the Senate. Led by the Committee on the Present Danger, whose analyses purported to show that SALT II would result in "a large imbalance in Russia's favor," the opposition argued that the treaty was a sellout of America's security and that President Carter and his negotiators had, in effect, been duped by their Soviet counterparts.[34]

The Soviet invasion of Afghanistan on Christmas Eve 1979 put virtually all of the US–Soviet detente relationship on ice. President Carter asked the Senate to defer ratification of SALT II and imposed a wide range of sanctions: The licensing of high technology exports to the USSR was suspended, and some recently granted licenses were revoked; fishing privileges for Soviet ships in US waters were severely curtailed; an embargo was placed on 17 million tons of grain already purchased by the Soviets but not yet shipped to them; planned openings of new American consular facilities were canceled; most of the Soviet–American economic and cultural exchanges then under consideration were deferred; US athletes were not permitted to compete in the Olympics being hosted by Moscow; and visa criteria were tightened for Soviet officials wanting to visit the United States. "While this invasion continues," explained Carter, "nations of the world cannot conduct business as usual with the Soviet Union."[35]

In his January 23, 1980, State of the Union address, the President said that the continuing Soviet occupation of Afghanistan "could pose the most serious threat to world peace since the Second World War. . . . Let our position

[32]Henry Kissinger, Statement of January 19, 1976, before the Subcommittee on African Affairs of the US Senate Committee on Foreign Relations, *Hearings on US Involvement in Civil War in Angola,* 94th Cong. 2d sess. (Washington, DC: GPO, 1976), pp. 14–23.
[33]Joint US-Soviet Communique in Connection with the signing of the SALT II Treaty, Department of State, *Vienna Summit* (Washington, DC: Department of State, 1979), General Foreign Policy Series 316, Publication 8985.
[34]Committee on the Present Danger, *Does the Official Case for the SALT II Treaty Hold up under Analysis?* (Washington, DC: GPO, 1980), issues of 14 January, 28 January, 18 February, and 14 April, 1980.
[35]For the various presidential announcements of sanctions on the USSR for its invasion of Afghanistan, *see Weekly Compilation of Presidential Documents,* Vol. 16 (Washington, DC: GPO, 1980), issues of 14 January, 28 January, 18 February, and 14 April, 1980.

be absolutely clear: Any attempt by any outside force to gain control of the Persian Gulf region will be regarded as an assault on the vital interests of the United States. It will be repelled by the use of any measures necessary, including military force."[36] The White House was pleased at the media's labeling of this statement as the "Carter Doctrine."

The revived concern in Washington over Soviet expansionism was reflected in the Carter administration's request to Congress for a 5 percent increase in the defense budget. Plans to organize a Rapid Deployment Force (RDF) were accelerated as were negotiations with Kenya, Oman, Somalia, and Egypt to provide service facilities for the RDF and other expanded US naval units in the region. Pakistan, presumably threatened by the Soviet military operations in Afghanistan, was offered $400 million in military aid.[37]

The White House also allowed the anti-Soviet thrust of the US rapprochement with China to surface more openly. National Security Advisor Brzezinski conducted negotiations with Pakistan and China for concerting aid to Afghan insurgents (dramatized in the world's press by a photo of Brzezinski at the Khyber Pass holding a Chinese-made automatic rifle). Secretary of Defense Harold Brown's January 1980 trip to China, although planned before the Soviets marched into Afghanistan, was accorded heightened strategic significance in both Washington and Beijing. Following Brown's discussions with Chinese defense officials, the Carter administration announced approval of previously restricted exports to China, including air defense radars, electronic countermeasure devices, military-type helicopters, long-distance communications equipment with military potential, and hundreds of items of advanced technology and military support equipment. "What had started as an exercise in evenhandedness [toward the USSR and China]," Brzezinski recalls in his memoirs, "by 1980 became demonstrably a tilt, driven by stark strategic realities."[38] Congress did its part by approving MFN trading status for China (while continuing to deny it to the USSR), giving a major fillip to Sino–American commerce, which rose to the unprecedented level of $5 billion by 1980.

The Soviet leadership was taken aback by the intensity of the Carter administration's reaction to Afghanistan, but not so much as to accede to Washington's demands for military withdrawal. Brezhnev charged that "the forces of imperialism have gone over to a counteroffensive against detente," but made it known to most of the other noncommunist governments that they need not be affected by the new estrangement between Moscow and Washington: The commerce the USSR was being denied by the United

[36]Jimmy Carter, State of the Union Address, January 23, 1980, *Weekly Compilation of Presidential Documents*, 28 January issue, pp. 194–203, quote from p. 197.
[37]On the US military measures in reaction to Afghanistan, *see* Brown, *The Faces of Power*, pp. 559–563; and Garthoff, *Detente and Confrontation*, pp. 972–975.
[38]Zbigniew Brzezinski, *Power and Principle: Memoirs of the National Security Adviser 1977–1981* (New York: Farrar-Straus-Giroux, 1983), pp. 423–425, quote on p. 425.

States it would attempt to recoup with expanded commerce with other Western countries.[39] The Europeans and Japanese, anxious for detente to continue and angry at the US government for unilaterally announcing the sanctions policy as if it were speaking for the whole coalition, were more than happy to respond to the new Soviet overtures.

The results were hardly what the Carter administration wanted. The Soviets continued to pour more troops and heavy military equipment into Afghanistan. Meanwhile, as US–Soviet trade dropped in the early 1980s to nearly a third of what it was in the late 1970s (US exports falling from $3.6 billion in 1979 to $1.5 billion in 1980), Soviet–West German trade expanded by nearly two-thirds, and Soviet–French trade increased 100 percent! The Japanese also increased their trade with the USSR by 35 percent.[40] And in the food grains sector, the Canadians and Australians were taking up the sales opportunities now denied to American farmers.

Ironically, the United States in attempting to punish the Soviets for their invasion of Afghanistan ended up punishing itself, at least in the commercial field. Even at the level of international politics, an event that might have been expected to reconsolidate the US-led coalition (the first direct use of Soviet military force since World War II outside of its immediate sphere of control) had precisely the opposite effect. It exposed the divergent interests in detente within the US coalition and provided the Soviets with new opportunities to attempt to decouple the West Europeans from the United States.

THE BIG CHILL BEFORE THE FINAL THAW

Despite the negative effects of Carter's sanctions policy on the US economy and international political leadership, the Reagan administration during most of its first term (1981–1984) continued not only to dismantle the remaining commercial bridges but also the military and arms control foundations of detente. This was the declared intent of the new administration, consistent with the Republican Party platform of 1980 and numerous public pronouncements by Ronald Reagan himself during his 12-year campaign for the presidency.

US military superiority over the USSR, rather than the *mutual* deterrence championed by the arms controllers, once again would be the basis from which to confront the Soviets with the consequences of attempting to impose their will on others. If the Kremlin was foolish enough to take up the challenge of a new arms race, so much the better, for this would deeply strain available Soviet resources, compel the USSR to dispense with long-delayed domestic modernization, and deny it the economic wherewithal to

---

[39]Garthoff, *Detente and Confrontation*, pp. 990–1002.
[40]*Ibid.*, p. 977; and Joan Edleman Spero, *The Politics of International Economic Relations* (New York: St. Martin's Press, 1985), p. 377.

sustain its empire. It should not be the job of the West to relieve the Kremlin of its resource allocation crunch by providing the Soviets with access to the relatively inexpensive quality goods and technologies produced in the capitalist world (especially those technologies that had potential military applications), and surely not to provide them with financial credits to make purchases beyond their current ability to pay. It was time to return to the pre-detente prohibitions on "trading with the enemy" and to restrictions on scientific and technological exchanges that could provide the Soviets a legitimate cover for espionage. These people in the Kremlin, after all, professed to be the heirs of Lenin, who had advised lying and cheating to undermine the Western democracies and who had gleefully prophesied that the capitalists would sell their executioner the rope by which they would be hanged.

The Reagan administration made a heroic try during its first few years in office to translate its ideologically conceived grand strategy into concrete policy: Arms control negotiations with the USSR were to be officially suspended until the United States (under a projected military buildup to cost $1.7 trillion over the next five years) was again in a position to "negotiate from strength." As it turned out, this criterion would not be strictly adhered to, as popular and allied pressures compelled the administration to resume arms control negotiations in the fall of 1981. Reagan's earliest arms proposals, however, were transparently unacceptable to the Russians—which was hardly surprising considering that they were the handiwork of Pentagon officials hostile to arms control. The arms control arena, featuring mainly public relations games, was at this point essentially a sideshow to the accelerating arms competition, involving new generations of "counterforce" war-fighting strategic weaponry on both sides, much of it concentrated on multiple warhead intercontinental ballistic missiles (ICBMs).

The underlying basis of the SALT accords of the 1970s, that both sides would restrict themselves to deterrence-only strategic arsenals and eschew the deployment of weapons designed to deny the other an "assured destruction" capability, was thrown overboard by President Reagan's surprise announcement in March 1983 that he was directing the Pentagon to develop weapons that could destroy strategic nuclear missiles launched against the United States. Reagan justified this Strategic Defense Initiative (SDI) on the grounds that the prevailing Mutual Assured Destruction concept was morally deficient in attempting to deter an enemy from attacking by threatening its population with extinction. "Wouldn't it be better to save lives than to avenge them?" he asked.[41]

Dubbed "Star Wars" in the popular media because some of the options for SDI that most appealed to Reagan contemplated the launching of antimissile weapons from spacecraft orbiting the Earth, the administration's plan to invest heavily in systems designed to hobble the opponents' strate-

[41]Ronald Reagan, Address to the Nation, Washington, DC, March 23, 1983. Text in Department of State, *Current Policy*, No. 472.

gic offensive capabilities was viewed by the Soviets as an effort to deny them an assured deterrent against a strategic attack from the United States. Most weapons experts doubted the feasibility of developing such an effective shield against nuclear attack, especially in the face of Soviet countermeasures to penetrate or confuse the antimissile defenses—which they would have high incentives to develop and deploy in order to keep their deterrent viable. The consequence of SDI, therefore, even as a research and development effort, was likely to be an action-reaction spiraling of new and expensive arms programs on both sides. The Kremlin, contemplating the resource and budgetary implications no less than the destabilizing effects on the nuclear balance of terror, regarded SDI as hostile in intent, despite Reagan's continuing insistence that its only purpose was to make strategic nuclear war obsolete.

On the trade restriction front, the Reagan administration in early 1981 tightened export controls on high-technology goods and tried to get allied countries to adopt similar measures, in particular to stop selling the Soviets equipment for their 2,600-mile trans-European gas pipeline project. But in apparent contradiction of the revived policy of making life miserable for the enemy, Reagan removed the embargo on grain sales to the USSR that Carter had imposed in response to the Afghanistan invasion. (This was a payment by Reagan of his political debt to the farm lobby, which had supported him in the 1980 election in return for his pledge to remove the embargo.)

Reagan was given ammunition for his attempt to revive the flagging anticommunist spirit in the coalition when the Kremlin at the end of 1981 sponsored harsh martial law measures by the Jaruzelski regime in Warsaw, Poland, including the Polish government's arrest of the dissident Solidarity union leader Lech Walesa, who had become something of a folk hero in the West. In addition to the imposition of a wide range of economic sanctions against the Polish government, Reagan, holding the Kremlin responsible for Jaruzelski's repressive moves, enlarged the list of prohibitions on US exports to the USSR, withdrew Soviet Aeroflot rights to use US airports, placed new restrictions on the access of Soviet ships to US ports, and placed virtually all existing energy, science, and technology agreements with the USSR under review, with the clear implication that they might be summarily halted. There was even a postponement of negotiations on a new US–Soviet long-term agreement on the purchase of US grains.[42]

Designed to make life difficult for the rival camp, the policy of sanctions escalation had the paradoxical effect of weakening the unity of the anticommunist coalition; for to be effective, most of the new sanctions required that other technologically capable countries and grain-exporting countries join in the restrictions. But the other relevant countries, including America's principal allies, had their own priorities and strategies; and Reagan's impatient ef-

[42]Ronald Reagan, Statement on sanctions being applied to the Soviet Union, December 29, 1981, *Weekly Compilation of Presidential Documents*, Vol. 17, No. 53, pp. 1429–1430.

forts to coerce the West Europeans into a concerted policy for restricting East–West commerce produced the most serious crisis in the coalition since the Suez crisis of 1956.

In 1980 and 1981 the governments of Germany, England, France, and Italy had been negotiating with the Kremlin to provide Western technology and financing for the construction of a Soviet pipeline for transporting natural gas from Russia to Western Europe. Despite cajoling from Washington, the European allies were in no mood to forego the job-generating orders for the pipeline equipment at this time of economic recession, particularly in light of the United States having recently cut back on its steel imports from the European Community. The allies did not take at all kindly to suggestions by Reagan administration officials that in the gas pipeline deal the Europeans were letting commercial considerations override the common security needs of the West. And they took special umbrage at the allegation that by becoming consumers of Soviet natural gas they would be making themselves susceptible to Soviet economic blackmail. At the most, they pointed out, supplies from Russia would constitute 5 percent of their total energy consumption, a gap that could be filled from other sources in the event of a cutoff from the East.

Not to be rebuffed, President Reagan issued instructions in the summer of 1982 prohibiting European-based subsidiaries of US companies from selling or delivering equipment to the USSR for the gas pipelines and banning even the use of American equipment or technology in the pipeline project by foreign companies. But the West Europeans would not be pushed around. The US extraterritorial prohibitions, they charged, were an infringement on national sovereignty. Even Prime Minister Margaret Thatcher dug in her heels. "The question," explained Reagan's usually loyal British friend, "is whether one very powerful nation can prevent existing contracts from being fulfilled. It think it is wrong to do that."[43] Reagan's second Secretary of State, George Shultz, was able to paper over the growing rift with the West Europeans by getting the NATO allies to broaden the list of technologies deemed to have military applications (and thus not to be sold to the USSR and its allies) in return for the United States looking the other way while the Europeans consummated their gas pipeline deal with the Soviet government.

In ultimately conceding to the preferences of the West Europeans in their gas deal with the Soviets, Reagan was adapting reluctantly to what he saw as a loss of moral fiber in the anticommunist alliance. He attempted to refurbish the slackening ideological crusade, however, by relying on his vaunted skills as the Great Communicator. In a rousing speech to the British Parliament he called for a new "crusade for freedom" to "leave Marxism–Leninism on the ash heap of history." Before American audiences the President

---

[43]Margaret Thatcher, remarks to the British House of Commons, July 1, 1982, quoted by James Feron, "Mrs. Thatcher Faults U.S. on Siberia Pipeline," *New York Times*, July 2, 1982.

became even more strident, calling the Soviet Union "the focus of evil in the modern world" and castigating US arms control advocates for implying that both sides were equally at fault in the Cold War. To "simply call the arms race a great misunderstanding," he charged, was "to ignore the facts of history and the aggressive impulses of an evil empire." It was "to remove yourself from the struggle between right and wrong and good and evil."[44]

THE SURPRISING REAGAN–GORBACHEV SYMBIOSIS

Yet something happened on the way to a renewed Cold War: the reassertion, once again, of domestic constraints on the superpower competition in both the United States and the Soviet Union.

Public opinion polls in the spring and summer of 1984 revealed that Reagan's most unpopular characteristic, looking toward the presidential election, was his harsh anti-Soviet stance. A worried Nancy Reagan, along with White House domestic political strategists, prevailed upon the President to make a series of conciliatory speeches and to let it be known that he wanted to open a high-level dialogue with the Soviet leaders.[45]

The troubled US economy was also a factor. Although a pre-election upturn in economic conditions helped Reagan win an overwhelming victory over his Democratic rival, Walter Mondale, the President was aware by the start of his second term in January 1985 that the enormous and growing federal national debt, by driving up interest rates, was making it virtually impossible to erase the country's embarrassing international trade deficit. Meanwhile, Japan, unburdened by huge defense obligations, was outpacing the United States in the production and marketing of attractive high-tech consumer goods. Reagan came to understand that even under the most optimistic "supply side" economic assumptions of increasing revenue without raising taxes, the federal budget could not be brought into balance without drastic cuts and expenditures, and this would require substantial reductions in defense outlays.

The growing realization among the President's inner circle that it would be unfeasible to implement Reagan's promise to reduce the role of the government in the life of the nation while pursuing a global "full court press" against the Soviets coincided with a changing of the guard in the Kremlin, following the death of Leonid Brezhnev, that brought Mikhail Gorbachev to power. Gorbachev's plans for reforming Soviet society required that the hu-

[44]Ronald Reagan, Address to the Members of the British Parliament, Palace of Westminister, June 8, 1982, in *Speaking My Mind: Collected Speeches* (New York: Simon and Schuster, 1989), pp. 108–120; Address before the National Association of Evangelicals, Orlando, Florida, March 8, 1983, *Weekly Compilation of Presidential Documents*, Vol. 19, No. 10, pp. 364–370.
[45]Michael K. Deaver, *Behind the Scenes* (New York: William Morrow, 1987).

man and material resources of the USSR be substantially transferred from foreign and military tasks to domestic tasks, and that this would require an international environment much less threatening to the Soviet Union than had heretofore prevailed.

Secretary of State Shultz, National Security Adviser Robert McFarlane, and White House Chief of Staff Donald Regan, with the support of Nancy Reagan (but over the objections of Secretary of Defense Caspar Weinberger and CIA Director William Casey), persuaded the President to meet personally with Gorbachev in what turned out to be a series of summit meetings: their warm first encounter in Geneva in November 1985; their dramatic and embarrassing altercation over SDI and nuclear disarmament in November 1986 at Reykjavik, Iceland; their Washington summit of December 1987 at which they signed a treaty banning intermediate-range nuclear forces (INF); the President's visit to Moscow at the end of May 1988, where the two leaders strolled arm in arm through Red Square like old friends and Reagan took advantage of the new openness to address Soviet audiences on the comparative superiority of the American system of democratic capitalism; and Gorbachev's "farewell" meeting with Reagan (attended also by President-elect George Bush) in New York in December 1988.

Reagan came home from his first meeting with Gorbachev in Geneva convinced that his counterpart was sincere in asking for an end to the arms race. The Secretary of Defense and the Director of Central Intelligence, however, remained skeptical, reflecting the dominant view in the national security establishment that Gorbachev was just the latest Soviet practitioner—albeit a more sophisticated one—of the game of getting the West to let down its guard. The concern of the national security professionals turned into intense anxiety as they watched the President at the Reykjavik summit, charmed and beguiled by his deft Soviet counterpart, grant the objective of *mutual* comprehensive nuclear disarmament. Former Secretary of Defense James Schlesinger inveighed against Reagan's "casual utopianism" of being "prepared apparently to . . . jettison . . . the entire Western system of security based on nuclear deterrence."[46]

Such criticisms, echoed also by NATO officials, were based on the premise that the global balance of power restraining Soviet international aggressiveness still depended crucially on the credibility of the Western (primarily US) threat to respond with overwhelming power, including nuclear weapons, to any Soviet military move against a country outside its sphere of control. To eliminate nuclear weapons from the equation, prior to rectifying the conventional force imbalance favoring the Soviets and their Warsaw Pact allies, would be to grant the Soviet side overall superiority in the global balance of power. The Soviets, not having to face the likelihood of military

---

[46]James Schlesinger, "Reykjavik and Revelations: A Turn of the Tide?" *Foreign Affairs: America and The World 1986*, Vol. 65, No. 3, pp. 426–446, quotes from p. 434.

conflict escalating to nuclear war, would be tempted to engage in aggression, under the assumption of being able to control the risks.

For the time being, however, Gorbachev himself prevented Reagan from agreeing to the kind of general nuclear disarmament that alarmed Pentagon and NATO strategists. The Soviet leader, by insisting that as a condition for any such agreement the United States would have to renounce SDI (the strategic project to which Reagan was most passionately attached), was in effect assuring there could be no serious negotiation of his proposals. Thus, near the end of the Reykjavik summit, when Gorbachev explicitly re-linked the renunciation of SDI to the grandiose schemes he and Reagan had been discussing, the American president responded in anger and accused the Russian of ruining their chance to make a huge breakthrough toward world peace.[47] Reagan's hardline critics were relieved but continued to worry, for the negotiating sequence at Reykjavik indicated that Gorbachev might be able to win Reagan over at any time simply by giving up the Soviet anti-SDI card.

Indeed, the reason negotiations on the intermediate-range nuclear forces were allowed to proceed to a successful conclusion after Reykjavik was precisely because Gorbachev de-linked an SDI ban from an INF treaty. The INF treaty, by removing only a particular category of nuclear weapons while leaving the bulk of the superpowers' massive intercontinental striking power intact, was by itself of marginal strategic significance. Still, to the hawks it carried an unsettling portent of Gorbachev's ability to manipulate the arms control arena to achieve a highly destabilizing general nuclear disarmament agreement (in advance of substantial reductions in conventional forces) virtually any time he chose to give in on SDI.

Gorbachev finally convinced even the skeptics of his sincerity in wanting to call a halt to the arms race, however, by his dramatic announcement to the UN General Assembly on December 7, 1988 that the USSR was proceeding forthwith to reduce its non-nuclear forces unilaterally. "We are present at the birth of a new model of ensuring security," said Gorbachev, "not through the build-up of arms, as was almost always the case in the past, but on the contrary, through their reduction on the basis of compromise."[48] Reagan felt vindicated in his intuition that a new leadership group had ascended in the Kremlin with whom it was possible to make peace.

Ironically, having begun his presidency ridiculing the value of negotiating with the Soviets, the most influential anti-detente politician on the American scene presided over and personally participated in more high-level negotiations between the United States and the Soviet Union than had

---

[47]For a detailed account of the Reykjavik summit, *see* John Newhouse, *War and Peace in the Nuclear Age* (New York: Knopf, 1989), pp. 394–99.
[48]Address by Mikhail Gorbachev at the Plenary Meeting of the Forty-Third Session of the United Nations General Assembly, December 7, 1988 (New York: Soviet Mission to the United Nations press release, December 7, 1988).

any of his predecessors. When asked about this dramatic turnabout in his approach to the Soviet Union, Reagan denied having changed his basic views. The "evil empire" rhetoric, he explained, had taken place in "another time, another era." The behavior of the Soviet government had changed, at least internationally, and "a great deal of it is due to the General Secretary, who I have found different than previous Soviet leaders have been."[49] In his memoirs, Reagan credits his policy of strength for making Gorbachev realize that the Soviet Union "couldn't continue spending so much of its wealth on weapons and an arms race" without courting "economic disaster." But he gave great credit to the Soviet leader for having "the intelligence to admit Communism was not working, the courage to battle for change, and, ultimately, the wisdom to introduce the beginnings of democracy, individual freedom, and free enterprise."[50]

---

[49]Ronald Reagan, President's News Conference, June 1, 1988, Moscow, *Weekly Compilation of Presidential Documents*, Vol. 24, No. 22, p. 728.
[50]Ronald Reagan, *An American Life* (New York: Simon and Schuster, 1990), pp. 707–708.

5

IMPLOSION
IN THE SOVIET SPHERE

The buildup of frustrations and tensions within a society often leads to explosive outward aggression—sometimes against those deemed to be the source of the society's ills, sometimes in an attempt to regenerate unity in a situation of imminent political disintegration, sometimes for psychological catharsis. Most observers of the Soviet system projected a similar process of inner frustration and tension leading to explosive outward aggression if and when its leaders started to become overwhelmed by the contradictions of their rigid Marxist–Leninist imperium. The dystopian literature on Marxist totalitarianism—most notably George Orwell's novel *1984* and Andrei Almalricks's *Will the Soviet Union Survive 1984?*—also prophesied such a dynamic.

It is rare that an ambitious great power will take the opposite approach and react to internal crises by turning in on itself; yet that is exactly what the USSR did under Mikhail Gorbachev. In concept, Gorbachev's *perestroika* was supposed to have been a rational response to the Soviet Union's structural problems; in implementation, however, long pent-up frustrations were released in a chain reaction of revolutionary reform that imploded the entire Soviet sphere, overwhelming Gorbachev's plans to manage basic economic and political change (his "revolution from above") in an experimental and pragmatic way.

The dramatic implosion of the late 1980s and early 1990s was entirely unexpected by leaders and populace alike within the Soviet sphere and by outside observers. Looking back, however, we can see a history of cracks and rumbles that we now know were symptoms of the massive cave-in that was in store for the top-heavy totalitarian system.

KHRUSHCHEV'S
DE-STALINIZATION EFFORT

Like Gorbachev three decades later, Nikita Khrushchev in the 1950s attempted to shore up the deteriorating authority of the Communist Party of the Soviet Union (CPSU) by distinguishing his regime from the brutal dictatorship of Josef Stalin. Khrushchev moved to lessen the Kremlin's heretofore totalitarian control over all aspects of life in the USSR and broaden opportunities for political participation and dissent. But when the reformist premier, in an address to the Twentieth Party Congress (1956), destroyed the myth of Stalin's wisdom he also weakened the Soviet party's role as the authoritative interpreter of Marxism–Leninism. The CPSU, after all, had been Stalin's main instrument for ensuring ideological conformity; and many of those still holding top leadership roles in the party (along with Khrushchev himself) had previously been functionaries under Stalin. Inevitably, the Khrushchev regime's legitimacy too was undermined by its exposure of Stalin's errors.

Khrushchev also moved early in his tenure as General Secretary to relax the imperial grip the Kremlin maintained over the East European countries. (A symbolic step was the Kremlin's reconciliation with President Tito of Yugoslavia.) But juxtaposed with the inadvertent delegitimization of CPSU authority resulting from de-Stalinization, the indication that a degree of pluralism now was to be allowed weakened Moscow's hegemony over the "socialist commonwealth" more rapidly that anyone, Khrushchev included, had anticipated.

THE CRISES OF 1956

In the fall of 1956, the Poles—getting ahead of themselves in the eyes of Khrushchev—threw off their regime of Kremlin lackeys and installed the nationalist communist Wladislaw Gomulka. The Polish communist party had become a hotbed of factionalism, with a large and growing reformist element demanding the democratization of decision-making and a relaxation of state censorship. The Kremlin was alarmed at the prospect of a radical unraveling of the communist system in Poland and threatened military intervention. But a Soviet invasion was stayed at the last moment by evidence of Gomulka's strong support in the working classes and the army for sustaining his nationalist communist regime. Khrushchev settled for Gomulka's assurances of moderate domestic reform and continued loyalty to the Warsaw Pact.

The Kremlin was less willing to tolerate a radical loosening of bonds by the Hungarian communists in 1956. In response to antigovernment and antipolice rioting and a general condition of political confusion, Khrushchev ordered an enlargement of Soviet military garrisons in the country. In the context of the news from Poland, this intervention only stimulated the formation of explicitly anti-Soviet revolutionary committees and workers' councils. A new nationalist government, headed by Imry Nagy and containing only three communists in its thirteen-member cabinet, negotiated a cease-fire and a withdrawal of Soviet troops from Budapest. The Nagy regime then announced that Hungary would no longer be a one-party state and would leave the Warsaw Pact. These acts clearly crossed the threshold of Kremlin tolerance for deviation. Khrushchev angrily poured military reinforcements into Hungary, set up an alternative government under Janos Kadar, and rolled tanks with heavy guns into Budapest to brutally mow down anti-Soviet demonstrators on the streets. Even so, massive strikes and underground resistance continued throughout the winter of 1956–1957, and some 200,000 refugees escaped into Austria.[1]

Looking back from the vantage point of the post–Cold War era, the significance of the 1956 crises in Poland and Hungary lies not so much in the Kremlin's brutal repression of independence among its satellites. (After all, bipolarity was then the order of the day; this was the Soviet sphere of control, and not surprisingly the United States under the Eisenhower administration, despite its "liberation" rhetoric, made no threat of counterintervention.) The significance lies rather in the early sign of the USSR's inability to sustain a legitimate empire even within its own immediate zone of dominance. The Kremlin, of course, could not bring itself to view the lessons of 1956 that starkly. But it was noteworthy and portentous that in the wake of the uprisings in Poland and Hungary there was no general reinstitution of Stalinism. Instead, having established the limits within which national communist self-determination had to be confined, Khrushchev embraced the doctrine of "many roads to socialism" with even greater commitment, in the hope of refurbishing the legitimacy of the Kremlin's hegemony in the communist world.

THE SUFFOCATION OF THE "PRAGUE SPRING" OF 1968

Twelve years later, in April 1968, the Kremlin again felt its control excessively threatened when the Czechoslovak communist party leaders announced a program of reforms to implement their concept of "socialism with a human face." There would be greater intraparty democracy; pluralism in the form of more autonomy for political parties, the parliament, and various agencies; increased civil rights, including freedom of assembly and association; a more decentralized federal structure to accommodate the

[1]Adam B. Ulam, *Expansion and Coexistence: The History of Soviet Foreign Policy* (New York: Praeger, 1968), pp. 389–396.

rights of Slovaks and other ethnic minorities; and comprehensive economic reforms. True to character, the Kremlin under CPSU General Secretary Leonid Brezhnev brutally repressed the Czech reformism.

The August 1968 Soviet invasion of their country was immediately condemned by all the top officials of the Czech government and party, and for a full week Czechs and Slovaks participated in a massive show of nonviolent resistance. Over the next few months, Party Secretary Alexander Dubcek, primarily to avoid a bloodbath and to secure the withdrawal of invasion forces, gradually bargained away the popular reforms to which his regime had committed itself earlier in the year. His efforts bought mainly time, the lives of millions of his countrymen who were ready to participate in a suicidal insurrection, and perhaps some restraint on Kremlin factions anxious to stamp out all traces of anti-Soviet nationalism. But the Soviet troops stayed. Meanwhile, Dubcek's domestic backing fragmented as militant nationalists accused him of selling out to the Kremlin. Moscow no doubt was playing a different game, cajoling and coercing Dubcek himself into carrying out "normalization" measures: namely, the suppression of political pluralism and civil liberties and the reversal of market-oriented economic reform—thus weakening his domestic support. Then, at the appropriate moment, Dubcek was replaced by a more subservient successor, Gustav Husak.[2]

As in 1956, the immediate fact of suppression of the "Prague Spring" in 1968 was less important to the long-term evolution of world politics than the fact that the Kremlin felt it had to use major military force against a member of its own camp to compel conformity. Brezhnev's draconian treatment of Czechoslovakia was all the more momentous for revealing that the cracks in the Soviet sphere were a manifestation of inherent contradictions in the Soviet system of organizing life within and among nations, and not attributable simply to Stalinist rigidity or the sudden thaw of the early Khrushchev period.

POLAND 1980–1981:
THE RISE OF "SOLIDARITY"
AND THE IMPOSITION OF MARTIAL LAW

Unlike the earlier anti-Soviet uprisings in Eastern Europe, the agitation for reforms in Poland that most threatened the Kremlin were not initiated by leading communist party intellectuals, but by worker organizations outside the party. The 1980 resistance by Polish workers was triggered by the government's announcement of yet another round of increases in meat prices.

---

[2]For a thorough and comprehensive analysis of the 1968 Czech crisis and the Soviet response, see Jiri Valenta, *Soviet Intervention in Czechoslovakia: Anatomy of a Decision* (Baltimore: Johns Hopkins University Press, 1979).

Protest strikes by workers spread all around the country. And in the port city of Gdansk the worker organization headed by Lech Walesa used the occasion to present a wider catalog of grievances and a list of twenty-one demands, some of which concerned the role of the trade union movement in the Polish political system. The head of the government and leader of the communist party, Edward Gierek, anxious to avoid a further slowdown of the economy in a period of domestic sluggishness and soaring foreign debt, granted most of the demands of Walesa's worker Solidarity (*Solidarnosc*) movement.

The historic agreement of August 31, 1980, signed in Gdansk by the Gierek government and Solidarity, required revolutionary changes in the norms of the professedly Marxist–Leninist society—notably the government's formal acknowledgement of an "independent and self-governing" trade union movement and a willingness to grant it the status of a bargaining agent for the workers' interests (according to Marxist–Leninist doctrine, the communist party was the workers' representative, and there was not supposed to be any class conflict in a party-run society between the managers of industry and the workers); the government's affirmation of Solidarity's right to strike; a relaxation of censorship by the regime; and a number of concessions to the Catholic church.

Hard-liners within the communist party regarded Gierek's August 1980 concessions to Solidarity as a negation of Leninist principles for the organization of a socialist state. Over the next few months, with support from Moscow, they deposed Gierek and installed General Wojciech Jaruzelski as head of the regime. But it would be no easy task to put put down Solidarity, which now claimed a membership of some 10 million (out of a country of 35 million), one million of whom were members of the communist party, which meant that about one-third of the party belonged to Solidarity!

Given such a massive polarization of the country, the Soviets could not sit idly by. Yet just as in the 1956 crisis, direct military intervention would carry enormous risks. It would surely arouse an intensely nationalistic reaction within the Polish military itself; and many units might well fight for the honor of the country against the Russians regardless of General Jaruzelski's stance.

Instead, the Kremlin decided to exploit Polish fears of a Soviet invasion by conducting major military maneuvers along Poland's borders in the spring of 1981. This allowed Jaruzelski to appeal to the common sense of wavering party members and broad segments of the Polish public by way of presenting himself as both a Polish nationalist *and* someone the Kremlin would have sufficient confidence in to maintain public order against the irresponsible elements pressing for overly rapid change.

The stage was thereby set for Jaruzelski to declare martial law on December 13, 1981, in the freezing cold of winter when Solidarity would have difficulty getting the masses to take to the streets. The military moved quickly to arrest Walesa and the rest of the movement's leadership, and throughout the country purges were conducted of "unreliable elements." There was little more than token resistance. Jaruzelski was now in a position of unchallenged power to "normalize" the political and economic situation, ostensibly without intervention by the Soviets but, in fact, on the basis of substantial Kremlin direction.[3]

Jaruzelski's imposition of martial law was widely condemned as a moral outrage by Western observers, and most of the governments in the industrial world imposed trading and financial restrictions on Poland. Mainly to curry favor with the West, Jaruzelski released Walesa from jail in November 1982 (but Solidarity was not restored to legal status). Martial law was lifted at the end of December 1982. Some Western countries thereupon reduced their economic sanctions against Poland, but the Reagan administration wanted more evidence of a genuine let-up in political repression by the Jaruzelski regime.

When a general amnesty was extended to all political prisoners in September 1986, the United States lifted most of its economic sanctions against Poland. Opportunities of Polish citizens to form political groups to express views in opposition to government policies, however, still remained more circumscribed than they were prior to the imposition of martial law; and large segments of the populace remained deeply alienated from the regime and the ruling party.

GORBACHEV'S PERESTROIKA— AT HOME AND ABROAD

When Mikhail Gorbachev became General Secretary of the Central Committee of the Communist Party of the Soviet Union in March 1985, he was convinced that "a major overhaul" was required of the Soviet political economy. As he put it in his 1987 book *Perestroika: New Thinking for Our Country and the World,*

> Something strange was taking place:
> . . . In the last fifteen years the national income growth rates had declined by more than a half and by the beginning of the eighties had fallen to a level close to economic stagnation. A country that was once quickly closing on the world's advanced nations began to lose one position after another. . . .
> An absurd situation was developing. The Soviet Union, the world's biggest producer of steel, raw materials, fuel, and energy, has shortfalls in them due to wasteful or inefficient use. One of the biggest producers of grain for food, it

---

[3]My account of the situation in Poland during the 1980–1981 period relies heavily on Andrzej Korbanski's chapter, "Poland," in Teresa Rakowska-Harmstone, ed., *Communism in Eastern Europe* (Bloomington: Indiana University Press, 1984), pp. 50–85.

nevertheless has to buy millions of tons of grain a year for fodder. We have the largest number of doctors and hospital beds per thousand of the population and, at the same time, there are glaring shortcomings in our health services. Our rockets can find Haley's comet and fly to Venus with amazing accuracy, but side by side with these scientific and technological triumphs is an obvious lack of efficiency in using scientific achievements for economic needs, and many Soviet household appliances are of poor quality.[4]

The program of *perestroika* (Russian for "restructuring") Gorbachev and his associates unveiled in the 1987 meetings of the Central Committee was presented as a revival and development of Lenin's ideas of "democratic centralism":

The reform is based on dramatically increased independence of enterprises and associations, their transition to full self-accounting and self-financing, and granting all appropriate rights to work collectives. They will now be fully responsible for efficient management and end results. A collective's profits will be directly proportionate to its efficiency.[5]

Since this plan for the revival of efficiency was dependent upon the intensification of "the human factor," explained Gorbachev—by which he meant dedicated initiative by people at every level of society—it required "efforts to . . . develop self-government and extend glasnost, that is openness, in the entire management network." Such basic restructuring, he insisted, was not, as some in the West mistakenly contended, incompatible with socialism. Rather,

More socialism means more democracy, openness and collectivism in everyday life, more culture and humanism in production, social and personal relations among people, more dignity and self-respect for the individual. . . .
We want more socialism and, therefore, more democracy.[6]

As it turned out, however, even Gorbachev underestimated the degree of restructuring that would be required. Some of his associates, coached by American advisers, urged a rapid conversion of the economy to full market capitalism; anything less, they argued, would only perpetuate the inefficiencies of the command economy that had brought the country to its current stagnation. And democracy, if Gorbachev was serious about it, demanded that the Communist Party relinquish its monopoly of power; nothing less than a multiparty system offering the people real choices among candidates and programs would suffice. Others went so far as to insist that true democracy must grant the right of the member republics to govern their own affairs, even to the point of secession from the Union if that was what their peoples wanted. Gorbachev at first adamantly opposed these more radical

[4]Mikhail Gorbachev, *Perestroika: New Thinking for Our Country and the World* (New York: Harper & Row, 1987), pp. 19, 21.
[5]*Ibid.*, p. 33.
[6]*Ibid.*, pp. 33, 37.

implications of *perestroika* and *glasnost*, especially anything smacking of the dismantling of the USSR; but by 1990, both the radical reformers and the Communist party reactionaries were saying "I told you so" as the fondest hopes of the former and the worst fears of the latter did indeed come to pass. Although an extraordinarily skillful political maneuverer, Gorbachev was unable to sustain his authority as the unraveling of the Soviet system outpaced his prophecies and plans: When party reactionaries staged a coup to depose him in the summer of 1991, it took the hero of the radicals, Boris Yeltsin, to abort the coup and put perestroika back on track—but it was now the fast track toward full market capitalism and self-determination for the republics that Gorbachev had resisted.

A related process of unintended effects outpacing original plans affected Gorbachev's new departures in foreign policy and constituted part of the rationale for the 1991 coup by the party reactionaries. Two fundamental foreign policy implications of *perestroika* were realistically drawn by Gorbachev and his trusted collaborator and foreign minister Eduard Shevardnadze: There could not be a sufficient reallocation of human energies and material resources toward domestic development tasks as long as the increasingly expensive US–Soviet arms competition continued. And there could be no substantial expansion of commerce with the industrial countries unless the East–West detente were deepened. Gorbachev and Shevardnadze correctly perceived that these two international requisites for domestically reforming the USSR could not be realized unless the West Europeans and the United States could be convinced that the Soviet Union no longer posed a threat to the West; and they understood that this carried the corollary of a creditable Kremlin willingness to drastically reduce the Soviet military presence in East Central Europe.

These foreign policy dimensions of what Gorbachev liked to call the "new thinking" were the centerpiece of his historic address to the UN General Assembly on December 7, 1988. "New realities are changing the entire world situation," he said. "The differences and contradictions inherited from the past are diminishing or being displaced. . . . Life is making us abandon established stereotypes and outdated views; it is making us discard illusions." It had become clear that

> the principle of freedom of choice is mandatory. Its non-recognition is fraught with extremely grave consequences for world peace.
>
> . . . Freedom of choice is a universal principle that should allow for no exceptions.
>
> It was not simply out of good intentions that we came to the conclusion that this principle is absolute. We were driven to it by an unbiased analysis of the objective trends of today.[7]

---

[7]Mikhail Gorbachev, Address at the Plenary Meeting of the Forty-Third Session of the United Nations General Assembly, 7 December, 1988 (Washington, DC: Embassy of the USSR, 1988).

It had also become obvious, said Gorbachev, that "the use or threat of force no longer can or must be an instrument of foreign policy." This was the meaning of the superpower disarmament process that had commenced in earnest with the treaty eliminating US and Soviet intermediate-range nuclear forces. "We are witnessing the emergence of a new historic reality—a turning away from the principle of superarmament to the principle of reasonable defense sufficiency." Gorbachev announced to an incredulous world that, in accord with this principle, the Soviet leadership had decided to *unilaterally* reduce its armed forces by 500,000 men and to withdraw and disband six tank divisions from Germany, Czechoslovakia, and Hungary by 1991, along with comparable reductions in artillery and combat aircraft from the European theater.[8]

In the ensuing months, the European dimension of the new Soviet foreign policy was elaborated further under the concept of "a common European home" or "common space," as Gorbachev sometimes called it, from the Atlantic to the Urals. The European space would no longer be bifurcated into opposed military blocs; although it would still feature mostly socialist states in the East and mostly capitalist states in the West, the two halves would be increasingly interlinked in networks of economic, technological, and scientific cooperation. The Conference on Security and Cooperation in Europe (CSCE) framework, rather than NATO and the Warsaw Pact or the European Community and COMECON, was to be the foundation of the "common European home," and, building on the CSCE, the door would remain open to participation by the United States and Canada.

A litmus test of the credibility of Gorbachev's expressed intention to build a cooperative greater Europe would be his willingness to renounce the Brezhnev Doctrine (the standing assertion by the Kremlin of its prerogative of intervening to prevent the overthrow of an established communist regime). While not explicitly naming the Brezhnev Doctrine, Gorbachev and Shevardnadze in their policies and rhetoric in the summer and fall of 1989, in effect did rescind it by refusing to apply military power to prevent Solidarity from assuming governmental power in Warsaw and by a series of statements affirming the right of national self-determination in Eastern Europe and renouncing the right to intervene militarily in the internal affairs of countries in the region. The Soviet leaders were sending a message to the governments and peoples in the "socialist commonwealth" that they were essentially on their own when it came to defining the socioeconomic and political systems under which they chose to live—a momentous reversal of decades of the Kremlin's role of imperial regional hegemon.

Suddenly, in every country in the bloc the distribution of effective power, which heretofore had been a function of the ruling communist party's ability to call on Soviet might to put down serious challengers, was now up for

---

[8]*Ibid.*

grabs. Country by country throughout Eastern Europe, the long-seething discontent and frustration of peoples whose culture and elementary human dignity had been repressed by local satraps of the alien imperial overlord were expressed in an epidemic of revolutionary, yet remarkably nonviolent, political upheavals:

In Poland.   The again-legalized Solidarity movement won a stunning victory over the communists in the parliamentary elections of June 1989, and was therefore allowed (with Gorbachev prodding Jaruzelski) to become part of, and rapidly assume control of, the government—a wholly unprecedented occurrence in the communist world!

It had been Jaruzelski's expectation that by allowing Solidarity and other groups to contest the ruling Polish United Workers' Party (PUWP) in the elections, which he was sure would be won handily by the PUWP, he would not only re-legitimize the communist-run government in the eyes of the nation's citizens but would earn the respect of both Gorbachev and the West. The elections would once again undercut the 1988–1989 flareup of overt opposition, as had the lifting of martial law in 1983 and the issuance of amnesty for political prisoners in 1986. But the decline of oppositional agitation after 1986 belied the festering resentment of the populace at the continuing decline in the economy and quality of life generally under the still-arrogant dictatorial regime. When given a chance to vote even in a limited way (although all of the 100 seats in the newly created Senate could be contested, opposition candidates were permitted for only 35 percent of the 460 lower seats), the Polish citizenry rendered an unambiguous repudiation of the PUWP communists. No PUWP candidates won any of the contested seats, and even uncontested PUWP leaders were repudiated by citizen refusals to mark their ballots for them. Solidarity, on the other hand, not only won overwhelmingly in the Senate, but also captured all but one of the lower house seats lost by the PUWP.

No longer able to form a viable government under the leadership of the communists, President Jaruzelski in August 1989 endorsed and received parliamentary support for a grand coalition government with Tadeusz Mazowiecki, a Catholic intellectual who had been influential in the founding of Solidarity, designated as prime minister. In the new government, communists were appointed to only four of the 23 cabinet positions.[9]

In East Germany.   It took barely half a year, from the summer of 1989 to January 1990, to change the Soviet empire's most strategically significant,

---

[9]Roger E. Kanet and Brian V. Souders, "Poland and the Soviet Union," in Richard F. Staar, ed., *East-Central Europe and the USSR* (New York: St. Martin's Press, 1991), pp. 125–145.

heavily fortified, and tightly controlled forward bulwark into a pliant supplicant for reunification with capitalist West Germany—one of history's all-time greatest surprises. To be sure, the potential had been there all along for the German *nation* to reassert its unity, perhaps explosively, and to break through the ideological and physical barriers that had kept it divided since the end of World War II. But since neither the Soviet Union nor the United States would tolerate a unified Germany within the other's coalition and had credibly threatened to go to war to prevent such an outcome—a war that would have subjected each of them to intolerable levels of destruction—both superpowers (despite official rhetoric favoring reunification) conspired, as it were, to sustain the bifurcation. This, indeed, was the function of the hated Berlin Wall. Erected in August 1961 by the Communist authorities to stanch the hemorrhaging flow of refugees from East Germany to West Germany through the city of Berlin, the ugly cement-block structure sealing off East Berlin from West Berlin was ritualistically deplored in the rhetoric of Western statespersons over the next twenty-eight years. But NATO strategists privately agreed with their Warsaw Pact counterparts that it was geopolitically stabilizing.

Similarly, at the level of *realpolitik* statecraft, the East–West detente agreements of the 1970s, which had included a mutual and worldwide legal recognition of the Federal Republic of Germany and the German Democratic Republic, were welcomed as a stabilizing legitimatization of the de facto post–World War II status quo of two very different German states. Paradoxically, however, the intended "normalization" of relations between the two Germanies intensified the determination of increasing numbers of citizens in both states to have done with their political separation; for the resulting expansion of commerce and interpersonal contact only heightened perceptions that this legacy of World War II was profoundly unnatural.

As popular desires to overcome the politically imposed division intensified during the early 1980s, scheduled official exchanges of visits by high-level delegations of the two states had to be periodically postponed, usually at the Kremlin's insistence, because of fears of uncontrollable popular demonstrations—especially in East Germany. But after 1987, with Gorbachev urging domestic reform and conciliatory East–West diplomacy on all members of the Soviet coalition, these roles were reversed: The East German Communist leadership, not the Kremlin, now became a drag on the pace of liberalization, while the popular currents for change in the German Democratic Republic drew inspiration from the reforms Gorbachev had set in motion in the Soviet Union itself and was encouraging in Poland, Hungary, and Czechoslovakia. The worried East German Communists censored from the country's press passages of Gorbachev's speeches they considered too liberal, but the information got through anyway via broadcasts the populace was able to pick up from the West. In May 1989, thousands of East Germans, disgusted with the unwillingness of their government to join the current of reform sweeping through the Soviet sphere, took advantage of the decision of the Hungarian government to remove its barbed wire barriers along the Austrian border, thus allowing East German refugees to make their way into West Germany through Austria. Over the next few months the numbers of refugees swelled to the tens of thousands, encamping temporarily in West German embassies in Hungary, Czechoslovakia, and Poland while awaiting entry visas from the government in Bonn.

Meanwhile, the incipient reform movement in West Germany was energized by reports that the Soviet and West German governments, during Gorbachev's June visit to the Federal Republic, had signed a joint declaration according

> unqualified recognition of the integrity and security of every state and its right to choose freely its own political system as well as unqualified adherence to the norms and principles of international law, *especially the right of peoples to self-determination.*[10]

On their television screens, East Germans saw the Soviet leader being welcomed by West German crowds as if he were a conquering hero.[11]

The tension between popular reformist pressures and the reactive rigidification of the East German Communist regime came to a head in early October 1989 surrounding the visit of Gorbachev to East Berlin for the German Democratic Republic's fortieth-anniversary celebrations. Crowds numbering in the hundreds of thousands took to the streets in Berlin, Leipzig, and Dresden. It was during this visit, according to Gorbachev's own accounts, that he realized that the Communist regime of the German Democratic Republic was no longer capable of governing. He let old-line party boss Erich Honecker know that Soviet troops stationed in Germany would not participate in any effort by the East German government to counter the demonstrations and warned his hosts that "life punishes whoever comes too late."[12]

The word spread among the populace that the Honecker government had been castrated by the Kremlin, and that henceforth it could be fearlessly defied. In mid-October, ten days after Gorbachev's visit, the Politburo installed Honecker's protege Egon Krenz in his stead. The reputed younger hardliner proceeded to pursue a concessionary policy—legalizing freedom of travel to the West, forcing many of Honecker's associates to resign, and promising free democratic elections.

Then on November 9, 1989, most dramatically and symbolically, the East German military, acting under directives from Krenz, began to dismantle the Berlin Wall. Undoubtedly conceived of by the Communists as a safety

---

[10]USSR-FRG June 1988 Declaration, quoted in Karl Kaiser, "Germany's Reunification," *Foreign Affairs: America and the World 1990/91*, Vol. 70. No. 1, pp. 179–205; quote on p. 183 (my emphasis).

[11]Robert Gerald Livingston, "Relinquishment of East Germany," in Kaiser, pp. 82–84.

[12]Livingston in Kaiser, p. 86.

valve, this sudden opening of the Wall, like the removal of a lid from a boiling kettle, only expanded the force of the turbulent pressures. Clearly, it was too late to salvage any legitimacy for the Communist regime. The urgent question for East Germany's neighbors now was how to contain the potentially explosive consequences of a total collapse of civic order, for the nightmare of the West Germans and the Soviets counterintervening had become all too real a prospect.

Despite decades of rhetorical posturing, neither the Kremlin nor the NATO governments were psychologically or politically prepared in 1990 for the reunification of their former World War II enemy. But the dangerous political meltdown in East Germany and the sudden mass flow of refugees into the German Federal Republic convinced Gorbachev and German Chancellor Helmut Kohl that they had no alternative. Gorbachev knew that Soviet military intervention was inconsistent with his grand strategy of ending the Cold War in order to concentrate on Soviet internal modernization. And Kohl realized that the exodus of millions of job-seekers from the dying East Germany would overstrain West Germany's society and polity.

The solution to the new dilemmas was to have West Germany assume economic and political responsibility for the reconstruction of the East, which meant—unavoidably—some form of federal, or at least confederal, structure for all of Germany. This would need to be made palatable to Germany's immediate neighbors and to the Soviet Union and the United States, however, by an overarching structure of post–Cold War relationships to embed a reunified Germany firmly in a security system that would preclude a revival of her previous hegemonic temptations.

What finally emerged approximated the basic requirement of reigning-in the new Germany, but hardly in the form that Gorbachev wanted. A reunified Germany could be noncommunist, as far as Gorbachev was concerned, but it should be neutral, substantially disarmed, and definitely not a member of any military alliance. His preferred institutional means for ensuring that the new Germany played a constructive role in the post–Cold War system was a strengthened Conference on Security and Cooperation in Europe. But the Bush administration, sensing that Gorbachev was negotiating from weakness, decided to push for all it could get, insisting (successfully) that a reunified Germany should be a member of NATO.

In Hungary.   Ironically, the Communist regime in Budapest, in opening its borders in the summer of 1969 to refugees from East Germany trying to make their way to Austria, hastened its own demise by giving oxygen to the flames of radical anticommunist reform then being lit throughout East Europe. Hungary's sloughing off of communist rule between 1988 and 1990 was less traumatic than the upheavals experienced by her sister members of the Warsaw Pact. Yet the disassociation from the Soviet Union proceeded farther and faster than either the ruling Hungarian Socialist Workers' Party or the Kremlin could have anticipated.

Being the bloc's pioneer during the 1970s and early 1980s with "market socialism" and commerce with the West, the regime in Budapest welcomed Gorbachev's *perestroika* as an emulation of their own New Economic Policy. Even so, the Hungarian Communist Party was wary of rejection in open elections similar to that suffered by the Polish communists. The currents of reform sweeping the Soviet sphere seemed retrospectively to validate the Hungarian revolution of 1956 and to delegitimatize the successor Kadar regime that had been brutally installed during the Soviet military occupation. In May 1988, the ruling Communist Party voted to replace Kadar with Karoly Grosz.

Try as they might, however, the Hungarian Communists could not absolve themselves of the legacy of 1956. In June 1989, when opposition groups, with the permission of the regime, exhumed the coffin of Imre Nagy (the executed leader of the 1956 revolt) from his anonymous grave and gave him a hero's funeral, four prominent communist party members respectfully attended despite being told that they would be unwelcome if they came as representatives of the party. Also in the summer of 1989, the post–Kadar leadership promised to hold free multiparty elections in 1990 and signed an agreement with the opposition groups to bring them into the planning on the forthcoming transition to multiparty rule. Desparately trying to stave off defeat in the elections, the ruling party (officially called the Hungarian Socialist Workers Party) changed its name to the Hungarian Socialist Party and purged its leadership of elements that the populace might too closely associate with the Kadar regime.[13]

The results of Hungary's first free election since World War II were unequivocal: The Socialist Party (the communists) won only 9 percent of the vote, while the center-right parties—the Christian Nationalists, Democratic Forum, and Independent Smallholders' Party, together garnering 53 percent of the vote—formed a new government. The principal opposition was now the liberal Free Democratic Party, with 24 percent of the vote.[14]

In Czechoslovakia.   For two decades following the violent Soviet repression of Dubcek and his "Prague Spring," dissident intellectuals and artists had courageously kept alive the flame of reform in a cultural underground. The Helsinki Final Act of 1975 (with its "Basket III" provisions on human rights) became a crucial lifeline to the outside world for the reformers. In February 1977 several hundred Czech citizens, citing their government's signature of the Helsinki Accords, issued a charter appealing to the regime to obey its own laws and international commitments. This dissident movement, calling itself "Charter 77," which became the most internationally admired of the "Helsinki watch" groups in Eastern Europe, was subject to pe-

---

[13]*See* Elie Abel, *The Shattered Bloc: Behind the Upheaval in Eastern Europe* (Boston: Houghton Mifflin, 1990), pp. 15–47.
[14]Ivo Banac, ed., *Eastern Europe in Revolution* (Ithaca: Cornell University Press, 1992), p. 8.

riodic brutal crackdowns by the insecure neo-Stalinist regime. One of the leaders of Charter 77 was playwright Vaclav Havel (later to be installed as Czechoslovakia's first post-Communist president). Havel and his colleagues were frequently thrown in jail for their subversive writings and speech, and when released they were subject to almost constant police surveillance.

Even as late as January 1989, Havel was sentenced to a nine-month term in prison (subsequently reduced to four months) for leading a group of human rights activists in a flower-laying ceremony at the spot where a Prague Spring dissident had committed suicide twenty-five years earlier. But the intransigent Czech Communist party was unable to hold back the tide of reform sweeping across the region. News of the June 1989 victory of Solidarity over the Communists in Poland, followed by Gorbachev's July 6 announcement in Strasbourg that all countries had a right to choose their social systems free of outside interference, galvanized the Czech democratic reformers. Emulating their East German counterparts, who during the summer and early fall had taken to the streets in Leipzig and East Berlin to topple the Honecher regime, Czechs by the tens of thousands filled the streets of Prague on October 28—the anniversary of the founding of the Czechoslovak Republic—to demand civil rights and democratic reforms. The handwriting on the wall was no longer only the graffiti of a small group of dissidents. Intimidated for the first time since 1947, the Communists held back from attempting to break up the demonstration. The next eight weeks featured the formation of Civic Forum in Prague and Public Against Violence in Bratislava, the associations of anti-Communist groups in both the Czech and Slovak parts of the country, who openly mobilized overwhelming numbers of citizens to bring the existing government to a standstill.[15]

Between November 20 and December 20, 1989, virtually every night was demonstration night in the public squares across the country, with the crowds in the larger cities swelling to the hundreds of thousands. Prodded by the Kremlin, members of the ruling politburo resigned during the last week in December and allowed members of the opposition organizations to assume seats in a newly constituted Federal Assembly, which then unanimously elected Vaclav Havel president of the Czechoslovak Republic. Gorbachev drove a final nail into the coffin of the Czech Communist party by characterizing the reforms of the "Prague Spring" Brezhnev had repressed twenty-one years before as "right at that time . . . and right now."[16]

In Romania. The Stalinist ruler Nicolae Ceausescu, openly defiant of Kremlin pressures to the last, was finally toppled and assassinated by angry dissidents on December 22, 1989, when the military refused his orders to vi-

---

[15]Abel, *The Shattered Bloc*, pp. 48–83. See also Tim D. Whipple, ed., *After the Velvet Revolution: Vaclav Havel and the New Leaders of Czechoslovakia Speak Out* (New York: Freedom House, 1991).
[16]Gorbachev quoted by Abel, *The Shattered Bloc*, p. 67.

olently repress the popular uprisings against his regime. This bloody end to the Communist dictatorship in Bucharest was a bitter but fitting climax for Ceausescu and the role he played so deftly for a quarter of a century—internationally, a courageous David standing against the Soviet Goliath; domestically, a brutal tyrant who would tolerate no opposition.

The high point of Ceausescu's popularity with Western governments was the 1968–1971 period, following his condemnation of the Soviet invasion of Czechoslovakia and the Brezhnev Doctrine justifying intervention against "anti-socialist" movements in Warsaw Pact countries. Ceausescu was a key intermediary in setting up the contacts between Henry Kissinger and Zhou En-Lai that led to the 1972 rapprochement between Washington and Beijing; and consistent with the Nixon–Kissinger *realpolitik* philosophy of ignoring the human rights record of regimes who were useful to the United States in the international arena, Romania qualified even prior to detente for US trading privileges and credits denied to others in the Soviet sphere.

In the 1988–1991 period, however, Ceausescu found himself in opposition to and the target of the Western-oriented self-determination movements in Eastern Europe, who this time were *encouraged* by a reform-minded Soviet leadership to throw off the shackles of communist orthodoxy. No longer a catalyst of the centrifugal forces, and fearing the contagious spread of democratic ideas into his tightly controlled society, the Romanian dictator clamped down ruthlessly on those who might be carrying the transnational virus of human rights and democracy; but his reactionary policies were now incompatible with the degree of openness to the outside world that even many of the regime's own top bureaucrats and military regarded as essential to the country's modernization. The violence that brought him down was thus part revolution in the streets and part palace coup.[17]

[17]Robert R. King, "The Future of Romanian–Soviet Relations in the Post-Ceausescu Era," in Richard F. Starr, ed., *East Central Europe and the USSR* (New York: St. Martin's Press, 1991), pp. 229–247.

6

THEORIES
ABOUT THE END
OF THE COLD WAR[1]

The Cold War era was over, most analysts and statespersons agree, by 1991. Some would date it earlier, say, November 1989, with the dismantling of the Berlin Wall. Others locate the end of the Cold War broadly in the 1989–1990 period, in a cluster of dramatic developments: Mikhail Gorbachev's retraction of Soviet control of Eastern Europe, the efforts to install market-oriented economies and multi-party systems throughout the region, the reunification of Germany, the assertion of political autonomy by the constituent republics of the Soviet Union.

Virtually none of this was predicted by scholars of international relations, experts on the USSR, or government officials. Even with current knowledge of *what* happened, it is still not clear *why* the momentous turn away from the Cold War came when it did or took the form that it did. The search for explanations will be a preoccupation of social scientists for decades to come.

The contest among alternative explanations for the demise of the Cold War has more than academic implications. The reasons that come to be widely accepted by scholars, policymakers, and publics can shape the behavior of countries in the post–Cold War era—just as the accepted explanations for the breakup of the grand alliance that defeated Nazi Germany became assumptions underpinning Cold War diplomacy for some four decades.

[1]This chapter is an adaptation of my article "Explaining the Transformation of World Politics," *International Journal*, Vol. XLVI (Spring 1991), pp. 207–219, and is published here with the permission of the Canadian Institute of International Affairs.

EXPLANATION #1:
"IMPERIAL OVERSTRETCH"

The end of the Cold War might be seen as a validation of the leit motif of historian Paul Kennedy's treatise, *The Rise and Fall of the Great Powers*, which showed how empires tend to enlarge their spheres of control to the point where their capabilities can no longer sustain their commitments. In attempting to preserve their spheres, the overextended imperiums become weakened in their power to compete with emerging international rivals and even experience a deterioration in their capacity for effective governance at the national core of their domains.[2]

The Kennedy book, published in 1987, gave scholarly legitimacy to views circulating simultaneously in the US policy community during the second Reagan administration and in the Kremlin under Gorbachev that the globally extensive superpower rivalry was sapping the best of the human and material resources of the two countries and allowing both of them to be overtaken by Japan and the West Europeans. Gorbachev clearly saw the Cold War as the principal obstacle to *perestroika*, the restructuring of the Soviet political economy. Some of Reagan's economic advisers too had become convinced that their domestic "revolution" was being subverted by the huge budgetary and trade deficits generated by the accelerating arms race. Seen in this light, the personal "chemistry" experienced by Reagan and Gorbachev at their summit meetings was (to coin a phrase) more metafiscal than metaphysical in origin.

International relations scholar Richard Rosecrance advanced a parallel thesis in *The Rise of the Trading State: Commerce and Conquest in the Modern World:* The declining influence of the United States and the Soviet Union in the late Cold War period relative to the rise in influence of Japan and the countries of Western Europe signaled a progressive transformation of the world system from one dominated by territorially based and militarily supported rivalries to a system in which countries best secure their values through participation in mutually beneficial international commerce. In a hopeful prognosis, Rosecrance looked forward to a gradual abandonment by the Cold War leaders of their now obsolescent confrontational rivalry—an adaptation on both sides to the requirements of effectiveness in the evolving trade-dominated world.[3]

[2]Paul Kennedy, *The Rise and Fall of the Great Powers: Economic Change and Military Conflict From 1500 to 2000* (New York: Random House, 1987).
[3]Richard Rosecrance, *The Rise of the Trading State: Commerce and Conquest in the Modern World* (New York: Basic Books, 1986).

EXPLANATION #2: "HEGEMONIC PEACE"

The preferred popular view in the United States that "we won" the Cold War finds congenial scholarly reinforcement in theories that locate the basic cause of system-wide order and relative peace (or disorder and pervasive war) in the presence or absence of a dominant great power that depends on the perpetuation of a peaceful international order for its own security and well-being—a great power with both the material resources and will to defend such an international order.

A number of schools of thought prominent today in the academic discipline of international relations support this basic explanation. Devotees of the "structural realist" theory propounded by Kenneth Waltz[4] hold that the post–World War II distribution of war-making capabilities determined the bipolarized Cold War rivalry. Accordingly, as it became clear to the Soviet side in the mid-1980s that they were unable to continue to generate the military capabilities required to stay at least equal with the US side, the Soviets rationally chose to opt out of the competition.

Less monotonic, but essentially similar, explanations are provided by the hegemony/leadership school, whose progenitors are historians Arnold Toynbee and Ludwig Dehio and political scientists Quincy Wright and A. F. K. Organski, and which was best represented in the 1980s by George Modelski and his associates in a series of publications attempting to explain "long cycles" of war and peace.[5] The closely related "hegemonic stability" school, based on concepts developed by the economist Charles Kindleberger and elaborated by political scientist Robert Gilpin, is mainly focused on the role of great powers in sustaining a liberal global economic order.[6]

From the perspective of most of the hegemony theorists, the global conflicts of the twentieth century were brought on by the demise of nineteenth century *Pax Britannica* and the resultant contest for world and regional hegemony that this opened up. As a consequence of World War II having eliminated Japan, Germany, Britain, and France as serious contenders, the two remaining "superpowers" were each able to establish hegemony in rival spheres of influence while undertaking an all-continents contest for world hegemony (Between 1945 and 1947, the United States, given the overwhelming economic and military superiority with which it emerged from World War II, could have aggressively and decisively assumed the role of global hegemon, but held back, for reasons not adequately explained in the

[4]Kenneth Waltz, *Theory of International Politics* (Reading, MA: Addison-Wesley, 1979).
[5]George Modelski, ed., *Exploring Long Cycles* (Boulder: Lynne Rienner, 1987). *See also* Joshua S. Goldstein, *Long Cycles: Prosperity and War in the Modern Age* (New Haven: Yale University Press, 1988).
[6]The most prominent international politics version of the "hegemonic stability" thesis is Robert Gilpin's *War and Change in World Politics* (New York: Cambridge University Press, 1981).

theory). The resulting Cold War persisted for four decades without exploding into World War III mainly because of mutual fears of the massive destruction that would ensue; but the required commitment of resources on both sides to prevent the other from gaining decisive geopolitical superiority finally sapped the strength of the Soviet Union internally—in some versions, the Soviet Union, lacking a sufficiently modernized economy, was never even close to being a fully capable challenger—leaving the United States, at last, the undisputed world political–military hegemon, ready to preside over a new era of essential peace among the great powers.[7]

Marxists and neo-Marxists (there are probably more of these today outside of the former Soviet sphere than within it) have in many respects a remarkably similar explanation for the demise of the Cold War—viewing it, however, as only a pause in the working out of the longer historical dialectic: The temporary winner is not the United States per se, but rather advanced corporate capitalism that, in the twentieth century had become increasingly headquartered in the United States. The current world ascendancy of advanced capitalism over its ineffective and premature challenge from the Leninists based in relatively backward Russia and the Maoists based in underdeveloped China has yet to play itself out fully before the inner contradictions of capitalism lead ultimately to its collapse and supplantation by a successor system.[8] Some neo-Marxist commentators have argued that the world system is experiencing merely a phony peace in the long struggle against capitalist domination, and that the situation may yet get worse (in the form of an exploitative absorption of the resources and peoples of Eastern Europe and the former Soviet Union into the capitalist periphery) before there is a global regrouping of "progressive" forces. Meanwhile, with the countervailing power of the USSR taken out of the picture, the prospect is for a period of intensified economic, political, and military intervention by the United States and other capitalist powers against their opponents in the Third World—the intervention by the Bush administration in the 1990–1991 Gulf Crisis on behalf of "a new world order" being only a harbinger of things to come.[9]

---

[7]It should be noted that Gilpin, for whom the test of hegemony is the success of the dominant great power in presiding over an open global economy, has been less sure of the ability of the United States to sustain the liberal world trading order it imposed following World War II. Now, as America's principal trading partners perceive less need for US military help in fending off an aggressive Soviet Union, a durable *Pax Americana* looks less and less plausible. Rather, Gilpin foresees an era of increasing mercantilistic rivalry between the United States, the West European countries and Japan in the advanced industrial world, and a stubborn reliance by Third World countries on illiberal protectionist measures—trends he found strongly emergent even before the evaporation of Cold War hostility.

[8]Immanuel Wallerstein, ed., *The Politics of the World Economy* (Cambridge: Cambridge University Press, 1984).

[9]Noam Chomsky, for example, in various public presentations around the Boston area in 1990, was a vigorous articulator of the thesis: Watch out! With the United States no longer inhibited by an anticapitalist superpower opponent, the world is in for its biggest binge of capitalist imperialism yet.

EXPLANATION #3:
THE GEIST WHOSE ZEIT HAS COME

The Imperial Overstretch and Hegemonic Peace theories obviously are too neat as explanations of the dramatic transformation of the Cold War system into the *post*–Cold War system. In giving overwhelming causative weight to changing international distributions of military and economic power (which are calculated and presumably responded to by governing elites), these theories fail to account for the fact that in Eastern Europe, at least, most of the pressures for fundamental change were generated and nurtured by dissident intellectuals, artists, youth groups, technocratic modernizers, would-be entrepreneurs, and (in Poland) labor leaders. To be sure, it was a series of demarches promulgated at the pinnacle of the Soviet hierarchy, by a new General Secretary of the Communist Party, that revamped the foreign and domestic priorities of the USSR and gave the green light to reformers throughout the Soviet sphere in Eastern Europe in 1989 and 1990 to establish new "self-determined" political and economic systems; but in these demarches, the Gorbachev regime (itself comprising many technocratic modernizers and closet dissidents who had risen to the top of the system) was responding at least as much to "forces from below" as to the changing "global correlation of forces."

Perhaps it is time to turn the philosopher Hegel's grand dialectic of history right-side-up from its upside-down position into which it was turned by Karl Marx; for haven't we been witnessing the global contagion of the culture of freedom—a higher synthesis, as it were, of the ideas of British Liberalism, the French Revolution, American democratic capitalism, and their various hybrids? This spirit of the times, or *Zeitgeist*, simply could not be contained, despite the efforts of the Soviet communists to quarantine the masses behind iron curtains and brick walls and to immunize their professional elites with "scientific" Marxism-Leninism.

But the idea of democratic capitalism has been around for a long time, and has been vigorously championed since World War II in opposition to socialism, especially its Marxist version—the other twentieth century candidate for the Geist Whose Ziet Has Come. We are still left with the question: *why now?* Why, in the space of less than three years, did the idea of structuring society around a free market economy and openly competitive pluralistic polity suddenly attain explosive popularity in the stronghold of its antithesis?

EXPLANATION #4: GORBACHEV AS A
GREAT MAN OF HISTORY

Unlike most social scientists, media pundits characteristically have few qualms about attributing momentous historical developments to the genius—constructive or malevolent—of particular personalities. Biography sells better than multivariate analysis. Napoleon Bonaparte brings on the age of the *nation*-state; Lenin makes Marxism a global political force; Franklin Roosevelt saves the United States from socialism; Hitler causes World War II; Stalin causes the Cold War; Gandhi and Nehru bring independence to India; Mao restores greatness to China; Martin Luther King transforms the American South; Margaret Thatcher undoes the British welfare state—this is the stuff of popular history.

Professional scholars tend to scoff at *Time* magazine's "Man of the Year" hyperbolies (Gorbachev was their "Man of the Decade" for the 1980s)—but perhaps too readily.

Gorbachev's policies and personality were inextricably of the "essence"—as generators and resultants—of the profound historical transformation of the late 1980s and early 1990s. Yet having almost single-handedly unleashed the creative forces imprisoned in the Soviet sphere of totalitarian polities and command economies, Gorbachev soon found himself caught up in unbridled stampedes toward political decentralization and economic privatization more swift and radical than he could have anticipated or was capable of modulating effectively.

Gorbachev was displaced, ironically, by another "larger-than-life" figure: his protege, Boris Yeltsin, the charismatic champion of full independence for Russia and other Soviet republics and an accelerated "shock therapy" transition to a capitalist economy.

Explanation #5: All of the Above (But None by Itself)

Perhaps the best explanation for the demise of the Cold War is that, like other major developments in world history, it emanated from multiple sources and was generated at multiple levels.

The competing Moscow-centered and Washington-centered imperiums were surely "overstretched" by the end of the period (explanation #1), but asymmetrically so, putting the United States in a position to make demands on the more rapidly disintegrating Soviet side (explanation #2). The fact that Marxist "East" capitulated to the capitalist "West" without another world war being fought to determine the victor—an anomaly in the history of world politics—is incomprehensible, however, without according substantial weight to the contagious spread of the democratic ideas across the East–West ideological divide (explanation #3), *and* the determination of a great leader, Mikhail Gorbachev, to peacefully accommodate to all of these forces (explanation #4).

In hindsight, none of this should have been so surprising, for the systems and subsystems that appear to be dominant and durable at any particular historical juncture are, in fact, quite open to one another and highly susceptible to either enhancement or disintegration: Causes and effects typically move back and forth from the material to the cultural realms, and between the transnational, international, subnational, and small group and individual levels. Stated another way, Cold War bipolarity was a global transnational political system (itself a subsystem of world society) superimposed on a nation-state system composed of volatile domestic subsystems. The multilevel interaction of political systems and subsystems was particularly stimulated by the impact of the technological revolution—the dramatic increase since World War II in the mobility of persons, goods, and information. The bipolar Cold War system, a rather artificial overlay on the inherently pluralistic and dynamic world society, was a historically bounded response to the power vacuums created by World War II. It embraced all of these levels and partook of all of these processes, but could never fully encompass them and was eventually eroded and collapsed by them.[10]

---

[10]I elaborate this theoretical model of dynamic system change in my *International Relations in a Changing Global Context: Toward a Theory of the World Polity* (Boulder: Westview Press, 1992). For an essentially similar approach, *see* James N. Roseanau, *Turbulence in World Politics: A Theory of Change and Continuity* (Princeton: Princeton University Press, 1990).

7

POST–COLD WAR
DISORDER

The end of the Cold War was hailed around the world as a blessing. It would virtually eliminate the prospect of a nuclear World War III. It would allow for substantial superpower disarmament, thus creating potential "peace dividends" (freed-up financial resources) that could be channeled to unmet socioeconomic needs. The relaxation of the compulsion in each Cold War camp to maintain solidarity vis-a-vis a common enemy would create openings for the assertion of national self-determination and human rights. But such developments would soon show themselves to have a shaky "down side" of new predicaments for world society and particular countries.

Forces frozen for decades, freed by the sudden thaw of the Cold War, would dislodge and disintegrate not only the huge military blocs that had been constructed by the superpowers but also many of the political controls within countries that had been keeping intercommunal animosities and conflicts over scarce resources within civil bounds. With the global struggle between the Marxists and the capitalists no longer the dominant axis of world politics, alignments and antagonisms would henceforth fluctuate in complicated and often unpredictable patterns, depending on the particular mix of issues—economic, territorial, ethnic, religious—that might percolate to the surface of international relations regionally or locally at the time.

Unable to count on protection from a superpower patron, but thereby also freed from the need to gain approval from the hegemon before engaging in moves with large international implications, former clients would be tempted to engage in unilateral action that could destabilize important regional or global systems. This was the systemic environment in which Iraq's Saddam Hussein, no longer constrained by how the Soviets might feel about it, and convinced that the Americans had other preoccupations, launched a massive invasion of Kuwait in August 1990.

The aftermath of the Cold War would also feature openly confrontational and frequently violent assertions by national, ethnic, and religious communal movements of their "right" to political autonomy, if not full independence. Readily repressed by the superpowers during the Cold War on grounds of strategic necessity (such movements in one's own camp were targets for infiltration by the rival camp), the contemporary flareup of militant communalism, often involving groups with "brothers" and "sisters" in a number of states, would create new risks of transborder warfare and interventions by threatened or expansionist powers. The breakout of virtually genocidal civil war in the former Yugoslavia in the early 1990s (see below) was a portent of the role such conflicts could play in the former Soviet Union and other regions.

CRISES OF POST–MARXIST MODERNIZATION

The attempt throughout the former Soviet camp suddenly to convert (through what has been called "shock therapy") from centralized command economies and totalitarian polities to free markets and democratic pluralism has been producing volatile reactions, sometimes even widespread societal convulsions, in many of the ex-Marxist states of Eurasia, including Russia itself. The rapid privatization of state industries, the removal of subsidies and price controls, and the opening of domestic markets to foreign competition have been accompanied by severe levels of unemployment, a drastic decline in purchasing power for large segments of the population, alarming scarcities of essential goods and services in some areas, and the rise of "black markets" and criminal syndicates. These hardships have in turn given rise to increasingly adamant demands, now able to make themselves felt through the democratic process, that vulnerable sectors of the economy be protected by the state and, in some cases, that the departure from socialism be fundamentally reassessed.

As of this writing there are increasing fears of authoritarian backlashes across Eurasia against the spreading chaos associated with rapid liberalization. Some observes in the West, convinced that Russia is too weakened to make another bid for world hegemony, would be content to let the ex-Marxist societies fend for themselves. But the option of simple isolationism in the West is an illusion. The combination of intercommunal conflict and depressed living conditions in the former Soviet sphere has maximized incentives for migration into the affluent industrialized countries. The unprecedented movement of peoples from East to West seeking economic betterment, added to the flow from South to North of refugees from poor or politically repressive Third World countries, has been engendering xenophobic reactions and new political instabilities in the Western democracies.

The Violent Dismemberment of Yugoslavia: A Portent of Things to Come

In the early post–World War II period Yugoslavia had been ahead of its time, so to speak, in exposing the fact that Cold War bipolarity was a flimsy geopolitical and ideological overlay on the deeper historical bases for amity and enmity among peoples. Once again, in the early post–Cold War period, it was Yugoslavia, with its ethnic and religious affinities and antagonisms, that demonstrated the superficiality of "new world order" designs premised on a revival of Westphalian principles of national sovereignty and mutual noninterference of states in each other's domestic affairs.

Yugoslavia's defection from the Soviet bloc in 1948 had marked not only the limits of Soviet imperialism but also the inappropriateness of the ideological view prominent in the United States that the Cold War was a universal struggle between the good (democratic capitalism) and the bad (totalitarian communism). Josip Broz Tito, the hero of the Yugoslav partisan resistance against Hitler and subsequently the defiant challenger to Stalin's effort to subordinate Yugoslavia into the Soviet sphere of control, was a Communist—but like Ho Chi Minh, who led the Vietnamese resistance against the Japanese, a nationalistic Communist. One of the founders of the Nonaligned Movement in the 1950s (along with India's Jawaharlal Nehru, Indonesia's Achmed Sukarno, Egypt's Gamal Abdel Nasser, and Ghana's Kwame Nkrumah), Tito led the way in showing, to the embarrassment of both the Soviet and American cold warriors, that proud peoples with their own cultures were not willing to serve as pawns in the power games of others.

Also, as far back as the early 1950s, Belgrade began to experiment with a less centralized and command-directed type of socialism than provided for in the Soviet model. Yugoslavia's relatively impressive achievements (as compared with other countries in the Soviet sphere) in the economic, scientific, and cultural fields could not go unrecognized by Stalin's successors, who felt compelled to concede that there might indeed be "many roads to socialism."

Yet what was admirable in the early stages of the Yugoslav pluralist challenge to Soviet totalitarian imperialism spun out of control after Tito's death in 1980. Tito's charisma and secular authoritarianism had provided the cohesive cement for the multinational/multireligious country precariously constructed after World War I out of the polyglot Slavic remnants of defeated Austria-Hungary and the disintegrating Ottoman Turkish empire—in Professor Steven Burg's words, "a patchwork of territories and peoples who were at the same time both united and divided by language, religion, culture, history, and political tradition."[1] Without Tito's strong hand, sepa-

---

[1]Steven L. Burg, *Conflict and Cohesion in Socialist Yugoslavia: Political Decision Making Since 1966* (Princeton: Princeton University Press, 1983), pp. 3–30, quote from p. 9. *See also* Paul Shoup, *Communism and the Yugoslav National Question* (New York: Columbia University Press, 1968).

ratist forces began to tear at both Yugoslavia's federal structure of government and the country's ruling party, the League of Communists of Yugoslavia (LCY). When the onset of a prolonged economic crisis in the 1980s exacerbated the competition between the regions, many LCY leaders found it difficult to resist the temptation to court popular support by championing greater political autonomy for their republics.[2]

Political leaders in the more modernized and affluent republics of Slovenia and Croatia, seeing autonomy as a means of keeping control over their own resources and not being compelled to bail out the less developed regions of the federation economically, were stimulated by the secession of the three Baltic republics from the USSR in 1990 to declare their own independence on June 25, 1991. Serbia, less developed economically but the dominant republic both politically and militarily, tried in the name of all-Yugoslav nationalism to put down the defections.

The federation's armed forces, commanded mostly by Serbs, were ordered into action in both Slovenia and Croatia. A half-hearted military operation against Slovenia was quickly given up. But bitter fighting ensued in Croatia where a large Serbian minority welcomed Belgrade's attempt to undo the republic's secession; a UN-brokered truce in January 1992, including a ban on outside shipment of arms to any of the republics, left more than a third of Croatia under Serbian military occupation.

Next came the paroxysm of violence in the Muslim-majority republic of Bosnia-Herzegovina, which declared its independence in April 1992. The large Serbian minority in Bosnia, backed by Belgrade, asserted their own independence from Bosnia and initiated a reign of terror (called "ethnic cleansing") against the Muslims to drive them out of the Serbian areas. A full-scale civil war ensued, including bombing and artillery siege-bombardment of the Bosnian capital city of Sarajevo by Bosnian Serbs armed by Serbia, provoking the United Nations to impose economic sanctions against Serbia. The Croats, also a sizable minority in Bosnia, initially sided with the Muslims against the Serbs but, as it looked like the republic might eventually have to be partitioned into ethnic enclaves, also began to stake out their own claims to dominance in some of the Croatian-majority areas of northern Bosnia.

If such intercommunal and interrepublic violence had erupted in Yugoslavia during the Cold War, the USSR would have been highly tempted to intervene, using the instability on the strategically crucial southwestern flank of the Warsaw Pact as a pretext for gaining the Russian presence on the shores of the Mediterranean that had eluded the Czars for centuries. But to forestall exactly this contingency, the United States and its NATO allies might well have engaged in a preemptive intervention of their own. Indeed,

---

[2]Steven L. Burg, "Political Structures," in Dennison Rustow, ed., *Yugoslavia: A Fractured Federalism* (Washington, DC: The Wilson Center Press, 1988), pp. 9–22; and Steven L. Burg, "Nationalism and Democratization in Yugoslavia," *The Washington Quarterly*, Autumn 1991, pp. 3–19.

the "Yugoslav Civil War" scenario was one of the standard pre–World War III crisis simulations staged in Cold War planning agencies to assess the effectiveness of their military and crisis-management capabilities.

Coming early in the post–Cold War period, however, the outbreak of civil war in Yugoslavia found the Kremlin devoid of the capability and will to intervene; and the White House was preoccupied with other priorities (the crisis in the Persian Gulf, dealing with Russia and the other ex-Soviet states, the 1992 elections) that prevented serious consideration of a major US role in the Balkans. The Europe-oriented multilateral organizations—even if they could have forged a consensus among members with varying historic ties to the different Yugoslav communities—were themselves in the throes of redefining their reasons for existence and were not capable of managing a coherent response. The Warsaw Pact had disbanded. Neither NATO nor the CSCE had sorted out its appropriate roles and powers for dealing with the internecine ethnicity conflicts that threatened to disrupt civil society, not just in Yugoslavia but across much of Eurasia.

World society, at the start of 1992, seemed paralyzed by its own basic anarchic structure and revived sovereignty norms (the *old* world order basis of the so-called "new world order") from dealing with this ominously prototypical post–Cold War crisis. Both the advocates of intervention and the advocates of letting the local forces battle things out feared the precedent the Yugoslav case might set for external involvement in similar ethnic conflicts in the former USSR and in Africa. But in the late spring of 1992, international media reports on Serbian atrocities, plus fears in diplomatic circles of a spread of the interethnic violence into Albania and Macedonia that could catalyze a confrontation between Greece and Turkey, galvanized more intrusive UN efforts to stop the fighting and mediate the conflicts over sovereignty and jurisdiction. In June, the Security Council authorized the deployment of UN peacekeepers to Sarejevo to reopen the airport and to assist in the delivery of food and medical supplies. And on August 13, the Security Council passed a stronger resolution authorizing the Secretary General to use "all measures necessary" to deliver relief supplies to the Muslim communities the Serbs had isolated in Sarajevo and other parts of Bosnia.

Still, with the UN peacekeepers inhibited from taking sides in the interethnic conflict by the terms of the Security Council mandate, and the major external powers constrained from deep involvement by domestic preoccupations and more weighty international interests, the unbalanced military situation in Bosnia allowed the Serbs to continue their brutal expansionary policies even while the international diplomatic community was becoming more active in trying to broker a settlement.

For the next few years, the center of diplomatic efforts to terminate the Bosnian civil war was the International Conference on the Former Yugoslavia (ICFY), sponsored by the United Nations and the European Community, and co-chaired by Cyrus Vance, representing the UN, and Lord

David Owen, representing the EC.[3] The ICFY had some limited success in persuading the warring communities and states to agree to a series of cease-fires (most of which quickly broke down) and to commit themselves, at least in principle, to avoid interfering with deliveries of humanitarian relief, to end the detention of civilians, to provide for the safety of refugees, and to keep their aircraft out of stipulated "no fly" zones. The ICFY was persistently stymied, however, in its crucial task of mediating the basic political conflict among the Croats, Serbs, and Muslims over the constitution and territorial demarcations of the Bosnian state. Chairmen Vance and Owen thanklessly carried the burden of trying to achieve a viable political settlement. Their main vehicle was a draft constitution for a decentralized Bosnian confederation that would please no one but which the three ethnic communities would hopefully find to be better than the continuation of genocidal bloodletting and brutality.

The Vance-Owen Plan, in its most prominent version, contemplated dividing Bosnia into ten provinces, reflecting mainly the geographic concentration of the principal ethnic groups; their precise location and shape would also be constrained by economic and security considerations. Three of the provinces would be Serbian, three Muslim, and three Croat. The tenth province would surround and include Sarajevo and would be designated as multi-ethnic. Minorities in each of the ethnic-majority provinces would be guaranteed full and equal rights and protection under the province's laws. During or following the peaceful consolidation of these territorial units, the constitutional structure of the new Bosnian confederation would be elaborated on in detail through negotiations among the provinces.

The Croats expressed a willingness to negotiate peace on the basis of the Vance-Owen Plan. The Serbs indicated they might negotiate under the premises of Vance-Owen, but only if the settlement would designate as "Serbian provinces" most of the territory they now controlled in Bosnia. The Muslims were adamantly opposed, however, even to versions of the Vance-Owen Plan that would require the Serbs to relinquish more than half of the area they had captured in the civil war, insisting that this would still confer legitimacy on the Serbian military aggression and "ethnic cleansing." The Muslims also objected to the loose confederal structure contemplated for Bosnia as a whole, seeing it as really nothing more than a partition of the country that would deny the Muslims (who prior to the civil war had been living throughout Bosnia) their right of democratic national self-determination; moreover, the Muslims viewed the plan for politically autonomous provinces as a ruse that would allow the Bosnian Serbs to merge their province with Serbia itself.

[3]Again, I draw heavily on the insights of my colleague Steven L. Burg for understanding the local and international politics of the Balkan crisis of the 1990s. Other scholars will need to await the forthcoming publication of his study on nationalism and democracy in post-communist Europe for The Twentieth Century Fund.

The Muslims were buttressed in their position by the cold shoulder the Clinton administration gave the Vance-Owen Plan in the spring and summer of 1993, and by the anti-Serb stance taken by the President and other high administration officials, especially their calls for a removal of the embargo on weapons shipments to the Bosnian Muslims, and their public discussion of the possibility of NATO air strikes in response to Serbian violations of various cease-fire arrangements. Meanwhile, the Serbs remained undeterred from grabbing more Bosnian territory, especially in light of statements by Clinton precluding the deployment of US ground forces to Bosnia except to help enforce a settlement already agreed to by the three sides. (The Clinton stance was opposed by other members of NATO and the UN Secretary General, on the grounds that arming the Muslims and/or air strikes against the Serbs would only drive the conflict to higher levels of violence, which in turn would endanger the UN peacekeepers on the ground). Indeed, the mixed signals from the Clinton administration gave the Serbs every incentive to prevent a negotiated settlement.

By the fall of 1993, the situation in Sarajevo and various Muslim holdouts in Bosnia was even worse for the Muslims than when the Vance-Owen Plan was first proposed. Lord Owen and a representative of the UN Secretariat (Vance had resigned) continued their mediational efforts under the auspices of the ICFY, but the international diplomatic community was increasingly pessimistic. The war-terminating alternatives appeared to have narrowed to at best a full partition of Bosnia into three countries reflecting the military status-quo on the ground and at worst at total victory by the Serbs. An additional reason for pessimism was the prospect of more active diplomatic involvement by Moscow on behalf of the Serbs following the strong showing in Russia of imperial-minded ultra-nationalists in the December 1993 parliamentary elections. The Serbs, it was feared, would be stiffened in their resistance to any substantial relinquishment of the territory they had conquered, knowing that the Yeltsin government could no longer afford to look wimpish before its own people when it came to supporting Russias's "Slavic brothers" in the Balkans. Meanwhile, the civil war continued to exact a terrible toll. By the turn of the year United Nations agencies were reporting more then 200,000 dead or missing since 1991 and 3,800,000 refugees.[4]

The crisis drew the major powers more deeply into its vortex in February 1994 as the world media focused on the carnage inflicted on the central market in Sarajevo by a mortar attack launched from the nearby hills. The exploding 120-mm shell killed 68 people and wounded over 200, the worst single attack on the captial in the civil war. Although UN investigators were unable to determine who fired the weapon, the response in words and actions from the United States and other NATO governments strongly implied that Serb artillery gunners, who had been holding the city under siege for

[4]Elizabeth Neuffer, "4 Million Seen at Risk in Balkans," *New York Times*, February 20, 1994.

months, were the culprits. Prodded by their outraged publics, the NATO governments issued an ultimatum to all the Bosnian belligerents (though the Serbs were obviously the main target) giving them ten days to remove or place under UN control all heavy weapons within a 20 kilometer radius of the center of Sarajevo; any such weapons not removed or turned over to the UN would be subject to strikes by NATO aircraft.[5]

The Yeltsin government, embarrassed at not having been a part of the international coalition that developed the response to the shelling of the Sarajevo market, moved quickly to inject itself into the diplomatic arena. Two days before the expiration of the deadline in the NATO ultimatum, the Russians announced that the Serbs had agreed to the terms of the ultimatum as a part of a deal with Moscow in which some 800 Russian peacekeeping troops would be moved into and around Sarajevo under the UN flag to enforce a cease-fire. In announcing this development, Russian Deputy Foreign Minister Vitaly Churkin warned: "I know there are some people in NATO who are advocating the strategy 'strike then negotiate.' In Bosnia-Herzegovina, there can be no such thing as strike and negotiate. You can have either negotiations or an all-out war."[6]

The Clinton administration and other NATO governments were left no choice but to publicly praise the Russians for their constructive intervention, particularly as UN monitors reported that the Serbs were complying with the terms of the ultimatum. But privately there was worry in NATO circles that the Russians, having interjected themselves as a peacekeeping presence between the belligerents, were now in a position to help the Serbs secure their already-achieved territorial gains against any coercive efforts to reverse them; this situation could also enhance Serbian bargaining power in subsequent negotiations to divide up Bosnia.

At the time of this writing (March 1994), the post–Cold War Balkan crisis was hardly at an end. There were announcements of a Muslim-Croat accord on a confederal arrangement for the parts of Bosnia under their control, but no suggestions that the Muslims had given up on their demands for a return to their jurisdiction of lands conquered by the Serbs. Various Muslim cities and towns remained under virtual siege by the Serbs (threatened by artillery that might well have been redeployed from Sarajevo), but NATO was not ready to issue Sarajevo-type ultimata on a country-wide basis, and the Clinton administration remained firm in its refusal to deploy US troops into Bosnia save for any purpose other than to help police a political settlement voluntarily entered into by the three ethnic communities. Would it make a difference, however, that the United States was now more actively involved,

---

[5]Roger Cohen, "NATO Gives Serbs a 10-Day Deadline to Withdraw Guns," *New York Times,* February 10, 1994. For background on the intra-NATO diplomacy, *see* Elaine Sciolino and Doughlas Jehl, "As U.S. Sought a Bosnia Policy, The French Offered a Good Idea," *New York Times,* February 14, 1994.
[6]Churkin quote from Fred Kaplan, "Russia Warns Against Air Strikes, Pledges Peacekeepers for Sarajevo," *Boston Globe,* February 19, 1994.

along with the Russians, in attempting to broker a settlement and to arrange cease-fires?

Presumably, if Washington and Moscow could operate in tandem in the Balkans as they had done recently, with success, in imposing war-terminating settlements in Angola and Namibia, Afghanistan, and Nicaragua, they ought to be able jointly to leverage a cessation of hostilities in Bosnia. But those cases of conflict resolution were themselves part of the process of ending the Cold War: the belligerents had been clients of the rival superpowers, advised by them, provisioned by them, as local proxies in the worldwide geopolitical and ideological struggle; consequently, when Washington and Moscow, in calling off the Cold War, instructed their respective clients to make peace with each other, the latter had no choice but to comply. By contrast, the civil war in Bosnia was prototypically a *post*-Cold War conflict, in which the clashing objectives of the belligerents were almost entirely self-generated; the communal conflicts were able to escalate into protracted open warfare precisely because, absent the Cold War, the major external powers were strategically indifferent to the violent disintegration of Yugoslavia.

The situation in the Balkans is thus both a symptom of the demise of the Cold War and a portent of public order and security problems that are likely to pervade the emerging world polity. As put by Steven Burg,

> The wars in former Yugoslavia have made it clear that principles and practices which provided a stable framework for international security in the era of the Cold War are no longer sufficient to preserve the peace. The principles of state sovereignty, territorial integrity, human rights, and self-determination embedded in the United Nations Charter and other United Nations documents, and developed in detail in the documents of the Conference on Security and Cooperation in Europe, have proven contradictory, or at least subject to contradictory interpretation. Moreover, the mounting human tragedy in Bosnia Herzegovina has revealed the inadequacies of decision-making principle, operational guidelines, and conflict management capabilities of Euro-Atlantic institutions such as the CSCE, NATO, and the European Community, as well as the United Nations.[7]

AN ENHANCED ROLE
FOR THE UNITED NATIONS?

The removal of the disciplining function of the superpower-led coalitions plus the inclination of the former Cold War rivals to forge new cooperative relationships has turned the attention of statespersons to the potential of the United Nations—only marginally relied on during the Cold War—for coun-

---

[7]Steven L. Burg, 1994 manuscript of study prepared for The Twentieth Century Fund, tentatively titled, *War or Peace? Nationalism, Democracy, and American Foreign Policy in Post-Communist Europe*, p. 176; quoted with permission of the author.

tering the threats to peace and security inherent in the emerging world disorder.

Before the end of the Cold War, the principal UN role in the peace and security field was in the form of narrowly defined peacekeeping operations: multinational military units with missions usually restricted to monitoring cease-fire or truce agreements (including typically military disengagement zones) already accepted by local belligerents.

Since 1989, however, the new opportunities and need for neutral international authorities have been reflected not only in an increased reliance on such peacekeeping forces but also in the deployment of UN civilian and military operatives with authority to assist in the establishment of provisional governments and the conduct of elections in situations of persisting political conflict (for example, the UN Transitional Assistance Group in Namibia, deployed in 1989, and most ambitiously, the UN Transitional Authority in Cambodia, established in 1991) and in the provision of relief to populations suffering as a consequence of local civil conflict (notably in Somalia starting in late 1992, where US armed forces, acting under the authority of UN resolutions, provided most of the initial help, and in Rwanda in 1994).

The outlines for an enhanced UN role, encompassing a broadened concept of peacekeeping plus greater utilization of its preventive diplomacy, peacemaking, and "peace-building" potentialities were drawn by Secretary General Boutros Boutros-Ghali in his April 1992 report, *An Agenda for Peace*, and in subsequent statements. Reflecting the sudden popular rediscovery, as it were, of the world organization, the Secretary General urged member governments to provide support—doctrinally and in tangible undertakings—for a wide range of enlarged UN capabilities, including:

- Violence-avoidance (fact-finding and early-warning missions, mediation and adjudication of disputes, the establishment of demilitarized zones, and "preventive deployment" of UN forces)

- Truce and cease-fire reinforcement (peace-observation and truce-supervision forces, sometimes deployed as a buffering presence in zones of disengagement, and in some cases with the authority to disarm local groups)

- Post-belligerency "peace-building" (elections supervision; technical assistance in administration, human-rights monitoring, and the like)

- Collective-security (military action by UN forces to counter aggression) and the maintenance by members of specially designated and trained units to be made available to the United Nations, as provided for in Article 43 of the Charter

While reiterating the Charter's respect for the sovereignty and integrity of the member states of the United Nations, the Secretary General insisted that

The time of absolute and exclusive sovereignty . . . has passed. It is the task of leaders of States today to understand this and to find a balance between the needs of good internal governance and the requirements of an ever more interdependent world. . . .

Globalism and nationalism need not be viewed as opposing trends, doomed to spur each other on to extremes of reaction. The healthy globalization of contemporary life requires in the first instance solid identities and fundamental freedoms. The sovereignty, territorial integrity and independence of States within the established international system, and the principle of self-determination for peoples, both of great value and importance, must not be permitted to work against each other in the period ahead.[8]

Easier said than done. Without amending the Charter, all UN peace and security missions—from peacekeeping to nation-building to collective security—still need authorization by the Security Council and are therefore subject to veto by any one of the five permanent members of the Council: The United States, Russia, China, Britain, and France. The fact that Russia and China are no longer enemies of the three western powers does not mean that they will see eye-to-eye with them, let alone with each other, on the policies required in any particular situation to terminate a war or resolve the precipitating disputes. Nor is it likely that the interests of the United States and its former Cold War allies, now more than ever shaped by their quite different constellations of international relationships, will often converge sufficiently to produce mandates for UN operations that would not be opposed by some of their significant international clients.

These complexities of the post-Cold War system have translated in the peace and security arena into disputes over the financing, contributions of military personnel, and command and control of UN forces.

The United Nations organization is in severe financial trouble, in large part because of the failure of members to pay the additional dues required to fund the many peacekeeping missions that the Security Council has authorized since 1987. Whereas in 1987, there were five active UN peacekeeping operations, employing some 10,000 UN soldiers at an annual draw on the UN budget of about $235 million, at the end of 1993, there were 18 peacekeeping operations, employing over 75,000 troops at a cost of more than $3 billion a year.[9] The UN budget from which these operations are funded comes from member contributions apportioned according to the relative wealth of the countries—an arrangement that has become a special target of the anti-UN coalition in the US Congress, and has resulted in the United States falling behind in its obligations by nearly $1 billion.

---

[8]Boutros Boutros-Ghali, *An Agenda for Peace: Preventive Diplomacy, Peacemaking and Peace-keeping* (New York: United Nations, 1992), quotes from pp. 9–10.
[9]Paul Lewis, "Reluctant Peacekeepers: Many U.N. Members Reconsider Role in Conflicts," *New York Times*, December 15, 1993.

The lack of adequate funds could restrict the composition of peacekeeping forces to those from countries who can and are willing to pay their own way. This might mean that the UN's ability to deploy units from countries like India, Ghana, Egypt, and Fiji (typically sources of experienced peacekeepers) would have to be substantially reduced, and units from the Nordic countries and Canada, for example, would need to be relied on more—a development that in many places would have the unfortunate result of mostly white UN troops policing people of color.[10]

Finally, the issue of the chain of command and control of multi-national UN forces has become a focus of concern in the United Nations and of debate within member governments as peacekeeping is transformed into active pacification and peace enforcement; for when national governments anticipate that their UN contingents may be ordered into battle, to kill and be killed, as happened in Somalia in 1993, they become reluctant to place the authority over the crucial tactical decisions entirely in the hands of military commanders directly responsible to the UN Secretary General and his deputies. Yet without a tightly centralized chain of command and responsibility in such circumstances, the national units are prone to operate at cross purposes and dangerously get in each other's way.

Faced with these complications, the Clinton administration (which Secretary General Boutros-Ghali had been heavily depending on for implementing his "Agenda") turned away from its early support for a stronger and enlarged UN peacekeeping capability.[11] In an address to the General Assembly, Clinton explained,

> our nation has begun asking harder questions about proposals for new peacekeeping missions. Is there a real threat to international peace? Does the proposed mission have clear objectives? Can an exit point be identified for those who will be asked to participate? How much will the mission cost? From now on the United Nations should address these questions before we vote and before the mission begins. . . .
>
> The United Nations simply cannot become engaged in every one of the world's conflicts. If the American people are to say yes to UN peacekeeping, the United Nations must know when to say no.[12]

Reiterating these points before the press, the President also insisted that prior to contributing US forces to any UN military operation,

---

[10]On how UN financing relates to the composition of peacekeeping forces, *see* Margaret P. Karns and Karen A. Mingst, "Maintaining International Peace and Security: UN Peacekeeping and Peacemaking," in Michael T. Klare and Daniel C. Thomas, eds., *World Security: Challenges for a New Century* (New York: St. Martin's Press, 1994), pp. 188–213.

[11]For background on the Clinton administration's shift away from a strong UN peacekeeping role, *see* Seyom Brown, *The Faces of Power: Constancy and Change in United States Foreign Policy From Truman to Clinton* (New York: Columbia University Press, 1994), pp. 592–594.

[12]President Clinton's Address to United Nations General Assembly, September 27, 1993, *Department of State Dispatch*, Vol. 4., No. 39.

I would want a clear understanding what the command and control was. [In Bosnia] I would want the NATO commander in charge of the operations. . . . And I would want a clear expression of support from the United States Congress. . . . We have to know how we are going to fund it, and then we would have to know that others were going to do their part as well.[13]

Hearing these reservations, the UN Secretary General was disappointed, but philosophical. "I am firmly committed to the concept of peace enforcement," he said. "It is essential if we are to strengthen international peace and security. But there is a new reality: member states are not ready for it. I must accept reality."[14]

This "new reality" and its underlying causes is the subject of Part Three of this book.

---

[13]Bill Clinton, press conference of September 27, 1993, quoted by Thomas L. Friedman, "Clinton at U.N. Lists Stiff Terms for Sending U.S. Force to Bosnia," *New York Times*, September 28, 1993.
[14]Boutros-Ghali, quoted by Lewis, "Reluctant Peacekeepers."

3

The Emerging World Polity: Essential Characteristics and Systemic Determinants

8

THE GLOBAL POLYARCHY

The post–Cold War era features a wide diversity of alignments and adversary relationships, formed around a myriad of issues: jurisdictional and territorial, economic, ecological, cultural, and moral. Lacking a dominant axis of cooperation and conflict, yet featuring both regional and functional enclaves of order, some coercively imposed, some voluntaristic, the world polity is more than ever a *polyarchy* in which national states, subnational groups, and transnational special interests and communities are vying for the support and loyalty of individuals, and in which conflicts are prosecuted and resolved primarily on the basis of ad hoc power plays and bargaining among combinations of these groups—combinations that vary from issue to issue. Today's adversary on the question of international navigation through straits, for example, will be tomorrow's coalition partner on the issue of whether sanctions should be imposed on Country X for its repression of a religious minority. Moreover, in the global polyarchy, "international" politics—the power game among nation-states—is no longer the overbearing determinant of who gets what, when, and how; rather, the international system in much of its behavior functions as one of the *sub*systems of a larger and more complex field of relationships.

The complexity and seeming unpredictability of the post–Cold War polyarchy might appear to negate the possibility of durable configurations of world politics. Yet there are certain configurations of cooperation and conflict and hierarchy and subordination that are so deeply embedded—materially and culturally—in history and contemporary life as to constitute basic parameters within which even the highly volatile polyarchic relationships can be expected to operate over the coming decades.

This chapter provides only an overview of the basic polyarchic patterns now emerging, leaving it to subsequent chapters to elaborate their underlying sources and manifestations in particular fields and sectors of world society.

POWER IN THE POLYARCHIC SYSTEM: WHO ARE THE MOVERS AND SHAKERS?

In the post–Cold War polyarchy the distribution of power—the capacity to influence the behavior of others—is strikingly different from what it was for most of the four decades following World War II. The difference is evident in at least two general interrelated features: (1) the diffusion of system-wide power to capitals and organizations beyond Washington and Moscow; and (2) the emergence of a wider array of issue-specific arenas of conflict and co-operation, each with its own pattern of alignment and rivalry. The second of these is partially a function of the first, but it also reinforces the first feature. The result is a more variegated lineup of "movers and shakers," with power rankings differing arena by arena, than that which dominated the system during the Cold War.

When world politics was pervaded by the enmity of the United States and the Soviet Union, each obsessed with preventing the other from obtaining military superiority, virtually every major international conflict or bargaining arena was transformed into an adjunct of the Cold War power competition. Economics and ideology were the handmaidens of geopolitical rivalry of the superpowers, neither of whom would allow its intra-alliance relationships or relationships with nonaligned states to interfere with the imperative of maintaining a sufficient balance of military power vis-à-vis the other superpower. Even states, political movements, or nongovernmental interest groups who wanted to keep apart from the Cold War rivalry were highly constrained by the realization that they were courting danger in challenging the will of Moscow or Washington and that in situations where either superpower might try to impose its will, the only recourse might be to seek the protection of the other.

The collapse of the Soviet Union in 1990–1991 and the consequent removal of the overriding incentive for the United States to be globally involved—which had been the containment of Soviet imperial expansion—changed not only the global distribution of usable power but also the ingredients of such power. The US–Soviet balance of power had been calculated essentially in terms of the military capabilities deployed by each and the credibility of their stated intentions to employ these capabilities on behalf of their international interests. The demise of the Cold War and the constriction of the objectives for which these erstwhile rival superpowers were willing to employ their military forces thus altered both the distribution of military power and the relative importance of different kinds of power in the international system. Most dramatic was the comparative rise in the influence of economic power—a realm in which the identity of the movers and shakers would be quite different from the rankings prevailing in the military arenas. Also significant, and somewhat surprising to many analysts, was the revival of the attractive (and repellent) power of ethnic, religious, and other cultural identifications as determinants of the post–Cold War patterns of alignment and antagonism, not merely as soft factors to be manipulated by the great military and economic imperialists.

Military Power

While the international distribution of military capability is not, as it used to be during the Cold War, a virtually sufficient indicator of the overall distribution of power in the world, it is still one of the crucial determinants of which countries can credibly defend their interests "when push comes to shove." Despite the relative increase in other kinds of power, it remains essential to know who are these world-class military powers—that is, which countries have military forces that not only give them wherewithal to unilaterally deter attacks upon themselves but also to make it likely that their intentions (ranging from staying completely aloof to intervening directly) with respect to major conflicts anywhere in the world will be taken into account by the belligerents and potential belligerents.

The end of the Cold War, while accompanied by numerous arms reduction agreements, still leaves the United States and Russia as such world-class military giants. Even after their mutual arms reduction agreements are implemented, each will retain enough weapons in its nuclear arsenal to virtually blow up the world.[1] The United States ranks way ahead of Russia in overall military power, however, because of the diversity, technological sophistication, and global mobility of the US general purpose forces and because Russia, preoccupied with internal and nearby security crises, is much less likely than the United States to make its forces available for world security missions—and the rest of the world knows this.

A second tier includes the other countries with strategic nuclear arsenals: China and the two European nuclear powers, France and Britain.

A third tier contains the two former world-class military powers, Japan and Germany, each of which has the potential (if it politically so decides) to rapidly raise itself into the second tier.

---

[1]Under the Strategic Arms Reduction Treaty (START) and follow-on obligations signed by Presidents Bush and Yeltsin in the early 1990s, each of the former rivals, at the end of the contemplated ten-year process of dismantling their strategic forces, would yet be able to launch roughly 3000 nuclear warheads more than halfway around the globe. *Each* of these 6000 nuclear warheads, on the average, contains a million tons of explosive power (which means that each warhead carries more than fifty times the destructive force of the bomb exploded on Hiroshima in 1945); Source: International Institute for Strategic Studies, *The Military Balance 1992–1993* (London: Brassey's, 1992). Under the START accords signed by Presidents Bush and Yeltsin in 1992, the United States would retain 3500 strategic warheads in the year 2003 and the Commonwealth of Independent States (the successor confederation to the USSR) would retain 2968. (The discrepancy reflects the fact that the Russian arsenal contains, on the average, warheads of greater megatonnage.)

Below these are the dozen or more countries with sophisticated and large enough military establishments to credibly defend themselves against opponents not among the nuclear Big Five. This category surely includes India and Israel, and arguably Nigeria, South Africa, Italy, Turkey, and Indonesia and North Korea, among others.

The following sketch of the military capabilities of particular countries in the top three tiers is not meant to be definitive, but only to provide points of reference for conjectures about the role of military power relative to other kinds of power in today's polyarchic world.

The United States as Post–Cold War "Superpower."   With Russia having sloughed off the Soviet Union's objective of being militarily capable of protecting and enlarging the global realm of Marxism–Leninism (including the support of "wars of national liberation" in the Third World), US officials have been unabashedly referring to the United States as the world's "only superpower." That status is self-evident and undisputable as long as power is defined solely in terms of the country's military forces relative to the military forces of other countries.

Russia's renunciation of rivalry with the United States allowed US national security and arms control planners to contemplate substantial reductions in the defense budget since the bulk of the US forces had been sized and designed to counter Soviet forces; but the defense budget adopted during the first year of the Clinton administration, while projecting a 35 percent drop in defense spending over the ensuing five years, was still premised on the need, after these reductions had been achieved, to spend some 13 percent of the federal budget (or over $250 billion each year) to provision the country's military requirements in the post–Cold War era.

The somewhat downsized military requirements, as defined by Secretary of Defense Les Aspin and approved by President Clinton, definitely bespoke of an intention to retain a global superpower role for the United States. The intelligence and military planning documents pointed to new and emergent security threats around the world that the United States could not ignore.

"The post cold-war world is decidedly not post nuclear," warned Secretary Aspin. In place of the rival strategic nuclear superpower, who had been a dependably cautious adversary, there were now three states plus Russia possessing nuclear weapons—none with particularly stable governments or totally reliable command and control systems. Southward, across the traditional "arc of crisis" of the Eurasian rimland, were three undeclared, but suspected, members of the nuclear club: Israel, India, and Pakistan. North Korea was threatening to withdraw from the nuclear nonproliferation treaty. Libya and other terrorist-supporting "rogue states," perhaps as many as twenty, were suspected of clandestine efforts to gain access to nuclear explosive devices. "In the past, we dealt with the nuclear threat from the Soviet Union through a combination of deterrence and arms control," observed the Secretary of Defense. "But the new possessors of nuclear weapons may not be deterrable." The nuclear threat is no longer the "single animal" it used to be. "It's a multi-headed monster."[2]

Nor was the US post–Cold War foreign policy establishment content to stand aloof from local wars that posed no clear and present danger to vital US interests. It was enough that such conflicts—and there appeared to be many in the offing—could escalate to the point where they could threaten general international peace and security. US general purpose forces generated by the Clinton administration accordingly called for capabilities hefty enough to fight a "regional conflict" of the size of the Persian Gulf War while participating in a conflict of comparable dimensions along with well-armed allies in another region—all of this simultaneously, of course, with being able to sustain air and naval dominance in and around North America, Central America and the Caribbean. The United States also intended to maintain military units capable of participation in international peacekeeping missions.[3]

Russia as Hobbled Military Giant.   The largest remnant of the dismembered USSR, Russia, having inherited the bulk of the Soviet Union's nuclear arsenal, most of its navy, and virtually all of its air force, is second only to the United States in overall military capability. But it is a military capability hobbled by the country's need to devote its material resources and human energies to the enormous process of transformation from authoritarian communism to democratic capitalism. It has been hobbled not only by the scarcity of resources but also by the fragmentation of political authority in post-Soviet Russia, which frustrates the inclinations of some of the Russian military for adventures beyond the area that was formerly the USSR.

The military establishment's indispensable role as domestic political stabilizer (without the loyalty of the military, President Yeltsin would have been unable to put down the violent rebellion by his parliamentary opponents at the end of September 1993) gives the military leadership significant leverage with both the existing regime and those who would depose it. Paradoxically, this requires that the military attend more closely to domestic law and order problems than to the external security and balance of power situations that are the military's unique and preferred preoccupations. Yet, to the extent that domestic law and order for Russia is part and parcel of its *federal* problem—the fact that Russia itself is made up of territorial entities with majority populations ethnically distinct from the Russians, and that these ethnic republics are susceptible to the independence fever that brought about the secession of some of their neighbors from the former USSR—the reassertion by Moscow of its historical imperial imperatives in reaction to the country's domestic instabilities is quite plausible.

[2]Michael Wines, "Aspin Orders Pentagon Overhaul of Strategy on Nuclear Weapons," *New York Times*, October 30, 1993.
[3]Secretary of Defense Les Aspin, *The Bottom-Up Review: Forces For A New Era* (Washington, DC: Department of Defense, 1993).

Moscow's new imperial vocation, if it arises, would more closely resemble the imperialism of the Czars (expansionism to secure the ramparts of the empire) rather than the messianic global imperialism of the Communists. But that "defensive" expansionism, particularly as it is likely to be expressed in the reassertion of the need for a sphere of influence over the Eurasian, largely Islamic peoples on Russia's southwestern peripheries, who would be tempted to obtain support from the Islamic states of the Middle East, portends a continuing preoccupation by Russia's leaders with at least the distribution of military capabilities in and around Eurasia. Russia, as a minimum, will probably feel compelled to maintain credible military superiority over any combination of Muslim countries, some of whom may obtain nuclear arsenals. Nor is Moscow likely to discount the possibility that in some future conflict China would weigh in on the side of Russia's Islamic opponents. It is questionable, however, whether the military, weakened by major budgetary cuts and reductions in personnel, is up to the task of internally policing the still-sprawling country while continuing to secure its vast borders against hostile neighbors.[4]

Russian defense officials, in making public in November 1993 their nuclear doctrine that allows for a strategic first strike in certain circumstances, appeared to be putting the world on notice that, despite the country's new time of troubles and need to keep conventional forces available for internal public order tasks, Russia remained a great power that it would be disastrous for others to provoke.[5]

China as Emerging Military Great Power.   China's position as the country with the largest army in the world, the strongest Asian military power, and the only Third World country with a major nuclear weapons capability has become more than ever a crucial component of both the regional and global balances of military power. During the Cold War, when Asia was a primary theater of the US–Soviet geopolitical rivalry, China's principal neighbors, as well as the regime in Beijing, could be reasonably confident that any major territorial expansion by China would be countered by either the United States or the Soviet Union—by the United States because China's expansion would enlarge the sphere of communism; by the Soviets because China's expansion would both challenge Soviet hegemonic aims in Asia and the Kremlin's determination to remain the polar center of the Marxist world. In the post–Cold War era, that calculus of power has changed.

Now, unless there were a direct encroachment by China on Russian territory or US military or economic assets in the region, the likelihood that Moscow or Washington would deploy major military force to counter Bei-

---

[4]Serge Schmemann, "Russia's Military: A Shriveled and Volatile Legacy," *New York Times*, November 28, 1993.
[5]Fred Kaplan, "Moscow Cites Right of Nuclear First Use," *Boston Globe*, November 4, 1993.

jing's power plays is not very high. Indeed, if the People's Republic of China becomes embroiled in military confrontations with her neighbors in some of their long-standing disputes (say, over control of the Spratly and Paracel archipelagos in the oil-rich areas of the South China Sea or over the demarcation of the Sino-Indian border), the inclination of the United States, Russia, and the European powers may well be to look the other way. Japan, facing the prospect of a long-term rivalry with China for Asian hegemony, might not want to stand idly by, but if Tokyo chose to oppose Beijing directly in such conflicts, she might not be able to count on Washington's backing.

These new geopolitical realities in Asia are underscored by the continuing buildup of China's military capabilities—aided by the competition among Russia, the United States, and other arms producers to sell their wares in the lucrative Chinese market. While the numerical strength of the People's Liberation Army declined in the 1980s from approximately 4 million troops to 3 million in the early 1990s, China has been modernizing its military capability, emphasizing, in addition to nuclear weapons, force projection capabilities based on ballistic missiles, long-range aircraft, and a "blue water" (deep ocean as distinct from only coastal) navy. Significantly, for its ability to function as a great power, China's military buildup is based more and more on an expansion of domestic production facilities rather than imports of complete weapons systems, with its imports concentrated on technologies that will contribute to its enhancement of indigenous military high-tech industry and weapons research and development.[6]

France and Britain. With the Cold War superpowers effectuating a mutual military disengagement from continental Europe, the military weight of France and Britain in at least the European balance of power, if not the global balance, would appear to have increased. A key indicator of how important a geopolitical role either intends to play in the post–Cold War era will be the emphasis it gives to modernizing its strategic nuclear arsenal. In the early 1990s, both countries appeared to be committed to going forward with quantitative and qualitative enhancements of their submarine-carried nuclear missiles and air-to-surface missiles.[7] But in late 1993, London began to have serious second thoughts.

Having withdrawn from the NATO command in the 1950s and developed a flexible military establishment capable of functioning apart from the United States, France was more prepared than Britain or Germany to take up the slack in Europe occasioned by the reduction of US forces in the region. She appears determined to be the dominant military power on the continent while continuing to maintain a quick-reaction intervention capability for responding to crises in her former African colonies.

[6]Michael T. Klare, "The Next Great Arms Race," *Foreign Affairs*, Vol. 72, No. 3 (Summer 1993) pp. 136–152.
[7]Yves Boyer, "French and British Nuclear Forces in an Era of Uncertainty," in Patrick J. Garrity and Steven A. Maaranen, eds., *Nuclear Weapons in the Changing World: Perspectives from Europe, Asia, and North America* (New York: Plenum Press, 1992), pp. 111–126.

Britain was more ambivalent. A strong peace movement saw the end of the Cold War as an opportunity for substantial military disarmament. Traditional power "realists," on the other hand, saw very different imperatives and opportunities in the retraction of Soviet and US spheres of influence: by maintaining and modernizing its strategic nuclear arsenal and force projection capabilities, Britain could once again protect its global commercial interests and access to energy supplies; it could also be in a position to reassert its historic role of holder of the balance against any attempt by France or Germany, or a revived Russia, to become the Eurasian military hegemon. The dominant view in the policy establishment was that at the least Britain should retain sufficient military power to hold its own vis-à-vis France and Germany in bargaining in the European Community on security issues. But in 1993, financial considerations and the need to devote considerable resources to "peacekeeping" in Northern Ireland were constricting these options, with the result that the government in November announced a scaling back of previous plans for a new generation of submarine-carried nuclear missiles.[8]

Germany.   Potentially the strongest European military power, Germany for the time being is constitutionally prohibited from possessing nuclear weapons and from deploying her forces out of the continental theater. But Germany does maintain a hefty conventional combat capability—the legacy of her position as the most exposed and front-line NATO member—including the largest number of troops of any of the European countries, as well as the most tanks and combat aircraft. In the post–Cold War period, with the demise of external threats to her security, Germany may not want to maintain such a large military establishment. But because Germany does not want to grant France the status of continental hegemon, Chancellor Kohl felt compelled to agree in 1992 to President Mitterrand's proposal of a Franco-German Corps. The French envision this "Eurocorps" as the embryo of an all-European security system that would obviate the need for the Germans to obtain their own nuclear arsenal and that, with a reduced US presence, Paris would lead; the Germans, on the other hand, hope through the Eurocorps or similar mechanisms to limit French unilateralism as an increasingly undisciplined NATO becomes less capable of providing an integrating function.

Japan.   Japan clearly has the material and technological resources to catapult, once again, into the category of great military powers. It would take an amendment of the demilitarization provisions of the Japanese constitution—particularly Article 9, by which "the Japanese people forever renounce war as a sovereign right of the nation and the threat or use of force as a means of settling international disputes" and promise "never" to possess "land, sea or

[8]"Britain Scaling Back Nuclear Missile Plans," *New York Times* (special unsigned report), November 16, 1993.

air forces, as well as other war potential." But after nearly a half century of military abstinence, the question of whether these constitutional proscriptions should be repealed has become a matter of intense debate in Japan.

Actually, under the label of "self-defense forces," Japan already maintains one of the largest and best equipped military establishments in Asia. But in accord with the constitution, it has denied itself any "power projection" capabilities such as long-range bombers or missiles, aircraft carriers, and other weapon systems required for combat distant from the homeland.

One of the considerations that could drive the Japanese to cross the threshold into full-blown military status is the need—as security guarantees from the United States lose credibility—to protect their oil tankers all along the routes to and from their Persian Gulf suppliers. Another stimulus to eventual rearmament, including nuclear weapons, could be the steady buildup of China into a front-ranking superpower. Nor could Japan ignore the attainment by North Korea of a nuclear weapons capability. Renewed tensions with Russia over the return of the northern islands or over navigational, fishing, environmental, and other jurisdictional claims in the seas between them would also add to the incentives for Japan to become a military power in its own right.

Moreover, fifty years of nonmilitary penance by Japan for her World War II aggressions appears to be just about all that her former adversaries feel she should have been held to. Especially from the United States, the Japanese have been hearing increasing hints, if not outright appeals, that Japan (in anticipation of being given a permanent seat on the United Nations Security Council) should assume a greater military role both for her own security and in collective security and international peacekeeping missions. Indeed, the Japanese policy elite have been stung by the international talk that they hope simply by a continuation of their "checkbook diplomacy" to buy themselves out of the burdens of full great power responsibility (as they did during the Gulf War).[9] It was largely to counter such embarrassing allegations that the Japanese government was able to get the Diet to pass a law in 1992 allowing the Self Defense Forces (SDF) to take a limited part in UN peacekeeping operations.

The new Japanese law on international peacekeeping, under which some 600 SDF engineers and construction troops were contributed in 1962 and 1963 to the UN peacekeeping operation in Cambodia, contains the following restrictions: No more than 2000 SDF troops can be deployed in UN operations at any time; they are prohibited from participating in "military activities" and must be confined to such missions as medical and refugee aid, transportation, infrastructure repair, election monitoring, and policing operations. They may carry light firearms that can be used only in self-defense. If any dispatch of SDF troops to perform functions permitted in the law even

[9]Colin Nickerson, "Japan Ponders a Larger Role in World Arena," *Boston Globe*, February 1, 1993.

risks involving them in actual military missions, the government must obtain specific authorization from the Diet before assigning them to such an operation.[10] Accordingly, an SDF peacekeeping contingent for Cambodia was acceptable, but not one for Somalia or the Balkans.

Economic Power: Importance and Distribution

Economic power has also always been one of the requisites of great power status for two elementary reasons: (1) A country's military power is crucially dependent on its ability to marshall the material and human resources required to sustain a large and technologically up-to-date defense establishment. (2) A country or corporate entity can exert influence in world society by virtue of its being a source of material goods and human services (including the provision of financial capital) that others want or being a lucrative market for what others have to sell.

Query: Can an actor wield great power in the contemporary world largely on the basis of its economic strength? Some analysts, Kenneth Waltz, for example, hold that "no state lacking in military ability to compete with other great powers has ever been ranked among them" and see nothing in the post–Cold War system that is likely to change this relationship.[11] Others, among them Richard Rosecrance, citing especially the influence Japan has achieved, and John Mueller, on the premise that war among the major industrialized countries has become obsolete, see economic power supplanting military power as the principal determinant of who gets what, when, and how in the contemporary world polity.[12] The reality, I contend, lies somewhere between these extremes.

Unlike the nineteenth century, when Britain was clearly the dominant country in economic power, or the four decades following World War II, in which the United States was supreme, the latter 1990s and the beginning of the twenty-first century, in the eyes of most economists, will feature a three-way race for ascendancy between the United States, Japan, and the European Community. Who will ultimately "win" this race is less important than is the prospect that the ongoing competition for dominance in the world's markets will profoundly affect the daily lives of people all around the globe—sometimes positively, sometimes negatively. Some sectors of the economy and some localities will be winners in terms of the goods and services enjoyed and the overall quality of life; others will be losers, both relatively and absolutely.

---

[10]International Institute for Strategic Studies, *Strategic Survey 1992–1993* (London: Brassey's, 1993), pp. 139–140.

[11]Kenneth N. Waltz, "The Emerging Structure of International Politics," *International Security*, Vol. 18, No. 2 (Fall 1993), p. 54.

[12]Richard Rosecrance, *The Rise of the Trading State: Conquest and Commerce in the Modern World* (New York: Basic Books, 1986); and John E. Mueller, *Retreat from Doomsday: The Obsolescence of Major War* (New York: Basic Books, 1989).

The Preeminence of the United States in the Global Economy.   In the first half of the 1990s, despite the relative gains of the other industrialized giants (Japan and the European Union) and weakness in various aspects of its productive base that portended an era of "decline," the United States, with a gross domestic product (GDP) of more than $5.5 trillion a year, still accounted for about 25 percent of the world's total production of goods and services.[13] Despite the relative gains by her principal competitors, the United States remains the greatest source of finance capital for other countries and continues to hold more voting power than any other country in the world's key financial institutions, the International Monetary Fund and the World Bank.

It is precisely because of the persisting dependence of the rest of the world on the health of the US economy—"when the United States sneezes the rest of the world catches cold"—that the country's huge trade deficits (averaging about $100 billion annually in the early 1990s) and its transformation from the world's largest creditor to the largest debtor have not been accompanied by victory dances by the Japanese and the Europeans, let alone by the peoples of the former Soviet Union and most Third World nations. The world's economic movers and shakers and professional economists fear that if the United States, in a period of severe recession and fearing an impending depression, were to severely reduce its purchases from other countries (normally about 14 percent of the world's exports) because it was unable to pay for them out of its own export earnings and if it were unable to pay its international creditors because of its own bankrupt finances, the whole world might be catalyzed into an economic depression. Indeed, this scary prospect has been invoked by US officials—implicitly, and at times explicitly—in international economic negotiations to pressure their counterparts not only to reduce their trade barriers but also to "heat up" their economies, by reducing interest rates and the like, so that the United States can get its own international trade and other international accounts back into balance.

Japan.   In some respects Japan was even more powerful economically than the United States in the early 1990s. Its $3.4 trillion GDP was still 60 percent of that of the United States; but on a per capita basis, it was producing more than 20 percent above the United States. Japan was the world's largest net creditor and was consistently earning the world's largest trade surplus year after year. Economist Lester Thurow summarizes the indicators of the country's dramatic economic growth:

> Where none of the fifteen largest banks in the world in 1970 were Japanese, ten of the largest fifteen banks in the world in 1990 were Japanese, and the top six were all Japanese. Japan had 5 percent of the American auto market in 1970; in

[13]World Bank, *World Development Report 1993* (New York: Oxford University Press, 1993), p. 243.

1990 it had 28 percent. In just twenty years' time, it completely wiped out the American consumer electronics industry. . . . In the last 15 years, after correcting for inflation, its growth rate was 75 percent greater than that of the United States and twice that of the European community.[14]

But Thurow is among those economists who foresee Japan's lead in economic growth—which has been largely export-led, rather than based mainly on the cultivation of her own domestic market—giving ground to the United States and Europe in the twenty-first century as North American and European trading areas are developed to counter Japanese exporting dominance.

In the intensifying competition for spheres of economic hegemony, Japan's efforts to balance the new economic regionalism in America and Europe by focusing on the countries of the Pacific Rim are not particularly welcomed by her Asian neighbors, still resentful of Tokyo's arrogant attempt to impose a Japanese-run "co-prosperity sphere" on the region in the 1930s and 1940s. Moreover, even on grounds of current economic self-interest, as pointed out by Thurow, "Korea and the Chinese based economies (mainland China, Taiwan, Hong Kong, and Singapore) may prefer to have special arrangements with their best market—the United States—rather than their chief rival—Japan."[15]

Europe as an Integrated Economy.   If the countries of the European Union, expanded to include the Scandinavians, Austrians, and former members of the Soviet camp, were to operate as an integrated economic group, this greater Europe (with a population of about 850 million) could well be the most economically powerful entity in world society. In the first half of the 1990s, the combined annual GDP of the West Europeans alone (including Britain and the Scandinavians, but omitting the former Communist countries) averaged nearly $7 trillion (more than 15 percent greater than that of the United States and almost twice as large as that of Japan). This was yet in the absence of full economic integration and the dynamic synergies such integration could produce.

There is, of course, considerable uncertainty and debate among economists over the effects on Europe's productivity—at least over the short term—of an attempt to comprehensively integrate greater Europe's very diverse economies. Pessimists contemplate that the economically and politically less developed regions (particularly in the former Sovietized states) will pull the others down, especially if expensive "social justice" policies are instituted for the community as a whole to subsidize the development of the backward areas. Optimists emphasize the positive: the ex-Communist areas

---

[14]Lester Thurow, *Head to Head: The Coming Economic Battle Among Japan, Europe, and America* (New York: Warner Books, 1993), p. 247.
[15]*Ibid.*, pp. 250–251.

have highly educated populations, especially in science and technology. As Thurow puts it,

> If the high science of the former Soviet Union and the production technologies of the German-speaking world are added to the design flair of Italy and France and a world-class London capital market efficiently directing funds to Europe's most productive areas, something unmatchable will have been created. The House of Europe could become a relatively self-contained, rapidly growing region that could sprint away from the rest of the pack.[16]

China: Twenty-First Century Economic Superpower?   The most dramatic growth in the size and global impact of a country's economy in the post–Cold War period has been experienced by China—prompting some experts to speculate that sometime during the first half of the next century China, with one-quarter of the world's people, may well supplant the United States, Japan, and Europe as the number-one economy in the world. These prognoses are based on trends established in the period 1988 to 1993 in China's GDP, market size, and international trade. According to World Bank estimates, if the economic performance of Hong Kong and Taiwan are added to that of the People's Republic (the assumption that such an integrated political economy will materialize before the end of the 1990s is quite plausible), the GDP of this "Greater China" could surpass that of the United States as early as the year 2002—despite China's low per capita income—and its annual imports would exceed Japan's by some $100 billion.[17]

India—Another Potential Heavyweight.   Second only to China in population, and perhaps pulling even by the year 2025 (some demographers predict an Indian population of 1.5 billion), India, with a GDP lower than Mexico's in the early 1990s, nevertheless has the potential of entering the ranks of the world's great economic powers before the middle of the twenty-first century. Her assets in this effort include well-educated professional classes and industrial and financial sectors whose technologists, scientists, and managers are comfortable participants in the capitalist global marketplace. Her principal liabilities are the country's soaring population growth, portending continuing low per capita income; and bitter political conflict within and between the Indian states among geographically concentrated ethnolinguistic and religious communities.[18] However, India's post-Gandhian elites, irreversibly modernists and cosmopolitans, are no less determined than their Chinese counterparts to be among the ranks of the great powers even if this means giving short shrift to distributive justice considerations along the way; nor do they appear inclined to allow overall economic

[16]*Ibid.*, p. 252.
[17]Nicolas D. Kristof, "The Rise of China," *Foreign Affairs*, Vol. 72, No. 5 (November/December 1993), pp. 59–74.
[18]Paul Kennedy, *Preparing for the Twenty-First Century* (New York: Random House, 1993), pp. 163–192.

growth to be slowed by environmental considerations. Yet even as a problem case—especially as industrialization on the population-glutted subcontinent portends massive consequences to the global environment—India can be expected to have substantial bargaining power vis-à-vis the more affluent industrialized countries, particularly when it comes to making it financially possible for India to adopt energy-efficient industrialization policies.

Light-Heavyweight Economies.   In some regions of the world, in addition to the great economic powers already discussed, there are one or two countries with sufficient economic weight to affect—positively or negatively—the overall prosperity of at least their region, if not also the world economy. Their cooperation, accordingly, is often required in trade, monetary, and investment consortia and in environmentally sustainable development programs. In North America, both Canada (with a GDP of over $500 billion in the early 1990s) and Mexico (with a GDP approaching $300 billion) are in this middle-ranking category, as is Brazil (GDP over $400 billion) in South America. The Asian countries in this category are Australia ($300 billion) and South Korea (over $280 billion).

Middleweights.   Finally, outside of the European group there are a number of countries in the GDP range of roughly $100 to $200 billion that, because of the specialized products and/or considerable purchasing power in the global market, are also treated with considerable respect by the economic movers and shakers. This category includes three large oil producers, Saudi Arabia, Iran, and Indonesia; mineral-rich South Africa; and Turkey, Argentina, Taiwan, and Thailand.

Internationally Powerful Nongovernmental Actors.   In the contemporary global economy, the power to generate and distribute wealth (itself a source of other forms of power) has been gravitating to various kinds of nongovernmental actors—most notably multinational corporations (MNCs), enterprise webs, and regional clusters of interdependent and coordinated economic activity—who have the capability to attract and make investments and to produce and deliver goods and services more efficiently than can be done by governments.

The typical globally active MNC comprises a family of firms directed by a home office located in one of the advanced industrial countries; its corporate subsidiaries are implanted around the world in countries where low "factor costs" (often resulting from low wage rates, relatively low corporate taxes, and a minimum of environmental regulation) are conducive to the least expensive production, thus allowing the MNC to market its goods and services globally at the most competitive prices. The largest MNCs each have a gross product larger than the GDP of many a middle-sized country. Thus, General Motors (with annual sales in the early 1990s exceeding $125 billion) outranks economically flourishing countries such as Taiwan, Switzerland,

and Austria; Royal Dutch Shell and Exxon (each with sales greater than $100 billion) outrank South Africa, Norway, Turkey, Argentina, and Thailand among others; General Electric and Hitachi (each with sales well over $50 billion a year) by this measure are more weighty economic actors than, for example, Pakistan, Israel, Malaysia, or Nigeria.[19]

Another breed of transnational conglomerates, primarily banks, investment houses, and money brokers, specialize in the management of capital—the life blood of every country's economy. The most effective entrepreneurs in this money arena often operate through multiple international partnerships and have financial ties to, and inside information on, all the world's major money markets. Such "enterprise webs" (Robert Reich's term) are thus strategically situated to obtain information early on changes in demand for products and services and contemplated shifts in national interest rates or currency values. This allows them to transfer huge financial investments in and out of countries to take advantage of demand shifts in anticipation of currency devaluation or upward revaluations by particular countries.[20] In the process, they can severely disrupt the economic stimulus or stabilization policies of the countries in which they operate. Japan is the host country for the headquarters of some of the largest of these enterprise webs, notably Dai-Ichi Kango Bank, Mitsui Taiyo Kobe Bank, Sumitomo Bank, and Mitsubishi Bank—each with assets approaching half a trillion dollars in value. The fourth-ranking financial giant is Germany's Deutsche Bank. Citicorp of New York ranks sixth, but probably is the leader when it comes to the scope of its global access and the range of financial services it can perform.[21]

A third type of powerful nongovernmental economic entity, overlapping and often in positive symbiosis with major MNCs and enterprise webs, consists of geographically concentrated clusters of economic activity, which may not fall within the borders of a particular country and in which the major sectors engage in a high degree of coordination to advance the prosperity of the region. The coordination may take place almost entirely through unofficial contacts and agreements among private firms, trade and labor associations, and the like, or it may also be strongly encouraged, even subsidized, by local or subnational governmental agencies and sometimes by transcountry commissions. Examples of such flourishing regional clusters are the San Diego and Tijuana corridor; the Hong Kong/South China complex (a highly interactive market connecting the free-enterprise haven of Hong Kong to Shenzhen, Zhuhai, Amoy, and Guangzhou); and the "growth

[19]The corporations' annual sales estimates are based on *Fortune* magazine's yearly listings. April 1993, the latest issue I consulted, showed General Motors' sales at $133 billion for the previous year and General Electric's at $62 billion.
[20]Robert B. Reich, *The Work of Nations: Preparing Ourselves for 21st-Century Capitalism* (New York: Knopf, 1991), pp. 87–135.
[21]Janet Lowe, *The Secret Empire: How 25 Multinationals Rule the World* (Homewood: Business One Irwin, 1993).

triangle" linking Singapore and some of the nearby islands of Indonesia.[22] These regions characteristically are not simply domestically oriented clusters of commercial interaction but are also important participants in international trade. Indeed, their economic intercourse is usually at least as much (if not more) with foreign buyers and sellers as with nationals of their host countries. And significantly, with respect to the emerging political economy of world society, they have begun to bargain as entities in global arenas.

Cartels.   The economy of the global polyarchy, which remains largely unregulated in comparison with domestic economic systems, provides a lot of room for collusion among particular industry groups across national lines to alter the market-determined supply and demand and price of the goods and services they produce, which may include dividing up the market among them. Sometimes the collusion is sponsored by governments and, in the case of state-run enterprises, actually conducted by governments. The objective of such collusionary cartels is to generate higher profits for their members than would occur simply on the basis of free market forces.

The most prominent of the producer cartels is the Organization of Petroleum Exporting Countries (OPEC). Through their membership in OPEC, twelve Third World countries whose economic condition is highly dependent on their earnings from international sales of petroleum products (Saudi Arabia, Iran, Iraq, Kuwait, the United Arab Emirates, Qatar, Libya, Indonesia, Venezuela, Ecuador, Nigeria, and Gabon) are committed to coordinate production quotas and minimum selling prices for their exportable oil. During the 1970s, when OPEC members produced about two-thirds of the world's exportable oil, their collusion on supply and price was a dominant force in the global economy. OPEC's ability to control supply and price declined in subsequent decades, however, largely as a result of the reactive increase in oil production by non-OPEC countries and deliberate cartel-breaking buyer stratagems by industrial-country importers. By the 1990s, OPEC controlled only about one-third of the world's petroleum export market and was losing the ability to prevent unilateral marketing policies by its members. (Iraq's invasion of Kuwait was motivated in part by Saddam Hussein's determination to punish Kuwait for depressing the market price of oil by violating OPEC's agreed production quotas.)

The cartelization efforts of other basic commodity producers in the Third World—for example, the exporters of cocoa, sugar, and cotton—have not been as successful as that of OPEC. Operating with a wider and less geographically concentrated number of suppliers and with commodities for which industrial countries have been able to develop synthetic substitutes, such commodity producer groups have lacked the requisites for maintain-

---

[22]Kenichi Ohmae, "The Rise of the Region State," *Foreign Affairs*, Vol. 72, No. 2 (Spring 1993), pp. 78–87.

ing discipline among their members in their sales and bargaining over terms of trade with consumer countries.

Transnational Industry Group Regimes.   In various fields where operating effectiveness requires a high degree of coordination among the multiple users of a common resource—such as the ocean, airspace, and the broadcasting frequency spectrum—it is characteristically industry leaders from the affluent and technologically advanced countries that set the rules and determine the allocations when there are scarcities. This is the situation in the International Maritime Organization, which is dominated by the large oceanic shipping lines, particularly as it promulgates navigational rules of the road (navigation lanes, traffic separation schemes, improvements in ship-to-ship communication, and internationally standardized licensing and training requirements for ships' officers). Similarly, the International Civil Aviation Organization, which is responsible for formulating standards for the safe use of the air corridors (including aircraft design specifications and air-traffic control procedures and personnel requirements), is basically the creature of the giant airline companies it is expected to regulate. This relationship between regulators and regulated also prevails in the International Telecommunication Union, particularly as the geosynchronous orbit in outer space is becoming a congested medium for deploying the most advanced communications equipment.

Transnational Professional Associations.   More and more, specialized professional and occupational groups also are organized across country and ideological lines. Physical scientists, academics in various fields, health care specialists, and althletes all have relatively permanent worldwide professional associations to represent their interests. For some occupational groups, the interests are bread-and-butter issues, and their transnational associations are designed to operate politically on the organs of social and economic policy of the various countries. (This is particularly the case with some labor unions whose members' jobs are dependent upon the decisions of multinational corporations, and who are attempting to strengthen their own capacity to coordinate pressures and bargain globally for job security, higher pay, improved working conditions, and other amenities).

The involved individuals—be they top executives of corporate subsidiaries located abroad, international labor union organizers, officers of one of the international scientific associations, or managers of an international telecommunications consortium—are likely to feel cross-pressured by the competing lines of professional and national identification and accountability to which they are subject. But in their multiple loyalties, these increasingly influential men and women are quintessentially of the generation of the emerging polyarchy.

Ideational Power

The ability to influence others and to prevail in conflicts with opponents in the world polity, no less than in the domestic polity, is dependent in large part on the attractive power of the ideas that bind people to one another in communities and impel them to sacrifice personal possessions and security, even their lives, in the service of the commonweal. As shown in the previous chapters, the formation and disintegration of the world's empires, the establishment and demise of hegemonic spheres of influence, and the maintenance by ordinary countries of their independence and way of life are functions not simply of the distribution of military and economic power. The deep commitments of people to the well-being of their community—the only durable cement of nations and empires—cannot be coerced or purchased. Over the long haul, it is ideas that bind more than chains or bank accounts; and human attachments lacking affection and moral concern tend to be perpetually on the market to the next bidder.[23]

States as Nations.   Each of the some 185 political entities in the world that are generally recognized as sovereign countries considers itself to be more than just a state, but also a "nation," in the sense of being a distinct people united at least by a shared historical experience, a set of values, and a common language. To assure that all people of the realm, despite their differences, are loyal to the nation-state, each country keeps the symbols of nationhood prominent—its flag and emblems, its oaths and anthems, and celebrations of its proudest historical moments and heroes.

The equation of country and nation has been an essential requisite of state viability since the latter part of the eighteenth century, given the fact that with industrialization and its attendant specialization of production, the provision of essential public goods, especially defense, has depended upon the capacity of elites to mobilize cooperative efforts from all sectors of society. And in democracies, operating according to the principle of the consent of the governed, the idea of "the national interest" is frequently invoked to counter special-interest demands antithetical to national security or sound macroeconomic policies.

In the contemporary polyarchic world, with citizens of most countries more than ever before able to establish and reestablish connections with ethnic "brothers" and "sisters" and professional colleagues in other countries, such state nationalism, though on the defensive, is still very much alive; indeed, it is often whipped up by governing groups and turned against those with divided loyalties, with the implication that their lack of patriotic enthusiasm is subversive and immoral.

---

[23]I like Kenneth Boulding's emphasis in his *The Three Faces of Power* (Newbury Park: Sage, 1989), on "integrative power" as distinguished from "threat power" and "economic power." He concludes that "The stick, the carrot, and the hug may all be necessary, but the greatest of these is the hug." (p. 250).

Transnational Ideational Communities.   Who is on whose side issue by issue in the global polyarchy often will be strongly determined by broadly dispersed ideational communities that transcend state borders and that comprise portions of some of the more coherent and geographically concentrated communities we usually call nations. Some of these transnational ideational communities are made up of devotees of a particular religion. Others may be the adherents of a particular secular ideology. Still others may assert the affinity of all (or a particular grouping of) people with common racial characteristics or those with common native languages.

Such trans-state communities can be the source of alliances between particular states in which the majority of the population and/or the ruling groups are members of the community. But ideational ties among transstate communities can also function to subvert existing governments. Sometimes, as is the case of the Marxist-Leninists or the Islamic fundamentalists, they have served as a tool of a particular state or alliance against their international enemies. Often they operate as totally nongovernmental movements of groups asserting their "human rights" against established regimes. Indeed, the ease with which people geographically remote from one another can come into contact, coupled with the universalization of the notion that no ethnic group, religious community, economic class, gender, or even age-cohort group has presumptive superiority over any other group, has led to all manner of mutual-support movements formed transnationally among people with particular characteristics trying to bring pressure on their respective governments to improve their lot.

A sampling of prominent transnational communities is provided in the following sections.

Islam.   Approximately one-eighth of the world's population profess to follow the teachings of the seventh century prophet Muhammad as recorded in the *Koran.* Concentrated in the crescent-shaped region extending from Morocco on the West Coast of Africa across to the Middle East and Southwest Asia and down into South Asia and then Indonesia, but claiming adherents in virtually every country, the community of Islam is fractionated into numerous sects. The majority, the Sunni, control most of the Arab countries of the Middle East; the largest minority, the Shi'ah (or Shiites), claiming some 20 million adherents, are in control of Iran, and are actively attempting in many Muslim lands to establish fundamentalist Islamic theocracies on the model of Iran. Defense of the community of Islam has been a rallying cry of militant Palestinians (not all of whom really are religious) in their efforts to garner transnational support for their campaign to establish a sovereign state of Palestine in territory controlled by Israel.

The Arabs.   The special bond among those who call themselves Arabian is ethno-cultural. A Semitic people, whose native language is Arabic, they constitute the majority population in Algeria, Bahrain, Egypt, Iraq, Jordan, Kuwait, Lebanon, Libya, Morocco, Oman, Qatar, Saudi Arabia, Sudan,

Syria, Tunisia, the United Arab Emirates, and Yemen. Although the vast majority of Arabs are Islamic (secular Arab modernists usually come from families that have adhered to the Muslim faith), less than 40 percent of the world's Muslims are Arab. Even in the Middle East, two of the most powerful countries with predominantly Islamic populations, Iran and Turkey, are non-Arab. Yet the myth of a larger Arab nation has frequently been a galvanizing force for common action among the diverse states and peoples of the region. It has been in the name of the brotherhood of all Arabs that Palestinian self-determination has been such a prominent catalyst of wars and terrorist campaigns against Israel. The charismatic Egyptian leader Gamel Abdel Nasser used the concept of Pan-Arabism to forge a strong anti-Israel coalition in the 1950s and even to effectuate a federal merger with Syria—the short-lived United Arab Republic. Iraq's Saddam Hussein, invoking Pan-Arab symbols, has aspired to be the Nasser of the 1980s and 1990s; but he ruined his chances by his invasion of Kuwait (a fellow Arab state), which split the Arab world and induced Saudi Arabia, Egypt, and Syria to join the US-led coalition to reverse the Iraqi aggression. Still, even after his defeat in the Gulf War of 1991, among the Arab masses of the Middle East, particularly the alienated urban poor displaced from their traditional moorings, Saddam continues to be widely seen in the vein of previous Arab heroes such as Nasser and Saladin.

The Roman Catholics.   About 12 percent of the world's population identifies with this branch of Christianity, which is organized hierarchically in a world church under the Pope (the bishop of Rome). In some countries the Church performs social welfare functions for its members that are not adequately performed by secular authorities; sometimes it serves as a protector (or even source) of political movements regarded as subversive of the established political order (as, for example, in Poland during the Cold War or Northern Ireland). The Church, through statements by the Pope and councils of bishops, promulgates rules of moral behavior supposed to be binding on all Catholics no matter where in the world they reside, prudently allowing for national cultural variations. Thus, to the extent that moral and political matters overlap (as they frequently do in totalitarian societies and as they sometimes do even in highly pluralistic societies, as, for example, with respect to birth control policies or the use of nuclear weapons in war), the fact that loyal Catholics are officials or constituents of any of the active political groups surely can affect the way the world polyarchy functions.

Other Christians.   The other large and globally dispersed Christian denominations, claiming overall some 400 million members, are not as hierarchically organized as the Roman Catholics, and thus their role in the polyarchy is subject to more local variation. Often their diversity and decentralized organization does not allow them to mobilize sufficient constituency pressure to have a substantial effect on public policy within large political units, for it is difficult to formulate a common "Christian" position on most issues. In certain localities, however, non-Catholic Christians will constitute a relatively unified force against perceived efforts by Catholics to dominate public policy and elite social roles; and in other places they will unite with Catholics against perceived efforts of non-Christians to ignore Christian values or discriminate against professed Christians.

World Jewry.   About three-quarters of the 15 million people who consider themselves Jews live outside of the state of Israel (over 6 million in the United States). Not all Jews are formally affiliated with one or another of the established branches of the Jewish religion (Orthodox, Conservative, Reform, or Reconstructionist), but most—with the exception of a few African and Asian Jewish communities—trace their ancestry back to the monotheistic Hebrews, one of the Semitic peoples that lived in the region of ancient Palestine; and most of the diaspora Jews, even if they do not have blood relatives in Israel, consider themselves nevertheless to be close cultural cousins of the contemporary Israelis. A substantial subset of the diaspora Jews are Zionists, in the sense of being strong supporters of the state of Israel, and therefore somewhat ambivalent in support of policies of their country of citizenship in cases of clashing policies between their country and Israel.

Pan-Africanism and the Black Diaspora.   The sense among the world's "blacks" (those with Negroid physiological characteristics) that they are a transnational community has two major manifestations: Pan Africanism among the post-colonial nation-states on the African continent; and the political support by blacks outside of Africa for the causes of their "brothers" and "sisters" in other countries. Since the 1960s, and especially among the 22 million black Americans, the rediscovery by diaspora blacks (many of whom are descendants of slaves) of their African ancestral roots has been reflected in the prideful adoption of African hairstyles and dress, efforts to learn African languages, and pressures to include courses in African history and contemporary culture in the core curricula of schools and colleges.

The "Eastern" Religions.   The largest of the religions whose followers are concentrated mainly in Asia (the Hinduism of some 800 million South Asians, mostly in India; the various forms of Buddhism practiced by nearly 300 million people distributed throughout the huge triangular area from Thailand to Japan to Indonesia; the more than 200 million Chinese some of them yet in the People's Republic, who adhere to Confucianism or Taoism; and the 60 million or so Japanese believers in Shinto) do affect the domestic social mores and legal systems of many of the countries of the region. But the co-religionists of these Eastern religions rarely act as a transnational political force, with a common set of demands on their respective national governments; nor, as much as do the Christians, Muslims, and Jews, do they cooperate in any substantial way across national boundaries to protect each other against hostile regimes.

Feminism. There is now a proliferation of transnational organizations among women who believe that the political regimes they live under have denied them the rights and power that men enjoy. Feminism covers a wide spectrum of beliefs and political aims, ranging from efforts to eliminate discrimination against women to militant movements to tear down male-dominated institutions. Some feminists want the traditional "male" roles of society, particularly the top positions in the government, military, and diplomatic services, to be as open to women as they have been to men; their heroines include not only Hillary Rodham Clinton and Norwegian Prime Minister Gro Harlem Brundtland, but also Margaret Thatcher, Indira Gandhi, and Golda Meir (all tough-minded, even militaristic, nationalists). Other feminists are convinced that the nation-state system and its principal bargaining instruments—coercive diplomacy and war—are quintessentially male and part and parcel of male dominance over females: Patriotism and patriarchy are seen to be mutually reinforcing; according to such radical feminists, liberation requires that both of these institutions be eliminated.

Gay and Lesbian Liberation. Since the late 1970s, homosexuals have become a visible political lobby in many national parliaments as well as in international governmental and nongovernmental organizations, sponsoring legislation and human rights convenants against discriminatory treatment of lesbians and gays around the world. Their transnational coalition-building has been facilitated by the International Lesbian and Gay Association (ILGA), founded in 1978. The ILGA claims responsibility for the World Health Organization's decision to eliminate homosexuality from the official international list of diseases, for Amnesty International's increased attention to the infringement of human rights on grounds of sexual preferences, and for getting various countries to decriminalize homosexuality. It is also one of the most active organizations internationally and domestically on behalf of the victims of AIDS.[24]

Again, this is only an illustrative sample of the proliferating transnational communities and identity groups. Among the others that could be included are the Hispanics, the environmentalists, human rights activists, peace activits, and so on.

Nations Without States. The idea that nations should have states of their own, the rallying cry of the American War for Independence against Britain and since then exploited by democrats and tyrants alike, has dramatically altered the world's political map twice since World War II: In the anticolonial revolutions of the 1950s and 1960s, it tripled the number of recognized coun-

---

[24]*See* Sylvia Borren's article on "Gay and Lesbian Politics," in Joel Krieger, ed., *The Oxford Companion to the Politics of the World* (New York: Oxford University Press, 1993), pp. 333–335.

tries from some 50 to more than 150. And in the early 1990s, it was the rationale for the breakup of the Soviet Union into fifteen separate sovereign republics. Neither of these epidemics of national self-determination has yet fully played itself out. The boundaries of most of the new states of the former colonial world still follow the lines of demarcation laid down by the European imperial powers, which cut across indigenous tribal and ethnocultural communities; many of these communities are today asserting that *they* should have states of their own. Similarly, the majority of the former Soviet republics are multinational countries containing ethnic minority populations resentful of some of the new "democratic" impositions (denigrating to the languages and cultures of the minorities) laid on them by the ethnic majorities.

Although all countries attempt to ensure that the peoples within their jurisdictions maintain a sense of belonging to one overarching nation, only a small proportion of the world's nations possess their own legally sovereign political jurisdiction. If a nation is defined as a population with a "distinctive and enduring collective identity based on cultural traits and lifeways that matter to them and to others with whom they interact,"[25] then by some counts the world contains anywhere from 3000 to 5000 nations. Yet there are less than 200 nation-states. Not all the nations without states are dissatisfied with being *sub*nations of the larger nation-states in which they reside. Those nations that are dissatisfied, in the sense of considering themselves systematically discriminated against by the nationality groups in control of their countries, and that have been expressing this dissatisfaction prominently in the form of political movements to rectify their disadvantages, number about 230 according to the Minorities at Risk Project sponsored by the United States Institute of Peace.[26] The Minorities at Risk Project further estimates that in 1990 members of these politicized subnations constituted over 17 percent of the world's population and that nearly three-quarters of the 127 largest countries contained at least one such disaffected community.[27] As many as forty of these politicized subnational communities have at one time or another over the past few decades asserted—sometimes violently—a right to secede from the nation-state of which they are a part.[28]

For the purposes of this chapter's overview of the global polyarchy, we need do no more here than mention examples of the most active political movements of this sort. The list includes the nations of the former Yugoslavia, who are still bloodying one another in Bosnia as this is being writ-

[25]Tedd Robert Gurr, *Minorities at Risk: A Global View of Ethnopolitical Conflicts* (Washington, DC: United States Institute of Peace Press, 1993), p. 3. The quoted definition is for what the Minorities at Risk Project calls "communal groups," but the project's concept of a communal group is a specialized term for what is commonly referred to as a nationality group.
[26]*Ibid.*, pp. 5–6.
[27]*Ibid.*, p. 10.
[28]For an analysis of the conditions under which ethno-tional conflicts are likely to explode into civil war, *see* Chapter 2 ("Why Communities Fight: Understanding Collective Violence") in Seyom Brown, *The Causes and Prevention of War* (New York: St. Martin's Press, 1994).

ten; the Palestinians living in the West Bank and the Gaza Strip; the Catholic vs. Protestant conflict in Northern Ireland; the Armenians in Azerbaijan; the Kurds of Iraq, Iran, and Turkey; the Muslims of Kashmir; the Hindu Tamils in Sri Lanka; the Tibetans vis-à-vis China; the Basques and Catalonians in Spain; and the Quebecois in Canada. These self-determination movements along with others will be discussed in more detail as a part of the analysis of human rights in Chapter 12.

ALTERNATIVE VISIONS
OF THE GLOBAL POLYARCHY

Most statespersons and analysts of the post–Cold War era understand that the world polity has become a polyarchy (as I have defined it here) even though they may not use the term.[29] For the time being, at least, the world lacks a dominant axis of political alignment and antagonism; coalition partners in one arena of policy may be opponents in another arena; geostrategic, commercial, and ideological considerations often function at cross-purposes; and power rankings vary from arena to arena; in some sectors of public policy, transnational nongovernmental organizations carry more weight than the national governments of many of the countries in which they operate.

Reflecting the diffusion of military and economic power, the shifting coalitions, and the variety of arenas in which bargaining is taking place, the emergent global polyarchy conceivably could assume one or another (or some hybrid) of the following configurations:

Residual Unipolarity

The configuration of global polyarchy most popular in the US foreign policy establishment, official and unofficial, is a residual of Cold War bipolarity, when the United States and the Soviet Union were military superpowers without peer (either, if it chose to, could convert its awesome destructive power into a trump card in its bargaining on a wide range of issues with any of the other countries) and the United States was undisputably Number One in the world economy. Thus, by default, the disintegration of the Soviet

[29]An influential book published in 1990, Joseph Nye's *Bound to Lead: The Changing Nature of American Power*, included my concept of polyarchy as one of four "visions" of the future—each of which Dr. Nye found inadequate. He was using these four visions as analytical foils against which he posed his own vision of United States leadership in a world of "complex interdependence." Nye's rendering of polyarchy, however, was considerably oversimplified from my formulation of the concept in the 1988 edition of *New Forces, Old Forces, and the Future of World Politics*; indeed, Nye's preferred vision, which subsumed the essential features of polyarchy, was fully consistent with the fuller version I had developed. I am now in a position to return the compliment by incorporating Nye's vision into my updated elaboration of polyarchy.

Union, and the constriction of Russia's geostrategic objectives to, at most, the maintenance of a sphere of influence congruent with the territorial ramparts of the former USSR, would seem to have left the United States as the world's "only remaining superpower"—President Bush's favorite formulation. Yet, increasingly since 1990, the US government has been compelled to accommodate to resistance by other governments—notably America's erstwhile allies in Western Europe and Japan—to any presumption by Washington that it has a continuing "right to lead" them, even on matters of international peace and security, let alone economics or human rights.

If there was a "unipolar moment" for the United States, it probably came (and went) with the Gulf War of 1990–1991, when President Bush, not needing to worry about Soviet counterintervention, was able to galvanize a broad coalition to assist the US military in humiliating a Middle Eastern bully who had perpetrated an act of blatant aggression against a defenseless state. But in subsequent international crises the fact of being both *the* world's military superpower and still outranking all other countries in GDP no longer gave the United States the degree of polar magnetism it possessed in the Gulf War.

In the Balkans from 1992 to 1994, members of the European Community, Japan, and Russia each had their own definitions of the interests that were at stake; and they were unwilling to defer to US leadership in either defining the common interest or concerting a multilateral response. Indeed, the United States on the one hand and the NATO core of the European Union (Britain, France, and Germany) on the other hand publicly accused each other of hypocrisy, if not cowardice, in their policies toward the civil war in Bosnia.

Additionally, there have been numerous open disagreements since the end of the Cold War between the United States and its industrial country partners, who previously were reluctant to display their major differences with Washington in front of the rest of the world. The post–Cold War rifts have been not only over trade, monetary, and global environmental issues, but also over the extent and kinds of assistance to provide Russian President Boris Yeltsin in his political and economic reforms; over the post–Cold War role and membership of NATO; over the appropriateness of denying normal commercial intercourse to China because of Beijing's human rights record and its lax arms sales and nuclear proliferation policies; and over the way to conduct "humanitarian" and "peacekeeping" interventions in Somalia and other such Third World trouble spots, especially the issue of the degree of control to be exercised by the United Nations. The United States as often as not fails to get its way in these disputes.

A revealing indicator of the degree of residual superpower influence the United States retains has been its circumscribed role in the Arab–Israeli peace process since the end of the Cold War. The "breakthrough event"— the September 1993 agreement of the Israeli government and the Palestine Liberation Organization (PLO) to negotiate with one another to effectuate a graduated transfer of power to the Palestinians in the West Bank and Gaza—took the Clinton administration unawares. The honest broker for this momentous diplomatic demarche was neither the United States nor Russia (the cosponsors of the post-Gulf War peace negotiations between the Israelis and moderate Palestinians), but Norway, in the person of Foreign Minister Johan Holst. President Clinton officiated at the White House ceremony for the formal signing by the Israeli and PLO leadership of their Declaration of Principles for handling the peace process; and continuing US support, especially in the form of financial incentives to draw other governments and the peoples of the region into cooperative webs of positive interdependence, would be crucial. Clearly, however, the role of the US government was more that of an after-the-fact facilitator rather than superpower impresario.[30]

The "West and the Rest"

A new (and in some respects ancient) variant of the "North-South" polarization of world society, which during the Cold War cut across "East–West" bipolarity, is the view that the industrialized West, having essentially won the global contest between market vs. nonmarket approaches to economic development, now faces a more profound *cultural* clash with some of the major civilizations of the Third World. This "clash-of-civilizations" school has representatives on both sides of the North–South divide.

The View from the Third World.   Many Third World ideologues see the persisting rich–poor gap between the industrialized and developing countries as the product of both Northern racism and continuing postcolonial economic exploitation. The Third World ideologues do, after all, have some historical justification for their views. Located mainly in the southern two-thirds of the globe, most of the Third World countries have indigenous cultures and languages that differ markedly from the European cultures and languages. The exceptions among the "southern" countries are Australia and New Zealand, whose indigenous populations were smaller than the European, mostly English, settler populations who took them over and stayed to make these lands, in effect, European countries.

Skeptics as to whether there really is a Third World can point to problems both in the logic of its definition and in evidence of a lack of consistent community cohesiveness: Either in concept or in practice, does it extend to the countries of North Africa? If so, then why not to the peoples on the northern littoral of the Mediterranean Sea who are racially very similar to the North Africans? Is Turkey in but Greece out? Does it include all of the Muslim countries of the Middle East, including the wealthy oil producers? Is China a

[30]*See* Seyom Brown, *The Faces of Power: Constancy and Change in United States Foreign Policy from Truman to Clinton* (New York: Columbia University Press, 1994), pp. 598–599.

Third World country? What about Japan? Are all blacks and Hispanics living in the United States a part of the Third World? What about the indigenous American "Indians"? What about the Asiatic and Muslim people living in the Soviet Union?

Granting such inconsistencies, most of the "southern" populations can claim to have suffered the similar historical experience of being forcibly incorporated into the empires of one or another of the major European powers between the fifteenth century and the early twentieth century—sometimes changing hands between different European overlords—and then having been kept in this colonial condition until they revolted against their imperial overlords in the post–World War II period. Exceptions are most of the countries of Central and South America, who became independent of Spain and Portugal earlier, during the 1820s. There were significant variations in this colonial experience, to be sure; but a common and deep-searing memory is that of having their indigenous cultures and religions treated as of little value, and often with disrespect, by their imperial European overlords.

The physiological distinctiveness (principally skin color) between the Southerners and their colonizers, as well as the fact that the Europeans disparaged the darker skins of the subjugated populations, not infrequently regarding them as inferior races, continues to provide the strongest bond among Third World nations who in other respects—religion, culture, contemporary ideological affinities—may be far apart or even antagonists.

These various experiences of Third World peoples that give them a sense of camaraderie against the rest of the world are reinforced by today's global North–South/rich–poor coalitions in international forums. The Southern coalition is often referred to as the "Group of 77" for the number of Third World countries that successfully lobbied in the 1960s for the creation of the United Nations Conference on Trade and Development (UNCTAD). Now numbering over 100 countries, this coalition is, to be sure, highly cross-pressured by conflicts of economic interests between those who produce certain commodities (particularly oil) and those who must import these commodities, between coastal states and landlocked states, and between those who have special associations with particular affluent countries (like the former British and French colonies) and those who do not. Yet the "Group of 77" periodically overcomes its internal differences to bargain on behalf of positions very important to some of its subgroups, particularly in universal-membership international bodies where one-county/one-vote procedures allow it to pass the resolutions it wants. Often the cement of the coalition when it holds together in a vote to support a particular resolution is not a rational calculation by each country of costs and benefits to tangible national interests, but rather the subjective bond of solidarity borne of common anger at having been tread upon for centuries by the arrogant Westerners.

The View from the "First World."   A mirror image of the romantic self-concept advanced by some Third Worlders appears in the widely discussed essay by influential political scientist Samuel P. Huntington, published in the Summer 1993 issue of *Foreign Affairs.* Contending that in the Post–Cold War era a "conflict between civilizations" has begun to supplant geopolitical, economic, and other forms of ideological conflict, Huntington forecasts that

> international relations . . . will increasingly be de-Westernized and become a game in which non-Western civilizations are actors and not simply objects; successful political, security, and economic international institutions are more likely to develop within civilizations than across civilizations; conflicts between groups in different civilizations will be more frequent, more sustained and more violent than conflicts between groups in the same civilization; violent conflicts between groups in different civilizations are the most likely and most dangerous source of escalation that could lead to global wars; the paramount axis of world politics will be the relations between "the West and the Rest"; the elites in some torn non-Western countries will try to make their countries part of the West, but in most cases face major obstacles to accomplishing this; a central focus of conflict for the immediate future will be between the West and several Islamic-Confucian states.[31]

Fellow political scientists from around the world have been exercised to challenge Professor Huntington's prognosis, and some incisive rejoinders have been published by *Foreign Affairs.* He has been most strongly taken to task for exaggerating the attractive force of Islamic fundamentalism for the peoples of the non-Western world, for grouping the very diverse cultural traditions of East Asia under the rubric of Confucianism, and for underestimating the pervasive impacts on Third World cultures of Western ways of industrialization, organizing markets, political institution-building, and thinking.[32]

Huntington has attempted to rebut these criticisms by arguing that he was not trying to account for everything of significance going on in world society, but rather to lay out "the elements of a post–Cold War paradigm" that comprehends many of the most important patterns of amity and enmity now emerging across the globe. He was primarily trying to offer an alternative to the naive view that the defeat of Soviet imperialism and the end of the Cold War meant the triumph of Western civilization based on the US model of market economics, pluralistic democracy, and individual rights. In the nineteenth and twentieth centuries Western culture was disseminated throughout the world by European colonialism and, particularly after World War II, by US hegemony. But, as Huntington puts it,

[31]Samuel P. Huntington, "The Clash of Civilizations?" *Foreign Affairs,* Vol. 72, No. 3 (Summer 1993), pp. 22–49; quote from p. 48. Huntington takes the phrase "The West and the Rest" from an article with that title written by Kishore Mahbubani (a Singapore government official), and appearing in *The National Interest,* Summer 1992, pp. 3–13.
[32]*See* comments on Huntington's thesis by Fouad Ajami, Robert L. Bartley, Liu Binyan, Jeane J. Kirkpatrick, and Kishore Mahbubai in *Foreign Affairs,* Vol. 72, No. 4 (September/October 1993), pp. 2–26.

European colonialism is over. American hegemony is receding. The erosion of Western culture follows, as indigenous, historically rooted mores, languages, beliefs and institutions reassert themselves. . . .

Civilizations unite and divide. . . . What ultimately counts for people is not political ideology or economic interest. Faith, family, blood, and belief are what people identify with and what they will fight and die for. And that is why the clash of civilizations is replacing the Cold War as the central phenomenon of global politics.[33]

In knocking down one obsolete universalistic paradigm, however, Huntington set up another in his postulate of a worldwide two-sided clash of Western and anti-Western civilizations. Even in his own formulation the paradigm has too many anomalies to stand: Where does he locate Japan, post-Soviet Russia, and secular Turkey, for example, or the Latin American countries? And what is the civilizational identity of Third World (Asian, African, Arab, Latino, etc.) citizens of the United States and the countries of Western Europe? If "faith, family, blood, and belief" are what unite and divide people, there would seem to be every reason to expect the emerging "clash of civilizations" to express itself globally in a polyarchic rather than a new bipolar configuration.

A World of Regions

A more differentiated vision than Huntington's of the world's basic international groupings and divisions focuses on five or six large geographically bound clusters of intense state-to-state and trans-state interaction. While largely the product of the material interdependencies of its constituent states and economic sectors, many of which cut across the world's major cultural groupings, the coherence and institutionalization of each regional system is, of course, affected by ideational affinities and antagonisms. But it will be primarily the basic and very practical economic and public safety benefits to the members of a region's regime (or regimes) that are likely, in the final analysis, to determine the extent and durability of their willingness to subordinate immediate self-interests to the interests of the regional community.

"Community" is the positive term for such regional systems, connoting cooperation for the commonweal that transcends narrow self-interest. "Bloc" is the negative term, connoting a combination against outsiders. Not surprisingly, both of these terms are applied to each of the major efforts at regional regime building now underway.

---

[33]Samuel P. Huntington, "If Not Civilizations, What? Paradigms of the Post-Cold War World," *Foreign Affairs*, Vol. 72, No. 5 (November/December, 1993), pp. 186–194, quotes from pp. 192 and 194.

The European Union.   The most advanced and generally most favorably regarded experiment in multi-national regionalism is the European Union (EU). The basic motive force for transforming the traditional European polity of rivalrous sovereign nation-states into a more integrated community has been economic—the principal objective being to harness and rationalize the productive resources of Europe so as to be able to compete more effectively in the global economy against the United States and Japan. A secondary motive, particularly of its early French founders in the aftermath of World War II, was to subjugate the Germans into a supranational regime to prevent their ever again trying to conquer Europe. These basic motives were for a time subsumed under the US-sponsored Marshall Plan for aiding the emergence of a strong and integrated Europe that could serve as a bulwark against Soviet expansion. The original primary and secondary motives are again very much in operation in the post–Cold War era. The United States, Japan, and Europe are now unabashedly economic rivals; and a reunited Germany is again warily regarded by its twice-burned neighbors as a potential aggressive imperialist.

Although during the first few decades of its existence, the European Community (as it was then called) could be treated primarily as an experiment in developing an integrated common market, the political implications of such economic integration that are now having to be faced were evident to the founders of the original instruments (the European Iron and Steel Community, begun in 1952, and the Treaty of Rome signed in 1957 by France, West Germany, Italy, Belgium, the Netherlands, and Luxembourg) that launched the project. Finally the Maastricht Treaty of 1991, in addition to clearing the path toward full economic integration, made explicit some of the unavoidable political corollaries of a true common market. Maastricht committed its twelve signatories not only to create a single currency and regional central bank by the end of the decade but also to accord the institutions of the Community (its intergovernmental Council, its executive Commission, and its directly elected Parliament) limited, yet unprecedented, authority over monetary policy, foreign affairs and defense policy, foreign trade, immigration, tourism, energy, the environment, transportation, labor relations, health policy, consumer protection, and human rights. On many of these subjects, major laws and directives developed by the Commission (more accountable than previously to the Parliament) would no longer require unanimous approval by all the member countries at the level of the intergovernmental Council, but could take effect on the basis of various majority-vote formulas. A controversial protocol annexed to the treaty further committed the Community, in the name of social equity, to reduce the gap in living standards between its affluent and poor areas by transferring financial resources to members with GDPs less than 90 percent of the Community's average. But to guard against these provisions being applied in ways that would substantially erode the sovereign prerogatives of member governments, the 1991 treaty and various follow-on agreements asserted the principle of "subsidiarity," which holds that the purposes of the Community should normally be achieved at the national level through national laws and instrumentalities and that action should be undertaken at the supranational level only when Community objectives "cannot be sufficiently achieved" by the member states or in those exceptional circumstances when they can be "better achieved" at the supranational level.[34]

In addition to the reluctance of some of the member countries to dilute their traditional sovereign prerogatives, one of the strongest breaks on the evolution of a federal European system is the prospect of having to enlarge the membership of the EU to accommodate not only Austria and the Scandanvian countries but also the countries of Eastern Europe recently liberated from the Soviet empire. Rather cynically, in fact, some of the core members—most blatantly the British government—have been advocating such enlargement in order to forestall the deeper transnational integration of national societies that would otherwise be in the offing.

Notwithstanding that the materialization of a fully-federated United States of Europe still seems a remote possibility, the region, by fits and starts, has been progressively coalescing and acting as a unit vis-à-vis the outside world on an increasingly broad range of issues. Particularly in external trade negotiations, most notably in the General Agreement on Tariffs and Trade (GATT) "rounds," and on matters such as the Common Agricultural Policy for protecting European farmers by imposing duties on cheaper American agricultural products entering the market, the Community has been able to speak with one voice. Accordingly, the United States and Japan are more and more seeing *Europe*, with a larger GDP and export earnings than either of them, as a singular competitor; and this is the principal stimulus for their own efforts to organize their own preferential trading regions.

North America.   The ratification in the winter of 1993–1994 of the North American Free Trade Agreement (NAFTA) by the United States, Mexico, and Canada marks a historic crossing of the threshold between the idea of North America as a US-propagated myth and the mutual official recognition and sponsorship of North America as a functioning economic community. The multilateral commitments in NAFTA, unlike those of the EU, are confined almost entirely to the realms of trade and investment policy, with the objective of removing most national barriers to commerce among the three countries. There is no serious contemplation of anything as ambitious as moving toward a common North American currency. Nor is there any contemplation of a common North American foreign policy.

---

[34]Walter Goldstein, "Europe After Maastrict," *Foreign Affairs*, Vol. 71, No. 5 (Winter 1992/93), pp. 117–132. For a capsule summary of the complicated treaty provisions see "What Does Maastrict Promise?" *New York Times*, September 20, 1992.

NAFTA has no provisions for coordinating immigration policies or harmonizing domestic social welfare programs; but to counter the fear of US labor unions that Mexico's low wages and permissive workplace standards would attract US industries to locate across the border and thus cause large layoffs in the United States, the Clinton administration persuaded the Mexicans to accept a "side agreement" on labor cooperation that committed the Mexican government to at least enforce its own minimum wage and child labor laws and to implement its own worker safety regulations. Similarly, another side agreement was attached to the treaty in response to the concerns of US environmentalists that Mexico's lax environmental controls on industry would attract US firms anxious to cut costs; this too committed Mexico to do a better job of enforcing its own laws. In perhaps the most innovative feature of the overall accord, both the environmental and labor side agreements created special multinational offices to investigate violations and to levy fines for abuses that were not remedied.[35]

The Western Hemisphere.   Hoping to build upon the successful negotiation of NAFTA, some elements in the US policy establishment are determined to keep alive a *Pan*-American vision, finding the idea of the hemispheric community a convenient counter to the "old worldism" the Europeans use to sustain their intra-European and ex-colonial special commercial relationships. The American hemisphere as a cultural unit, however, is largely mythological—based on a mystical fusion of the obsolescent geopolitics of the Monroe Doctrine, the self-determination movements against Spain, and the love–hate relationship of Latin Americans and Canadians for the United States. For their part, the Canadians and the Latins have cooperated in sustaining the myth for purposes of inducing the United States to treat them equitably rather than on the basis of its superior economic and military power, and to support their interests in international forums. Whether or not the Pan-American idea can be sustained in the post–Cold War era, the Europeans and Japanese are likely to leave no stone unturned in their own efforts to cultivate economic opportunities in the increasingly lucrative Latin American market, and their success will be partly a function of the persisting resentment in the hemisphere of US hegemonic pretentions, both in the economic and cultural spheres.

The Pacific Rim.   The world's fastest growing trading region since the late 1970s comprises the countries bordering and surrounded by the Pacific Ocean—hardly a surprising fact, since it includes, among others, Japan, China, Taiwan, Hong Kong, South Korea, and Singapore, in addition to the United States and Canada. Because it is so vast and contains countries that also belong to other regional groupings, it can never become an exclusive protectionist block; and as yet its major members have rebuffed appeals

---

[35]"What's What in the Trade Pact," *New York Times,* November 14, 1993.

from the United States to form a common market area of preferential intraregional "free trade." But because of their multiple and dynamic interdependencies, the countries of the region have constituted themselves into a consultative forum on Asia Pacific Economic Cooperation (APEC), which meets annually on at least the finance minister level.

A major attraction of the APEC grouping for many of its Asian members is that it provides them with an arena for regional economic cooperation and mutual accountability that is not dominated by Japan. Although Japan might want to organize an EAFTA (East Asian Free Trade Area) to counterbalance NAFTA, the less powerful countries of the region would find such a venture to be too reminiscent of Tokyo's pre–World War II East Asian "coprosperity sphere." By according prominence to the APEC arena they can avoid subordinating themselves to Japan without having to openly rebuff her and/or without having to compromise their Asian identity by seeking the protection of the United States.

Southeast Asia.   The Association of Southeast Asian Nations (ASEAN) functions as a weak but enduring regional subsystem within the larger Asia–Pacific region. A legacy of the Cold War, and of the Vietnam war in particular, the six-member organization (the Philippines, Indonesia, Brunei, Malaysia, Singapore, and Thailand) still excludes the communist states of Indochina. But unlike its parent organization, the Southeast Asia Treaty Organization (SEATO), one of the regional anti-Communist alliances formed and dominated by the United States, ASEAN conceives of itself as an indigenous Third World grouping and also excludes extraregional countries (even Australia and New Zealand) from its membership. Even though ASEAN is the most successful regional association among Third World states, there is virtually no prospect that it can achieve the degree of integration obtained by the European Union. There is a basic racial similarity among the peoples of the region, but the differences in national culture are large: Indonesia is predominantly Muslim; Thailand is 95 percent Buddhist; and the Philippines is 75 percent Roman Catholic. The only language in which all can communicate with one another is English, but not because of a common colonial experience. Indonesia was part of the Dutch empire; Singapore and Malaysia were mostly under British control; the Philippines were under Spanish and then US rule; and Thailand has been an independent country for over two centuries. ASEAN has evolved about as far as it can into a regime for coordinating member policies on matters of trade liberalization, currency exchange, air and sea transportation, immigration and refugees, and the control of illegal drugs and other contraband. Its members are increasingly involved in commerce with countries outside of ASEAN, but they are committed to at least consult with each other on matters where an extraregional arrangement might contradict their commitment to intraregional accountability.

Africa.   Some leaders of the anticolonial movement in sub-Sahara Africa, most notably Kwame Nkrumah of Ghana, had envisioned that the attainment of independence for each of the nations would be followed by an eradication of the borders the imperial powers had imposed across the continent's ethnic and tribal groupings, and the formation of a United Africa, or at least a federation of new political jurisdictions that were congruent with the location of indigenous nations. But any attempt to implement this Pan-African ideal in the postcolonial era was seen by most of Nkrumah's fellow African statesmen as too disruptive of their own power and authority within each of their newly independent countries, and providing the former colonial powers and the Cold War superpowers with pretexts for "neocolonial" intervention. Accordingly, the Organization of African Unity (OAU), in its charter and resolutions, while affirming the "solidarity" of the African nations in their continuing common struggle against the legacies of colonialism, has also explicitly accepted, with a few exceptions, the state boundaries left by the departing European powers. Jealous of their recently acquired independence, the new states of Africa are for the most part also defenders of the traditional Westphalian norms of national sovereignty and mutual non-interference by countries in one another's domestic affairs, an exception being international sanctions to rid the continent of the last vestiges of colonialism such as the apartheid system in South Africa. The OAU has served on occasion as an effective mechanism for mediating inter-African conflicts over access to commonly used resources (irrigation waters, fisheries, and the like) and for developing common African positions on international development issues. There is no expectation, however, that its members will give it any supranational powers in the foreseeable future.

The Special Case of NATO

Although the end of the Cold War should have made obsolete the coalitions and organizations that were that conflict's special creatures, one of them has taken on a life of its own and is determined not to expire. The institutions of the Soviet-led coalition are dead: The Warsaw Pact had a formal funeral; the Socialist Commonwealth and its economic arm, COMECON, have closed up shop; and no one except historians any longer mentions the transnationally subversive Comintern. The amorphous "free world coalition" too—the sometimes embarrassing global melange of democracies and dictatorships whose only qualification for membership was their willingness to follow Washington's lead in fighting international communism—has lost its reason for existence. Even the Nonaligned Movement (the 100 or so countries, mostly in the Third World, that did not want to be defined as an ally of either Cold War superpower) is moribund; the "nonaligned" continue to convene periodically but do not appear able to find a new role that would justify the expenses of their annual convocations and secretariat organization.

The post–Cold War anomaly is the North Atlantic Treaty Organization (NATO) which, despite the seeming geopolitical irrationality of its continuance, was sustained in 1994 through the "Partnership for Peace" demarche of the Clinton administration.

Having been the principal institutional expression of the US-led anti-Soviet coalition, NATO's survival required that it redefine its objectives and missions and that it open up its membership to match its revised reasons for existence. But if NATO attempted to become more congruent with the emerging global polyarchy and thus took on functions that were also the primary responsibility of other international institutions, the question would inevitably arise: Why NATO? Was it realistic to expect the organization to successfully shed its Cold War aura of being a Northern and Western *alliance against* a common threat from the East? Wouldn't this require membership even for Russia? And wouldn't that so dilute the organization's identity and mission to make it virtually indistinguishable from the pan-European Conference on Security and Cooperation in Europe (CSCE), not to speak of the absurdity of retaining the name "North Atlantic"?

Undaunted by the conceptual and potential practical contradictions, NATO's champions—and there were many in Western capitals for whom the organization had become a way of life—worked assiduously to fashion imaginative proposals for expanding NATO's objectives and membership. Those that found most favor at the top levels of the Clinton administration featured enlarging the alliance's areas of potential intervention to encompass East Central Europe (the area between Germany and Russia) and the Mediterranean/Middle Eastern "arc of crisis"; diversifying the organization's role from that of only collective military deterrence and defense to the provision also of conflict resolution and control services, crisis management, peacekeeping, and peacemaking (the latter to include elections supervision and assistance in establishing and protecting the institutions of democratic governance); and progressively broadening its current membership to include (in addition to the current sixteen), in the first stage, Poland, Hungary, and the Czech Republic, followed by at least an associate status for Slovakia, the Baltic states, Ukraine, and possibly some of the other former republics of the USSR, leading eventually to the incorporation into the alliance of a stable, democratic, and nonexpansionist Russia. Such a design and sequential enlargement of NATO, it was argued, will provide the best assurance against a resurgence of Russian imperialism.[36]

Not surprisingly, such proposals did not go down well in Moscow, even with those leaders who were dedicated to democratic reform and greater integration of the Russian economy with the capitalist West. For the offer of NATO membership first to the East Europeans, the Ukrainians, and the Baltics has all the appearances, despite insistent disclaimers from Western

---

[36]*See* Ronald D. Adams, Richard L. Kugler, and E. Stephen Larrabee, "Building a New NATO," *Foreign Affairs*, Vol. 72, No. 4 (September/October 1993), pp. 28–40.

capitals, of a grand encircling coalition against Russia. Strong objections were voiced by Boris Yeltsin and other pro-Western officials that for the West to enhance NATO in this way would play into the hands of both the ultra-nationalist Russians and the unreconstructed Marxist–Leninists, and thus contribute to the very resurgence of aggressive Russian imperialism it was designed to prevent.[37]

Objections of a different kind—stressing the incompatibility with the emerging global polyarchy of such designs for enhancing NATO—were raised in some Western circles. Reflecting these, Owen Harries argued that

> NATO does not remotely resemble a great power, with well-defined interests over a range of issues and a well-developed will of its own. Each major European power has its own interests and concerns; what Germany deems vital to its security and prosperity, England may regard as peripheral. To insist on joint intervention in such a case would only create friction where none previously existed.
>
> At a time when the core purpose of the alliance—mutual protection against the direct military threat posed by a clearly defined adversary—has lost much of its . . . binding power, an effort to save NATO by finding a new role for it might end up having the effect of hastening the alliance's demise.[38]

Hoping to transcend these various objections, President Clinton gained the assent of his West European conferees at the January 1994 NATO summit meeting for an offer to the East Europeans to enter into "Partnership for Peace" arrangements considerably short of actual membership in the alliance. Each "partner" would negotiate individually with NATO to establish a mode of consultations on security threats and to institute joint training and field exercises for possible peacemaking efforts. The first arrangements were to be negotiated with Poland, Hungary, the Czech Republic, and Slovakia, but the invitation to enter into such negotiations was extended to all the successor states of the Soviet Union (including Russia) and all former members of the Warsaw Pact. Neither President Lech Walesa of Poland nor President Vaclav Havel of the Czech Republic were happy with Clinton's explanation that he did not want to "draw a line between East and West that could create a self-fulfilling prophecy of confrontation[39];" but they were offered the Partnership for Peace essentially on a take-it-or-leave-it basis, and thus had no realistic alternative but to sign on. With the Poles and the Czechs acceding, the others—even the Russians, who had initially opposed any eastward outreach by NATO as hostile—were almost certain to ask to come on board.

Former Secretary of State Henry Kissinger, watching all this post–Cold War NATO gamesmanship from the sidelines, criticized the Parnership for

---

[37]Stephen Erlanger, "Russian Warning Over Bigger NATO," *New York Times*, November 26, 1993.

[38]Owen Harries, "The Collapse of 'The West,'" *Foreign Affairs*, Vol. 72, No. 4 (September/October 1993), pp. 44–45.

[39]Remarks by Bill Clinton to the North Atlantic Council in Brussels, Belgium, January 10, 1994, *Weekly Compilation of Presidential Documents*, Vol. 30, No. 2, pp. 21–23.

Peace for "equating the victims of Soviet and Russian imperialism with its perpetrators." Giving Russia a stake in the stability of Europe through encouraging commercial, scientific, scientific, and cultural exchange was important, he maintained, and this could be accomplished through the CSCE and related institutions; but drawing Russia, even informally, into a continent-wide collective security association would be counterproductive. In Kissinger's words,

> If the Partnership for Peace is to be made an aspect of NATO, it may well undermine the Atlantic Alliance by diverting it into activities unrelated to any realistic security mission, magnifying the insecurity of Eastern Europe, and yet, being sufficiently ambiguous, fail to placate Russia. Indeed, the Partnership for Peace runs the risk of being treated as irrelevant, if not dangerous, by the potential victims of aggression while being treated in Asia as an ethnic club directed primarily against China and Japan.[40]

Despite such risks, the inclination on the part of the national security officials of the major Western governments as of this writing is decidedly towards broadening NATO's role, geographically and functionally—but experimentally, and with prudential deference to Russian sensitivities.

All of the associations I have discussed in this chapter are contending for adherence among the diverse peoples of the world. A serious attempt to ascertain which of these associations will be the most durable and influential over the long run in determining who gets what, when, and how—including who fights against whom and who makes peace with whom—requires a more deeply cutting analysis of the underlying sources of the visible affinities and antagonisms. Such basic analysis is the task of the following chapters.

[40]Henry Kissinger, *Diplomacy* (New York: Simon & Schuster, 1994), pp. 824–825.

9

THE IMPACT OF SCIENCE AND TECHNOLOGY ON COMMUNITY

The membership, location, structure, and ways of life of human communities are highly determined by nature's "givens": the planet's material and biological makeup and its environment. The dimensions of human communities are also profoundly affected by the remarkable capacity of human beings, as distinct from other creatures, to transform what has been given to them by nature or God. Who can communicate with whom, who can easily exchange goods and services with whom, who can injure or destroy whom, and who can survive disease and produce healthy offspring will at any point in history substantially define the shape of human communities and their durability. It is hardly surprising, therefore, that the twentieth century's scientific and technological revolutions—particularly their applications in communications, transportation, war, industrial and agricultural processes, and disease prevention and control—are playing havoc with the traditional national-community basis of the world polity.

THE MOBILITY OF PEOPLE, MATERIALS, AND INFORMATION

Many of the scientific advances and new technological applications of the twentieth century have had their most dramatic cumulative or synergistic effects in the fields of transportation and communication, radically altering the role of location, distance, and topographic barriers in human affairs. From the standpoint of the physics of moving persons, things, and ideas, the whole Earth is already a community. The degree to which the Earth community has been activated to form concrete cooperative relationships, however, lags far behind what is now physically possible and rapidly becoming cost-effective in economic terms. The reasons for this sluggish response are almost all political, not physical.[1]

Transportation

If distance is measured by the time it takes to move from place to place, then the size of the world has indeed been shrinking at a phenomenal rate since the emergence of the modern nation-state system (dated roughly from the time of the French Revolution and the inauguration of George Washington as the first president of the United States). In 1789, it still took a few years to circumnavigate the globe with the fastest sailing ships; horses were the principal means of rapid overland transit; and traveling 25 miles a day in a horse-drawn carriage was considered to be very fast. By the 1880s, steam engines had compressed the distance–time ratio to as much as 250 miles a day over the ocean (about two weeks from New York to London) and some 500 miles a day by rail locomotive. Now it takes only a day to fly around the world in a jet aircraft, and astronauts in spacecraft can orbit the Earth 16 times each 24 hours.[2]

But even though the movement of people and goods between countries and continents today can be virtually as rapid as between neighboring cities, international travel is frequently still a time-consuming and expensive operation—mainly for political reasons: Countries remain determined to keep final control over who and what enter their territory, for to lose such control would be in effect to lose control over fundamental social and economic processes.

Relatively unpoliced national borders, such as between Canada and the United States and among the countries of the European Union, are rare. The more prevalent response to the expanding international mobility of persons and things has been for countries to thicken their apparatus of inspections and controls at most points of trans-border entry and exit. Typically, national land frontiers are fenced, and transit between countries is funneled through a few officially manned checkpoints. The physically accessible ocean coasts of most countries are heavily patrolled and guarded, not only against contraband in weapons, drugs, and other banned goods, but also to prevent "boat people" refugees from clandestine entry. Aircraft are not allowed to penetrate the airspace above a country without prior authorization from that country's aviation agencies. National governments retain sovereign control over all landings and takeoffs from their territory. International

---

[1]A wide-ranging survey of developments that have turned the world into a community at the material level is provided by Lester R. Brown, *World Without Borders* (New York: Random House, 1972).
[2]On the transportation revolution, *see* John McHale, *The Future of the Future* (New York: George Braziller, 1969), Chapter 1; and Hal Hellman, *Transportation and the World of the Future* (New York: M. Evans and Company, 1968).

travellers must submit to sometimes elaborate procedures of identification and inspection of themselves and their baggage when entering and/or leaving. Almost all countries require foreign visitors or even those simply in transit to produce proof of citizenship of their country of origin and may deny entry to citizens of countries with which they do not maintain friendly relations. Some governments require considerable advance application for foreign visitors and will frequently deny visas for unspecified security or political reasons. In the 1970s and 1980s, responding to the increase of terrorist acts by transnationally mobile militants, there was a worldwide tightening of these various controls on national ingress and egress. Commercial cargo transport is subject to even more elborate systems of national surveillance and permissions at points of entry, applying customs charges, rigid product and packaging specifications, and other nontariff barriers to implement national policies designed to protect various economic sectors from unwanted foreign competition.

Such tension between the mobility that technology allows and the mobility that societies will countenance has become a central issue in both international and domestic politics. Everywhere the physical ease with which people and goods can circulate among countries presses against the barriers to their free circulation, with the result that the barriers have become more and more politically controversial and economically costly to maintain. As will be discussed in *Chapter 11*, the material costs of maintaining the barriers, including the opportunity costs of contact and commerce foregone, bear differently on certain countries and sectors of society. Especially where tourism has become a large earner of foreign exchange, which is the case in many developing countries, visa and customs regulations that may discourage foreign visitors are matters of intense debate in national parliaments and bureaucracies, often pitting cultural traditionalists and xenophobes against the entrepreneurial middle classes and cosmopolitan elites.

In most countries the transportation industries and allied interest and occupational groups tend to constitute an active lobby against cumbersome regulations on the international mobility of people and goods. But where such regulations are obviously required for reasons of safety, orderly commerce, environmental protection, or domestic political order, the transportation interests tend to prefer assigning a greater role to the specialized international organizations operating in the transportation field: the International Maritime Organization (IMO) for sea transport and the International Civil Aviation Organization (ICAO) for air transport. The national and industry delegates to these institutions, while looking out for the interests of their home industries, are motivated to facilitate and expand international transportation and therefore to work cooperatively, knowing that if they do not resolve their differences at the international level, uncoordinated and unstandardized domestic regulations, often reflecting protectionist interests, will proliferate to constrict international mobility and increase transportation costs.

Communication

The compression of spatial relationships, as dramatic as it has been in the transportation field, is even more dramatic in the field of communication. Before the invention of the telegraph in 1840, all information had to be transmitted on material documents carried by people or shipped in containers, so the distance–time ratios were exactly the same for communication as they were for transportation. Today, using Earth-orbiting communications satellites as relays, electronically processed sounds, visual imagery, and documents can be sent almost instantaneously from any point on earth to any other point.

Fax Me a Revolution.   The availability to individuals worldwide of telephonic facsimile transmission equipment (fax machines) has dramatically enlarged the ability of groups to mobilize opposition to governments while increasing the economic and political costs to governments of attempting to repress dissidence. The political potential of this new technology was previewed in the *Tiananmen* Square uprising in Beijing in the summer of 1989, where student leaders of the "democracy movement" in Beijing, utilizing the fax equipment then available in the city's international hotels, were able to link up with dissident groups not only in Shanghai and other large Chinese cities, but also with supportive Chinese students in US and European universities. Until the time they were sealed off by a wall of infantry and tanks, the students in Tiananmen Square were able to break the monopoly possessed by the totalitarian government on communication with the outside world: Global media reporting on the fate of the uprising were informed by students on the spot, and the Tiananmen dissidents were in turn fed information on their international support. The proliferation of computer "internet" links is an additional resource now available to such dissidents.

Direct International Broadcasting.   Another politically consequential technological innovation is the Direct Broadcasting Satellite (DBS), which, along with improvements in reception technology, allows an international broadcaster to transmit programs directly to households that possess a satellite dish or that are connected by cable to such equipment. Using as few as three of these satellites, appropriately positioned 22,300 miles above the surface of the Earth (in the so-called geostationary orbit where the inertial motion of the spacecraft keeps it roughly over the same spot on the revolving Earth below), a broadcasting corporation or country with the required advanced technologies could beam a program simultaneously to the populations of every country in the world. International Telecommunication Union rules adopted in 1979 put some constraints on such unlimited broadcasting through the assignment of particular orbital slots, broadcast frequencies, and "cones of transmission" to each country, which provide the basis for mutual restraint and accountability. But the new technologies now coming into use by powerful broadcasters allow those who want to receive their broadcasts to pull them across any such assigned electronic jurisdictions.

As put by the Director of the British Broadcasting System,

> DBS will, in effect, create proximity between far-flung points; all countries across oceans and cultures could become as Canada to the United States, as Ireland to Britain, as the other islands of the Caribbean to Cuba. The economics of communications satellites . . . destroy geography. . . .
>
> With a working DBS, we could all become each other's neighbors, with everything that implies, to be enriched, influenced, and irritated by each other. In that sense, we may all become Canadians now.[3]

Countries that for cultural, political, or economic reasons want to maintain control over the broadcasts received by their populations have three options: electronic interference with unwanted broadcasts ("jamming"); controls on the reception equipment they allow their own citizens; or international regulations that the powerful broadcasters will respect.

While the technology of jamming has also been making strides, effective interference with broadcasts from space requires expensive and complex equipment. Only a handful of advanced countries appear capable of developing electronic anti-DBS capabilities. The developing countries, among which are many of the governments most worried about the harmful political or cultural effects of foreign television programs, would have difficulty in obtaining jamming capabilities without outside help.[4] A government lacking effective means of jamming unwanted broadcasts can still counter the new DBS technology by allowing individuals to possess only specially altered receiving equipment to filter out all broadcasts on nonapproved networks; but this approach puts the government visibly in the role of censor and requires intrusive and heavy inspection of private buildings to suppress the inevitable black market in illicit receiving sets—a policy hardly conducive to the popularity of a government among its citizenry.[5]

The third course—that of trying to develop an internationally acceptable regime to regulate direct broadcasting across national borders—is favored by a majority of countries. The principal holdout against such a regime is the United States, on the grounds of international "freedom of information."

The essential feature of most of the regulatory regime proposals under consideration in the UN Committee on the Peaceful Uses of Outer Space is the requirement of prior consent by the government of the country that

[3]David Webster, "Direct Broadcast Satellites; Proximity, Sovereignty and National Identity," *Foreign Affairs,* Vol. 62, No. 5 (Summer 1984), p. 240.
[4]Seyom Brown, Nina Cornell, Larry Fabian, and Edith Brown Weiss, *Regimes for the Ocean, Outer Space, and Weather* (Washington, DC: Brookings, 1976), pp. 153–154.
[5]The proliferation of equipment in India allowing individuals to receive CNN and other Western programs is described in Edward Gargan, "TV Comes in on a Dish, and India Gobbles It Up," *New York Times,* October 29, 1991.

would receive broadcasts. The consent requirement might be applied to an overall arrangement between the broadcaster and receiver country to allow relatively unrestricted broadcasting and reception; alternatively, the receiving country's government might be accorded prior consent rights on program content.

The most vociferous proponents of a rigid prior consent regime are many of the Muslim theocratic states of the Middle East. Some Western democracies—notably Canada and Sweden—are also part of the coalition in favor of receiver-country choice, fearing inundation by broadcasters from the technological giants. The United States, virtually isolated on this issue but whose cooperation is needed for any consent regime to be viable, takes the doctrinal highroad, invoking Article 19 of the Universal Declaration of Human Rights, which asserts the right "to receive and impart information and ideas through any media regardless of frontiers." Meanwhile, the diplomatic impasse tends to favor those with powerful broadcasting capabilities. US broadcasters already have what amounts to worlwide coverage. Israel and Jordan compete in beaming news broadcasts to each other.[6]

The global neighborhood exists at the technological level in the field of telecommunication. At the legal, political—and moral—levels, however, there are hardly any global community norms (analogous to the broadcasting rules in national communities) for ensuring that users of the electromagnetic spectrum are mutually respectful and accountable to each other for what is seen and heard.

Observation Technologies. Synergistic developments in communications, photography, and other observational techniques, combined with advances in space satellite technology, have also made it possible for those in possession of the advanced capabilities to obtain detailed information on human and natural activities and phenomena the world over. The increases in remote sensing power, similar to the increases in broadcasting power, are having both positive and negative effects on how the world's peoples relate to each other.

The powerful new sensing technologies can identify a wide range of electromagnetic energy emissions from the Earth's natural features and from human activity and structures. The energy is emitted, reflected, or scattered at distinctive wavelengths by each particular surface or atmospheric feature; and each of these unique "signatures" can be minutely analyzed with cameras and other instruments sensitive to radiation to detect changes in structure or activity.

The technological breakthroughs in this field since World War II have greatly facilitated the remote surveillance of the following phenomena:

[6]Webster, "Direct Broadcast Satellites," p. 1166.

- Military deployments and activity (enhancing the prospects for verifiable arms limitation agreements and reducing opportunities for surprise attack)

- Meteorological conditions (allowing for better forecasting of weather and climate patterns, including timely warnings of hurricanes, blizzards, and other damaging occurrences)

- Ocean surface and subsurface conditions (providing for better ocean resource management, particularly in fisheries and petroleum exploitation and for the control of ocean pollution)

- Geological characteristics of land masses (permitting more accurate mapping and location of commercially exploitable minerals and fossil fuels)

- Soil conditions, pest infestations, and the availability of irrigation (when combined with better weather and climate forecasting, allowing for more comprehensive and accurate forecasts and crop yields)

- Patterns of urban, rural, and coastal zone land use (providing the basis for economically sound and ecologically responsible development plans and projects)

Ideally, the availability of continuous information of threatening military deployments and on the condition of the Earth's ecologies, geology, and environment should be to everyone's benefit. But the reality of the uneven possession among countries of the sensing and information-processing technologies, as with direct broadcasting technologies, has led to fears on the part of the technologically less-developed countries that their relative lack of access to the information can hurt them militarily and economically; and these fears have been translated into demands for restrictions and international management of remote-sensing technologies—demands that the United States and other technologically well-endowed countries have been stoutly resisting.

Many developing countries fear the loss of their recently won sovereignty. Traditionally, nations have been able to control information about their military preparations, land use, and natural resources by controlling foreign access to their territory. Even with the advent of surveillance from aircraft, host-country prerogatives were retained: Airspace was considered an extension of landspace, and foreign overflights, whatever their purpose, were considered illegal unless the state under surveillance consented—a principle embodied in standard international legal theory and practice.

The increasing reliance on surveillance from spacecraft, however, has rendered anachronistic the traditional international law on territorial sovereignty. There is no way of drawing lines of territorial jurisdiction up into space from the continually revolving Earth and therefore no way of determining just when foreign spacecraft are engaged in "overflight" of national territory. Yet the sovereignty of countries under surveillance from space surely *is* being violated. And the negative consequences to some target countries indeed can be tangible and substantial.

A developing country in negotiations with a mining corporation for exploratory drilling rights in its territory can be at a major bargaining disadvantage if the corporation initially knows more about the local geology and location of mineral deposits than do the indigenous experts, particularly if the host country is even ignorant of the fact that the corporation has such knowledge. Moreover, reconnaissance that is supposed to be primarily for producing information on resources and environmental conditions will also—by design or simply as a byproduct—obtain information on the observed country's military capabilities.[7]

Understandably, countries unable to deploy or rent surveillance time on another country's observational spacecraft see many of the innovations in remote-sensing technology as enlarging the gap between the affluent and the poor countries and even as dangerous to their security. As in the direct broadcasting field, resolutions have been introduced in the United Nations to prohibit satellite sensing of a country's land areas and zones of ocean jurisdiction without that country's consent. But just as understandably, countries with a head start in the relevant technologies claim that a prior consent regime is both retrogressive and unworkable.

Countries with observational spacecraft have attempted to cater to developing-country concerns by selling the nonmilitary information obtained from their reconnaissance satellites and by providing assistance in photo interpretation and other information processing to countries that need it. The space powers have also helped other countries to build and launch their own satellites. These technical assistance measures, however, have only partly overcome the deep-seated suspicion by the technologically lagging countries that they are being continually spied on from space and that much of the information thus obtained can be used against them—commercially and militarily.

Congestion on the Frequency Spectrum and Satellite Orbits.   The proliferation of communications satellites in outer space has been turning preferred segments of the electromagnetic broadcasting spectrum and slots on the orbit 22,300 miles from Earth into scarce resources. The users of these resources have not been able to escape the realization that they constitute an interdependent community, since if the pressure on the resources continues unabated, there will be too much mutual interference with broadcast signals from closely positioned spacecraft to allow any of them to function efficiently. Accordingly, current and prospective users, acting through the International Telecommunication Union, have adopted detailed rules for allo-

---

[7]On the overlapping military and civilian uses of observational space satellites, *see* Anthony Dolman, *Resources, Regimes, World Order* (New York: Pergamon Press, 1981), pp. 310–313.

cating the spectrum and preferred orbits and for the design of space communications systems so as to prevent the unnecessary use of these resources.[8]

The lower orbits utilized by manned spacecraft and low-flying observation and scientific satellites are subject to congestion of a more dangerous kind: the orbiting debris from inactive payloads, abandoned nuclear reactors, spent rocket stages, and tests. These bits of debris may now number in the 70,000s, ranging from 1 to 10 centimeters in diameter. But travelling at 22,000 miles an hour, even the smallest bits can do tremendous damage if they collide with spacecraft. A 1990 Office of Technology Assessment report, "Orbital Debris: A Space Environment Problem," concluded that "existing international treaties and agreements are inadequate for minimizing the generation of orbital debris or controlling its effects" and recommended consideration of an international treaty specifically devoted to the problem.[9]

DEMOGRAPHIC CRISES

The size, distribution, and density of the planet's population and major population groups have also been dramatically affected by the century's revolutions in science and technology. Industrialization, new agricultural processes, and disease control have combined to produce overall exponential growth in the number of humans—a population "explosion" that is placing a critical strain on essential natural resources in various regions of the globe.

Additionally, uneven population growth and poverty (often a symptom of "*over*population") are stimulating politically destabilizing patterns of migration into the world's more affluent societies. Germany, for example, is having trouble grappling with increasing incidents of harrassment, sometimes violent, on the part of native Germans against the growing influx of immigrants from Eastern Europe, the former Soviet Union, Africa, Southeast Asia, and the Middle East. There are over five million immigrants and refugees living in Germany, and the government has been spending some $6 billion a year to support them. The neo-Nazi "skinhead" youth movement has been feeding off the fear of indigenous local populations that the new foreigners are competing for scarce jobs and social welfare services. Fearful of a revival of extreme nationalism and ethnic prejudice after decades of attempting to atone for the genocidal racism of the Hitler regime, even the democratically committed centrist political parties now support tight restrictions on immigration, despite the negative implications for human rights issues.[10]

---

[8]Brown et al., *Regimes for the Ocean, Outer Space and Weather*, pp. 176–196.
[9]William J. Broad, "Experts Say Space Junk May Create Peril by 2000," *New York Times*, October 12, 1990.
[10]Stephen Kinzer, "A Wave of Attacks on Foreign Migrants Ignites German Fear," *New York Times*, October 1, 1991.

In France, resentment directed at foreign migrants is the principal source of popular support for Jean-Marie Le Pen's xenophobic National Front. As in Germany, centrists and even leftist parties, fearful that Le Pen and other right-wing nationalists will reap most of the political benefits of the growing xenophobia, have supported legislation to restrict immigration and to get the European Union to strengthen controls on refugees, particularly from poor Third World areas, that have been flooding into Western Europe.[11]

In combination with the century's dominant modes of industrialization and energy consumption, these demographic trends, if unabated, will not only exacerbate interethnic and racial conflict in many regions, but could also jeopardize the life-sustaining ecological balances in many parts of the world and even the Earth's entire biosphere. The demographic crisis thus invokes what may turn out to be the twenty-first century's most contentious political question—namely, what are the most appropriate political communities for dealing with the planet's "commons" and how should they be structured?

ANARCHY OR COMMUNITY IN THE "COMMONS"?

The term "commons," as used in contemporary international discourse, is derived, by analogy, from the nineteenth century English pattern of allowing cattle open access and free use to grazing land abutting the households of the local villagers. Today's principal *international* commons are outer space; the moon and other celestial bodies; the biosphere; the atmosphere; the great oceans; internationally shared seas, lakes, and river systems; Antarctica; and various of the Earth's interlinked plant and animal ecologies. Modern technologies have made these realms susceptible to intensive use and exploitation by humans and therefore subject to the kind of "tragedy of the commons" that befell the English village grazing lands when individual villagers increased the size of their herds to the point where the commons was severely overgrazed and everyone suffered.[12]

A number of disastrous modern commons tragedies are in the offing—if humans do not alter their prevailing industrial and technological habits—including a dangerous thinning of the Earth's ozone envelope, the excessive "greenhouse" warming of the Earth's climate, the death of major aquatic ecosystems, the degradations of previously fertile croplands, the poisoning of the air breathed by large populations, and the still-unknown effects of reducing the planet's biological diversity. Many of these potential tragedies are discussed in Chapter 10 along with other ecological issues.

[11]Alan Riding, "Immigrant Unrest Alarming French," *New York Times,* June 23, 1991.
[12]Garrett Hardin, "The Tragedy of the Commons," *Science,* 3 December 1968, pp. 1243–1248. *See also* Hardin's *Exploring New Ethics for Survival: The Voyage of the Spaceship Beagle* (New York: Viking, 1972), p. 254.

10

THE RISE OF ECOPOLITICS

One of the traditional functions of the state is to oversee the use of natural resources on which a community depends for its well-being. This inevitably has involved politically contentious issues of property rights and the obligations of owners to neighbors and to the community as a whole (including future generations). It also has involved equitable access and use rules for the "commons," namely those areas and resources considered to be the indivisible province of all members of a community of users—traditionally, rivers and oceans and their harvestable resources; more recently, it includes the atmosphere, outer space, and biological species whose health and survival are connected directly or indirectly with human welfare.

The new politics of ecology is in many respects a continuation of the traditional politics of natural resource use, but in some respects, especially in the domain of international politics, the issues and the challenges they pose to existing political norms and structures are unprecedented.

First of all, what's new about the politics of ecology is the concept of ecology itself—its frame of reference: A natural *ecology*, as distinguished from a natural resource, is, by definition, a set of highly interrelated (and usually also interdependent) phenomena. The new ecological consciousness is precisely the recognition that the planet's animal and plant life and/or the water, soil, and air are not simply resources to be used by humans but are all, along with the humans, likely to be impacting on one another in a complicated pattern of feedback relationships. Nature's "givens" and human constructions are part of the *environment* of any human community; but the human community and its behavior are also part of the environment of the other phenomena, affecting their health and well-being, which, in turn, affect (positively or negatively) the human community's condition. The biological and physical sciences have been illuminating these ecological relationships as have the everyday experiences of humans of the massive

187

impacts that their own inventions and actions are having on the natural environments on which they depend.

Second, and highly interactive with the interdependence of various types of phenomena, is the wide *geographic scope* of the ecological interdependencies of which humans have become conscious and over which they have come into conflict. In earlier times, to be sure, there were out-of-jurisdiction "ecological" effects (mostly in the form of the depletion or contamination of water resources downstream by upstream users in rivers, lakes, and seacoasts) that prompted neighboring states to negotiate or fight over access and use rights to the shared resources. In the contemporary period, the traditional sources of political strife over water and land-based food resources have been joined by conflicts over what is being done to the air that flows across jurisdictions. There is also awareness of the extent to which the waste disposal practices of human communities are subjecting huge seas, like the Mediterranean, and even the great world oceans to severe ecological degradation. These regional and intercontinental threats, when combined with the new scientific estimates and popular fears of catastrophic disturbances to the planet's life-sustaining biospheric balances resulting from human activities around the world, have begun to engender widespread recognition that some of the most crucial ecological interdependencies are truly *global* in scope, that the whole Earth is in effect a commons, and that therefore all of humankind has become, like it or not, an interdependent community for mutual harm or beneficial cooperation.

The rest of this chapter traces the sources and political implications in various fields of this rising consciousness of humankind's ecologically embedded condition.

Marine Biologists Sound the Alarm

A benchmark in the rising ecological consciousness was Rachel Carson's 1962 best-selling book *Silent Spring*, which vividly reflected the findings of marine biologists on how mindless and narrowly self-interested uses of the seas were profoundly disturbing the ocean's natural ecologies in ways that could jeopardize the food supplies and health of large segments of the Earth's human population.[1] These concerns were heightened in 1967 by reports of the widespread death of aquatic animals and plants caused by the oil spill when the supertanker *Torrey Canyon* ran aground. Finally, the rise of a full-blown environmentalist movement in the United States can be dated from 1969 and the media coverage of the lethal effects on ocean ecology along the Pacific coast resulting from a leak in the Union Oil Company's rig in the Santa Barbara Channel. Over the next few years numerous publications, television documentaries, and legislative hearings alerted newly at-

[1]Rachel Carson, *Silent Spring* (Boston: Houghton Mifflin, 1962).

tentive publics worldwide that not only accidents, but "normal" activities—fishing, beachfront residential and recreational development, the dumping of wastes, the tank-washing procedures of oil tankers, drilling in the seabed, seismic explosions, thermal heat transfers from power stations, and the atmospheric transfer to the oceans of agricultural pesticides—were despoiling the seas. Meteorologists, aware of the crucial function the great world ocean (covering 70 percent of the Earth's surface) plays in absorbing carbon dioxide from the atmosphere, began to worry about the effects of widespread marine pollution of the Earth's climate.

The decade of the 1960s may well be looked back on as the period when human society experienced a "paradigmatic shift" in its view of the sea. As put by the oceanographer Edward Wenk, Jr., "The Community of nations began to recognize that all peoples cluster on continental islands embedded in the vast ocean, that man's activities are intimately linked to the sea, and that the planet represents a closed ecological system wherein ostensible local events may have widely distributed effects."[2] A Resources for the Future study expressed the growing concern:

> We know all too little of how the sea and its biotic communities impinge on global ecology, but there is every reason to treat this relationship with great respect. Instead we utilize the sea thoughtlessly as the ultimate sink for all sorts of debris and chemicals generated on land and transmitted by air and water."[3]

The strain humans have been putting on sea-centered ecological relationships is most evident in semienclosed parts of the world's great oceans. The following vivid account of the degradation of the Mediterranean Sea illustrates the problem:

> Surely Neptune never anticipated that Homer's fabled "wine dark waters" would one day become a colossal toilet bowl and waste tank. Every year, 85 percent of the raw sewage from 44 million residents and 100 million tourists is dumped directly into the Mediterranean Sea. Inundated as they are, the Mediterranean waters that under normal circumstances could purify and oxidize human wastes now breed infectious diseases such as cholera, typhoid, viral hepatitis and dysentery. Pollutants from land-based industry smother sea floor organisms in a deadly gray ooze. Overfishing, water and noise pollution have dramatically reduced fish stocks and threatened species. The food chain is thoroughly contaminated. The Mediterranean is dying.[4]

This stark account was written before assessment could be made of the results of the Mediterranean Action Plan started in the 1970s under the auspices of the United Nations to rescue the dying sea. The so-called Med Plan

[2]Edward Wenk, Jr., *The Politics of the Ocean* (Seattle: University of Washington Press, 1972), p. 423.
[3]Sterling Brubaker, *To Live on Earth: Man and His Environment in Perspective* (Washington, DC: Resources for the Future, 1972), p. 148.
[4]Douglas LaValle, "Mediterranean Sea: Just How Much Can It Take?" *Greenpeace Examiner*, Vol. 11, No. 2 (June 1986), pp. 13–14.

was one of the multilateral initiatives resulting from commitments made by governments at the 1972 Stockholm Conference on the Environment to do something, not just complain, about the planet's ecological predicaments.

STOCKHOLM 1972

The United Nations Conference on the Environment, meeting in Stockholm in 1972, elevated the protection of the Earth's basic ecologies to a primary concern of international statecraft and authorized a new permanently sitting global agency, the United Nations Environmental Program (UNEP), to stimulate international cooperation in this field. But the UNEP, despite the vigorous leadership of its first Secretary General, Maurice Strong, was provided with few carrots (financial resources) and no punitive sticks whatsoever with which to induce adherence to its resolutions. The most important role of the UNEP was to be a catalyst and clearing house for environmental scientists and other professionals to interact as an "epistemic community" of common knowledge and commitment and to reinforce one another's influence within their respective countries.[5]

By the tenth anniversary of the Stockholm Conference the world media were full of reports of unhealthy air pollution levels, acid rain, oil-drenched coasts, dying seas and lakes, poisoned fish, and contaminated food chains—all of this symptomatic of the transborder communities of mutual vulnerability wrought by the industrial and technological revolutions. But there was as yet little progress in devising transborder legal and political instruments with spans of control congruent with these communities of mutual vulnerability. That would begin to come during the next decade, which would produce a set of wide-ranging instruments for signature by the heads of state at the 1992 "Earth Summit" (see pp. 199–202).

ACID RAIN: A PROTOTYPICAL INTERNATIONAL "EXTERNALITY" PROBLEM

The lack of ecological consciousness allows some of the damaging effects of productive activity to be put out of sight and out of mind when firms or nations calculate the costs and benefits of particular enterprises and projects—what economists call the "externality" factor. But sometimes such externalities strike too close to home, causing pain to those in the immediate community of the source activity; and when the perpetrators are discovered, corrective action is imposed by local political jurisdictions. This dynamic

[5]On the role of transnational "epistemic communities" in forging international cooperation on environmental policy, *see* Peter Haas, *Saving the Mediterranean: The Politics of International Environmental Cooperation* (New York: Columbia University Press, 1990).

generated a good deal of legislation in the United States, Canada, and Western Europe in the 1960s and 1970s against sources of smog and other air pollution that were making life uncomfortable and unhealthy for people living and working in urban industrial centers. The sources included preeminently coal-burning power plants emitting sulfur dioxide and cars and trucks emitting nitrogen oxides. But ironically, the corrective legislation aimed at the sources of the sulfur dioxide emissions, namely, that the coal-burning plants install higher smokestacks so that the effluents could be dissipated in the atmosphere, gave rise to a new externality problem in the form of acid precipitation.

The problem is that higher-altitude emissions of sulfur remain suspended in the air long enough to become absorbed in moving weather fronts and to be converted by sunlight and water vapor into acidic compounds. The noxious compounds can travel for thousands of miles before falling to the ground as rain or snow or fog (sometimes even as a dry dust). If this "acid rain" falls into freshwater lakes, it can deplete the calcium in the bone structure of fish and can interfere with their reproductive processes; the acidity can also cause chemical reactions in the subsoil of lakes and the reactions inject aluminum and other heavy minerals into water, clogging up the gills of fish and suffocating them. On land, acid rain can damage the foliage of crops and arrest the growth of trees; it can also corrode steel bridges and railroad tracks and the marble and limestone surfaces of buildings.[6]

Because of the characteristic movements of weather fronts, much of the acid rain falling on eastern Canada originates in the American midwestern industrial heartland. In Europe, about half of all deposits of sulfur come across national boundaries, with the Scandinavian countries in particular having to absorb damaging amounts of acid rain originating in Germany, France, and especially Britain.[7]

The principle that countries must be accountable to one another for such obvious transboundary pollution has been affirmed in numerous international environmental conferences, beginning with the Stockholm declaration of the 1972 United Nations Conference on the Environment. Many countries have now formally assumed such an obligation in subscribing to the International Treaty on Long-Range Transboundary Air Pollution, which entered into force in 1983. But the working out of respective obligations for corrective action, let alone liabilities for damage, has been very sluggish in this field. Thus, thirteen countries, including the United States, Britain, and Poland, refused to sign the 1985 Protocol on the Reduction of Sulfur Emissions of Their Transboundary Fluxes by at Least 30 Percent (less cumbersomely known as the Helsinki Protocol). The Helsinki 30 Percent Protocol

[6]Bernard J. Nebel, *Environmental Science: The Way the World Works* (Englewood Cliffs: Prentice-Hall, 1990), pp. 321–336.
[7]The World Bank, *World Bank Development Report 1992: Development and the Environment* (New York: Oxford University Press, 1992), p. 135.

received sufficient ratifications to come into force in 1987, but without the adherence of the three countries who by themselves were responsible for 30 percent of the world's sulfur dioxide emissions![8]

MEGA-TECHNOLOGICAL ACCIDENTS AND THE QUESTION OF INTERNATIONAL ACCOUNTABILITY

The enlarged consciousness of transborder ecological interdependencies has a normative corollary, which is gradually becoming a part of world law; namely, that countries and nongovernmental actors shall be held accountable for the peacetime injuries they inflict upon foreign populations and property. The case for a codification of such an accountability principle was strengthened by two disastrous accidents in the mid-1980s: the release of poison gas in December 1984 from a Union Carbide pesticide plant in India, and the explosion and meltdown in the Soviet Union's Chernobyl nuclear power facility in April 1986.

The Bhopal Disaster.   About 2000 people in the immediate vicinity of the Union Carbide pesticide factory at Bhopal, India, were killed by an escaping cloud of methyl isocyanate gas, which fortunately was blown away from the city of Bhopal itself (where nearly one million people live); however, 30,000 people downwind were exposed to the lethal substance, and a considerable percentage of them would suffer serious long-term effects in the form of pneumonia, emphysema, asthma, bronchitis, or pneumonia.[9] Preliminary investigations by the government of India supported allegations that the Union Carbide company negligence was responsible for the disaster. The next question was in which country's court system should the company be sued: in India, the location of the accident, or in the United States, the location of the home offices of the multinational chemical corporation? Lawyers representing the victims finally decided to press the claims of the victims in the US courts in the expectation of being awarded more substantial damages. In this case, the US courts granted that they had jurisdiction (and finally awarded damages); but they might have refused jurisdiction, as they have in roughly analogous cases; nor could it be expected, in the absence of a general treaty on international accountability, that other countries would allow such international litigation in their courts.

---

[8]Gareth Porter and Janet Welsh Brown, *Global Environmental Politics* (Boulder: Westview, 1991), pp. 71–74. *See also* Caldwell, *International Environmental Policy, Emergence and Dimensions* (Durham: Duke University Press, 1990) pp. 224–225.
[9]Sanjy Hazarika, "India Police Seize Factory Records of Union Carbide," *New York Times*, December 7, 1984; Walter Sullivan, "Health Crisis Could Last Many Years, Experts Say," *New York Times*, December 7, 1984.

Chernobyl.   The gap between the harms people can suffer across international boundaries and human society's means for ensuring the accountability of those responsible for the injuries was even more starkly exposed by the Chernobyl nuclear power plant meltdown in April 1986. Neighboring countries in the path of the radioactive cloud escaping from the fire raging at the Soviet nuclear facility did not even know that a terrible accident had occurred until two days after the explosion when scientists in Sweden and Finland discovered abnormal levels of radioactivity in their own atmosphere. As the Soviet government over the next few days reluctantly revealed details on the nature of the disaster, West European health authorities advised their populations about the dangers of consuming milk and fresh produce, and the European Community banned agricultural imports from the Soviet Union and Eastern Europe. In Finland atmospheric radiation levels reached ten times the normal amounts, in Sweden and Denmark fives times the normal, and in Norway 60 percent above normal. The radioactive fallout in Paris some 10 days after the accident was as high as it had been during the period of the most intense nuclear weapons testing in the atmosphere in 1963.[10]

Though fewer than 100 people working in and near the Chernobyl facility died from immediate exposure to lethal doses of radioactivity, physicists and medical experts predicted that the nuclear accident would cause tens of thousands of deaths in the USSR and Eastern Europe over the next several decades.[11]

The heightened sense of intersocietal vulnerability to such accidents was reflected in various unilateral actions by national governments in 1986: Austria dismantled its Zwentendorf nuclear power plant and Vienna brought pressure on Bonn not to start work on a planned West German nuclear power plant at Wackersdorf. The Saarland government and the city of Trier initiated legal action against Electricité de France to ensure that France would apply safety standards as rigorous as West Germany's in the French company's nuclear plant just across the Franco-German border. The Danish parliament demanded that the Swedes close down a nuclear facility barely 20 kilometers from Copenhagen. Observing these reactions, the British publication *The World Today* commented: "Thus for many countries and especially individual cities the policies of foreign neighbors may be as important as their own governments."[12]

One positive result of the Chernobyl disaster was a new willingness of the Soviet Union to concert with the United States and other Western governments in tightening up International Atomic Energy safety standards

[10]Ellen Dudley, "In the Aftermath of Chernobyl: Contamination, Upheaval, and Loss," *Nucleus,* Vol. 8, No. 3 (Fall 1986) (publication of the Union of Concerned Scientists), pp. 3, 5.

[11]*See* the *New York Times* from April 29, 1986 to May 15, 1986 for extensive reporting on the Chernobyl nuclear accident.

[12]"The Chernobyl Effect," *The World Today,* Vol. 42, No. 7 (July 1986), p. 110.

and safeguard procedures in nuclear power plants. Stimulated by Chernobyl, efforts have been undertaken in cognizant international agencies, such as the World Health Organization and the Food and Agricultural Organization, to improve their reporting and information dissemination on accidents and natural disasters of international scope.[13]

DEALING WITH THE DEPLETION
OF THE OZONE LAYER

In the mid 1970s, scientific reports on what was happening to the Earth's ozone layer produced a *do something!* attitude on the part of publics and elites. The fears were triggered by scientific research showing a dramatic thinning of the envelope of ozone concentrated in the stratosphere 9 to 30 miles above the Earth that shields the planet's living organisms from harmful ultraviolet radiation. Atmospheric scientists found that a huge hole had developed in the ozone layer over Antarctica and appeared to be widening so as to expose the populated areas in the southern hemisphere to ultraviolet rays; such ozone depletion could also occur at the North Pole and affect the northern hemisphere. Biologists worried that without sufficient filtering by the ozone layer, the ultraviolet rays reaching the Earth's surface would severely increase the incidence of skin cancer and damage DNA cells. The unscreened rays would also wipe out varieties of plankton and fish larvae floating near the ocean surface and diminish crop yields.[14]

Some of the scientists studying the problem advanced the hypothesis in 1974 that the protective ozone layer was being destroyed by industrially produced chlorofluorocarbons (CFCs). Presumably, the CFCs most responsible were being injected into the atmosphere by aerosol propellants used in hair sprays, spray paints, perfumes, deodorants, and other lubricants; by refrigerators, freezers, and air conditioners; by fire extinguishers; by solvents used in dry cleaning and in the manufacture of computers and other electronic products; and by the blowing agents used to produce foam cushions and packaging substances.[15]

Despite objections by the involved industries, the United States and a few other industrial countries, responding to a growing body of scientific evidence and popular pressures, were moved in the late 1970s to legislate controls on some of the ozone-destroying agents. And in the early 1980s there were increasing calls for an international treaty—initially opposed by the US government—to mandate reductions in CFC outputs. But some five hun-

---

[13]John F. Ahearne, "Implications of the Chernobyl Nuclear Accident," *Resources,* No. 86 (Winter 1987) (publication of Resources for the Future), pp. 10–12.

[14]James Gleick, "Hole in Ozone Over South Pole Worries Scientists," *New York Times,* July 29, 1986 (science section).

[15]Dianne Dumanoski, "Scientists Say Ozone Threat Is Worsening," *Boston Globe,* September 15, 1986 (science section).

dred of the US companies affected by the domestic legislation, now anxious to rectify their international competitive disadvantages, formed the Alliance for Responsible CFC Policy to lobby for international controls. Following this turnaround by influential US companies, the pro-business Reagan administration changed from an opponent of an international abatement treaty to a supporter. In 1986 and 1987 the US Department of State disseminated information through all of its embassies on the threat CFCs posed to the ozone layer. In other countries where strong environmental movements had produced anti-CFC legislation a similar dynamic operated to convert the affected industries into champions of international controls so as to achieve a "level playing field" with those countries lacking domestic CFC abatement laws. Thus it came about that a core group of industrial countries, including the United States, were now willing to cooperate with the effort of the UNEP to get them to negotiate an international CFC control regime.[16]

The result was a set of international instruments—the Vienna Convention for the Protection of the Ozone Layer (1985), the Montreal Protocol on Substances That Deplete the Ozone Layer (1987), and the London Revisions to the Montreal Protocol (1990)—that, in the words of Mostafa Tolba, head of the UNEP, opened "a new chapter in the history of international relations."[17] The parties to these agreements have committed themselves to totally phase out the production of CFCs and halons (another substance discovered to be depleting the ozone layer) by January 1, 2000, with the exception that a developing country who would suffer economic hardship from such a total phaseout can apply for a ten-year extension, provided that its annual production of the offending substances is kept below 0.3 kilogram per capita. The London Revisions also established a "Multilateral Fund," to be supplied by the more affluent parties, to finance the acquisition of appropriate technologies by developing countries to help them convert to ozone-safe industries and goods.[18]

THE ISSUE OF GLOBAL WARMING

The environmental public-interest constituency that was responsible for the establishment of the international ozone protection regime has been encountering greater difficulties in generating national legislation and international accords that could make a comparable contribution to abating the other looming threat to the essential life-sustaining conditions on the planet: the

[16]See Richard Elliot Benedick, *Ozone Diplomacy: New Directions in Safeguarding the Planet* (Cambridge: Harvard University Press, 1991). *See also* Edward A. Parson, "Protecting the Ozone Layer," in Pater M. Haas, Robert O. Keohane, and Mark A. Levy, eds., *Institutions for the Earth: Sources of Effective Environmental Protection* (Cambridge: MIT Press, 1993), pp. 3–73.
[17]Musrafa Tolba, quoted by Benedick, *loc cit.*, p.196.
[18]The texts of the agreements that constitute the international regime for protecting the ozone layer are included in the appendix of Benedick, *Ozone Diplomacy*.

prospect of excessive rises in the Earth's average temperature. The planetary climatic conditions conducive to the survival of plant and animal life result from the balance between the heat from the sun that is absorbed by the Earth's surface and the heat that is reflected back out of the atmosphere. For decades, however, meteorologists have been warning that the buildup of an atmospheric belt of concentrations of chemical substances, predominantly carbon dioxide from the burning of fossil fuels, is changing the planet's basic temperature balance by blocking the escape of heat back into space—the so-called greenhouse effect. Other major causes of the buildup of carbon dioxide in the atmosphere are large-scale deforestation (the foliage absorbs carbon dioxide) and, potentially, the pollution of the oceans (which serve as a major sink for carbon dioxide and a source of oxygen).

A principal worry of the concerned scientists is that the resulting warming of the Earth could melt the polar ice masses and change precipitation patterns sufficiently to produce a rise in the level of the oceans that would result in inundation of many of the world's major cities. Some previously frigid regions might benefit by having more moderate temperatures, but others would experience desertification.[19]

In 1985 scientists from twenty-nine countries met to pool their knowledge of these phenomena under the auspices of the World Meteorological Organization, the UNEP, and the International Council of Scientific Unions. Their deliberations, plus reports of international scientific panels convened by the US National Academy of Sciences and the National Aeronautics and Space Administration, produced a rather solid (albeit far from total) consensus among meteorologists and atmospheric scientists that human practices had already contributed significantly to an ominous global warming trend and that, because of the population explosion and worldwide industrialization, the rate of warming was destined to accelerate in the future, probably at as much as twice the rate in the next thirty years as in the previous 130 years.[20]

Although some scientists studying the problem remain skeptical of the proposition that human activities rather than natural phenomena such as volcanic eruptions have been a principal cause of the long-term climatic trends, and there is considerable argument over the projected rates of warming in some of the standard international assessments, almost all of them grant that there are a wide range of plausible effects that the human contribution to atmospheric carbon dioxide levels may be having on the world's climate, and that some of them *could* be both catastrophic and irreversible.

[19]Kenneth A. Dahlberg, "Environment as a Global Issue," in Kenneth A. Dahlberg, Marvin S. Soros, Anne Thompson Feraru, James E. Harf, and Thomas Trout, *Environment and the Global Arena: Actors, Values, Policies, and Futures* (Durham: Duke University Press, 1985), pp. 25–27.
[20]United States Senate, Subcommittee on Toxic Substances and Environmental Oversight, *Global Warming: Hearing*, December 10, 1985 (Washington, DC: Government Printing Office, 1985). *See also* Philip Shabecoff, "Scientists Warn of Effects of Human Activity on Atmosphere, *New York Times,* January 13, 1986.

When it comes to policies for limiting or reversing the carbon dioxide buildup, however, there is as yet little convergence, analogous to what happened with respect to the ozone issue, on an abatement regime capable of dealing adequately with the major sources of the threat. Thus the United Nations Framework Convention on Climate Change, signed by 154 countries at the 1992 Rio Conference (see below), while embracing the *goal* of restoring greenhouse gas emissions to 1990 levels by the year 2000, did not commit signatories to specific levels.[21] Even if the goal were met, the buildup of carbon dioxide would continue, albeit at the 1990 rate instead of at the greater rate forecast under the assumption of a continuing worldwide increase in energy consumption. This rather innocuous undertaking reflects the fact that many of the sources of the carbon dioxide buildup, unlike the case of CFCs, are not simply specific manufacturing processes and machines for which technological substitutes can quite easily be found. Rather, the particulate effluents that are the principal contributors to the thickening atmospheric envelope of carbon dioxide come mostly from the burning of fossil fuels—the most basic means of producing the energy that is the life blood of so many of the activities that are central to the way of life of contemporary industrial society: vehicular transport (ground, air, and sea); lighting and communication systems; temperature control systems; and most of the manufacturing processes for the foods, clothing, and hard goods that people consume. This is why the per capita emissions of carbon dioxide in the affluent countries are so much higher than they are in the low-income and middle-income countries. The average citizen in the United States, for example, is responsible for emitting almost 25 times as much carbon dioxide as the average citizen of India. Indeed, the United States alone, with under 5 percent of the world's population, produces over 30 percent of the world's carbon dioxide emissions.[22]

Should the affluent countries change their lifestyles so as to drastically reduce their energy consumption? And what about the overpopulated developing countries, say India and China (who together make up nearly 40 percent of the world's population)—should they be dissuaded from petroleum-based industrialization policies in light of the likely destabilizing effects on the Earth's climate? Or should the technologically advanced countries attempt to counter the threat by massive investments now in projects to develop "clean" energy systems (for example, thermal and solar power) for themselves and for the developing countries? The potentially huge consequences of a too-little–too-late approach to the uncertainties about the

---

[21]*United Nations Framework Convention on Climate Change* (1992). For analysis *see* Edward A. Parson, Peter M. Haas, and Marc A. Levy, "A Summary of the Major Documents Signed at the Earth Summit and the Global Forum," *Environment*, Vol. 34, No. 8 (October 1992), pp. 12–13.
[22]World Bank, *World Development Report 1992: Development and the Environment* (New York: Oxford University Press, 1992), p. 204.

greenhouse effect *logically* point to drastic choices of this sort.[23] But the market interventions and economic dislocations that would have to be associated with any of these alternatives have thus far rendered them politically infeasible.

"SUSTAINABLE DEVELOPMENT" AS A NEW GLOBAL ETHIC

A further maturation of popular, official, and general intellectual views about global ecological relationships would be necessary to make politically feasible the changes in economic behavior that increasing portions of the international science community regard as logically required to maintain a healthy biosphere. The essential features of such a "paradigmatic shift" were outlined in the 1987 report to the United Nations by its specially appointed, distinguished persons World Commission on Environment and Development. The report of the World Commission (often called the Brundtland Commission, after its chairperson, Norway's Gro Harlem Brundtland) confronted the political, intellectual, and moral sources of the world's predicament head on:

> The Earth is one but the world is not. We all depend on one biosphere for sustaining our lives. Yet each community, each country, strives for survival and prosperity with little regard for its impact on others. Some consume the Earth's resources at a rate that would leave little for future generations. Others, many more in number, consume far too little and live with the prospect of hunger, squalor, disease, and early death.[24]

A principal contribution of the Brundtland Commission was to challenge the presumed antithesis between economic development and environmental care, a concern especially of many Third World economists, worried that the new ecology-preservation imperatives being touted by environmentalists in the United States and Europe would slow down and make more costly the industrialization of their countries. The Brundtland Commission's central concept of *sustainable development* was directly responsive to this concern. The imperative for affluent as well as poor countries, industrial as well as primarily agricultural societies, said the Commission, was "the integration of environment policies and development strategies."

Far from urging a cessation of economic growth, the Commission called for "a new era of growth in which developing countries play a large role and reap large benefits." In particular, "development that is sustainable has to

---

[23]For a systematic elucidation of the logical world development alternatives, *see*, for example, Donella H. Meadows, Dennis L. Meadows, and Jorgen Randers, *Beyond the Limits: Confronting Global Collapse, Envisioning a Sustainable Future* (Post Mills, VT: Chelsea Green, 1992).
[24]The World Commission on Environment and Development, *Our Common Future* (New York: Oxford University Press, 1987), p. 27.

address the problem of the large numbers of people who live in absolute poverty . . . [for] poverty reduces people's capacity to use resources in a sustainable manner; it intensifies pressure on the environment." But policymakers guided by the concept of sustainable development "will necessarily work to assure that growing economies remain firmly attached to their ecological roots and that these roots are protected and nurtured so that they may support growth over the long term."

While recognizing that economic and social systems and ecological conditions differ widely among countries and that each nation will have to work out its own sustainable development policy, the Brundtland Commission was equally insistent that no country can develop in isolation from others. The pursuit of sustainable development, it concluded, "requires a new orientation in international relations."[25]

Responding to the Brundtland Commission's recommendations, the United Nations called a World Conference on Environment and Development, to convene in Rio de Janeiro in June 1992. The Conference Secretary General, Maurice Strong, articulated its mandate:

> The Earth Summit will be asked to adopt an Agenda for the 21st Century, setting out an internationally agreed work program, including targets for national and international performance . . . [and] new international conventions on climate change, forestry, and biodiversity. . . . The summit will be asked to provide developing countries with access to additional financial resources . . . and environmentally sound technologies to enable them to implement the conventions and to integrate environment into their future development. It will also be asked to consider far-reaching reforms of the international system.[26]

THE ACCOMPLISHMENTS OF THE 1992 EARTH SUMMIT

The largest official international conference ever, the United Nations Conference on Environment and Development, held in Rio de Janeiro in the summer of 1992, was attended by 8000 delegates representing 178 national governments, and featured appearances by over 100 heads of state.[27] It also provided a forum for 3000 accredited representatives of nongovernmental organizations.

Two international treaties were signed at the Rio Earth Summit:

[25]The World Commission, *Our Common Future,* quotes from pp. 28–40.
[26]Maurice Strong, "Introduction," to a report to the Trilateral Commission on the tasks of the 1992 UN Conference: Jim MacNeil, Pieter Winsemiuns, and Taizo Yakishiji, *Beyond Interdependence: The Meshing of the World's Economy and the Earth's Ecology* (New York: Oxford University Press, 1991), pp. x–xi.
[27]My discussion of the 1992 Earth Summit in this section relies heavily on the excellent summary report by Parson, Haas, and Levy, in *Environment* (cited in note 21 on page 197).

The United Nations Framework Convention on Climate Change (discussed above), while lacking specific emission targets, commits its signatories to work toward the objective of "stabilization of greenhouse-gas concentrations in the atmosphere at a level that would prevent dangerous . . . interference with the climate system," leaving it to subsequent negotiations and national legislation to establish the means for achieving the stabilization objective. It also provides for funding mechanisms to assist the poor countries in sustainable development strategies that would be consistent with this objective.

The Convention on Biological Diversity requires national governments to develop plans for protecting biologically rich natural habitats and extinction-threatened species within their jurisdictions. The Diversity Convention also requires countries to ensure access to the biologically rich habitats by commercial firms and institutes that are engaged in legitimate biomedical research and product development, but the source countries will retain the right of "prior consent" to such access; moreover, revenues from such exploitation are to be shared equitably with the source countries on the basis of agreements to be negotiated for each situation (this last provision caused the US government, represented by the Bush administration, to balk at signing the convention at Rio; but the Clinton administration indicated in 1993 that it was ready to sign).

The Rio Conference also voted approval of three documents: The Rio Declaration, a Forest Principles Statement, and Agenda 21.

The Rio Declaration, comprising 27 "principles," was championed especially by the Third World delegations. It emphasizes the *development* side of the sustainable development philosophy (Principle 3 stipulates a "right to development") and the "sovereign right" of states to exploit their own resources; but due recognition is accorded as well to the concept of sustainability in principles asserting the integral connection between environmental protection and economic development and endorsing "appropriate demographic policies." One of its provisions, the "polluter pays" principle, could well become a subject of many international disputes in the future.

The Authoritative Statement of Principles on the World's Forests is a weakly worded nonbinding agreement that falls far short of even the rhetorical language of early drafts committing countries to preserve more of their forests. Developing countries that earn considerable foreign exchange from marketing lumber and wood products (led by India and Malaysia) lobbied successfully to eliminate language that would make national governments accountable to international environmental agencies for how they managed their forest resources. The result, commented the Environmental and Energy Study Institute, was "a set of principles which emphasizes sovereign rights to exploit forest resources and thus tends to legitimate existing policies of some countries that imperil those resources."[28]

---

[28]Gareth Porter with Inji Islam, *The Road from Rio: An Agenda for U.S. Follow–up to the Earth Summit* (Washington, DC: Environment and Energy Study Institute, 1992), p. 6.

Agenda 21 is regarded by many environmentalists as potentially the most important document to come out of the Earth Summit. Although also a nonbinding agreement, it lays out a comprehensive set of action imperatives that the Rio countries who voted for it are pledged to implement. In 39 chapters and some 400 pages it calls upon national governments to institute a wide range of particular policies including, for example:

- The removal of subsidies that are inconsistent with sustainable development (such as those that allow for below-cost timber sales and budgetary subsidies for fossil fuels)

- The adoption of community-based approaches to sustainable development that will involve locally affected groups, including indigenous peoples, in the determination of land and water rights and natural resource management rules

- The commencement of negotiations on an international convention to combat desertification

- The establishment of a United Nations Sustainable Development Commission to monitor progress by governments in implementing their Agenda 21 commitments and to coordinate the work of the various international institutions whose missions and projects impact on sustainable development objectives

Following Rio, it would fall primarily to the Sustainable Development Commission to ensure that global sustainable development was more than simply a paradigm on paper. The new institution's ability to perform this role, however, would depend crucially on support from the affluent and powerful countries, particularly the United States.

A year after the Earth Summit the signs were positive that the Sustainable Development Commission might indeed be gaining the capacity to play the central and galvanizing role contemplated for it by its founders. A principal reason for the new optimism was the fresh approach taken by the Clinton administration to issues that had previously divided the industrial countries from the Third World coalition. Indicative of the new approach was a demarche by the US delegation to the Commission on the matter of financing the transfer of environmentally appropriate technology to the developing countries. The United States was now discussing such financial assistance, not as a Third World demand that needed to be resisted by the affluent countries but as a moral and practical imperative in the service of humankind's common interests. Malaysia's Razali Ismail, the chairman of the Commission, called it "a sea change," the beginning of the end of "the developed world versus the developing world."[29]

---

[29]William K. Stevens, "Panel on Ecology Showing Progress," *New York Times,* June 26, 1993.

Still, there is a long way to go toward translating the new consciousness of ecological interdependence into something more than an obligation by the rich countries to help the poor countries achieve sustainable development. The larger imperative—the political and legal institutionalization of mutual accountability relationships congruent with multiple lines of mutual dependence of the peoples of the Earth on each other and on the health of the biosphere—has yet to find a sufficiently influential constituency. But there are stirrings. In most of the industrialized countries, "Green" political parties are finding a place on the ballot, in some cases getting their candidates elected to public office. Increasingly, these parties are communicating with their counterparts in other countries, and they have begun to transnationally coordinate informational and lobbying activities in their respective national legislatures and in international forums.

11

ECONOMIC TRANSNATIONALISM

Most of the technological developments discussed in Chapter 9 are expanding and thickening the economic interdependence of countries, linking their industries, economic sectors, and buyers and sellers of goods and services. "As almost every factor of production—money, technology, factories, and equipment—moves effortlessly across borders," wrote Robert Reich in 1991, "the very idea of an American economy is becoming meaningless, as are the notions of an American corporation, American capital, American products, and American technology. A similar transformation is affecting every other nation."[1] Accordingly, the arenas for determining winners and losers in the world market and in domestic markets are increasingly transnational. In all countries, relationships between governments and markets are affected, as are the issues and instruments of their foreign policies. And in some countries the backlash against the new economic transnationalism is bitter and severe.

More than the legal–constitutional forms of national sovereignty are at stake. The ability of a country to ensure that public safety, orderly commerce, social justice, and cultural integrity are sustained within its territory is undermined when national policies for regulating the national market can be ignored or overwhelmed by buyers, sellers, and investors unaccountable to the legal institutions of the country. Thus, although the end of the Cold War was widely held to be a victory for free market capitalism and an opportunity to dismantle the market-distorting controls on private enterprise associated with the national-security state, it did not easily translate into a rapid worldwide dismantling of national barriers to commerce. Rather, the hoped-for opportunities for expanding free transnational commerce have

---

[1]Robert B. Reich, *The Work of Nations: Preparing Ourselves for 21st-Century Capitalism* (New York: Knopf, 1991), p. 8.

been accompanied by the intensification of the long-standing universal political battle—within countries and among countries—between those who expect to thrive in an open global economy and those who perceive they will be at a disadvantage.

THE CHAMPIONS
OF THE TRANSNATIONAL MARKET

The new economic transnationalism is basically all to the good, say devotees of the "neoclassical" school of political economy that provides the intellectual rationale for free market capitalism: From their point of view, anything that prevents individuals or firms from buying as cheaply as possible and selling to the highest bidder anywhere in the world is unjust. An open global market for trade and investment—or as close an approximation to it as possible—supposedly will result in the greatest good for the greatest number of people.

Today's neoclassical champions of the new economic transnationalism can claim a distinguished intellectual tradition. Their classical forebears include the brilliant sixteenth century Spanish Dominican scholar, Francisco de Vitoria (who articulated the "natural law" right of merchants to trade freely in foreign countries and the corresponding duty of foreign governments not to interfere with them); the French political philosopher, Baron de Montesquieu (who wrote in *The Spirit of the Laws* that "one nation should never exclude another from trading with it, except for very great reasons"); Immanuel Kant (who in *Perpetual Peace* argued that open commerce between nations was strongly conducive to the peaceful resolution of conflict); the eighteenth century French Physiocrats (who insisted on absolute property rights for individuals and argued that the state's primary functions were to guarantee contracts and to ensure free trade between individuals across all provincial and national borders); and, of course, the great early philosophers of economic liberalism, Adam Smith and David Ricardo.[2]

Adam Smith's masterpiece on political economy, *The Wealth of Nations*, published in 1776, was influenced by the *laissez-faire* ideas of the French Physiocrats, although he opposed their agrarianist denigration of the new urban-based industrialism. Smith postulated a self-regulating market that produces what people want at prices they are prepared to pay. As long as there is free competition among producers (including laborers in hiring out their brawn and brains), the natural interaction between supply, demand, and price will work to produce and distribute society's amenities more efficiently and fairly than could any government agency. Smith saw in industri-

---

[2]My characterization of the ideas of the early advocates of universal free trade relies on Stephen C. Neff, *Friends But No Allies: Economic Liberalism and the Law of Nations* (New York: Columbia University Press, 1990), pp. 19–20, 28–35.

alization, with its specialization of labor, the engine of perpetual economic growth and increasing abundance for all, since individuals and firms would be producing and refining their productive techniques for those particular parts of the goods and services that they could produce most efficiently. By extension, larger international markets in which nations specialized in producing what they could do best would add to each nation's wealth and to the overall well-being of the human population. The essential corollary was that nations should be able to trade freely with one another for these various products.[3]

It remained for another Englishman, David Ricardo, in his 1817 treatise *Principles of Political Economy and Taxation,* to elaborate the theory of comparative advantage that to this day (with some refinements) provides the most widely invoked rationale for free trade among nations. Like Smith, Ricardo held that "the pursuit of individual advantage is admirably connected with the universal good of the whole." The aggregated economic behavior of individuals within nations under "a system of perfectly free commerce" results in each country devoting its capital and labor to such productive enterprises that it can produce most efficiently for its home and foreign markets. This system of free competition and global specialization of production "diffuses general benefit, and binds together, by one common tie of interest and intercourse, the universal society of nations throughout the civilized world."[4] In its contemporary "neoclassical" expressions, the theory holds that a nation's success in specializing in particular products is determined not only by its comparative advantage for such production in the standard factors of capital, labor, and natural resources, but also of management and technology. The contemporary neoclassicists admit that free trade can induce economic dislocations and occasionally severe relative differences in the rate of economic growth between countries, particularly in periods of rapid technological change. The sudden development of a new "high tech" product or a chemical synthetic substitute for a standard raw material, for example, can price certain countries out of the international economy literally overnight. But today's neoclassicists see such dislocations as only temporary transitions to new configurations of international specialization and are as committed as their predecessors to the proposition that over the long run "individual and international welfare is maximized by economic specialization and free trade."[5]

---

[3]Adam Smith, *An Inquiry into the Nature and Causes of the Wealth of Nations* [1776] (New York: Modern Library, 1937). For interpretation and location of Smith's ideas in the history of economic thought, *see* Robert L. Heilbroner, *The Worldly Philosophers: The Lives, Times, and Ideas of the Great Economic Thinkers* (New York: Simon and Schuster, 1953), pp. 33–66.

[4]David Ricardo, *Principles of Political Economy and Taxation* [1817] in *The Works of David Ricardo* (London: John Murray, 1871), pp. 75–76, quoted by Robert Gilpin, *The Political Economy of International Relations* (Princeton: Princeton University Press, 1987), p. 174.

[5]Gilpin, p. 179. (It should be noted that Gilpin is not himself a devotee of the neoclassical school.)

Is there any historical evidence that supports the optimistic prognoses of the philosophers of free trade? The most impressive attempt to apply the philosophy to the realm of practical statecraft occurred during the period of British economic hegemony in the nineteenth century. The party of the commercial classes, having won control of the government at a time of prosperity and flourishing trade, launched the world's first great experiment in international economic liberalism with their repeal in 1846 of the tariff on imported grain. This would drive Britain's marginal grain producers out of business as 80 percent of the British population shifted over to the consumption of cheaper food imported from other countries. As characterized by Richard Rosecrance, "this was not an altruistic policy" on Britain's part.

> Under the law of comparative advantage, it allowed her to concentrate on an industrial and exporting strategy and to nourish her citizens with grain from America, Australia, and New Zealand. . . . Britain, in other words, reversed the mercantilist practices of the previous century. Cheap raw materials would now be the fuel for British industry, and inexpensive food would provide energy for the British worker. England's specialization in one realm would allow others to specialize in different ones, and free trade between them would benefit all.[6]

The reversal of mercantilism included elimination of most protective tariffs, removal of the ban on the export of advanced technology, and the ending of the "imperial preferences" system under which Britain gave preference to the imports of her colonies over similar goods of equal or lesser price from other countries. For a time the strategy worked—at least to Britain's advantage. By 1860, the United Kingdom was conducting two-fifths of the world's trade in manufactured goods, and over one-third of the world's merchant ships flew the British flag.[7]

A century after a proud Great Britain, with its repeal of the Corn Laws, attempted to lead the world in removing state barriers to international commerce, the United States, the only great power to survive World War II with its industrial base intact, launched another grand effort to transform the world (at least the noncommunist part of it) into one huge market for free enterprise. The foundational planning for this idealistic yet for the United States self-serving project was the handiwork of Secretary of State Cordell Hull, a latter-day true believer in Adam Smith's vision of world peace through world trade. The principal lesson that Hull and his fellow economic liberals drew from the collapse of the world trading system during the first half of the twentieth century was that the interstate economic order, left to the devices of governments acting out of considerations of short-term domestic popularity, was prone to disastrous disequilibria. National govern-

---

[6]Richard Rosecrance, *The Rise of the Trading State: Commerce and Conquest in the Modern World* (New York: Basic Books, 1986), p. 91.
[7]Paul Kennedy, *The Rise and Fall of the Great Powers: Economic Change and Military Conflict from 1500 to 2000* (New York: Random House, 1987), pp. 151–153.

ments needed to be institutionally locked into international commitments that would insulate them against the inevitable protectionist demands of their constituents during times of economic uncertainty or recession. The result was the famous "Bretton Woods" institutional triad of the General Agreement on Tariffs and Trade, the International Monetary Fund, and the World Bank.

With the objective of universally coordinating the reduction and eventual removal of barriers to international commerce, the General Agreement on Tariffs and Trade (GATT) committed its signatories to a reciprocal lowering of tariffs and to equal market access for all trading partners (the so-called most-favored nation principle). Recognizing that a country finding itself at a competitive disadvantage in the trading arena might be tempted to unilaterally devalue the international exchange value of its currency—the functional equivalent of a tax on imports (and a subsidy for its exports)—all members of the International Monetary Fund (IMF) were required to peg their currencies to a mutually agreed price of gold and to refrain from changes in currency values that were not authorized by the IMF's Board of Governors; but recognizing also that participation in such a genuine global market would periodically subject a country to balance-of-payment deficits (when the value of its imports exceeded its export earnings), the IMF would maintain a pool of contributed funds on which countries temporarily in severe arrears in their international payments could draw to regain equilibrium. Longer-term economic growth deficiencies could be remedied by borrowing from the World Bank to finance development projects.

All of these instruments were supposed to work in tandem to give eventual reality to the dream of a worldwide transnational economy of open borders, a global free market in which individuals and firms pursuing their self-interests would ultimately advance the well-being of all.

PROTECTIONIST REACTIONS

Both the champions and critics of a truly free market understand, however, that it is designed to work and produce its presumably great social benefits through the operation of a painful (for some) "Darwinian" process: Only the fittest—those who can produce most efficiently what others want to buy—survive and thrive; the inefficient must shape up or expire. The problem is that such a stark process of "natural selection" can destroy the social and moral basis of community. Even in the most primitive human societies, some provision is made for tending to the basic needs of at least the young, the old, and the infirm who are unable to compete effectively for scarce resources. And in the contemporary world, every country (often the result of historic domestic battles) maintains a complex of special safeguards against the market's cruel indifference to who gets what, when, and how.

Consequently, as existing safeguards for the less-competitive economic sectors within national societies or, for the less well-endowed countries within global society, are undermined or avoided by big players in the transnational economy, political reactions set in. Groups who fear they will lose in the open transnational market coalesce within countries, and sometimes across national borders, to strengthen their increasingly vulnerable protections. Moreover, on the grounds of needing to remain self-sufficient in an anarchic (and therefore potentially hostile) world, even the governments of well-endowed and powerful countries usually will oppose opening up their economies fully to the vagaries of the global market.

Such protectionism, no less than economic transnationalism, also has an impressive tradition in statecraft and political theory. Economic nationalists can seek support in the classics of moral philosophy. Plato and Aristotle saw the self-sufficient *polis* (city-state) as the form of society most conducive to justice. They argued that external trade, by creating habits of dependence on foreigners, would undermine *autarkeia* (self-rule), and therefore should be kept to the minimum necessary to supplement natural deficiencies in resources. Medieval political theorists, most notably Thomas Aquinas, revived the Hellenic ideal of civil society based on economically self-sufficient city-states. The official cosmopolitan theology of the Catholic Church, however, was more equivocal on matters of political economy than was Aquinas, recognizing that interstate trade not only linked together the parts of the Christian commonwealth but also gave the Church indirect authority over secular matters via its role in interpreting the usury prohibitions and other religiously based rules of fair commerce.[8]

The transmutation of the highly decentralized feudal society of medieval Europe into larger states was stimulated by the need for systems of governance that would match the widening and thickening networks of capitalist commerce in sixteenth and seventeenth century Europe. But the dimensions of the evolving political units, many of which were finally consolidated in the late Middle Ages in religious wars between Protestants and Catholics and had their "territorial integrity" legitimatized in the Peace of Westphalia (1648), would remain substantially smaller than the Roman and other ancient empires. With their territorial jurisdictions now reasonably appropriate for the civic order needs of evolving networks of industry, trade, and banking, the countries of Europe settled into a pattern of government-managed interstate economic rivalry for the next two centuries—the so-called Age of Mercantilism.

Although transborder trade, a good deal of it transcontinental, was very much a part of the mercantilist ethos, it was essentially state-directed trade, with the objective of enhancing the power and wealth of the country as a whole. The increase in power and wealth was not left to the "unseen hand"

---

[8]For the ancient and medieval antecedents of modern protectionism, see Neff, *Friends But No Allies*, pp. 11–20.

of the free market that, according to its advocates, would render the general good out of the pursuit by individuals of their self-interest. Rather, the mercantilist state got its hands into the economy in heavy and visible ways, purposefully manipulating the behavior of its firms and citizens abroad and the activities of foreigners in the domestic market through government regulations, taxes, funding, and other subsidies. The governments worked in close alliance with great overseas trading companies that often acted as the leading edge of the state's colonial expansion.

For the mercantilist states, "free" trade meant the *freedom of each government* to manage its country's commercial relationships in its own interest. The most important consideration was how such trade would add to the military and/or economic power of the country vis-à-vis its rivals. The second-ranking consideration was how the country's own prosperity would be affected. The security and well-being of others or of humankind as a whole were no more than tertiary considerations or afterthoughts, if indeed they were taken into account at all.

The mercantilist orientation was consistent with and largely reinforced by the foundational treatises on international law, most of which were written during the seventeenth and eighteenth centuries. Hugo Grotius, generally regarded as the father of international law, was himself a legal counsel for the Dutch East India Company. In his *Commentary on the Law of Prize and Booty,* written in 1605, Grotius (a supporter of Dutch commercial expansion) argued that every state had the sovereign right to decide whether or not to engage in foreign trade and with whom it would trade.[9] A century after the Peace of Westphalia, building on the theories of Grotius and the actual practice of states, the field of international law came into full maturity in the writings of the German jurist Christian Wolf. In his 1749 treatise, *The Law of Nations Treated According to a Scientific Method,* Wolf asserted that the commercial acts of a state are acts of "pure power" and thus subject to the unfettered will of the state. In pursuing its economic interests, as in defending its territorial integrity, a state's duty to itself overrides its duties to other countries.

Across the Atlantic, the "federalists" in control of the newly independent United States of America discarded the economic ideas of the Physiocrats by which the colonies had justified their opposition to British rule. Mercantilism was more in accord with the imperatives of the new nation's own industrialization and continental development, which would require the protection of a wide array of American "infant industries" against competitive manufactures from the more developed industries of Europe. Secretary of the Treasury Alexander Hamilton's 1791 *Report on the Subject of Manufactures,* with its justification of tariffs to support balanced indigenous industrialization in the service of basic national self-sufficiency, found a receptive

[9]Neff, p. 24.

audience in Europe as well, where it became standard reading in academies and treasury ministries. Influenced by Hamilton's ideas, Friedrich List and the German Historical School of economic analysis led the mid-nineteenth century intellectual reaction against the free-trade ideas then being championed by the British.

List's treatise, the *National System of Political Economy*, published in 1841 and widely regarded as the antithesis to Smith's *Wealth of Nations*, argued that free trade was the luxury of already-industrialized countries with diverse economies. For other countries, like Germany and the United States, the path to industrial affluence and power required tariffs to keep lower-priced foreign goods from displacing domestic manufactures.[10] This was the period when Marx and other socialists were propagating their radical critiques of capitalism and agitating among the working classes to wrest control of governments from the national bourgeoisie. In Germany, the increasing threat of socialist revolution was preempted by the Listian social welfare and protectionist policies instituted by Chancellor Otto von Bismarck in 1879—foreshadowing the social democratic and nationalist reactions in Europe and the Americas to the economic depressions of the twentieth century.

In the twentieth century, with expanding political enfranchisement of more and more economic classes of society, national public policies in most countries have featured a variety of measures for public management of the economy in the service of social justice norms that the free market could not be expected to service. Although the more extreme experiments in political control over the economy, such as the Marxist state socialism instituted in the Soviet Union, have been almost universally discarded as hopelessly inefficient, a wide spectrum of market-management regimes prevails around the world, from social democracies like Sweden and Germany to corporatist states like Japan. Even the United States and Britain, who in the 1980s tried to substantially deregulate their economies, have retained many of the "safety nets" installed during their social democracy phases (the middle 1930s through the late 1970s) for ensuring minimal welfare to those left behind in the market competition. And all national governments today administer a rather heavy menu of health and safety and environmental controls on private enterprise.

Typically, such interferences with the free market have been opposed by elements in society who anticipate being winners in the unfettered economy: the winners in the last round of competition and/or those already in possession of resources they believe will give them the mobility and flexibility to come out on top in forthcoming rounds of the competition. The battles between those optimistic about their chances in the free market and those who do not trust the market to provide adequately for their well-being, let

---

[10]On Hamilton's ideas and their influence, *see* Gilpin, *The Political Economy of International Relations*, pp. 180–183; for List's ideas, *see* Neff, *Friends But No Allies* pp. 65–66.

alone produce equitable outcomes, have been waged predominantly in the domestic political arena, where one-person, one-vote electoral systems have frequently reflected the anxieties of the relatively less competitive economic sectors. The resulting rules governing the market have been expressed for the most part in *domestic* laws. International law, such as it is—being largely a body of doctrines formulated in defense of the state sovereignty system— tends basically to defer to the domestically oriented commercial laws of each country. Consequently, the transnational economic arena, happily for the big players, remains relatively unregulated.

The existence of these two increasingly incongruent domains of the world economy—relatively controlled domestic markets on the one hand and comparatively unpoliced transnational networks of buyers and sellers of goods, services, and money on the other hand—is a glaring expression of the inability of the world polity as currently structured to ensure thus far that what happens in the economic arena serves broad public interests and does not run roughshod over the uncompetitive elements of the human population.

THE EUROPEAN UNION

Although the primary impetus for turning Europe into a common market has come from the advanced industrial sectors that are characteristically antiregulation, the evolution of the multinational market into a genuine European *community* spells the eventual replication at the level of the Union of the intersectoral accountability and social justice norms that constrain laissez-faire capitalism at the level of the nation-state. The freedom of firms to buy and sell and invest in a European market integrated by a common currency and banking system will predictably stimulate community-wide controls on monopolization as well as community-wide laws on bank interest rates and arrangements for handling foreign capital flows, direct investments, and trade beyond the Union. Labor unions, if they are not to be denuded of collective-bargaining strength against management (which has the mobility to operate throughout the Union) will have to develop community-wide strategies and organizations and mutual help in supporting candidates for public office in their respective national parliaments and in the European parliament. The prospect is for increasing community-wide legislation of common health, safety, and social welfare policies of the kind that have evolved over the centuries in national markets to constrain the activities of the entrepreneurial sectors; but, as with the national markets, the European Union's social justice policies are unlikely to be instituted without major political battles along the way. And as with such national legislation, the political unit within which such struggles to humanize the market have been won—in this case the multinational European Union—is, as a result of the process, likely to be all the more protective against unaccountable outsiders penetrating the evolved political economy.

Some of the accountability arrangements, however, on grounds of both justice and practicality, are more appropriately contemplated for transregional or global levels of interaction. This is particularly the case for some of the high-technology communication and transportation industries, which, by their very nature, are joint users of the *planet's* "commons," and therefore require coordination, if not authoritative allocation of resources, across continents and through outer space. As discussed in the Conclusion, some of the most prominent international accountability institutions, such as the International Telecommunication Union and the International Maritime Organization, perform these functions.

CONTENTION OVER THE ROLE OF MULTINATIONAL CORPORATIONS

The tension between the new economic transnationalism and the concerns of nationalists has been particularly evident in many countries of the Third World in the contention over the advantages and disadvantages of a policy of hospitality to multinational corporations (MNCs).

The *proponents* often make the following claims:

- Multinational firms bring financial resources into countries that the host governments and indigenous private sectors would otherwise not be able to obtain. Thus, by the latter half of the 1980s some $20 billion annually in investments in developing countries (22 percent of all funds flowing in) were in the form of investments by MNCs.[11]

- Because of the risk capital, advanced technology, and skilled personnel a large multinational firm can move into a host country, it can establish facilities in previously underdeveloped areas—constructing roads, bringing in electricity and water, setting up local suppliers of goods and services—thereby generating new centers of industry, employment, and economic growth.

- By locally hiring and training workers, technologists, and managerial personnel, the multinational subsidiaries contribute to the diversification of skills and talents within the host-country population and thus to the country's overall development.

- By creating indigenous markets and consumer demand for new lines of goods and services, the MNCs provide an established, relatively low-risk environment for indigenous entrepreneurs (with less risk capital at their disposal) to start their own businesses.

[11]Joan Edelman Spero, *The Politics of International Economic Relations* (New York: St. Martin's Press, 1990), p. 240.

The *opponents* counter with the following complaints:

- The managers of local subsidiaries of MNCs, appointed by and expected to maximize returns to the parent company, have no compelling sense of responsibility or accountability to the host society and therefore are prone to make investment, production, and marketing decisions distortive of the host-country's economic planning.

- The multinational subsidiaries often develop sectors or localities in the host country that draw local talent and financial resources away from sectors and localities that may be in greater need of greater development.

- The new industries brought into a host country by MNCs frequently use advanced capital-intensive technologies whose effects can be pernicious in at least two respects: (1) Their greater efficiency over indigenous industries in similar product lines destroys local competition and discourages the development of local technological capabilities; and (2) their reduced need for human labor worsens unemployment problems that are particularly severe in most of the developing countries.

- The multinational enterprises provide a funnel and mechanisms for an excessive outflow of capital from the host countries through repayments of loans extended to local and private enterprises by the MNCs, special royalties and fees paid to the subsidiary, the disguised repatriation of profits to avoid host-country taxes, and intracorporate trade (purchases of goods and services among the various divisions of a multiproduct MNC instead of purchases within the host-country market)—the latter accounting for more than half of all US international trade in 1990, for example.[12]

- Because a congenial host-country political and economic environment is the key determinant of whether an MNC will transfer in its capital and technology, the corporations have a high interest in the makeup of the host-country governments and their policies; they often will exploit their strategic position within the host-country's economy and among its elite elements to ensure the passage of favorable legislation and the perpetuation of friendly regimes. Occasionally, this intervention goes as far as financial bribery and/or covert conspiracy to install or destabilize particular ruling groups.

- Finally, the transnationalization of economies through the agency of MNCs carries along with it the cultural mores and values of the advanced industrial societies that are the locus of the parent corporations. In the process, indigenous ways of life—including religious practices,

[12]Reich, *The Work of Nations*, p. 114.

languages, and arts and crafts—are often overwhelmed. The euphemism for this impact is "modernization." The negative characterization is "neoimperialism," which is also a connotation carried in the Latin American term *dependencia*.

Despite the criticisms, the MNCs are flourishing. The postures struck against them by Third World leaders are largely rhetorical—a politically necessary element of nationalism—rather than real, as evidenced by the ubiquitous existence of subsidiaries enjoying local tax breaks and other incentives designed to attract and keep them. National economic competition, even mercantilism, paradoxically, turns out to be a rather reliable protection for the MNCs to operate with a minimum of regulation.

Will the ability of the giant multinational firms and international financial networks to affect who gets what, when, and how in world society stimulate efforts to bring them into greater accountability to those whom they affect? If the past two or three decades are looked to for portents of the direction of political responses, nationalist reactions can be expected in most countries. These reactions range from taxes on income earned out of country to barriers to imports of products manufactured by foreign subsidiaries of MNCs. Such measures are likely to reflect the concerns of various groups that feel threatened: labor unions reacting to the loss of jobs to countries with lower wages and poor working conditions; smaller and less mobile corporations unable to take advantage of foreign site locations where the factors of production make for lower-cost operations; and cultural nationalists opposed to the materialistic homogenization of their societies into the global market. Efforts to regulate the MNCs may also be supported by broader public interest and populist constituencies moved by "social justice" concepts.

The best hope for subjecting MNCs and other big players in the transnational economy to public interest accountability lies in the transnational mobilization of multilateral restraints on their freedom of action. This is more likely to happen first in regional common markets—in particular the European Union—rather than universally, although there has been some activity in UN forums.

TENSION BETWEEN FREE-MARKET GLOBALISM AND ENVIRONMENTALISM

The new consciousness of the ways in which market-determined applications of technology are endangering the health of ecosystems (see Chapter 10) has begun to generate national legislation to make firms active in the transnational economy accountable to environmental interests. Predictably, some champions of economic transnationalism have started to fight back, with the invocation of GATT rules against the unilateral imposition of non-tariff barriers.

A case in point has been the comparatively lax environmental laws of Mexico, which became an issue in the controversy over the North American Free Trade Agreement (NAFTA). Labor unions and small business associations in the United States, which are not normally noted for their proenvironmental stances but were now worried about loss of jobs and sales to firms in Mexico that employ cheaper labor, allied with environmental interest groups to oppose such an enlarged common American market unless Mexico first corrected its neglect of environmental values. Mexico (along with Venezuela) has also been a target of Congressional legislation banning the importation of tuna from countries whose tuna-fishing fleets were killing dolphins—legislation that a GATT panel in September 1991 found to be in violation of its rules on reducing trade barriers. Congressional sponsors of the restrictions on tuna imports alleged that the Bush administration was using the GATT arena to circumvent US health, safety, and environmental laws. Senator John Kerry of Massachusetts saw the episode as part of the "confrontation . . . between trade laws and our ability to protect the environmental interests not only of the US, but of the world."[13]

Another issue has been the legitimacy of export controls on logs or wood products, measures favored by environmentalists to slow the cutting of rain forests (a major cause of the carbon dioxide buildup that is promoting global warming). Japan, a major importer of lumber, has been particularly adamant against such controls, charging they violate key provisions of the GATT.

Part of the problem has been the tendency of MNCs, in locating subsidiary manufacturing plants in countries where the factors of production allow them to keep costs down, to favor countries that place the least inhibitions on the pollution of air, waters, soils, etc. (a phenomenon critics have called "the export of pollution"). Products manufactured "efficiently" in such regulation-free locales are then marketed internationally at competitive prices. Increasingly, however, environmental public interest groups, sometimes in alliance with national labor and business groups angry at the price advantages obtained by the importers, are sponsoring national laws to discourage the sales of such products. An example is the effort by the US copper industry, operating under legislation that requires the alteration of copper smelters so that they would capture most of the sulfur used in the production of their products, to get Congress to approve levies on copper imports from foreign industries that do not have to bear the costs of such smelter alteration.[14]

[13]Dianne Dumanoski, "Free Trade Laws Could Undo Pacts on Environment, *Boston Globe,* October 7, 1991. *See also* Keith Schneider, "Balancing Nature's Claims and International Free Trade," *New York Times,* January 19, 1992.
[14]Gareth Porter and Janet Welsh Brown, *Global Environmental Politics* (Boulder: Westview, 1991), pp. 138–139.

An effective coalition of environmental and industry interests will some-times form after the fact of environmental legislation originally opposed by the affected industries. Such indeed has been the result of the domestic and international prohibitions on the chlorofluorocarbon (CFC)-producing in-dustrial processes and products threatening the planet's ozone layer. Indus-tries in countries whose governments have banned CFCs have become part of the domestic and international lobbying effort to ensure that industries in countries not adhering to the prohibitions are not allowed to freely market their products.[15]

A momentous confrontation appears to be looming over the issue of grenhouse warming, however, between economic transnationalists who want maximum freedom of commerce and the enlarging constituency of those concerned with the health of the planet's environment. Without re-strictions on the international trade and consumption of sources of energy that produce carbon dioxide (primarily oil and coal), and without subsidiza-tion of development of alternative clean sources of energy (primarily solar and wind power), human communities the world over are unlikely to con-vert to clean energy systems in time to avoid the disastrous ecological effects of the warming that, as outlined in Chapter 10, the continuing buildup of at-mospheric carbon dioxide levels is expected to produce in the twenty-first century. The restrictions and subsidies, typically, will need to be imposed by national governments—ideally, in accord with internationally negotiated protocols designed to equitably allocate the burdens of conversion—in the form of import and consumption taxes to discourage the use of fossil fuels and research and development contracts and tax breaks as incentives to en-trepreneurial investments in the new energy systems.[16] Moreover, because national producers who get a jump on others in developing cost-effective clean energy systems are likely to find ready buyers for their systems around the world, new and powerful coalitions favoring active "mercan-tilist" support from their respective governments are likely to emerge in most of the industrial countries.

---

[15]Richard Elliot Benedick, *Ozone Diplomacy: New Directions in Safeguarding the Planet* (Cam-bridge: Harvard University, Press, 1991).
[16]For the range of anti-greenhouse measures contemplated, *see* World Resources Institute, *Greenhouse Warming: Negotiating a Global Regime* (Washington, DC: World Resources Institute, 1991).

12

THE RIGHTS
OF INDIVIDUALS
AND COMMUNITIES
VIS-À-VIS NATION-STATES

It is not only the increasing penetration and leaping of state borders by mobile goods, persons, and information that is undermining the "territorial integrity" of nation-states. The capacity of national governments to maintain sovereign authority over what happens within their jurisdictions is also being weakened by the worldwide popular embrace of the idea that a government is legitimate only to the extent that it rests on the noncoerced consent of the governed and secures their basic "human rights."

As with environmentalism, the so-called human rights *movement* is an inchoate phenomenon, encompassing a wide diversity of interests and groups. But its diverse elements tend to coalesce around two philosophical poles that are themselves at odds in many respects: One camp gives primacy to the rights of individuals; the other emphasizes the rights of "peoples" or coherent communities within or transcending existing states. The first expresses universalistic sentiments, derives its philosophical arguments from cosmopolitanism and natural-rights liberalism, and propagates the idea that each human being simply by virtue of being human has an equal claim to the same basic rights as any other human being. The second gives vent to communal and ethnocentric impulses, finds intellectual justification in communitarian schools of thought, and features the concept of "self-determination" in mobilizing political support.

The two human rights camps overlap in their common insistence that governments are legitimate and deserving of respect only if they in fact represent the people within their jurisdictions. But, ironically, this core human rights principle, having galvanized the national independence movements that toppled the great European empires and, more recently, the Soviet empire, is now playing havoc with the nation-state system it helped to create. Almost all countries today contain some ethnic or nationality groups who have caught the human rights/self-determination fever and who are challenging the legitimacy of the state within which they reside.

IDEAS AND INSTITUTIONS SHAPING THE HUMAN RIGHTS STRUGGLE[1]

Historically, some of the most dramatic shakeups of the prevailing international order have been the result of a temporary fusion of revolutionary groups with differing views over whether individuals or communities are the primary possessors of human rights. The revolutionaries have deferred their differences at these defining historical junctures, combining against the perceived common source of their plight: the human rights–denying rulers of their respective countries. In response, the guardians of "international law and order" (regardless of their views about social justice within states) have often found themselves in a *realpolitik* alliance—sometimes explicit, sometimes tacit—with domestic conservatives.

The Revolt of the American Colonies

An early example of the system-disrupting potential of the human rights idea was the revolt of the American colonies against British rule. Drawing heavily on the writings of the British philosopher John Locke, the American Declaration of Independence proclaimed

> that all Men are created equal, that they are endowed by their Creator with certain unalienable Rights, that among these are Life, Liberty, and the Pursuit of Happiness—That to secure these rights, Governments are instituted among Men, deriving their just Powers from the Consent of the Governed, that whenever any Form of Government becomes destructive of these Ends, it is the Right of the People to alter or abolish it, and to institute new Government. . . .[2]

On the one hand, the Declaration claimed even divine dispensation for its assertion of unalienable rights for every person; on the other hand, it lodged the right of revolutionary action in the collectivity ("the people") that was denied representation in the British Parliament. The target, however, was unambiguous—namely, the oppressive and unrepresentative British imperial system—as was the goal of instituting full self-government in America. There was the implication, perhaps naive, that the post-colonial system of governance would simultaneously be representative of the people and protect the rights of all individuals. It was left until later (after the success of the revolution, and at the stage of having to form a new government) to resolve the potential contradictions between individual rights and the requisites of viable nation-statehood.

---

[1]This section on the history of the human rights movement draws on material in the chapter "Human Rights vs. States Rights" in my *International Relations in a Changing Global System: Toward a Theory of the World Polity* (Boulder: Westview, 1992), pp. 101–114.
[2]*A Declaration by the Representatives of the United States of America, In Congress Assembled*, July 4, 1776.

As it turned out, these contradictions were never fully resolved. The original version of the Constitution of the United States formulated by the Constitutional Convention was essentially a compromise among the new nation's diverse states and economic sectors to ensure each of them adequate representation in the federal Union. But the Constitution could not obtain sufficient votes for ratification until it was amended with a Bill of Rights protecting individuals against the excesses of governmental power. Supporting the campaign to amend the proposed Constitution, Thomas Jefferson argued that a "bill of rights is what people are entitled to against every government on earth."[3]

The Bill of Rights did not prevent the newly instituted American government, now bent on consolidating its power, from passing Alien and Sedition Acts against subversive internal dissent—foreshadowing the pattern seen in later successful anticolonial movements for "national self-determination." The post-independence recrudescence in America of the notion that the rights of individuals can only be realized in a well-ordered state, and that therefore reasons of state must often override the claims of individuals, was consistent with the general reaction among philosophers and statespersons worldwide against the "reign of terror" perpetrated in the name of the "Rights of Man" by the revolutionary French government. Nor did the newest nation-state, while shunning entangling alliances, hesitate to take its place in the society of nation-states or endorse the interstate society's norms of sovereignty and mutual noninterference in one another's domestic affairs.

The European Conservative Reaction to the French Revolution and Napoleon's Imperialism

In Europe, reacting to the excesses of the French Revolution and Napoleon Bonaparte's incitement of anti-government liberal/nationalist uprisings throughout Europe (which Napoleon used as a pretext for French imperialist aggression), the great powers, through their nineteenth century "Concert," attempted to restore a conservative statecraft of mutually respectful relations among sovereign governments. Moderate statecraft at the government-to-government level, however, was unable to prevent new human rights battles, fueled by the republican, democratic, and socialist ideologies of the nineteenth century, from sometimes exploding into revolutionary violence (in France in 1839 and throughout much of continental Europe in 1848).

[3]Jefferson's letter to Madison, quoted by Richard Pierre Claude and Burns H. Weston, eds., *Human Rights in the World Community* (Philadelphia: University of Pennsylvania Press, 1989), p. 4. Weston's lead essay in this volume provides a succinct overview of the historical development of human rights ideas.

There were even defections by conservative statesmen from their Concert of Europe commitments of mutual respect, mutual restraint, and mutual help among governments to put down radical domestic uprisings. The opportunities to weaken a rival imperial power in its sphere of control, particularly when the dissidents demanding their rights were of the same ethnic grouping as one's own citizenry, were sometimes too tempting to resist. Yet for most of the century the prevailing *realpolitik* norms (reinforced by orthodox scholarly writing in international law and diplomacy) were by and large observed: Governing elites remained either indifferent to how their counterparts in other countries dealt with rights issues or actively assisted their fellow conservatives to preserve law and order.

By the beginning of the twentieth century, however, the disintegration of the Turkish-ruled Ottoman Empire juxtaposed with the declining power of the neighboring Austro-Hungarian Empire gave an unprecedented opening for the Slavic peoples in the Balkans (themselves divided among diverse ethno-linguistic groups) to demand their basic human rights—preeminently the right of national self-determination. When the autocratic Czar of Russia, perceiving a great opportunity to expand Russia's sphere of influence under the banner of pan-Slavism, began to aid and abet secessionist wars against the Austrians and the Turks, Austria (fearing a radical disintegration of its imperial realm) enlisted the help of Germany in countering the independence movements in the Balkans. Thus was created the combustible cauldron that was ignited into World War I by the assassination of the Austrian Archduke Ferdinand during his July 1914 visit to Sarajevo, a hotbed of Serbian nationalism.

The Legitimation of National Self-Determination after World War I

One of the lessons that President Woodrow Wilson and other liberals around the world drew from the events that precipitated World War I was that conflicts between the rights of peoples and the rights of states could no longer be left to the balance-of-power mechanisms of the nation-state system to control. If new orgies of violence were to be avoided, imperial states that were losing legitimacy with their subjects would have to be induced to allow genuine national self-determination in their realms. Various minorities treaties and a system of mandates and trusteeships requiring the preparation of some of the world's colonized peoples for self-government were instituted under the League of Nations. But the League's mechanisms for managing national self-determination proved ineffective, since the League itself was too deeply embedded in the state-sovereignty system. No individuals or non-governmental groups had "standing to sue," as it were, for their rights. No League agency could have access to any part of the territory of a country or a segment of its population unless such access was officially permitted by the national government of that country. Nor could the Permanent Court of International Justice hold any state accountable to the terms of a treaty it had not signed. Moreover, states could refuse to accept the jurisdiction of the Court.

The pent-up frustrations of aggrieved groups, having virtually no legitimate international outlets, were, no less than prior to World War I, easy targets for mobilization by demagogues. Once again, world war was precipitated by powerful states cynically exploiting communal "human rights" issues: the anticolonial, antiracist themes in the Japanese expansionary power plays in Asia; the national self-determination justifications employed by Hitler for his "Anschluss" of Austria and his absorption of the Sudetenland in Czechoslovakia.

The Precedent of the Nuremberg War Crimes Tribunal

The view that a national government can be held accountable by the rest of the world for how it treats its own people was officially endorsed by the US government and some of its allies when they convened a tribunal in Nuremberg to try Nazi officials not only for starting World War II but also for perpetrating acts of genocide upon civilian populations under their control, particularly the "holocaust" against some 6 million Jews. The Nuremberg Tribunal convicted top political and military officials of the German state of committing and conspiring to commit "war crimes," "crimes against the peace," and "crimes against humanity." The legally controversial nature of the trials was underscored by Britain's unwillingness to associate herself with the charge of "crimes against humanity." The British government agreed that "war crimes" and "crimes against the peace" could be derived from treaties on the laws of war and from peace pacts to which the German and Japanese governments had been parties; but the British found no "laws of humanity" from which to derive crimes against humanity. The US and French jurists, however, invoked *natural* law and "just war" concepts (proscribing disproportionate destruction and attacks on noncombatants) in support of the Nuremberg findings that, in particular, the Nazi death-camp murders of millions of Jews constituted a gross crime against humanity.[4] In the words of the Tribunal's charter,

> CRIMES AGAINST HUMANITY . . . [include] murder, extermination, enslavement, deportation, and other inhumane acts committed against any civilian population, before or during the war, or persecutions on political, racial or religious grounds in execution of or in connection with any crime within the jurisdiction of the Tribunal, whether or not in violation of the domestic law of the country where perpetrated.[5]

[4]Donald A. Wells, *War Crimes and Laws of War* (Lanham: York, 1991), pp. 109–126.
[5]The text of the Nuremberg "Crimes Against Humanity" count is from Victor H. Bernstein, *Final Judgment: The Story of Nuremberg* (New York: Boni & Gaer, 1947).

The Nuremberg Tribunal (and a similar tribunal set up to try Japanese officials) went further than any international agency had ever gone in subordinating the actions of nation-states to a presumed higher law of the human community—a law comprising enforceable rights and obligations for *all* individuals by virtue of their membership in the human race.

Even so, the Nuremberg precedent was worrisome to some human rights advocates insofar as it was a trial of the vanquished by victors who themselves had engaged in arguably disproportionate acts of violence: the fire-bombing of German and Japanese population centers and the US use of atomic weapons against Hiroshima and Nagasaki. The victors failed to subject their own potentially criminal acts to an international judgmental process analogous to the trial they imposed on their defeated enemies.

Although the international legal fraternity continues to debate the legitimacy of the Nuremberg and Tokyo tribunals, one of their legacies was the adoption in 1948 by the UN General Assembly of the Convention on the Prevention and Punishment of the Crime of Genocide. The Convention outlaws "acts committed with the intent to destroy, in whole or in part, a national, ethnic, racial or religious group," including not only killing members of the group, but also causing "serious bodily or mental harm" or deliberately "inflicting on the group conditions likely to bring about its physical destruction."[6] It is under the Genocide Convention that the UN has set up a tribunal to investigate war crimes in the civil war in Bosnia.

The United Nations Human Rights Regime

Well before the full extent of Nazi atrocities were exposed at Nuremberg, it was a foregone conclusion that the post–World War II order would give unprecedented emphasis to human rights. The democracies in the anti-Axis coalition, in order to sustain public enthusiasm for the war effort, claimed to be fighting Germany and Japan not only with the geopolitical motive of preventing these aggressor states from becoming imperial hegemons but equally to allow all peoples to enjoy the freedoms proclaimed in the Atlantic Charter by US President Franklin Roosevelt and British Prime Minister Winston Churchill. The claim exceeded the reality. Neither the Soviet Union nor the European colonial members of the anti-Axis coalition intended to extend such freedoms to all the peoples within their jurisdictions. And there is evidence in the diplomatic record that Roosevelt was more of a *realpolitik* international statesman than his democratic rhetoric indicated. But the expectations, once raised, could not be treated lightly after the war.

Thus the Charter of the United Nations, in addition to its overriding function of preserving international peace and security, gives preambular

---

[6]*Convention on the Prevention and Punishment of the Crime of Genocide*, 78 United Nations Treaty Series 277 (adopted December 9, 1948; entered into force January 12, 1951), Article II.

prominence to the signatories' determination "to reaffirm faith in funda-mental human rights, in the dignity and worth of the human person, [and] in the equal rights of men and women. . . ." And one of the basic purposes of the Organization enumerated in Article 1 is "To achieve international co-op-eration in . . . promoting and encouraging respect for human rights and for fundamental freedoms for all without distinction as to race, sex, language, or religion."

Still, the statespersons and international lawyers who drafted and con-structed the United Nations had no intention of eroding the sovereignty of the nation-states in the name of human rights. Accordingly, Article 2, Sec-tion 7 assures that "Nothing contained in the present Charter shall authorize the United Nations to intervene in matters which are essentially within the domestic jurisdiction of any state or shall require Members to submit such matters to settlement under the present Charter." Notably, the reiterated obligation in Article 55 to promote "universal respect for, and observance of, human rights and fundamental freedoms for all" is presented as a *means* of ensuring the conditions of stability and well-being necessary for peace and security, not as an end equal in value to peace and security.[7]

The UN Charter's circumscribed human rights provisions lagged behind the growing popular support in the aftermath of World War II for rights-based democracy. The liberal democratic ethos could not be denied and was given *its* "charter" in the form of the Universal Declaration of Human Rights adopted by the General Assembly in 1948.

The Universal Declaration was an omnibus collection, without clear pri-oritization, of virtually all the human rights demands that were being di-rected at governments around the world, from demands that governments not interfere with civil liberties to demands that governments guarantee everyone basic amenities like jobs, education, and health care. Because the Declaration was not a treaty requiring ratification by member governments, but only a resolution of the UN General Assembly, it is not, in a formal sense, international *law*. Even so, as pointed out by Louis Henkin,

> Adoption of the Declaration confirmed that the international political system had accepted human rights as a systemic value, and had given it prime place on its political agendas. The international agenda was mainly promotional, as the U.N. Charter had projected, but occasionally, and increasingly, it became also normative and "judgmental."[8]

Building on the Universal Declaration as their imprimatur, the transna-tional human rights constituency pressed the United Nations General As-

[7]*Charter of the United Nations* (signed at San Francisco June 26, 1945; entered into force October 24, 1945).
[8]Louis Henkin, "Law and Politics in International Relations," in Robert L. Rothstein, ed., *The Evolution of Theory in International Relations: Essays in Honor of William T. R. Fox* (Columbia, SC: University of South Carolina Press, 1991), p. 177.

sembly to pass resolutions somewhat more binding on member governments. Four such instruments were adopted in the mid-1960s: The International Covenant on Civil and Political Rights (ratified at the time of this writing by some ninety countries); The International Covenant on Economic, Social, and Cultural Rights (ratified by some 100 countries); the International Convention on the Elimination of All Forms of Racial Discrimination (ratified by some 150 countries); and—the most innovative of all—the Optional Protocol to the International Covenant on Civil and Political Rights (ratified as yet by only 37 countries).[9] The Optional Protocol created the United Nations Human Rights Committee and empowered it to consider written petitions directly from *individuals* who claim that their rights enumerated in the Covenant on Civil and Political Rights have been violated—with the proviso that the claimants must first "have exhausted all domestic remedies."[10] The Committee may hold hearings and issue findings, but these findings are informational only and do not have the force of law. This cluster of basic covenants, increasingly referred to as the "International Bill of Rights," in turn spawned a multitude of specialized and regional human rights conventions and forums.[11]

Most of the human rights activity in recent years, however, has been generated by nongovernmental groups and has bypassed the United Nations and other intergovernmental arenas as being too constrained by procedural deferences to the sovereignty principle to act effectively in cases where individuals and aggrieved groups are seeking redress against their governments. This nongovernmental activity is discussed below (see pages 240–241).

The European Human Rights Regime

The most progress toward holding national governments to international standards of human rights has taken place under the auspices of the Council of Europe. The Council's members (twenty-one at last count) are also parties to the European Convention for the Protection of Human Rights and Fundamental Freedoms. The European Convention established a Commission on Human Rights with authority to receive petitions "from any person, nongovernmental organization or group of individuals claiming to be the victim

[9]*International Covenant on Civil and Political Rights,* and *Optional Protocol to the International Covenant on Civil and Political Rights,* 9 United Nations Treaty Series 171 (both adopted 1966, entered into force 1976); *International Covenant on Economic, Social and Cultural Rights,* 993 United Nations Treaty Series 3 (adopted 1966, entered into force 1976); and *International Convention on the Elimination of All Forms of Racial Discrimination,* 660 United Nations Treaty Series 195 (adopted 1966, entered into force 1969).
[10]*Optional Protocol,* Article 2.
[11]Myers S. McDougal, Harold D. Lasswell, and Lung-Chu Chen, *Human Rights and World Public Order: The Basic Policies of an International Law of Human Dignity* (New Haven: Yale University Press, 1980); *see also* Richard Pierre Claude and Burns H. Weston, eds., *Human Rights in the World Community: Issues and Action* (Philadelphia: University of Pennsylvania Press, 1989).

of a violation by one of the High Contracting Parties of the rights set forth in this Convention, provided that the High Contracting Party against which the complaint has been lodged has declared that it recognizes the competence of the Commission to receive such petitions."[12] (Most of the members of the Council of Europe have signed such declarations.) In such cases, the petitioner and the involved governments are obligated to cooperate with the Commission's investigation.

If the European Human Rights Commission is unable to secure a settlement among the parties to a dispute, it draws up a report stating "its opinion as to whether the facts found disclose a breach by the State concerned of its obligations under the Convention,"[13] and proposes next steps to the Ministers of the Council. These next steps may include referring the case to the European Human Rights Court, also established by the Convention. Only states or the Commission (which can represent individual petitioners) have standing before the Court as plaintiffs. But an individual or nongovernmental group that can get the Commission to back its complaint or find a friendly government to do so can usually obtain a hearing by the Court, since most of the member governments have accepted the Court's compulsory jurisdiction. The seven-judge tribunal has the authority to find a member government to be in conflict with its obligations under the Convention. Moreover, according to the Convention, "the decision of the Court shall, if necessary, afford just satisfaction to the injured party."[14]

An authoritative study of regional human rights regimes published in 1989 found "that the European regime has been genuinely receptive to processing human rights grievances." But the study also reported that over 95 percent of all petitions are screened out during the process and concluded that even in this comparatively progressive system "statist imperatives [still] tend to outweigh the values of human dignity."[15]

An opportunity for expanding the Council of Europe's human rights regime would appear to have emerged out of the 1989 collapse of the Soviet empire in Eastern Europe. The disintegration of the Communist sphere of control was in large part the accomplishment of reform groups operating in the name of the human rights provisions of the 1975 Helsinki Accords (the 1975 Final Act of the 35-country Conference on Security and Cooperation in Europe), which had been signed, but not honored, by the Kremlin and its satellite governments in Eastern Europe.[16] But any formal broadening of

---

[12]*European Convention for the Protection of Human Rights and Fundamental Freedoms,* 213 United Nations Treaty Series 221, Article 25 (signed 1950, entered into force 1953).
[13]*Ibid.,* Article 46.
[14]*Ibid.,* Article 50.
[15]Burns H. Weston, Robin Ann Lukes, and Kelley M. Hnatt, "Regional Human Rights Regimes: A Comparison and Appraisal," in Claude and Weston, *Human Rights in the World Community,* pp. 209–211.
[16]*Conference on Security and Cooperation in Europe, Final Act,* Department of State Publication 8826, General Foreign Policy Series 298, 1975, especially Article VII ("Respect for Human Rights and Fundamental Freedoms, Including the Freedom of Thought, Conscience, Religion or Belief"), and Article VIII ("Equal Rights and Self-Determination of Peoples").

membership in the Council of Europe to now include the non-Communist East European governments, like the contemplated broadening of member-ship in the European Union, is controversial, for it could dilute the degree of consensus on various issues that has been achieved in the 21-member Coun-cil. Moreover, as discussed below, another legacy of the 1989–1991 anticom-munist revolutions (which were in substantial part *nationalistic* revolutions) is the atavistic return to intercommunal hostilities in many of the states of the former Soviet empire.

CONTEMPORARY SELF-DETERMINATION AND INTERCOMMUNAL CONFLICTS

The widespread sympathy among political liberals in the the affluent indus-trial countries for victims of oppression around the world has often failed to differentiate between demands for ethno-national liberation and demands for individual freedom. The fact that the Third World anti-colonial move-ments of the 1950–1970 period and then the anti-Soviet and anti-Communist revolutions of 1989–1991 combined both types of demands produced a pop-ular confusion in the West; and this confusion was reinforced, if not manip-ulated, by makers of foreign policy in order to gain public and legislative backing for various international initiatives and programs.

A parallel set of confusions during the Cold War era appeared in quarters of academic social science that dealt with questions of economic and politi-cal development. Many of the most influential theories of "modernization" assumed that industrialization and democratization, by stimulating the ver-tical and horizontal mobility and intermingling of groups within society, would substantially reduce the class and ethnic cleavages that typically breed revolution and intercommunal violence. A good deal of scholarly writing thus reinforced the dominant popular and official formula holding that national independence plus economic growth plus political democracy equals the maximization of human rights, and that therefore all of these ought to be pursued simultaneously.

The contemporary political turmoil in the post-colonial, post-Soviet worlds, and also in many parts of the advanced industrial world, has not conformed to these popular, scholarly, or official expectations.

Turmoil in the Third World

In most Third World countries, with the necessity of maintaining solidarity in struggles for self-determination against the colonial powers now re-moved, the ethnic heterogeneity of the population has turned the issues of the location of borders and of constitutional and representational structure into explosive contests over which indigenous "nations" now have the right to lord it over others.[17] A sampling of such conflicts follows:[18]

- *India.* The numerous political autonomy movements in India and the frequent outbreaks of violence among its ethno-linguistic and religious groups are no surprise to anyone familiar with the country's history and sociopolitical demography. Indeed, the leaders of India's independence movement knew that probably their most difficult task after the British departed would be to keep their huge multinational/multireligious country from being consumed by intercommunal conflict. Events were to prove them right from the very start, as terrible Hindu–Muslim riots accompanied the partition of the subcontinent into Islamic Pakistan and secular India. The wholesale disintegration of the country into over a dozen nation-states has been averted by a considerable devolution of governing authority to the states of the Union and through modification of their borders to make them as congruent as possible with the location of the principal ethno-linguistic communities. Still, some of the peoples—most insistently the Sikhs of the Punjab and the Nagas and the Assamese in the northeast—have continued to demand even more autonomy, at times violently, to the point of provoking military occupation by the Indian government. The Indian self-determination problem that has attracted the most international attention is that of predominantly Muslim Kashmir, whose status has provoked war between India and Pakistan (requiring UN mediation and peacekeeping), and could do so again.

- *Sri Lanka.* More than 20,000 Sri Lankans have died in the conflict being waged off and on since 1983 between the government run by the Buddhist Sinhalese community (nearly 75 percent of the population) and the mostly Hindu Tamils in the north and east of the island (about 14 percent of the population). Militant Tamils have not only been demanding a state of their own but have also tried to forcibly depose the Sinhalese government.

- *Indonesia.* People in the East Timor region of Indonesia, since obtaining independence from Portugal in 1975 (nearly two decades after the

---

[17]*See* Donald L. Horowitz, *Ethnic Groups in Conflict* (Berkeley: University of California Press, 1985).

[18]For a more comprehensive list and detailed analysis, *see* Morton H. Halperin and David J. Scheffer with Patricia L. Small, *Self-Determination in the New World Order* (Washington, DC: Carnegie Endowment for International Peace, 1992). *See also* Ted Robert Gurr, *Minorities at Risk: A Global View of Ethnopolitical Conflicts* (Washington, DC: United States Institute of Peace Press, 1993).

Dutch relinquished their holdings in the rest of the Indonesian archipelago), have been waging a second war for independence against Jakarta so that they can finally have a sovereign nation-state of their own. As many as 200,000 East Timorese are estimated to have died thus far in this conflict.

- *The Kurds.* The 25 million Kurds, a distinct ethno-linguistic people, proud to claim Saladin (the Islamic anti-Crusades hero) as one of its own, are currently a large minority in four adjacent countries: Turkey, where they are 20 percent of the population; Iran, where they are 10 percent; and Iraq, where they are over 15 percent. Having sought since the 1920s to establish an independent Kurdistan, their self-determination movement has survived repression in each of the countries of their domicile. Their plight again came to the attention of the larger world community at the time of the 1990–1992 Gulf War, which they saw as an opportunity to seek greater autonomy, at least in Iraq. Brutalized by Saddam Hussein, Kurdish refugees from Iraq have been turned back at the borders of neighboring states who are no less willing to allow substantial autonomy to the Kurds within their jurisdictions. Their situation remains a combustible problem for the entire region.

- *Sudan.* For much of the period since gaining independence in 1956, this largest of all the countries in Africa has been convulsed in a polarized struggle between its mostly animist or Christianized southerners (about one-fourth of the population) and its predominantly Arab-speaking and Muslim northerners. Since the intensification of the civil war in the late 1980s, the country's economic development has been paralyzed, resulting in mass starvation and an exodus of destitute refugees.

- *Nigeria.* Although the central government militarily smashed the Biafran secession in the 1960s, Nigeria has continued to be wracked by inter-ethnic violence among its 250 ethnic groups. In recent years, the worst and largest of these intercommunal animosities has pitted the more affluent Christians of the south (about 18 percent of the population) against the Muslim majority who dominate the country.

- *Ethiopia.* A 30-year-long secessionist rebellion by the province of Eritrea, causing over 500,000 deaths, led in the early 1990s to a de facto independent state within Ethiopia. Final establishment of an Eritrean sovereign state was to be consummated following an internationally monitored referendum in 1993. Other regionally concentrated ethnic groups in Ethiopia (the largest being the Oromo) have been encouraged by Eritrea's success and are also agitating for autonomy.

- *Rwanda.* The majority Hutus (about 90 percent of the population) are in a chronic civil war against the minority Tutsis (about 9 percent of the population); in 1994 the killing reached genocidal proportions.

The Palestinian "Intifada"

The contemporary expression of the Palestinian community's demand that Israel relinquish control over territories it occupied in the 1967 Arab–Israeli war—particularly the Gaza Strip, the West Bank, and East Jerusalem—the *intifada* (Arabic for uprising) involves militant, but more or less spontaneous, direct action, sometimes violent, by the Palestinians against Israeli authorities in the territories to make continued Israeli occupation untenable. Arising out of prolonged frustration at the failure of diplomacy to advance the prospect of an autonomous Palestinian state, the intifada temporarily appeared to lose its reason for existence in the fall of 1993 as the Israeli government and the Palestine Liberation Organization (PLO) signed their historic agreement to institute transitional autonomy arrangements for the West Bank and Gaza. But at the time of this writing, the ability of extremists on both sides to retard the implementation of the Israel–PLO accords has been accompanied by a renewed flareup of intifada protests.

The Epidemic of Ethnic Conflicts in the Former Soviet Empire

The numerous outbreaks in the 1990s of ethnic strife between and within the states formerly part of the Soviet sphere of control—an epidemic that followed almost immediately the collapse of the autocratic Communist regimes imposed from Moscow—gave the lie to the Marxist-Leninist myth that the dictatorship of the proletariat would abolish racial and nationalistic conflict. Throughout the communist era, ethnic rivalries seethed beneath brittle political structures in the USSR and Eastern Europe—a deeply implanted legacy that Soviet imperialism was unable to suppress.

The Soviet Union itself was a conglomeration of about one hundred linguistically distinct ethnic groups, some of whom harbored historical grievances against domination by greater Russia. To preempt future trouble, Lenin proclaimed the right to national self-determination, and in the 1920s the Soviet regime granted formal autonomy to the major national minorities, creating constituent republics. The Soviet republics were not really sovereign, however. The Bolsheviks viewed full national self-determination as disruptive of the socialist state; and formal autonomy was merely a characteristic Leninist stratagem of co-optation. In each case, in strict interpretation of Marxist-Leninist orthodoxy, the language, symbols, and folk art of the nationality were brought into the service of the Communist party, which remained highly centralized and uniform throughout the USSR.

The Kremlin's nationalities policy was actually one of Russification and compulsory assimilation where Marxists believe it counts most: the socioeconomic infrastructure. The constitutional recognition of cultural differences, however, allowed the regime to excuse uneven development of the various regions on the grounds that they were incompletely assimilated. But most of the non-Russian republics regarded this as a transparent ruse, which only added to their determination to someday extract themselves from the Soviet empire.[19] They got their chance earlier than expected: With the retraction of Soviet power from Eastern Europe in 1990, the three Baltic states—Latvia, Lithuania, and Estonia—whose forced post–World War II annexation by Stalin was never recognized as legal by the West, declared their intention to secede from the Soviet Union. Belarus, Ukraine, and Russia itself (under President Boris Yeltsin) were next to secede from the USSR, compelling the Union's formal dissolution and supplantation in December 1991 by the loosely organized Commonwealth of Independent States.

With the doctrine that nations should have states of their own now legitimized, the process of ethno-national self-determination had an open field to work its disruptive effects.

What Was the USSR.   The problem is that the newly sovereign members of the former Union of Soviet Socialist Republics are themselves all multinational societies; moreover, in most of the non-Russian states a significant portion of the population is Russian. More than 30 percent of the populations of Estonia and Latvia are ethnic Russians, whom Moscow alleges have been discriminated against, and which is why Russian troops, even though no longer officially welcome, have not been completely withdrawn from these states. Ukraine, fiercely nationalist and second only to Russia in military and economic power among the former republics of the USSR, is over 20 percent Russian. The Crimea, largely populated by Russians but now a part of Ukraine, shows signs of becoming "another Yugoslavia.'"

Many of the most intense intercommunal conflicts are on Russia's southern periphery, where ethnic groups with a Muslim orientation are fighting groups who identify with the Orthodox Christian church. These situations are especially combustible in that they carry the danger of intervention from one or a combination of Islamic Middle Eastern nations, which Russia might perceive to threaten her security interests. The conflict in Azerbaijan over Nagorno-Karabakh is of this type: A mostly Christian Armenian enclave within largely Muslim Azerbaijan, Nagorno-Karabakh voted in 1991 to secede from Azerbaijan and to merge with neighboring Armenia—a vote that provoked violence between the Muslims and Christians in Nagorno-

[19]Harry Schwartz, "Tensions in Brezhnev's Realm," *New York Times*, March 29, 1971; "The Ukraine Stirs," *The Economist*, February 26, 1972. *See also* "Special Issue: Nationalities and Nationalism in the USSR," *Problems of Communism*, Vol. 16, No. 5 (September-October 1967); and Erich Goldhagen, ed., *Ethnic Minorities in the Soviet Union* (New York: Praeger, 1968).

Karabakh and then military intervention by the Azerbaijani government to coercively reverse the secession. Temporary cease-fires mediated by Moscow have broken down, and well over 10,000 people have died in the fighting. An ominous turn was taken in 1993 as the Azerbaijani Armenian militia, well supplied by Armenia proper, consolidated their hold on Nagorno-Karabakh and drove on to "liberate" Armenia's other Christian-Armenian areas, including Nakhichevan, which is bounded in the north by Armenia and in the south by Turkey and Iran. Turkish officials have threatened war against Armenia if that country's troops intervene, a contingency that could also draw in Iran, a rival of Turkey's for influence in Azerbaijan.

Russia Itself.   The government of the Russian federation itself claims to comprise 20 republics. But two of these—Cheschen-Ingusheitia and Tatarstan—have refused to sign Russia's 1992 federal constitutive treaty, and there are secessionist rumblings in other regions as well, such as Siberia and Kaliningrad. Resource-rich Tatarstan's demand to be an independent state is particularly troubling to Moscow for sociocultural and well as economic reasons: Of the republic's some 3.5 million inhabitants, 49 percent are Tatars (a Turkic-speaking Muslim ethnic group), but 43 percent are Russian; and the Tatar people in the republic are only 30 percent of the entire Tatar community, the rest of which is dispersed among other republics of the Russian south.[20]

Eastern Europe.   With the demise of the Cold War and the loosening of Communist-state controls on national and ethnic movements, the countries with the greatest prospect of a recrudescence of destabilizing self-determination demands were Yugoslavia, Czechoslovakia, and Hungary. Also, the German-speaking population in Western Poland was a possible future trouble-spot if Germany ever chose to make their ethnicity a cause for reconsidering the Polish-German border. The explosion of ethnic conflict into a full-blown civil war in Yugoslavia is discussed on pages 128–134.

Czechoslovakia, an artificial creation of the World War I peace settlement, avoided a future of bitter conflict between its mostly Czech and Moravian western parts and its mostly Slovak eastern parts by peacefully deciding in 1992 (through a vote of its central parliament) to dissolve into two countries: the Czech Republic and Slovakia. The lack of congruence between existing international borders and the location of ethnic Hungarians is likely to be a source of increasing trouble for Hungary's neighbors, including Slovakia (which contains 400,000 Hungarians), Serbia (which also has about 400,000), and, most ominously, Romania (which harbors some 2 million Hungarians in Transylvania). In each of these areas political movements

[20]Victoria Pope, "Tatarstan: Descendants of Genghis Khan Are Marching," *U.S. News & World Report,* February 24, 1992.

have been agitating for reunion with Hungary. The official position of the Hungarian government is that it does not want to change existing borders. But sentiment for making the larger Hungarian nation a whole state is definitely a growing factor in Hungary's politics. "Although I am the legally elected leader of 10 million Hungarians," Prime Minister Josef Antail has been quoted as saying, "in my heart I feel I am the leader of 15 million Hungarians."[21]

In the Industrialized West

The flareup of ethnic self-determination movements in Western Europe and North America after 1950 was a surprise, not only to governments but also to social scientists who had expected to see a decrease in subnational dissidence within the modern industrialized countries in the second half of the twentieth century. Consolidation of the polity was widely thought to be a correlate of industrialization; populations would be homogenized within the nation-state, as transportation and communication networks made for rapid interchange of goods and ideas; and rising standards of living would accelerate the assimilation of the previously ethnic ghetto poor into the larger culture.[22]

It was supposed that in free enterprise societies, the expanding economy and desire for jobs in the technological sectors would encourage national integration by stimulating internal migrations to the urban centers, demands from all segments of society for education in the new knowledge and skills, and attempts by ethnic subcultures to assimilate the general culture of the dominant society.

But the new mobility of persons, goods, and ideas has paradoxically stimulated ethnic separatism. Political leaders of particular communities can more easily mobilize sentiment and support of their constituents, especially when the community feels discriminated against by the central state apparatus. Relatively underprivileged ethnic groups, when they are daily exposed via the mass media to the apparent privileges of the majority, have become more receptive to the idea that they are indeed victims of unjust discrimination. The fact that industrialization has also raised the absolute level of goods and services available to all groups in the society does little to relieve this perception of injustice and often exacerbates it. It is the perception of *relative* deprivation that is crucial to the mobilization of group jealousies; and the realization that, even in an economy of abundance, the room at the top is limited, and the competition for status and power increases the higher one climbs, engenders intense bitterness among cultural groups that are up-

[21]Jonathan Kaufman, "Europe Hears Beat of Nationalism Anew From Hungarians," *Boston Globe*, July 7, 1993.
[22]The mistaken expectations are analyzed by Arend Lijphart, "Political Theories and the Explanation of Ethnic Conflict in the Western World: Falsified Predictions and Plausible Postdictions," in Milton J. Esman, ed., *Ethnic Conflict in the Western World* (Ithaca: Cornell University Press, 1977), pp. 46–78.

wardly mobile. Their bitterness is often reflected in systematic discrimination against those on the status rungs just below.[23]

When a group that considers itself deprived is differentiated by a number of cultural factors—say, language, religion, concentration in certain occupations, or physical traits and geographic clustering—the situation is ripe for that group to be politicized and to demand autonomy or annexation by a neighboring state where the group will be part of the ruling majority.

Again, a sampling:

Catholics vs. Protestants in Northern Ireland.   Constituting less than 40 percent of a population more than 60 percent Protestant, the Catholics in Northern Ireland have been agitating, often violently, for a rectification of their minority status, which they regard as being artificially imposed on them by predominantly Protestant Britain. If all of Ireland were one nation-state (that is, if Northern Ireland were merged with the predominantly Catholic Irish Republic), the Catholics, constituting 76 percent of the entire island's population, would provide the ruling majority for the whole country. Thus, from the perspective of the Catholics, the 1921 "solution" to the eight-century long, often bloody history of Anglo-Irish and religious conflict was unjust from the start: Under the 1921 partition, the southern and western two-thirds of the country, over 90 percent Catholic, were granted the status of a self-governing dominion; but the northeastern one-third of the country where 85 percent of Ireland's Protestant minority reside was kept out of the Irish Republic and preserved as a Protestant-majority province of the United Kingdom. Understandably, from the point of view of the Protestants the 1921 partition was an eminently fair resolution of the otherwise interminable civil war between the two religious groups.

As it turned out, however, the 1921 partition only deflected the violent civil conflict from the whole island, where the Protestant minority would be battling for its rights against the Catholic majority, into Northern Ireland, where the now-minority Catholics have been battling against the province's Protestant majority, whom they charge with preempting the best living areas and jobs and in many other ways perpetuating a regime uncongenial to the Catholic way of life. Extremely militant Catholics in both parts of Ireland have never reconciled themselves to the 1921 partition and have conspired in outlawed societies to make Northern Ireland ungovernable, often resorting to terroristic acts and harassments to provoke violent encounters between the two religious communities.[24] The situation deteriorated so severely in the late 1960s and early 1970s, that in 1972 the British government was driven to reinstitute direct rule from London. Concerned people in England and abroad were compelled to reconsider whether the only way of

[23]Gurr, *Minorities at Risk*, pp. 123–138.
[24]J. C. Beckett, "Northern Ireland," *Journal of Contemporary History*, Vol. 6, No. 1 (1971), pp. 121–134.

avoiding intensified rounds of intercommunal terrorism and even full-scale civil war would be to acquiesce to the militant Catholics' demands for the separation of Northern Ireland from Britain and some sort of federation with the South.

In 1985, after more than a decade of failed mediational and diplomatic efforts, the British government and the Republic of Ireland signed an agreement that would give the government in Dublin a consultative voice on a wide range of policy decisions affecting Northern Ireland. The 1985 accord was denounced by Protestant party leaders from Northern Ireland sitting in the British parliament as providing the southern Catholics with "covert joint authority" with Britain over the northern counties and charged that it was transparently a first step toward the united Ireland that the Protestants could not accept. Militant Catholics denounced the agreement for the opposite reasons: In signing it the Irish Republic recognized British sovereignty over Northern Ireland and in return got a consultative role that in reality was responsibility without appropriate power.[25]

Since the 1985 accord, however, the essential sociopolitical situation in Northern Ireland has not changed. Catholics and Protestants continue to segregate themselves in different parts of the cities and towns. The Catholics, egged on by their militant leaders, continue vehemently to express their sense of alienation and underprivileged status. The Irish Republican Army continues to demand a plebiscite throughout greater Ireland on the issue of Ulster's incorporation into the Republic of Ireland. Radical Unionists in the Protestant community continue to demand full union with Britain. And intercommunal terrorist acts have not abated.

Once again, in 1993, the deteriorating situation produced a new effort by moderates in the United Kingdom and the Republic of Ireland to resolve the conflict. In December 1993, prime ministers John Major of Britain and Albert Reynolds of Ireland signed a declaration of general principles calling for a renunciation of violence by all parties and reaffirming that the two governments "will uphold the democratic wish of a greater number of the people of Northern Ireland on the issue of whether they prefer to support the Union or a sovereign united Ireland." The document also contained an agreement by the British government to the proposition that "it is for the people of the island of Ireland alone, by agreement between the two parts respectively, to exercise their right of self-determination on the basis of consent, freely and concurrently given, North and South, to bring about a united Ireland, if that is their wish."[26] Skeptics doubted that the gaps in and between these two statements were any closer to being bridged than in the past; but optimists pointed to a number of factors conducive to a breakthrough to peace, or at least to compromise: The end of the Cold War reduces the strategic signifi-

[25]Jo Thomas, "Anglo-Irish Agreement Pits Both Ends Against the Middle," *New York Times*, November 24, 1985.
[26]Excerpts from the text of the joint declaration by the British and Irish prime ministers, *New York Times*, December 16, 1993. *See* accompanying article by John Darnton.

cance to Britain of Northern Ireland as a forward defense outpost against potential Soviet forays around Scandinavia; and the British are becoming increasingly impatient with the financial strain of continuing to police and tend to the economic development of Ulster. The tremendous burdens the Germans have been suffering since 1991 as a result of reunification is not lost on Dublin, nor is there much enthusiasm for the prospect of having to take over the role from Britain of suppressing intercommunal violence in Ulster. But what federal or confederal arrangements all of this implies still need to be negotiated at the state-to-state level and then made acceptable to the religious communities of Northern Ireland.

The Flemish-Walloon Rivalry in Belgium.   In Belgium, a bitter historic polarization of society along ethnic and linguistic lines periodically threatens to overwhelm other bases of political alignment that have sustained this bicultural nation-state. The 5.5 million Dutch-speaking Flemings in the traditionally agricultural north have for centuries resented the dominance of the 4 million French-speaking Walloons of the more industrialized south. Their linguistic differences became the central political issue between the two communities in the 1830s when French was made the official language of the new kingdom of Belgium. Henceforth, facility in the French language, to the disadvantage of the Flemings, was essential to professional advancement in both the public and private sectors. The post-1950 industrialization of some of the Flemish areas and the accompanying northward migrations of the Walloons into Flemish border areas and cities exacerbated the interethnic animosities.[27]

During the 1970s and 1980s, the Belgian parliament transformed the heretofore highly centralized government into more of a federal system of four ethno-linguistic regions:.[28] A Flemish (Dutch) area; a Walloon (French) area; a small German-speaking area; and Brussels, which is bilingual. Each region has autonomy over language use and local social/cultural matters. The 1991 elections increased the strength of parties demanding even further devolution of power to the regions. It is unpredictable at this point whether the devolution of additional governing authority to the linguistically defined regions will defuse the country's interethnic conflict or whether it will merely whet the appetite of the communal extremists and lead eventually to the breakup of Belgium into two nation-states.[29]

[27]Derek W. Urwin, "Social Cleavages and Political Parties in Belgium: Problems of Institutionalization, *Political Studies*, Vol. 18, No. 3 (September 1970), pp. 320–340.
[28]Louis L. Snyder, *Global Mini-Nationalisms: Autonomy or Independence* (Westport, Conn: Greenwood Press, 1982), pp. 85–94.
[29]Some analysts see the development of other occupational, class, ideological, and regional affiliations in Belgium as becoming more, or at least no less, salient in Belgian politics than the conflict between the Flemish and the Walloons, and forecast that these proliferating cross-cutting associations augur well for the perpetuation of a generally well-functioning nation-state. *See*, for example, Aristide R. Zolberg, "Splitting the Difference: Federalization without Federalism in Belgium, " in Esman, *Ethnic Conflict in the Western World*, pp. 103–142.

Basque Separatism.   Resistance to assimilation into the larger nation-states in which they reside has been a chronic political preoccupation of the Basques, a linguistically and culturally distinct population of over 1 million living just north and south of the Pyrenees mountain range between Spain and France. About 90 percent of the Basques live on the Spanish side of the border. Exposure to the outside world, including the example of the Irish, Flemish, and Quebec independence movements and, since 1990, the disinte-gration of the USSR, has had intensive political impact on the four Spanish Basque provinces, where contemporary demands for independence echo Spain's long history of regionalist/centralist conflict.[30] (The Catalans, an-other distinct ethno-linguistic community on the French-Spanish border, have been engaged in a similar campaign to maintain their cultural and po-litical autonomy.)

As part of Spain's evolution toward full democracy after the death of dic-tator Francisco Franco in 1975, the Constitution of 1978 divided the country into 17 regional "automies." Under the new Spanish constitution, the Basques, like the peoples of other regions, have increasingly assumed power over schools, taxation, and local economic development. But Basque politi-cal extremists, worried that their compatriots would settle for half a loaf, particularly during the economic depression the region was suffering, esca-lated their demands for total independence and stepped up terrorist attacks against Spanish officials and local industrialists and businessmen who wanted constructive cooperation with the new democratic modernizers in Madrid.

The militants' terrorist strategy is designed both to provoke the Spanish government into repressive reactions, so as to justify the claim that fair treat-ment of the Basques can never be had from Madrid, and to take credit for whatever additional concessions to local autonomy the central government may choose to make to avoid further extremism. As of this writing, how-ever, it appears that the Basque moderates who believe autonomy within the Spanish state makes more economic and political sense than full inde-pendence have the ascendancy in the Basque provinces.[31]

Secessionist Pressures in Quebec.   The fact that over 6 million Canadians out of a total Canadian population of 28 million trace their ancestry back to France and continue to regard French, rather than English, as their first lan-guage, and that more than 5 million of them live in Quebec (which has a to-

---

[30]Stanley Payne, "Catalan and Basque Nationalism," *Journal of Contemporary History*, Vol. 6, No. 1 (1971), pp. 15–51.
[31]Snyder, *Global Mini-Nationalisms*, pp. 101–110. For reportage on the persistence of Basque ter-rorism into the middle 1980s, *see* Edward Schumacher, "No End in Sight for Basque Terrorism," *New York Times*, August 26, 1986. For the early 1990s, *see* "Spain's Nationalists Press for Inde-pendence," *New York Times*, September 22, 1991.

tal population of 7.2 million) has been a persisting source of potential dis-ruption of the Canadian federal system. Beginning in 1963 with the found-ing of the *Rassemblement pour l'independence nationale*, Quebec's secession from the Canadian federal union has been an openly proclaimed objective of influential elements of the province's elite. Public opinion surveys show that only 35 percent of Quebec's population actually favor secession, but some 60 percent support a maximum amount of autonomy within the Canadian fed-eration, including total control of all matters cultural, especially with respect to laws mandating the use of the French language.[32] The growing political self-consciousness among Canada's indigenous (pre-European) peoples is another brake on Quebec's full secession, for the Cree and Inuit tribes who inhabit Quebec's northern regions have made it clear that if Quebec leaves Canada, they will secede from Quebec.

The zenith of Quebec secessionist nationalism was the election of the Parti Québecois (PQ) into power in 1976 under the leadership of René Lévesque. But faced with the practical problems of just when and how to ef-fectuate secession, the economic and political costs of the rupture, and then of going it alone compelled the PQ to modify the objective to "sover-eignty/association"—political independence but economic association with the rest of Canada in a common market.

When the concept of secession was put to a vote in a 1980 provincial ref-erendum, it was rejected by 60 percent of the voters. But in 1982 when Canada enacted its first constitution, Quebec refused to sign. In 1985 the PQ lost control of the provincial government to the Liberal Party, also a cham-pion of greater autonomy for Quebec, but within a reformed Canadian fed-eration.[33] Efforts to work out a special formula (such as the Meech Lake Ac-cord of 1990) by which Quebec could satisfy its demands for distinctiveness have been strongly opposed by some of the other provinces as violating the principle of the constitutional equality of the Canadian provinces; frustrated and angry, the Quebec electorate returned the cessationist PQ to power in 1994.

A Global Phenomenon

The ethnic self-determination movements briefly described above are just a sampling of a phenomenon that has become a worldwide challenge to the viability of the nation-state system as a whole. Only one in ten of the world's countries are ethnically homogeneous; three-quarters of the countries have ethnic minorities that make up over 5 percent of the population; and in one-tenth of the countries at least 40 percent of the population is distinct from

[32]Colin Nickerson, "A Separatist Fervor in Quebec," *Boston Globe*, October 20, 1993.
[33]Ivo D. Duchacek, "Quebec: A U.S. Neighbor—A Community Unlike Any Other: Dyadic Fed-eralism and Its Confederal Ingredients," A paper for the University Consortium for Research on North America, Conference on Canadian-United States Relations, Fletcher School of Law and Diplomacy, October 1986.

the dominant ethnic group.[34] In almost every nation-state industrialization and economic development have visibly benefited some regions, ethnic groups, or classes more than others, and the disadvantaged are prone to see themselves as victims of systematic discrimination by the privileged groups. In some countries where the poorer ethnic elements are in the majority or are special beneficiaries of redistribution programs, the better-off ethnic groups are also prone to become alienated from the existing nation-state. Such situations provide an opportunity for ethnic or class leaders to step forward and demand power in addition to programs, and to promote the heady notion that things would be better if the distinctive group designed and operated its own sociopolitical system.

Not all of the would-be separate nations, however, are strong enough in numbers or command enough resources to carry through a full-blown secessionist revolution on their own. Consequently, although ethnic self-reliance is the ideal that holds them together, many militant vanguards are tempted to seek allies among other aggrieved groups at home or abroad that are severely alienated from the dominant culture, or with separatist movements in other countries or sometimes with foreign nation-states that also oppose the existing national government.

One response by aggrieved people who are suffering political persecution and/or economic deprivation and are unable to obtain redress within their countries of domicile is simply to leave and to attempt to settle in another country. In some cases, however, this can transfer inter-ethnic conflict into the other country whose majority population also may be unprepared psychologically and politically to deal constructively with the resulting cultural tensions and economic burdens.

The Migration Issue

As pointed out in Chapter 9, the fact that the population explosion is having its most severe impacts in the poorer countries is a primary reason, along with political repression, for the swelling rivers of migrants across national borders in the search of a better life. In its 1993 report, the United Nations Population Fund estimated there were some 100 million migrants around the globe, 37 million of whom fled their home countries to escape violence, starvation, or unlivable environmental conditions.[35] This problem will not go away and is bound to get worse in the decades ahead. In the affluent

---

[34]*See* Gunnar P. Nielson, "States and 'Nation-Groups': A Global Taxonomy," in Edward A. Tiryakian and Ronald Rogowski, *New Nationalisms of the Developed West* (Boston: Allen & Unwin, 1985), pp. 27–56.
[35]*See Boston Globe* editorial, "The Human Crisis of Our Age," July 11, 1993; and Tim Zimmerman, "A Cry From the Wretched." *U.S. News & World Report,* November 30, 1992, pp. 36–38.

Western countries in particular, one of the consequences has been to elevate the question of immigration policy to the top of the political agenda.[36]

In the democracies of Western Europe and North America, the majority populations have been polarizing over the extent to which criteria for immigration and citizenship for refugees, and even for admitting temporary laborers, should be restricted more than they have been in the recent past. Nationalist parties—the Vlaams Blok in Belgium, the National Front in France, the Lombardi League in Italy, Die Republikaner in Germany, the Freedom Party in Austria—have been attracting popular support and gaining strength in their countries' parliaments on the basis of platforms that unabashedly sound the alarm against the dilution of the national culture by immigrants from the Third World. Violent encounters between paramilitary ultranationalist youth groups (most notoriously the neo-Nazi "skin heads" in Germany) and residents with non-European ethnic characteristics, who have begun to defend themselves against harassment, are played upon by the officially recognized right-wing parties to engender fear in the populace at large that law and order requires the restoration of sociocultural homogeneity. Although European Union leaders at their December 1991 Maastricht conference signed a statement warning that "the manifestations of racism and xenophobia are steadily growing in Europe," they were sufficiently concerned about the nationalistic backlashes in their countries during 1992 to delay their earlier pledge to remove passport controls among the continental European countries scheduled for January 1, 1993.

Even in the United States, under a Democratic president whose election campaign castigated his predecessor for callously turning away Haitian and other Third World exiles from political oppression, the government, supported by Congress and organized labor, has instituted stringent implementation of immigration controls that were originally designed as Cold War screens against subversives. And public opinion has been increasingly supportive of tightening the restrictions (a *New York Times*/CBS News Poll in the summer of 1993 showed 61 percent of the respondents favoring a decrease in immigration).[37] The ostensible reasons advanced by those in favor of reinstating restrictive policies are economic—to prevent the loss of jobs by American citizens to desperate immigrants (legal and illegal) willing to work for any wage, and to reduce the social welfare and health costs to the country of having to care for the influx of destitute people from all around the world. A publicly unarticulated populist sentiment underneath these pressures is the desire to arrest the rapid change in the "complexion" of US

[36]Myron Weiner, ed., *International Migration and Security* (Boulder: Westview Press, 1993.)
[37]Seth Mydans, "Poll Finds Tide of Immigration Brings Hostility," *New York Times*, June 27, 1993.

society from being predominantly Caucasian and unilingual to becoming a microcosm of world society. Human rights advocates of a largely open immigration policy, like their counterparts in Europe, are now on the defensive against the new xenophobia.

TRANSNATIONAL AGITATION FOR INDIVIDUAL RIGHTS

A counterpoint to the the post–Cold War politics of ethnicity, at times contradicting it, has been the growth of transnational nongovernmental activity on behalf of individuals whose basic rights (presumably universally valid) are violated by the states, nations, or other communities in which they live. The spearheads of this effort include lay organizations such as Amnesty International and Human Rights Watch, semiofficial organizations such as the International Committee of the Red Cross, and professional associations such as the International Commission of Jurists.

The perceived need and opportunity for nongovernmental action in this field is a product of the conservatism of national governments and intergovernmental organizations when it comes to challenging the sovereignty norm of the nation-state system. Consistent with this norm, national governments and the international organizations to which they belong are reluctant to become advocates on behalf of individuals who are citizens of another country—unless such advocacy is a considered strategy designed to embarrass the other country's ruling regime. If governments are friendly toward each other, one government may on occasion quietly intercede with another's officials on behalf of individuals whose family or professional associates are concerned about their well-being, but almost never in a case that has become an international cause célèbre.

Typically, the nongovernmental human rights organizations like Amnesty, using their transnational memberships and worldwide contacts, gather information on individuals reported to be missing or maltreated precisely in those cases where a government is presumed to be at fault or negligent. This information is then fed back to the involved government, and inquiries are made in an effort to verify the allegations. In the process, the offending government is alerted to the fact that the victim has international advocates who could bring the case to the attention of the world's official international organizations, the media, and the publics and parliaments around the world, thereby negatively affecting that government's international relationships. Moreover, if Amnesty, for example, discovers a pattern of violations of the rights of individuals by a particular country, it will report this pattern to cognizant international agencies such as the International Human Rights Commission and also will publish an analysis of that country's behavior in reports available to the general public.

Thus, Amnesty International's 1993 report cited 163 countries for human rights violations, totaling over 3000 cases of torture, arbitrary imprisonment, disappearance, political killing, and the death penalty. Some of the most notorious offenders like Syria and North Korea are dictatorships and might seem to be immune from the negative publicity. But others, while highly autocratic and resentful of foreign prying—China, for one—may be attempting to overcome poor human rights reputations so as to qualify for normal trading relationships with the United States and other countries. And there are governments that can be deeply wounded by reports calling into question their claim to be democracies. Mexico, trying to build a reputation of being a worthy partner of Canada and the United States in the North American community, could not have been happy with Amnesty's allegations that

> Torture was frequently used by [Mexico's] law-enforcement agents, particularly the state judicial police, throughout the country. Most of the victims were criminal suspects but some—including leaders of indigenous communities and human rights activists—were apparently targeted solely for their peaceful political activities. . . .
>
> Scores of people were arbitrarily detained and ill-treated by security forces in the context of land disputes and during peaceful demonstrations. . . .[38]

Even democracies proud of their human rights records have come in for specific criticisms by Amnesty. The United States, for example, was cited (among other things) for its frequent use of the death penalty, for various cases of brutality and racial discrimination against prisoners by corrections officials, and for forcibly returning thousands of Haitian asylum-seekers to Haiti without a hearing.[39] And the Netherlands, for many liberals a model of an enlightened democracy, was criticized for failing to sufficiently investigate reports of torture and ill-treatment of prisoners in the Netherlands Antilles and Aruba, two of its Caribbean possessions.[40]

THE NEW ACCOUNTABILITY

Clearly, the era of world politics when national governments did not have to be accountable to anyone but themselves for how they treated their citizens is coming to an end. But the norms and structures of accountability that will be featured in the new era are still to be determined. In the emergent world polity, who will have primary standing as claimants and sources of rights—individuals, non-governmental collectivities, or states? And which kinds of rights will be accorded primacy—political and civil rights? Economic and social welfare rights? Finally, can these inherently controversial issues be

[38]*Amnesty International Report 1993* (New York: Amnesty International, 1993), pp. 207–210.
[39]*Ibid.*, pp. 301–304.
[40]*Ibid.*, pp. 220–221.

addressed in universalistic terms, applicable to individuals and peoples of all cultures, or must the international guardians of human rights always defer to the particular cultural traditions and circumstances of the world's diverse nations and ethnic groups as interpreted by their own authorities?

While the answers to these questions remain highly debatable, what has moved beyond debate to the point of being accepted as a foundational norm of the contemporary world polity is the obligation of all peoples to subject their human rights practices to international scrutiny and discussion. This consensus was ratified in December 1993 in the form of an agreement by the members of the United Nations to appoint a High Commissioner of Human Rights charged with the responsibility for ensuring respect for human rights around the world. The High Commissioner and his or her staff would not have the power to compel adherence to particular human rights principles, but, mirroring the functions of some of the nongovernmental groups such as Amnesty International, and drawing on their investigations, the new office can itself investigate and publicize questionable human rights practices and report them to the UN General Assembly and other world bodies. In creating this office, and by the terms of its mandate, the countries of the world have officially overridden objections by some Third World ideologues that the human rights idea is a Western conceit imposed by neoimperialists on the rest of the world. But the mandate makes a concession in the direction of a pluralistic rather than a unified view of human rights by requiring the UN Secretary General to appoint a high commissioner with "knowledge and understanding of diverse cultures."[41]

R. J. Vincent, a sage British scholar of international relations, in his 1986 book, *Human Rights and International Relations,* anticipated the current ferment in his recognition of

> the reality of a transnational world from which proposals about the rights of humans come. . . . Individuals and groups other than states have forced themselves on the attention of international society, and the international law of human rights has been both the response to this and the handle for further progress.[42]

Those blind to this new reality, wrote Professor Vincent, "may be missing a transformation from international relations to world politics as significant as that which established the society of states, and for which the idea of human rights is a kind of midwife."[43]

---

[41]Paul Lewis, "U.N. Agrees to Create Human Rights Commissioner," *New York Times,* December 14, 1993.

[42]R. J. Vincent, *Human Rights and International Relations* (New York: Cambridge University Press, 1986), pp. 151–152.

[43]*Ibid.,* p. 128.

13

THE PROBLEM OF INCONGRUENCE[1]

A well-functioning political system normally features an essential congruence between, on the one hand, the effective authority possessed by society's governing institutions and, on the other hand, the behavior that must be constrained by government in order to maintain or further society's values. By contrast, where behavior escapes needed governmental constraints—as it so often does today in the global nation-state system—we do not have a well-functioning political system.

Congruence, in this sense, does not imply heavy intervention by government to control human behavior throughout the society; political congruence can exist in sufficient measure where there are relatively permissive or laissez-faire regimes—which in many situations may well be the most conducive to the realization of a society's values. But the concept does imply at least a *capacity* of government to provide sanctions and incentives to constrain the behavior of elements of society as required to maintain society's essential structure and norms. Indeed, the lack of capacity for such governance, especially if this deficiency is widely perceived throughout the society, is one of the conditions conducive to political violence. Without enforceable rules for managing conflict, those whose interests clash have little to rely on besides raw power to constrain their adversaries from simply grabbing and taking.

THE TRADITIONAL SOVEREIGN STATE SYSTEM

For some three centuries the world's political system has been premised on a particular pattern of governance/society congruence: the expectation that the most intensive patterns of human interaction would take place within

---

[1]This chapter borrows substantially from Chapter 8 of my *International Relations in a Changing Global System: Toward a Theory of the World Polity* (Boulder: Westview Press, 1992), pp. 115–130. Sections of that chapter are reprinted here with permission of Westview Press.

territorially defined jurisdictions, each having its own regime of governance (or "state") with sovereign authority over what happened in its jurisdiction, and that this sovereignty would be recognized and respected by the other states. Attempts to intervene in another's jurisdiction would be considered illegitimate, and even grounds for war.

As described in Chapter 1, each of the presumably sovereign states in the nation-state system is expected to control events within its jurisdiction so as to ensure the performance of basic societal functions: the protection of persons and property from physical attack; the enforcement of laws and contracts; the orderly exchange of goods and services; the husbanding of resources essential to the healthy survival of the population; and the maintenance of the society's cultural, moral, and legal norms, including the rights and obligations of individuals and standards of distributive justice.

In the traditional, somewhat idealized configuration of the system, these basic functions of society and governance were to be performed and provisioned almost entirely *within* each of the sovereign nation-states. Accordingly, international or transnational interactions could be relatively sparse and managed for the most part by negotiation or periodically (in cases of conflict unresolvable through peaceful bargaining) by war. Looking at the world from this perspective, there was no crucial incongruence between the configuration of global society and the anarchic structure of global governance: Global society itself was compartmentalized into national enclaves of human interaction that conformed essentially to the territorial and legally recognized jurisdictions of the states in the system. The nation-states were willing to take their chances in the anarchic world polity when it came to handling international relations, in preference to subordinating the sovereignty of their territorial units to "supranational" governing bodies purporting to act on behalf of some larger inchoate international community, let alone a nonexistent worldwide community of humankind.

THE CONTEMPORARY PATTERN

Today's world hardly conforms to the traditional picture of a global society of sovereign nation-states interacting with each other mainly at the margins of their existence. Rather, it features a growing incongruence between the dynamic trans-jurisdictional mobility of persons, things, and information and the comparatively static institutions of national governance—to the point where the anarchically structured nation-state system is virtually in crisis. This approaching systemic crisis is an expression of increasing incongruities worldwide in society/governance relations along five dimensions: (1) the protection of community values vs. the destructiveness of warfare, (2) the behavior of the economy vs. the structure of the polity, (3) the location of ecological systems vs. political boundaries, (4) ethnic or religious identifications vs. loyalty to a given nation-state, and (5) human rights vs. state sovereignty norms.

The Incongruity of War with Community Values

The nation-state system, being essentially of anarchic structure, has required that each country (acting on its own or with assistance from allies) be able to credibly threaten military action to protect its independent existence and highly valued interests. But when going to war involves placing the national community at high risk of virtually total destruction, which today's military technology makes all too likely, an intolerable disproportion arises between the ends and the means of foreign policy: No foreign interests, save perhaps those essential to the defense of the homeland itself, are worth the destruction of one's entire national community. As the disproportion grows between the values that are supposed to be protected by the exercise of military power and the values that must be risked in a big war, the international system of presumably sovereign nation-states is fundamentally undermined in its principal sustaining mechanism—the balance of power: Countries lacking sufficient military force of their own to deter provocations from an enemy armed with awesome destructive capabilities are no longer able to count on allies to redress the threatening imbalance of power. Formal "mutual security" pacts are coming to be widely regarded as hollow commitments, unlikely to be honored at moments of truth. The North Atlantic Treaty Organization and the Warsaw Pact, under the impact of Mutual Assured Destruction capabilities, were experiencing this profound crisis of credibility just at the time that the demise of the US–Soviet rivalry rescued them from facing up to their strategic obsolescence.

In parallel with the crisis of confidence over the viability of alliance commitments, there is a growing worldwide understanding that a war on the dimensions of either World War I or World War II fought with the weapons now in the arsenals of major states could put the survival of the entire human species in jeopardy. Accordingly, a global "community" does now exist (in both elite and popular perceptions) with respect to at least the shared vital interest in avoiding such a war. But there is still no effective institutionalization of that global community interest. The United Nations Organization is the closest the world has come to such institutionalization, yet the UN clearly lacks the power to constrain the behavior of the actors in a position to catalyze the species-threatening holocaust. (The Security Council's authorization of members' use of military force in 1991 in response to Iraq's invasion of Kuwait was not an adequate test of the UN's capacity for collective security actions against great powers.) Unlike the nation-states themselves, whose governments are assumed to monopolize the legitimate violence capabilities of the national community, the putative global survival community has no comparable monopolization of violence capabilities.

In short, contemporary world society still operates with a growing incongruity at the most fundamental level: (1) the inherited political/legal forms for securing the physical survival of national communities; and (2) the vulnerability of these communities to genocidal destruction at each other's hands—a mutual vulnerability that (despite some flirtation with the fantasy

of strategic population-defense systems) the inherited political/legal entities, as long as they maintain their sovereign autonomy, have no real power
to overcome.

The Incongruity of Economy and Polity

While in individual countries there is often substantial congruence between
the economy and the polity (it is commonplace to refer to the political economy of a country), at the trans-country level the economy increasingly functions at cross purposes with the polity—the nation-state system and its legal
norms of national sovereignty and noninterference by foreigners into a
country's domestic affairs. This is an incongruence with fundamental implications for the durability of the nation-based structure of the world's political system. When a country's policies for regulating national markets can be
avoided or overwhelmed by transnational buyers, sellers, and investors, the
national polity is eroded at its very essence: the capacity to sustain (within
the country's borders) public safety and health, orderly commerce, social
justice, and the integrity of the national culture.

The growing incongruence between transnational economy and national
polity is a basically irreversible trend, emanating from the irrepressible efforts by humans to increase the range and ease of exchanging goods, services, and ideas. As shown in Chapter 9, the intelligence and inventiveness
of the human species, in enhancing the mobility of persons, things, and information, has been radically transforming the meanings of both natural geographical space and artificial political borders.

More than ever before, in fields central to the economic functioning and
well-being of a country, investors and producers and sellers and buyers are
thickly linked in networks of interdependence with their customers or suppliers in other countries. In some of these fields (for example, telecommunications broadcasting, oceanic shipping, air transport, and international
banking) the networks of interdependence have given rise to formal organizations representing governments and private industry groups, with the latter frequently playing the most influential roles. In other fields (for example,
petroleum, basic agricultural commodities, and electronics hardware and
software) the relations between producers and consumers—sometimes involving negative interdependencies—are intensely bargained out, through
cooperative negotiations or coercive threats, with transnational interests often colluding in price, supply, and market-share arrangements and to bring
pressure on their respective national governments.

Multinational/multiproduct firms are both the creatures and exploiters
of the new mobility and interdependencies. Manufacturing and sales of the
products of these corporations take place worldwide, making the board-
rooms of some of these multinationals today's functional equivalents of the
imperial chambers of previous centuries: By their unilateral "sovereign" decisions to invest capital here or there, to build roads and seaports, or to pull

up stakes for a more congenial locale, these *neo*-imperialists can drastically affect the life chances of people the world over (positively or negatively), often with less political, let alone legally enforceable, accountability than even the old mercantilist imperialists.

The dynamic transnationalism of the contemporary global economy has been producing a new transnational axis of political alignment, cutting across not only the post–World War II East–West, North–South groupings of countries but also political party and interest-group alignments within countries that heretofore have focused primarily on the roles government should play in the domestic economy. On the one side of the new alignment are those entrepreneurs, professionals, farmers, and blue-collar workers who see themselves benefiting from the increasing mobility of persons, goods, information, and money and who are willing to take their chances in the larger markets this is creating; they stand for global free trade and the removal of domestic barriers to transnational commerce. On the other side are those fearful of losing, at least in the short run, if compelled to compete in a fully open international economy: those who, largely as a result of special governmental subsidies and barriers to foreign competitors, have been able to sustain a protected niche in the domestic market.

The much lamented lack of "party discipline" in the domestic politics of most countries, as well as the disintegration of some of the most important interstate coalitions of recent decades—the North Atlantic economic community, the Soviet-led COMECON grouping, the Organization of Petroleum Exporting Countries (OPEC), and the Third World "Group of 77"— are all attributable, at least in part, to this growing incongruence between the new transnational relationships in the emergent global economy and the dominant associational bases of the polity in the traditional nation-state system.

Even efforts to achieve a new congruence between economy and polity on a regional basis, most prominently thus far in the European Union, are in danger of being overwhelmed by the rapid globalization of economic interdependencies and the transnational/transregional political alignments this is spawning.

The Incongruity of Ecology and Polity

The earth's natural ecological patterns—the interdependencies among plant and animal life and the geological and meteorological environment—have often directly influenced the location and form of organized human communities; but ignorance, short-sighted indifference to the long-term effects of their current disruptions of nature, and territorial conflicts between human communities have just as often made for a substantial lack of match between the spatial dimensions of human communities and the world's basic ecological patterns. Indeed with our growing technological capabilities for altering nature's "givens," most territorially specific political jurisdictions, originally formed in part to harness an area's natural ecologies, are becoming less and less congruent with dimensions of the ecologies that are being perturbed.

Some of the perturbed ecologies are global in scope: the stratospheric ozone layer that screens out cancer-producing sunrays; the planet's envelope of gases and particulate matter that, by controlling how much of the warmth the earth receives from the sun is retained within the atmosphere and how much is allowed to escape, has been responsible for the climatic conditions that have sustained human life. Other more tangible and immediately visible disturbances are to rivers, seas, forests, airsheds, and concentrations of animal and plant life that are used in common or depended upon by the populations of different countries.

The resulting international disputes are of the kind that historically have been least susceptible to noncoercive diplomatic resolution in the anarchic world polity. To the traditional war-provoking conflicts over rights to navigate, fish, or divert the waters of rivers, lakes, or seas used in common by various countries we now have added conflicts over the pouring of effluents into such bodies of water that can degrade their value for other users. Similarly, the growing awareness of how the injection of industrial byproducts into the planet's other highly mobile medium—the atmosphere—can severely injure agricultural productivity as well as cause life-threatening human illness in neighboring populations has multiplied the opportunities for nations to get angry at one another. In addition, trans-border injuries caused by mega-accidents such as nuclear power-plant meltdowns and oil-tanker spills further expose the inadequacy of the existing international political/legal order to handle the interdependencies and mutual vulnerabilities of peoples across national lines.

Writes Jessica Tuchman Mathews, Vice President of the World Resources Institute,

> Put bluntly, our accepted definition of the limits of national sovereignty as coinciding with national borders is obsolete. The government of Bangladesh, no matter how hard it tries, cannot prevent tragic floods [without] . . . active cooperation from Nepal and India. The government of Canada cannot protect its water resources from acid rain without collaboration with the United States. Eighteen diverse nations share the heavily polluted Mediterranean Sea. . . . Indeed, the costs and benefits of alternative policies cannot often be accurately judged without considering the region rather than the nation.[2]

As indicated in Chapter 10, a series of dramatic environmental disasters since the 1960s and new scientific attention to the planet's vital ecological relationships have generated public awareness of some of the glaring incongruities that exist between the location of important ecologies and the jurisdictions of the nations they affect. The spreading popular recognition that concerted multi-state efforts are required to deal with many of the most con-

---

[2]Jessica Tuchman Mathews, "Redefining Security," *Foreign Affairs*, Vol. 68, No. 2 (Spring 1989), pp. 162–177; quote from pp. 174–175.

sequential ecological threats to human health and well-being was reflected in the 1992 "Earth Summit" at Rio de Janeiro, especially in the Convention on Climate Change, the Convention on Biodiversity, the Statement on the World's Forests, and Agenda 21.

Even the new ecological consciousness expressed in the Rio conference, however, has not yet been sufficient to overcome the political/legal lag behind the material realities of ecological interdependence.

The Incongruity of Nation and State

The world polity, while commonly referred to as a "nation-state system," has never been in a condition in which most nations have states of their own and the borders of most states encompass the nations they purport to represent. To be sure, each of the world's recognized countries—unless in the throes of a civil war—normally comprises both a state and a nation congruent with its territorial jurisdiction: a country-wide set of institutions and officials with at least the legal writ (if not actual power and authority) of supreme governance throughout the territory; and a country-wide set of symbols, rituals, and myths reflecting (or designed to create) a common and distinctive cultural identity among the inhabitants of the territory. But in any slice of time, some of the world's many ethnic groups who consider themselves to be culturally distinct "nations" will have members that are a significant portion of the population of more than one country; and almost every country will contain some such ethnic groups who are not substantially assimilated into the dominant culture, perceiving themselves to be a distinct nation within the larger nation-state, and in some cases even alienated from the country's dominant ethnic groups.

These incongruities, on the one hand, between the shape of countries that purport to be the dominant focus of national loyalties for their populations and, on the other hand, the living spaces occupied by peoples with alternative national loyalties, have played havoc with established political boundaries throughout modern history. One of the principal precipitants of war has been the effort by one or another of the nations that have been fragmented by existing boundary lines and/or compelled to adopt the cultural ways of the dominant ethnic group of their state to redraw existing political jurisdictions so as to match their strongest national loyalties.

Some world order reformers have proposed that this cause of war could be largely eliminated through "national self-determination" plebiscites (a dream of President Woodrow Wilson). But unless such plebiscites include arrangements to allow the losers to obtain citizenship in a jurisdiction in which *they* would be in the majority, this determination by vote of the basic national identity of each nation-state could still leave just as many alienated minority subnations within states as before. Plebiscites might eliminate some regimes in which an ethnic or religious minority previously lorded it over a majority of different ethnic or religious makeup; but, assuming the perpetuation of the state-sovereignty system, there would be no guarantees against the newly installed majorities tyrannizing the now-deposed minorities unless such guarantees were specifically provided in the constitutions of particular countries.

Contrary to conventional expectations, neither democratization nor modernization has, in the aggregate, forged greater congruence between the nations and states of the world. Indeed, some of the bitterest communal conflicts have occurred in democratic polities: Catholics against Protestants in Northern Ireland; the Flemish-Walloon rivalry in Belgium; separatist agitation by the Francophone Québécois of Canada. It was the dismantling of the centralized Soviet autocracy in the late 1980s and early 1990s that permitted the flareup of fanatic separatist nationalism in the Baltic states, Ukraine, and Kazakhstan, violent communal strife among rivalrous ethnic groups in the southern Soviet republics of Azerbaijan and Georgia, the assertion of independence from the USSR by the huge Russian republic, and even nationalist/ethnic uprisings against the newly independent republics. Similarly, the brutal intercommunal conflict in the Balkans in the early 1990s was one of the products of the democratization of Yugoslavia following the death of Communist dictator Josep Tito.

Modernization and democratization, rather than assimilating diverse ethnic groups into a homogenized greater nation, often put previously dispersed or repressed members of ethnic subcultures in touch with their "brothers" and "sisters" and provide communal leaders with both the technical wherewithal and the philosophical justification to mobilize such groups to assert their collective "rights." Increased literacy, mobility, and exposure to the standards of living enjoyed by other groups can generate feelings of relative deprivation which are translated into demands for rectification—either through redistribution of society's privileges and amenities or by granting political autonomy to the aggrieved ethnic group.[3]

In sum, nations (being states of mind more than territorial entities or tangible government institutions) are constantly in the process of forming and re-forming in response to changes in the interaction and dependency patterns among human groups—patterns that under the impact of new technologies are being altered more dramatically and swiftly than ever before. The national identities by which the peoples of the world differentiate themselves at any point in time may give way to alternative national groupings in subsequent periods, making them intensely uncomfortable with governments premised on the primacy of the older national identities. The congruence of nation and state, where it does exist, is fortuitous; and particularly with the new mobility of people and ideas, nation-states are becoming increasingly unstable as foundational units of the world's political system.

[3]See Ted Robert Gurr, *Why Men Rebel* (Princeton: Princeton University Press, 1970; and Samuel P. Huntington, "Civil Violence and the Process of Development," *Adelphi Papers* (London: International Institute for Strategic Studies), No. 83 (December 1981).

The Incongruity of Basic Human Rights and State-Sovereignty Norms

The idea that every human being, simply by virtue of being human, has certain basic rights vis-à-vis all other human beings and that governments are created to secure these rights—in other words, that all individuals are "naturally" endowed with rights, but governments and other collectivities possess merely artificial and recallable powers—is at tension with the foundations of the nation-state system. This "rights of man" theory (an impetus for and mobilizer of the eighteenth century American and French revolutions, the twentieth century decolonization movements, and the 1989–1990 "revolution" in Eastern Europe against Marxist-Leninist regimes) contradicts the philosophy, still dominant among statespersons and international relations theorists, that human rights have no independent existence outside of well-ordered states.

The established state-centric view, which has roots extending back to Plato and Aristotle and which was elaborated variously by St. Thomas Aquinas, Edmund Burke, and John Stuart Mill, with contemporary expressions as diverse as Walter Lippmann, Michael Walzer, William Buckley, and Diang Xiaophing, holds that a stable and durable political community is at least the necessary context for, if not the source of, individual rights. The implication (sometimes made explicit) is that the existing governing institutions of the recognized national polities must be respected as the agencies for making the sometimes painful trade-offs and allocations among various rights claimants within each country. For each country is assumed to comprise a people with a special history and evolved culture, even if multi-ethnic, which is embodied in its political system, and which it is the state's role to nourish and protect against outsiders. Unless the government in power forfeits this trust by extreme (virtually genocidal) measures against its citizenry or by so trampling on the rights of significant minorities that it provokes civil war or secession, foreigners (including those who purport to represent the "international community") have no grounds for intervening. Additionally, according to this view, international stability and peace require that national governments forebear from supporting rights claimants within another state's borders. (Here we have the "realpolitik" justification for the Bush administration's aloof stance toward the Chinese government's massacre of student demonstrators in Tiananmen Square in the summer of 1989.)

The traditional state-centric view, however, has come under increasing assault in recent decades, both from intellectuals and from the international facts of life. The biological and social sciences confirm the commonality, despite cultural differences, of the basic human needs of subsistence, security, love, and (in varying manifestations) dignity of the person. The proposition that all of us, by the fact of being human, have a right to at least minimal satisfaction of these needs has come to command nearly universal assent. The intellectually derived correlative that servicing such basic human rights is the principal task of human polities, and that the worth of any polity is a function of how well it does in this task, has put the legitimacy of all extant polities up for grabs, so to speak. Whether or not particular nation-states and their prevailing territorial demarcations do indeed merit the badge of political legitimacy is, according to this view, subject to continuing assessment; accordingly, neither today's governments nor today's borders are sacrosanct. Moreover, those currently located outside of existing jurisdictions may well have a claim to be part of the relevant community of human rights assessors; this is particularly the case where ethnic, religious, ideological, class, occupational, and professional "brothers" and "sisters" are in intense communication with each other across national borders.

Thus, the increasing mobility of persons and ideas, along with the mobility of economic goods and services, is creating more than societies of material interdependence incongruent with the political–legal jurisdictions of the nation-state system; it is also creating (or re-creating) transnational, transborder community identities and political loyalties. At best (for the persisting primacy of the nation-state system), the transnational human rights constituencies will be expressed merely in cross-cutting associations of individuals and groups who, when it comes to determined assertion of their claimed rights, nevertheless will be inclined to accept the dispensations rendered by the national legal and political system in which they reside. At worst, the transnational human rights constituencies will openly challenge and defy the authority of the nation–state based political systems to render legitimate dispensations; and through civil disobedience or violence, perhaps organized transnationally, they will prevent the established polities from functioning effectively.

The world's human population thus approaches the twenty-first century AD, after more than 5,000 years of experimenting with various forms of political organization, in a rather confused and disoriented condition. With its genius for altering the material characteristics of the natural universe having far outpaced its creativity in the sociopolitical realms, its very survival as a species is increasingly in jeopardy. Yet there are some hopeful signs of possible political adaptation. The requirements and opportunities for positive political evolution are outlined in the Conclusion.

CONCLUSION:
THE FUTURE
OF WORLD POLITICS

Cumulatively, the dominant and durable post–Cold War trends—the press of the world's human population and global industrialization on the planet's resources; the widening and deepening of the material interdependence of peoples; the growth of economic transnationalism; the increasing worldwide mobility of people and information; and the contagion of human rights ideas—are producing a global polyarchy in which national states, subnational groups, and transnational interests and communities are vying for the support and loyalty of individuals and conflicts are prosecuted and resolved primarily on the basis of ad hoc power plays and bargaining among shifting combinations of these groups. In this emerging polyarchy there is once again, as has occurred at other chaotic periods in the history of the world polity, a growing incongruence between governance and society. The institutions with the greatest coercive capabilities—national governments—are losing the capacity to adequately represent and serve the basic needs of the communities within their jurisdictions, and consequently they are losing a good deal of their legitimate authority, which, in addition to their coercive capabilities, has been the essence of their political power.

There are three basic responses to the growing incongruence between governance and society. One is to try to restore the declining authority of the still-dominant institutions of governance; in the case of the contemporary world polity, this would mean arresting the erosion of the sovereignty of national governments. Another response is one of relaxed indifference—laissez-faire—letting events take their "natural" course, which in today's world means accepting as facts of life the spreading alienation and violence between winners and losers in the economic and political marketplace. A third response is to attempt to enhance the authority and accountability of institutions that are congruent with the most important interactions taking place in society, creating new institutions where necessary; in the case of the polyarchic world society, such institutions, more and more, would need to transcend, yet operate within, the jurisdictions of the existing nation-states.

If my basic analysis of the sources of the contemporary crisis of incongruence is correct, then the first approach—the attempt to renew the sovereignty of national governments—will prove to be inadequate, if not counterproductive, especially if it involves trying to reverse trends that are the product of deep human needs and irrepressible advances in science and technology. Efforts to compel these trends to conform worldwide to the traditional norms and structures of the nation-state system will in many places require a degree of coercion incompatible with the legitimate authority required for viable governance.

If today's volatile currents are left to take their own course, however, without substantial normative and institutional channeling, the emerging polyarchy could degenerate into full-blown anarchy, in which any community hoping to survive, let alone protect its range of interests, would seek to acquire independent capabilities for self-defense. In the contemporary world, this might include nuclear or other genocidal weapons capable of detering adversaries from intolerable provocations. With world order in the process of total collapse, a desperate effort to restore the system of sovereignty-protecting nation-states, even though outdated, might appear to be the only tolerable alternative. In the nation-state system, the population of the world is at least supposed to be divided into definable jurisdictions jealously controlled by national governments, each responsible for what the people under its jurisdiction do internationally. Deterrent threats directed at such political entities still might have a chance of working.[1] But in a totally unregulated polyarchy, the inability of national governments to be in fact sovereign within their jurisdictions and the existence of many subnational and transnational groups who are accountable only to themselves, portends a chaotically insecure world—a world in which weapons of mass destruction would be available to groups who are not squeamish about using terror to achieve their ends and who are too internationally mobile to be targets of effective deterrent or retaliatory strategies.

The third basic approach—proactively adapting the institutions and processes of governance to the world's evolving polyarchy rather than attempting to make the polyarchy fit back into the traditional state system—would be both a more just and realistic way to deal with the worsening crisis of incongruence. It would be more just because (as outlined below) it would be animated and constrained by essential requirements of political and legal accountability. With accountability its normative core, it should involve less coercion than the alternatives; as such, it is also more realistic, for its governance structures would have a better chance of operating with the legitimate authority they require to exercise their powers.

---

[1]Confidence that sovereign national governments, even when (or particularly when) armed with nuclear weapons, will act responsibly and rationally and therefore will be deterred from military adventures against each other, underlies the arguments of Kenneth Waltz that the proliferation of nuclear weapons to many countries might not be so bad after all. *See* his "What Will the Spread of Nuclear Weapons Do to the World?" in John Kerry King, ed., *The International Political Effects of the Spread of Nuclear Weapons* (Washington, DC: Government Printing Office, 1979), pp. 165–196. In a somewhat more refined and qualified way, Waltz reiterated this argument in a 1993 article, "The Emerging Structure of International Politics," *International Security*, Vol. 18, No. 2 (Fall 1993), pp. 44–79.

THE GLOBALIZATION OF ACCOUNTABILITY

The third response to the dangerous implications of global polyarchy envisions a world polity with a substantially greater amount of accountability across national borders than now exists—mutual accountability among governments, accountability by governments to people living in other countries, accountability by non-governmental actors for how they affect people around the world.

The normative core of such a globalized accountability system would be the principle that *those who can or do substantially affect the security or well-being of others (especially by inflicting harm) are assumed to be accountable to those they can or do affect.* The accountability principle would apply both "horizontally" (to relations *among* communities) and "vertically" (to relationships *within* communities and institutions).[2]

So defined, the accountability principle opens up more questions than it answers and begs for further elaboration. But so do the traditional principles of international relations, including those of state sovereignty and noninterference in domestic affairs that underlie the nation-state system; these too are abstractions capable of multiple and often contradictory interpretations and applications.

Granted the ambiguities and complications, an evolving yet basic shift in world politics and world law is contemplated, a shift away from the traditional emphasis on protecting the sovereign rights of states vis-à-vis one another and toward the new imperative of holding states and other powerful entities accountable, across national borders, for the way they affect people's lives.

The projected accountability system does not imply the obsolescence of the nation-state. National governments are likely to remain the most powerful agencies in world politics as far ahead as we can see. It does, however, imply an increasing subordination of the sovereignty norms of the nation-state system to the basic accountability principle. Additionally, the evolving accountability system would feature an enhancement of the international political and legal status of various international organizations, transnational associations, and subnational groups plus the empowerment of individuals to seek redress internationally for basic rights denied them in their national societies.

The political and legal arrangements for implementing the basic accountability principle exhibit a wide array of configurations. They can be expected to vary according to (1) the degree of accountability actors are

---

[2]I borrow the concepts of *horizontal* and *vertical* accountability from Robert C. Johansen, "Building World Security: The Need for Strengthened International Institutions," in Michael T. Klare and Daniel C. Thomas, eds., *World Security: Challenges for a New Century* (New York: St. Martin's Press, 1994), pp. 372–397.

willing to accept, ranging from the most minimal of obligations to keep the affected or potentially affected informed of what is being (or will be) done to them to enforceable agreements not to act without the approval of the affected parties; (2) the extent of institutionalization, ranging from ad hoc meetings between those who can and do affect one another (meetings in which information and/or threats are exchanged and/or behavioral adjustments are negotiated, after which the parties go home) to permanently sitting legislative, administrative, and judicial institutions; (3) the rules for membership, representation, and decision-making in the various accountability institutions; and (4) the relationship of such accountability arrangements to the established institutions of the nation-states and existing international institutions.

The implementation questions—political, legal, and moral—are thus as complex as they are wide-ranging. Few of the answers can be be derived directly from the core accountability principle or from other standard principles of political or legal philosophy. As with analogous questions in domestic political systems, most of the answers will have to be worked out through practical bargaining processes among the groups that set up and participate in particular regimes.[3]

Take, for example, a typical international water-use dispute: One of the countries through which a major river flows encourages the development of new communities and industries along the banks of the river and this severely depletes the supply of uncontaminated water to communities downstream, some of which are in neighboring countries. The accountability principle tells us that the downstream communities hurt by the effects of the development projects upstream ought to have some influence over those projects. But through what political instrumentalities should such influence be brought to bear? The standard answer would be that the aggrieved downstream communities should work through their respective national governments to negotiate an equitable water-use treaty with the country responsible for the upstream projects. The problem with this standard prescription in such situations is that unless the aggrieved communities have a lot of influence in the governments of the neighboring states, those governments are unlikely to give the issue prominence in their diplomatic interactions with the offending state; moreover, even where the aggrieved communities have been successful in a number of neighboring states to get the issue on the diplomatic agenda, the fact of varying constituency interests in each of the countries will make it very difficult for these states to concert their bargaining strategies toward the offending state. To ensure that their inter-

---

[3]For insights on how theory and practice will have to feed each other in the global elaboration of what I call "accountability regimes," *see* Marvin S. Soroos, *Beyond Sovereignty: The Challenge of Global Policy* (Columbia: University of South Carolina Press, 1986).

ests are appropriately and vigorously represented, the aggrieved communities will probably have to mobilize themselves into a trans-state pressure group (in our example, perhaps a water users' association)—if at all possible, encompassing allies in the offending state—to directly assert their demands on the relevant governments.

The increasing involvement of such trans-state organizations in transborder matters (in the literature they are more frequently referred to by the terms "transnational" or "international nongovernmental organizations" [INGOs]) opens up additional issues of representation. This is especially so when official national or international agencies are prodded to accord relevant communities more direct participation in the policy process than is normally provided through the institutions of the nation-state system. What if there are a number of INGOs active in a particular policy arena, each claiming to be the appropriate agents of the same or overlapping communities? Should each of them be given a consultative voice? And if one or more of these transnational communities or INGOs are provided a formal role in the policy process, should they be required to select their representatives through free and democratically run elections, or should each community be permitted its own system of selection? Again, there is no universally applicable answer to these questions that can be derived from the basic accountability principle. The determination of the mode of representation best able to serve the principle will be specific to each field and situation and will be the result of political bargaining among states and communities more than the result of abstract reasoning.

SOME PRELIMINARY SCAFFOLDING

Fortunately, when it comes to the actual construction of accountability relationships we need not start from totally unprepared ground. Rudimentary international accountability frameworks already exist and are functioning, at least marginally, in the fields of collective security, peacekeeping, arms control, international commerce, international transportation and communications, environmental management, and human rights. In each of these realms, states and nongovernmental actors have discovered that there often are "positive sum" benefits to be achieved through institutionalized mutual accountability in comparison with the absolute losses they will suffer if they persist in acting unilaterally and ad hoc out of a compulsion to maintain a relative advantage over their rivals. They have found it is to their advantage to mutually commit one another to certain norms and rules, even if only to establish predictability in one another's behavior; in some cases they have also been able to reap the benefits of economies of specialization and scale through such institutionalized accountability.[4]

Accountability for the Use of Force

The dispute resolution, collective security, and peacekeeping provisions of the UN Charter (and their precursors in the League of Nations) involve commitments of member states not to resort to military force against one another prior to obtaining authorization from the world organization, unless such unilateral action is absolutely necessary for self-defense; moreover, in all instances of time-urgent self-defense, members are supposed to reestablish their accountability to the Security Council as soon as possible.

During the Cold War, with the Security Council virtually paralyzed by the hostility between the superpowers, members tended to absolve themselves of the need to be accountable to the UN when their vital national interests were at stake, and to rely, as of old, on the international system's traditional mechanisms of alliances and the balance of power. Even so, they would exploit every chance to operate under the legitmating mantle of the world organization (as the United States did at the outset of the Korean War because of the temporary absence of the Soviet Union from the Security Council) and would seek to pass resolutions condemning their rivals' use of force in the absence of UN authorization (a device used by the Soviets and their allies against US interventions in Latin America and by the United States and its allies against Soviet interventions in East Europe). An anomaly at the time, but an advance indication of how the UN might come to be used after the Cold War, was the joint US-Soviet sponsorship of resolutions condemning the British-French-Israeli invasion of Egypt in the 1956 Suez crisis and providing for the deployment into the region of a multinational peace observation force under UN command.

In the post–Cold War era, accountability to the UN for any use of force internationally, whether or not the force is under UN command, is increasingly asserted by statespersons to be an imperative of world order. And, indeed, this has started to be a standard process in such cases, as, for example,

---

[4]Such international regimes are created and maintained even in the essentially anarchic nation-state system, observes a prominent theorist of the phenomenon, because they "facilitate agreements by raising the anticipated costs of violating others' . . . rights, by altering the transaction costs through the clustering of issues, and by providing reliable information to members." Robert O. Keohane, *After Hegemony: Cooperation and Discord in the World Political Economy* (Princeton: Princeton University Press, 1984), quote from p. 97. Insights on international regime creation and maintenance can also be found in Kenneth Oye, ed., *Cooperation Under Anarchy* (Princeton: Princeton University Press, 1986); Stephen D. Krasner, ed., *International Regimes* (Ithaca: Cornell University Press, 1983; and Oran Young, *International Cooperation: Building Regimes for Natural Resources and the Environment* (Ithaca: Cornell University Press, 1989).

in the Gulf War of 1990–1991 (where the Bush administration kept returning to the Security Council for legitimization of its threats and war aims against Iraq, even while insisting on maximum US autonomy for the conduct of military operations); in the "humanitarian" military operations in Somalia during the 1992–1994 period; and in the peace enforcement actions by NATO in Bosnia in 1994.

Accountability up and down the UN chain of command, from units in the field, to commanders directly responsible to the Secretary General, and back to the Security Council, is, of course, the expected modus operandi for "peacekeeping," "peace making," and "peace-enforcement" actions undertaken and run by the world organization. This is not to say that the accountability arrangements for such UN operations are automatic or instituted without controversy, especially in cases where nationally contributed troops may need to engage in actual battle; the point, rather, is that more and more world society is becoming accustomed to debating about the ways of ensuring international accountability for the international application of military power—not as an anomaly, but as an essential feature of world public order.

Accountability for Types and Numbers of Weapons and Troops

Even in this field, a traditional preserve of state sovereignty, the trend since World War II has been one of increasing accountability by national governments to each other and to international agencies to confirm adherence to treaties restricting military deployments in particular realms (such as the seabed and outer space) and prohibiting signatories from possessing and/or transferring to other countries certain types of weapons (notably nuclear, chemical, and biological).

The most elaborate accountability regime in the arms control field is the nuclear "safeguards" system of the International Atomic Energy Agency (IAEA). In order to make sure that signatories of the Treaty on the Non-Proliferation of Nuclear Weapons (NPT) do not violate its provisions, the NPT requires each state without nuclear weapons to negotiate an agreement with the IAEA declaring all of its peaceful nuclear materials and facilities and arranging for periodic IAEA inspections to confirm that none of the declared materials and facilities are being used for weapons development or production. The examples of Iraq in 1991–92 and North Korea in 1993 refusing to declare suspicious looking facilities and growing concerns that India and Pakistan are concealing active nuclear weapons programs have prompted pressures from the arms control community to give the IAEA more intrusive "full-scope" inspection capabilities; but many of the potential nuclear weapons states, located mainly in the Third World, are balking at the implications for their sovereignty and are objecting to what they claim is a double standard on the part of the five presumably "legitimate" nuclear weapons states who have not faithfully adhered to their NPT obligations to negotiate their own nuclear disarmament.[5]

Because of the political and technical difficulties of ensuring full accountability by potential recipients of prohibited weapons and materials, regimes to prevent their proliferation require international accountability by the potential suppliers as well. This has been one of the glaring holes in the NPT, and the effort to plug it by the formation of a voluntary association of nuclear materials exporters ("London Suppliers Group," now comprising 27 countries) has thus far been quite ineffective, in large measure due to the lack of a multilateral monitoring regime.

The need and difficulty of making weapons suppliers accountable to one another and to the larger international community also has become more evident in the post–Cold War era with respect to limiting the sales of sophisticated missiles and their components. Concerned particularly with the export of technologies that would permit recipients to develop ballistic missiles capable of carrying nuclear and other unconventional payloads, the Group of Seven industrialized countries announced in 1987 that they were entering into a Missile Technology Control Regime (MTCR) that would obligate them to restrict such exports. Seventeen other countries have joined the MTCR since 1987, and Russia has agreed to act in accord with the spirit of the regime; but some known exporters of missile components, such as China and North Korea, have been unwilling to respect the MTCR guidelines. The MTCR is an example of a weak accountability regime in that it has no monitoring or verification capabilities, and member governments are not even bound by a formal treaty.[6]

Another manifestation of the growth of international accountability in the military realm is the corpus of bilateral arms control agreements that have been negotiated between the two nuclear superpowers. The Strategic Arms Limitation Talks (SALT) of the early 1970s produced a series of pacts, notably the anti-ballistic missile (ABM) treaty and the agreement limiting offensive strategic weapons, that were designed to discourage either side from trying to attain a decisive first-strike capability; for such a bid by one or the other, or both, it came to be realized, would not only dangerously destabilize mutual deterrence but would also drive the military budgets of both countries to levels neither could tolerate. Henceforth, Washington and Moscow agreed, they would be accountable to one another for the size and characteristics of their strategic arsenals, and this mutual accountability would be institutionalized in the form of a standing consultative commission staffed by military experts of both sides to review complaints of noncompliance.

---

[5]Peter van Ham, *Managing Non-Proliferation Regimes in the 1990s: Power, Politics, and Policies* (New York: Council on Foreign Relations Press, 1994.)
[6]*Ibid.*, pp. 24–27.

The SALT precedent of the United States and Russia having to answer to one another for their military programs has been carried forward into their post–Cold War agreements to substantially reduce their armed forces. Some of these, notably the Strategic Arms Reduction Treaties (START) of 1992 and 1993, provide for visits to each other's weapons storage sites to mutually verify adherence to the terms of the agreements.

Accountability for Actions Affecting the Condition of the World Economy

The economic actions of states and private corporations are already constrained, albeit in quite limited ways, by institutions and rules of international accountability. Paradoxically, it has been the most transnationally active elements in the private sector (who normally tend to *oppose* regulation) that have been the principal champions of the world economy's most prominent intergovernmental institutions: the General Agreement on Tariffs and Trade (GATT), renamed the World Trade Organization (WTO) in 1994; and the International Monetary Fund (IMF). The paradox is explained by the fact that these global institutions, while fostering greater "horizontal" accountability among the governments and corporations who dominate the world economy, are even further removed from "vertical" (democratic) accountability than are the economic policy-making institutions of the nation-states.

Established at the end of World War II, the two premier global economic institutions are both mandated, as a minimum, to discourage countries from adopting the kind of national-protectionist policies that did so much to bring on the devastating economic depression of the 1930s; maximally, they are supposed to stimulate the evolution of an integrated global free market.

The GATT, now **WTO,** has been attempting to serve these objectives through two types of accountability processes: First, it hosts multilateral trade negotiation "rounds" to induce its members, now numbering 125, to reciprocally eliminate most of their tariff and non-tariff barriers to transnational commerce (the latest, the Uruguay Round, concluded in April 1994 with a treaty mandating reductions in tariffs on manufactured goods by 37 percent and cuts in farm subsidies by 21 percent; the April 1994 accord also bars countries from restricting competition by foreigners in most service industries, including computer software and advertising).[7] Second, the WTO maintains dispute settlement panels from which members are expected to seek substantive judgments and/or authorization for any retaliatory measures they plan to apply against countries alleged to be violating the existing

---

[7]Alan Riding, "7 Years of Struggle as 109 Nations Sign Trade Accord," *New York Times*, April 16, 1994.

accords (the 1994 treaty enhances the role of the panels in the direction of making it illegal for countries to ignore their judgments or to retaliate against one another without prior WTO authorization).

The IMF owes its existence in large part to the realization by powerful champions of the free market that the regulation and reduction of tariffs and non-tariff barriers provided through the GATT/WTO are insufficient to sustain an open global trading system. One of the lessons of the Great Depression was that an institutionalized system of international accountability with respect to monetary policies is also essential for a healthy world economy, for if countries can alter the international exchange value of their currencies at will, thereby increasing the price of foreign products in one's domestic market while decreasing the price of one's products in the global market, it will be all too easy for them to subvert free trade agreements in this way—in effect, conducting "beggar thy neighbor" tariff wars by other means. Accordingly, the monetary regime created by the United States and its allies for the post–World War II world provided that the currency values of all countries would be pegged to the US dollar at nonfluctuating rates of exchange and that the value of the dollar would remain stable in relation to an ounce of gold; alterations in these designated international exchange rates would have to be mutually agreed to by members of the regime.This "fixed-rate" regime has been modified over the years, however, in order to accommodate to the persistence of a good deal of unilateral and market-determined revision in currency values. (The current regime countenances such exchange-rate fluctuations within certain bands or stipulated ranges.)

The IMF at its founding was also given the responsibility of providing financial help to countries suffering temporary imbalances in their international accounts (an expected result of export–import imbalances that are natural from time to time in a free and competitive international market). In recent decades, this economic stabilization function of the IMF has been broadened to encompass financial help to countries attempting to overcome fundamental structural problems. Consistent with the IMF's basic philosophy and mission of husbanding the emergence of a global free market, it has made such structural assistance conditional on recipients adopting economic policies that will reduce the role of the state in their economies and that will allow free enterprise, including foreign private investments, to flourish. Such "conditionality" (as it has come to be called) has brought the IMF into a position of intrusive influence over the economic development strategies being pursued in many Third World countries and in the former Soviet states. The recipients are required to be directly accountable to the world's central banker, as it were, for what they are doing with their loans. Many are resentful at what they regard as violations of their national sovereignty and are urging that they be accorded a greater say in the Fund's policy-making processes, so as to make the loan criteria more responsive to their unique needs and cultural traditions, which in turn would make the

IMF reciprocally more accountable to its clients.[8] But as the IMF becomes less of a rich country club (which has already begun to happen), the world's affluent movers and shakers are likely to attempt to bypass the Fund's more broadened accountability relationships by conducting their serious deliberations in other more exclusive multilateral clubs, such as the Group of Seven (which has also begun to happen).

Understandably, the less affluent countries would prefer to have global economic policies set by the general-membership forums of the United Nations where the one-nation–one-vote rule normally applies. These institutions, not surprisingly, have been the source of the various UN resolutions, covenants, and charters postulating various ways in which the affluent countries should be accountable to the poorer countries. For example, Third World demands for a new international economic order that would institute a system of price supports for basic commodity exports and other "distributive justice" controls on the international market emanated from the UN Conference on Trade and Development (UNCTAD), an organ of the UN General Assembly; and the controversial design and decision rules of the International Seabed Authority, giving Third World mineral producers a virtual veto over the international licensing of deep-sea mining companies, was the product of the universal-membership Law of the Sea negotiating forum.

Accountability for the Use of the "Commons"

In the Law of the Sea negotiations, the insistence by Third World countries that all countries should have an equal say was based on UN resolutions claiming that the deep ocean beyond national jurisdiction, like outer space, was part of "the common heritage of mankind." The traditions of both international and domestic law support the contention that the rules of use for such "commons" areas are to be formulated jointly by the community of users and implemented in the interest of all of them. But the legal traditions also allow for a range of governance options.

Where the resources of a commons are abundant or nonexhaustible, the accountability arrangements among members of the user community may involve only minimal periodic consultations for exceptional situations of users getting in each other's way. This is still considered to be the case (perhaps wrongly) for much of outer space.

---

[8]Votes in the IMF are allocated to members according to the size of their financial contributions (their "subscriptions"), which in turn are determined on the basis of a country's wealth; but even the judgments on the appropriate size of each country's subscription, and thus the number of its votes, are made by those who currently hold a preponderance of the votes. Actually, formal voting rarely takes place; decisions normally are arrived at on the basis of deliberations among the Fund's board of directors and staff, leading to a "consensus" reflecting the views of those who would be able to marshall the votes if that became necessary—namely, the United States and its principal allies among the advanced industrial countries.

Where a commons contains scarce resources, however, the accountability arrangements among the members of the user community can be quite elaborate and institutionalized in the form of resource-management authorities. This came to be the case by the second half of the twentieth century for many of the resources of the ocean that in the past were thought to be exempt from scarcity considerations.

The imperatives of heavier international commons management that first began to be widely accepted in the case of the ocean are now under consideration as well for other international commons: inland seas, rivers, airspace, the atmosphere, weather and climate, rain forests, interlinked plant and animal ecologies, the stratosphere—indeed, the whole biospheric envelope that sustains healthy life on Earth. In all of these fields, heavy international accountability and management imperatives have arisen due to technological developments that are expanding and intensifying the use and exploitation of resources on which communities in more than one country depend for their well-being.

The 1992 "Earth Summit" in Rio de Janeiro on environment and development, a UN conference attended by more than 150 countries (100 of which were represented by their heads of state) and 1,400 nongovernmental organizations, was the most dramatic expression yet of the attention the world polity has begun to give to commons management issues. The treaties and other international instruments signed at Rio (see Chapter 10) left a lot to be worked out with respect to accountability processes and institutions; but as the conference secretary-general Maurice Strong told the delegates, "The Earth Summit is not an end in itself, but a new beginning. The measures you agree on here will be but first steps on a new pathway to our common future. Thus, the results of this conference will ultimately depend on the credibility and effectiveness of its follow-up."[9]

The coolness of the Bush administration to the new initiatives in international accountability launched at Rio did not augur well for the kind of follow-up the UN officials were calling for. For if the United States held back when it came to financial and institutional implementation of the Rio initiatives, particularly the commitments to assist Third World countries in environmentally sound "sustainable" development, it was doubtful that the other industrialized countries would be inclined to take up the burden on their own. A positive assumption of cooperative responsibility by the United States government, however, was announced in 1994 by the more environmentally oriented Clinton administration. Vice President Gore revealed that the United States and its Group of Seven partners would contribute $2 billion to the Global Environmental Facility (GEF), the funding

[9]Address of Maurice Strong at the opening of the UN Conference on Environment and Development, Rio de Janeiro, Brazil, June 3, 1992, quoted by Peter M. Haas, Marc A. Levy, and Edward A. Parson, "Appraising the Earth Summit," *Environment*, Vol. 34, No. 8 (October 1992), p. 7.

agency jointly administered by the United Nations Environmental Program and the World Bank and that had become the principal source of funds for sustainable development projects in the Third World. The United States also endorsed restructuring the GEF to give the developing countries more influence on its decisions than they have in funding agencies such as the World Bank and the IMF where the principal donors, through weighted voting arrangements, are left in commanding control.[10]

Institutionalized accountability relationships are also becoming more widespread and prominent in the management of international transportation and communications. Many of the the transportation and communications "highways" are located in or traverse the world's other commons (the ocean, rivers, airspace, and outer space); but they are appropriately regarded as international commons in their own right, in the sense of being essential resources that are normally supposed to be available without discrimination to all members of the international community. As with the environmental/ecological commons, the twentieth century's revolutions in transportation and communications technologies have rendered anachronistic the open-access free-use regimes that traditionally prevailed on international navigation routes and broadcast airwaves; for the proliferation of new uses and users has been producing levels of congestion in many areas that are counterproductive if not dangerous. As a consequence, the cognizant international organizations—such as the International Maritime Organization (for ocean shipping and navigation), the International Civil Aviation Organization (for air traffic), and the International Telecommunication Union (for electronic broadcasting)—are more than ever preoccupied with devising globally standardized "rules of the road" and pressuring national governments and industry groups to organize and fund the necessary enforcement. The most glaring deficiency in some of these accountability arrangements is the lack of sufficient procedural and institutional mechanisms for handling conflicts among different *types* of users of an international commons who are getting in each other's way: petroleum companies and shippers vs. fishing fleets vs. coastal recreation facilities and boats vs. waste-disposal pipelines; the airline industry (and their need of expanded airport facilities) vs. communities covetous of an existing ecological environment; orbiting telecommunications platforms vs. meteorological facilities vs. military reconnaissance satellites. It is difficult enough within countries to resolve such intersectoral conflicts; their peaceful resolution among states and transnational interests calls for uniquely innovative political leadership and institution-building.

[10]The GEF will henceforth operate with a complex "double majority" voting system in which decisions will require the support of at least 60 percent of the members who have contributed 60 percent of the agency's funds—a reform that various lay-environmental groups claim still does not allow recipient governments and communities sufficient opportunity to shape the programs that will be affecting them. Paul Lewis, "Rich Nations Plan $2 Billion for Environment," *New York Times*, March 17, 1994.

Accountability for Human Rights Violations

The growth of accountability in the human rights field in recent decades, in contrast to the accountability relationships appearing in other fields, has been less at the level of county-to-county relationships than in government-to-citizen relationships within countries. This reflects the still-strong determination of nation-states above all to ward off attempts by other nations to interfere in their domestic affairs, even in the face of the universal spread of the democratic human rights ethos that governments are legitimate only to the extent that they rest on the consent of the governed.

Although most governments have formally subscribed to the corpus of human rights covenants adopted by the UN General Assembly and various regional inter-governmental organizations (see Chapter 12), they continue, consistent with the traditional norms of the nation-state system, to shy away from calling one another to account in these forums except in cases of egregious systematic violations that have become a cause célèbre of domestic human rights constituencies and "watch groups" with strong transnational connections. The result is the enormous gap between the official governmental rhetoric of international accountability on human rights and the actuality of such accountability. Thus, in international forums we frequently hear governments profusely asserting their adherence to international human rights *norms,* while rejecting attempts to make them (the national governments) legally accountable to international human rights *institutions.*

There has been some limited progress in recent years, however, toward giving international human rights agencies authority to at least officially monitor the performance of countries to ascertain the extent to which they are adhering to the human rights norms they have formally embraced. The European Human Rights Commission, described in Chapter 12, has the authority to receive petitions from nongovernmental groups and individuals claiming to be victims of human rights violations, to investigate such claims, and to issue recommendations in such cases. The Commission also has the authority to refer difficult cases to the European Human Rights Court, and this tribunal has the authority to formally find a member government to be in conflict with its human rights obligations. Redress, of course, still remains in the hands of the member government. The capacity of the UN Commission on Human Rights to emulate the example of the European Commission is more problematical, given the sometimes extreme resistance of many Third World countries to any dilution of their legal sovereignty. Even so, its procedures have been gradually evolving so as to allow it to investigate complaints about human rights conditions in particular countries, although it is still precluded from taking official cognizance of individual cases.[11]

---

[11]Jack Donnelly, *International Human Rights* (Boulder: Westview Press, 1993), pp. 57–63.

All in all, meaningful international accountability in the human rights field remains a distant goal. Excepting some of the procedures in the European human rights regime, individuals, supposedly the primary holders of human rights, still have virtually no legal standing in the official forums of the international community to hold their own governments to account for human rights violations. This means that those who believe they have been denied their human rights by the official agencies of their country must try to obtain redress through their own country's national channels of appeal, and if this fails, they have no further legal recourse.

THE GROWING INFLUENCE OF NONGOVERNMENTAL ORGANIZATIONS

Much of the contemporary impetus for making governments accountable for the effects of their actions on populations outside of their jurisdictions has come from nongovernmental organizations. This is to be expected, for nongovernmental organizations are a common feature of the public policy process within domestic polities, especially democracies, pressing their views on both legislative and administrative agencies and on political parties and sometimes even organizing themselves as political parties and running their members for political office. When such groups perceive that their interests and/or their members in other countries (for many of them are organized transnationally) will be affected by the policies of particular governments, they are likely to attempt to influence such internationally impacting policies. Accordingly, as the countries and sectors of world society have become more and more interdependent, it has become commonplace for nongovernmental groups representing similar communities in their various countries to closely coordinate their policies and to constitute (or reconstitute) themselves as international nongovernmental organizations (INGOs).[12]

Just as national governments and the European Union have found various ways of legitimizing and formalizing the role of nongovernmental organizations in the policy process, so too in the global arena an increasing number of official intergovernmental organizations have accorded "consultative" status to INGOs. This is particularly so in the specialized agencies operating in technical fields like communications, transportation, and, in-

[12]Social scientists studying the proliferation of INGOs have counted some 23,000 as of the early 1990s. *See* Paul Ghils, "International Civil Society: International Non-Governmental Organizations in the International System," *International Social Science Journal*, Vol. 44, No. 3 (August 1992), pp. 417–431. The counted INGOs are those that have formally registered themselves with international or national agencies; the "informal" INGOs are of course some multiple of that number.

creasingly, environmental management, where the expertise provided by the INGOs has become indispensable in the formulation and implementation of agency policies. INGOs have also become progressively more active, and have been given consultative status, in various treaty-negotiating forums in these fields, often providing drafts of provisions that are sponsored by the official delegates of countries and are later formally adopted. Moreover, some of the most important negotiation- and coalition-building in such negotiations is conducted "behind the scenes," so to speak, by the INGOs representing different constituencies.[13]

It is not only as sources of technical expertise, however, that INGOs are becoming crucial participants in the international policy process. Their ability to represent the "grass roots" and in turn to build popular support for the policies they favor is often what humanizes and democratizes international arenas that otherwise would be too elitist and far·removed from public consciousness and accountability. Notably, this legitimizing function was built into the design of the 1992 "Earth Summit," not only through the certification of certain INGO representatives as consultants to the official delegations but also in the form of an adjunct "Global Forum" for nongovernmental environmental groups. Unwieldy and sometimes unruly, the Global Forum nonetheless tended to reflect the polyarchic constituencies that brought pressures on their governments to hold the Earth Summit and that would have to be relied on to generate public support in their countries for the follow-up national and local programs that would be required to implement the new global accords. These support-building and policy-implementing functions of the nongovernmental groups, in developing countries as well as in the advanced industrial world, were given special emphasis in "Agenda 21," the ambitious and comprehensive outline of national actions and international cooperation approved at Rio as targets for accomplishment by the start of the twenty-first century.[14]

THE CONSTITUENTS
OF THE WORLD POLITY

The world polity is in the process of self transformation—out of the traditional nation-state system and into a system more congruent with the contemporary global polyarchy. The shape and essential constitution of the

[13]The impact of INGOs on public international policy by their provision of technical expertise and specialized information has been conceptualized by some political scientists as an "epistemic community" role. *See* especially the special issue of *International Organization*, Vol. 46, No. 1 (Winter 1992) on "Knowledge, Power, and International Policy Coordination," edited by Peter M. Haas.

[14]*See* Gareth Porter with Inju Islam, *The Road From Rio: An Agenda for U.S. Follow-up to the Earth Summit* (Washington, DC: Environmental and Energy Study Institute, 1992); and James Gustave Speth, "A Post-Rio Compact," *Foreign Policy*, No. 88 (Fall 1992), pp. 143–161.

emerging world polity have not been predetermined by history but will grow out of the choices that its constituents make from here on.

Who *are* the constituents of the emerging world polity? The conclusion of this study (in today's vernacular, "the bottom line") is that all of us—no matter where we may live in the world, whatever our national or religious identification, whatever our gender, color, class, or occupation—are its constituents. We are its constituents in the multiple meanings of that term: as parts of the whole, as its architects and builders, and as those who have the right and obligation to determine its basic policies and elect its officials.

Realistically, in performing these constituent functions many of us will choose to work through the official instrumentalities of the nation-state and the nation-state system that still dominates many of the arenas of the world polity. Others among us may choose to work primarily through nongovernmental organizations that we can more directly influence and that we believe better represent our particular interests than do the governmental agencies of the countries in which we live. Some of us (scholars, writers, artists) may choose to exercise our constituent functions as independently as possible, without relying on political brokers or agents to represent us in the world polity.

Out of this ferment, which it is our fate to have inherited as late twentieth century inhabitants of this planet, will come a polity that is perhaps more orderly and just than the existing polyarchy.

The future of world politics is up to us.

INDEX